Dear Lou—

Here's some ins, ⟨...⟩
on the literary tradition of the
Pioneer Valley. Happy reading.

Love,
Mom

THE
PIONEER VALLEY
READER

THE PIONEER VALLEY READER

PROSE AND POETRY FROM NEW ENGLAND'S HEARTLAND

James C. O'Connell, Editor
Ruth Owen Jones, Picture Researcher

Foreword by Richard Todd

Berkshire House Publishers
Stockbridge, Massachusetts

Editor: Sarah Novak
Cover and book design: Jane McWhorter
Cover art and frontispiece: Michael McCurdy

Library of Congress Cataloging-in-Publication Data

The Pioneer Valley reader : prose and poetry from New England's heartland /
James C. O'Connell, editor ; Ruth Owen Jones, picture researcher ; foreword by
Richard Todd.
        p.   cm.
Includes bibliographical references (p.)
    ISBN 0-936399-71-6
    1. American literature—Massachusetts—Pioneer Valley. 2. Pioneer Valley
    (Mass.)—Literary collections. 3. Massachusetts—Literary collections.
    4. Connecticut River Valley—Literary collections. 5. New England—Literary
    collections. I. O'Connell, James C.
PS548.M4P526   1995
810.9'97442—dc20
                                                            95-8414
                                                               CIP

Berkshire House books are available at substantial discounts for bulk purchases by
corporations and other organizations for promotions and premiums. Special
personalized editions can also be produced in large quantities. For more information:

Berkshire House Publishers
PO Box 297
Stockbridge, Massachusetts 01262

Printed in the United States of America
10 9 8 7 6 5 4 3 2 1

(This copyright page, with permissions and copyrights for Pioneer Valley Reader
selections, continues on p. 357.)

Contents

Foreword

That a little place like the one that is our subject, a small valley in a small state, should deserve its own literary anthology may seem to the reader improbable. It *is* improbable, but so too is the art and the scope of the writers that the Pioneer Valley has nurtured. Dominant literary figures in each era of its more than three centuries of history have lived here, from Edward Taylor to Richard Wilbur. Scores of enduring minor writers have grown up in the Valley or found it a convenient refuge. And at least one writer occupies a transcendent category, the woman whom many call the greatest of American poets, Emily Dickinson.

Comparisons are odious, but one could name many a large and populous state, indeed many regions, that have contributed far less to American letters than has the Valley. Literature has been the local "product." If poems were peaches, or silicon chips, we'd be rich. We *are* rich, but in unspendable capital; in this, of course, like much of New England.

In the public imagination New England culture has been synonymous with Boston. But Boston has been an editor, a teacher, a patron. Genius has lived in the country — in Concord, the Berkshires, and the Pioneer Valley. And as James O'Connell points out in his introduction to this excellent anthology, the Valley, more than other literary corners, has kept its distance from the Hub of the Universe. Geography played its part, but ideas proved higher than hills. The Valley clung longer to Puritanism, renewing its faith with Jonathan Edwards's help, in the late 18th century. Amherst College was founded, in 1821, partly in fear of the dangerous Unitarianism in Cambridge that threatened to seduce the minds of local boys.

The central genius of the Valley, Emily Dickinson, was a prism refracting the white light of the past into modern hues. Despite her quarrels with religion, she honored the aesthetic lineaments of Puritanism, an unadorned style and a passionate relationship with the universe. Her voice was both older and newer than the language of commerce that was coming to dominate the world, including this part of it. It mocked rolling, periodic phrasing, it subverted pomposity, and re-declared the force of the individual consciousness. It was a celebration of the self as buoyant, if not so loud, as Emerson's.

She also incidentally taught us a way to see, and for those of us who live in the Valley our immediate world is in fact not quite immediate; we see it with her help. There comes a time in late summer when the sun begins noticeably to slip away from this latitude, starting the season of soft light, and I wake up thinking of the Dickinson image, "the morns are meeker than they were." (I don't *say* this, mind you, just think it.) And her various celebrations of anonymity have given us a certain exaltation (sometimes, let's face it, a snootiness) about the valuable provinciality of our place.

The Valley has changed not just in a century but in a generation, in a decade. Media-borne culture conspires to blur identity, here as else-where. Some thirty years ago the Interstate sliced across the view that Thomas Cole had painted from the summit of Mount Holyoke. But today even someone passing through on that hated highway knows himself to be in a distinct place. We are still organized by the river and held by the hills. And we are brightened and deepened by the presence of old houses, fields, customs.

But what binds us together most is nothing more than language. We live in the shade of a long overhanging bough of literary tradition. Poet is a plausible occupation here, no odder than roofer, indeed almost certainly more common. Bookstores and libraries abound. Each year it seems that more and more graduates from the "Five Colleges" simply move out of the dorm and into town, unwilling to leave their intellectual home. A high self-awareness about language fills the air, sometimes comically so (just attend a faculty meeting), but at its best the place enjoys an unaffected ease with literary things.

Not long ago a scholarly fellow "discovered" some 500 new poems by Emily Dickinson. They were buried, he said, in her letters. He had found images there, and meter — surely, then, these were poems!

Needless to say, this gent did not come from the Valley, where the infusion of poetry into daily life is still felt not to be an aberration but a happy fact of nature.

This book celebrates a place that has remained a place by the power of words.

— Richard Todd

Introduction

Explaining the Pioneer Valley

This book is about the Connecticut River Valley in Massachusetts. The region is nicknamed the "Pioneer Valley," reflecting its role as America's first frontier. This title dates from the 1940s, when the Pioneer Valley Association was established to promote tourism in Hampden, Hampshire, and Franklin Counties. For many who live here, the region is simply called "The Valley." For optimists or satirists, it is "The Happy Valley."

The Pioneer Valley has a geography, history, and culture distinct from the rest of Massachusetts and distinct from the stretches of the Connecticut Valley in Vermont and New Hampshire and in Connecticut. The Pioneer Valley is separated into two major sections divided by the Mount Tom–Mount Holyoke ranges — rural and academic north of the range around Northampton and Amherst and urban and industrial south of the range in Greater Springfield.

This anthology undertakes to explain this region through the writings of famous writers and public figures who have lived in or visited the Valley. The criterion for inclusion is that each piece must describe some facet of Pioneer Valley life and it must be good reading. By organizing these readings under certain themes, this *Reader* structures a dialogue about the Valley's history and what it has meant to various writers.

The range of writers who have lived in the Pioneer Valley includes Emily Dickinson, Edward Bellamy, Richard Wilbur, Sylvia Plath, Joseph Brodsky, James Tate, and Tracy Kidder. Visitors have included Ralph Waldo Emerson, Henry Wadsworth Longfellow, Charles Dickens, and Henry James.

There have been distinct strands of writing about the Pioneer Valley — one has depicted the region as archetypically American and another has emphasized "counter" cultural strains. The Valley has served as a microcosm for many aspects of the American experience, while engendering more than its share of creative activity, worldly repudiation, and challenges to the accepted order.

The themes that have emerged in the Pioneer Valley are big ones. The Valley was the first inland frontier, a place distinct from Boston and the Atlantic Coast. It has exemplified many of the strains of independence and challenges to traditional authority that also characterized the settlement of the American West. Throughout its history, the Pioneer Valley has been a seedbed of such reform initiatives as Jonathan Edwards's Great Awakening, Shays's Rebellion, abolitionism, women's education, Edward Bellamy's utopian critique of industrial society, and the commune and anti-nuclear movements of the 1970s. The region's Puritan seriousness, higher education, scenic beauty, and remoteness have nourished writers and thinkers of all kinds. The Valley has been a place to pursue one's unique voice out of the mainstream of American life.

Yet much writing on the Pioneer Valley celebrates its prototypical American dimensions. In the nineteenth century, travelers and artists used the picturesque landscape around Northampton, particularly the vista from Mt. Holyoke, to represent the bountiful blessings that Nature had bestowed on Americans. Since then, the Valley's scenic beauty has inspired a long line of poets and painters. Springfield has been regarded as the quintessential "hometown," nostalgically remembered by the likes of Larry O'Brien, Leo Durocher, and Timothy Leary. Calvin Coolidge's political career in Northampton demonstrated how a small-town boy could grow up to become President. Tracy Kidder's award-winning studies on home-building, public education, and nursing homes are all set in the Pioneer Valley.

Several writers have used the Pioneer Valley to represent some essential American quality. Henry James's *Roderick Hudson* opens with a description of provincial American life, as lived at Northampton. Before the embarkation of Roderick Hudson and Rowland Mallet for Rome and the serious pursuit of the arts, the two Americans stroll through the Northampton meadows to the banks of the Connecticut:

> Rowland watched the shadows on Mount Holyoke, listened to the gurgle of the river, and sniffed the balsam of the pines. A gentle breeze had begun to tickle their summits, and brought the smell of the mown grass across from the elm-dotted river meadows. . . . "This is an American day, an American landscape, an American atmosphere. It certainly has its merits, and some day when I am shivering with ague in classic Italy, I shall accuse myself of having slighted them."

Novelist Thomas Pynchon muses on a lost opportunity that the colonial Pioneer Valley represented for America. In *Gravity's Rainbow*, he reflects on a fictional William Slothrop (aka William Pynchon, founder of Springfield and colorful ancestor of Thomas Pynchon), a free, earthy, decidedly non-Puritanical character in a wistful account: "Could he have been the fork in the road America never took, the singular point she jumped the wrong way from?"

Frontier Origins

The Pioneer Valley's singularity originated in the seventeenth century, when the region was the country's first inland frontier. Some histo-

rians have argued that the frontier, with its emphasis on new beginnings
and self-determination, was the fundamental force in shaping American
culture. Certainly, much of the American frontier experience is evident in
the Pioneer Valley, where English Puritan civilization confronted the
Indians and the French.

Both John Pynchon's letter about the burning of Springfield in 1675
and John Williams's account of the 1704 Indian-French raid on Deerfield
indicate the formative stages of the confrontational English mentality
towards Indians. Ironically, the last Indian attack on Deerfield, in 1746,
was the subject of the first poem published by an African-American —
"The Bars Fight," by Lucy Terry Prince, a slave from Deerfield.

In the frontier tradition, Springfield founding father William Pynchon
asserted his independence by seceding from the Connecticut Colony
almost as soon as it was established. Remaining within the Massachusetts
Bay Colony, Pynchon resisted the control of Boston as much as possible
until he was driven out on charges of heresy.

When Yale President Timothy Dwight visited the Valley in 1806, he
recognized its distinct character: "the inhabitants of this valley . . . possess
a common character, and in all different states resemble each other more
than their fellow citizens who live on the Coast resemble them." Dwight
considered the Connecticut Valley one of the most prosperous and civi-
lized regions in the new nation.

The Other Massachusetts

Ever since the frontier era, the Pioneer Valley's geographical separa-
tion from Boston has encouraged independent thinking and a conscious
tendency to distinguish the region from the "Hub of the Universe." Tony
Hiss, in *The Experience of Place*, identifies the psychological divide be-
tween Western and Eastern Massachusetts when he reports planner Rob-
ert Yaro's observation:

> Many state officials who work in Boston, for instance, think of
> Massachusetts as the United States in miniature, and for some of
> them the Connecticut River Valley is in the boonies, a place as far
> away as the Great Plains. 'How's your view of the Rockies?' is a
> typical statehouse joke.

Nowhere was the split between east and west more dramatic than in
Shays's Rebellion. In 1786-1787, Western Massachusetts farmers forced
into bankruptcy by Boston bankers took up arms against the state gov-
ernment to halt the foreclosures. So frightened were the national elite that
George Washington, Alexander Hamilton, and others initiated efforts for
a stronger national government and a U.S. Constitution.

Remoteness has provided the Valley the freedom to experiment and develop an independent approach to things. The Valley missed some of the cultural trends of the Coast, clinging longer to traditions of Puritanism. Jonathan Edwards, the influential Northampton Calvinist theologian, initiated the Great Awakening in the 1730s to counter the liberalizing doctrinal tendencies being promoted in Boston.

The relative isolation of the Pioneer Valley nurtured the development of distinct poetic voices, encouraging escapes and fresh starts. Emily Dickinson is the quintessential Pioneer Valley poet, a recluse who did not leave her family's home during the last twenty-one years of her life. Dickinson published only seven of her 1,750 poems in her lifetime. She wrote that she was "rich in disdain for Bostonians and Boston" and feared, when staying there for eye treatment in 1864, the city's capacity to "silence" her poetry. Critic Alfred Kazin argues that Emily Dickinson became America's first modern writer, in part, because she could cultivate her consciousness far from the brittle urban sophistication.

The finest poet of colonial America was Westfield minister Edward Taylor, who wrote extensive religious poetry that was never published until the twentieth century. Frederick Tuckerman, who critic Edmund Wilson called "one of the few fine original poets of the later nineteenth century in the United States," was another recluse poet, a Boston lawyer who retired to Greenfield to write poetry and study botany and astronomy. Twentieth-century Amherst poet, Robert Francis, resembled Thoreau in his solitary, spare life and his total commitment to writing.

Seedbed for Reform

The Pioneer Valley's persistent strain of moral purpose and impetus for renewal, introduced by the Puritans, has given rise to numerous political and social reform movements, from the Great Awakening and Shays's Rebellion to women's education reforms at Mount Holyoke and Smith.

John Brown conceived his plans for leading a slave insurrection during his years as a merchant in Springfield and shared them with black abolitionist Frederick Douglass. *Springfield Republican* editor Samuel Bowles II and Congressman George Ashmun helped establish the Republican Party and its abolitionist platform. Frederick Douglass and Sojourner Truth, the first black woman lecturer, became members of a utopian industrial community in Florence called the Northampton Association of Education and Industry. Women's advocate and abolitionist Lydia Maria Child lived in Northampton during these years. In 1840s Northampton, Dr. Sylvester Graham became an early proponent of the healthy lifestyle, advocating coarsely-ground whole wheat flour (for "Graham crackers"), a vegetable diet, cold showers, hard mattresses, and abstinence.

Latter nineteenth-century Springfield saw the Reverend Washington Gladden help develop the "Social Gospel," exchanging the Puritanical acceptance of man's depravity for a more compassionate effort to ameliorate the sufferings of exploited workers. Springfield journalist Edward Bellamy turned concern for the plight of the urban poor into the influential utopian manifesto *Looking Backward.*

The 1960s and 1970s witnessed a blossoming of idealism in the Five College Area. Communes such as The Farm in Montague produced such anti-nuclear activists as Harvey Wasserman and Sam Lovejoy. The Renaissance Community (Gill), the Sirius Community (Shutesbury), and the Brotherhood of the Spirit (Turners Falls) have been other Upper Valley "intentional" communities. The Traprock Peace Center, in Deerfield, and the Leverett Peace Pagoda have promoted anti-war activism. Randy Kehler and Betsy Corner, of Colrain, have been prominent tax resisters protesting American militarism. Feminists and lesbians such as Adrienne Rich have used the area as a base for writing and consciousness-raising. The campus of the University of Massachusetts at Amherst has been the scene of much student activism, often around racial issues. Some observe that the Upper Valley is one of the few places left in America with traces of the counterculture.

The Five College Area

Intellectual and educational life has particularly deep roots in Northampton and Amherst. Puritan ministers, most notably Jonathan Edwards, fostered a strong tradition of learning in the colonial era. Just up the hills in Cummington, William Cullen Bryant wrote the first internationally recognized American poetry — "Thanatopsis" and "Inscription for the Entrance to a Wood." In 1819, lexicographer Noah Webster and other orthodox Congregationalists established Amherst College, the first of the "Five Colleges."

The Pioneer Valley is the birthplace of women's higher education in America. Mary Lyon established the Mount Holyoke Seminary in 1837 to train women as teachers. Emily Dickinson chronicled Mount Holyoke's 1847-1848 academic year, the last before Miss Lyon passed away. Another of the "Seven Sisters" is Smith College, founded in 1875 to offer a curriculum equal to the best of any men's college. Smith's longtime feminist heritage is evident in such graduates as Sylvia Plath, Betty Friedan, and Gloria Steinem (Nancy Reagan and Barbara Bush are also alumnae). Former Smith President Jill Ker Conway offers a spirited defense of women's colleges in her memoir *True North.*

Other area educational experiments have included Northampton's Clarke School for the Deaf (1867), the first oral, residential school for the deaf in America, and Hampshire College (1970), the non-traditional "fifth" of the Five Colleges, profiled in the *Reader* by Chip Brown.

Valley education has also had its more traditional side, as exemplified by Deerfield Academy, the noted prep school. In this *Reader*, alumni writers John McPhee and Edward Hoagland take contrasting views on how Deerfield has molded boys.

The University of Massachusetts at Amherst has solidified the region's status as an educational mecca. Originally established as the Massachusetts Agricultural College, it became a full-scale university after World War II, mushrooming from 725 students in 1945 to 10,000 in 1964 to 25,000 in 1972. The campus's hodgepodge of high-style Sixties Modern architecture is described by Patricia Wright. UMass has attracted nationally renowned faculty members such as writers James Tate, Paul Mariani, John Edgar Wideman, and Madeleine Blais, and has acquired a reputation for political disputation. Julius Lester's *Lovesong* tells about the controversy at UMass over his course on blacks and Jews.

The proximity of prestigious educational institutions to beautiful rural New England towns has attracted many writers and artists. Ray Stannard Baker (pen-named "David Grayson"), influential journalist and historian, wrote paean after ode to the rural beauties of Amherst in the first half of this century. Mary Heaton Vorse's family spent their summers in Amherst during the late nineteenth century. Pulitzer Prize-winning poet Archibald MacLeish maintained a second home in Conway for more than fifty years, writing poems about the local scene. The Five Colleges have attracted such faculty luminaries as Robert Frost (Amherst College), Richard Wilbur and W.H. Auden (Smith College), and Joseph Brodsky (Mt. Holyoke College). One of the largest concentrations of artists and craftsmen in America is currently active in Northampton, Amherst, and the surrounding towns.

Much has been written about the groves of academe and their role in the local communities. Eleanor Lipman's *The Way Men Act* describes the experience of a woman without a degree in the snobby fictional college town of Harrow (aka Northampton). Richard Todd sends up Northampton's consumer trendiness in "Notes from the Transcendental Valley." Madeleine Blais, with *In These Girls, Hope Is a Muscle*, perfectly captures Amherst's "self-absorbed loftiness."

Springfield and Holyoke: Normative Places

Springfield is entirely different. It is a normative place, the first "Springfield" to be established in America. There are thirty-nine Springfields scattered across the country, more than any other place name. There also is a "Springfield Estates," a "Falls," "Spring," "Woods," "Park," "Acres,"

"Corner," and "Mills." The setting for both "Father Knows Best" and "The Simpsons" is "Springfield." For more than a century, Springfield, Massachusetts, has been known by the homely sobriquet: "City of Homes."

Springfield, Mass., is a place to be from. Talented people ripen in Springfield, then move away to bigger cities to make their fortune. Back in Springfield, the locals boast of who made good. The *Springfield Union News* runs a column by Tom Shea that chronicles the successes of ex-Springfielders. Chauvinists recite the litany of successful local boys and girls: Taj Mahal, Julia Sanderson, Eleanor Powell, Larry O'Brien, John V. Shea III, Nick Buonicanti, Vinny DelNegro.

Many writings on Springfield are recollections of innocence or the loss of it. Dr. Seuss (Theodore Geisel) set his first children's book, *And to Think That I Saw It on Mulberry Street*, on a street in Springfield. Timothy Leary tells of his cut-up days at Classical High School. David Black recounts with some fondness his father's attempts to organize a teacher's union at the same Classical High. Larry O'Brien narrates his political epiphany of introducing the young Jack Kennedy to Springfield during the 1952 U.S. Senate race. Former Governor Foster Furcolo (aka John Foster) limns the comic outlines of local ward politics. Daniel Okrent uses Springfield to demonstrate how 1960s urban renewal tore the heart out of many American cities.

In Springfield, sports has exhibited some All-American qualities. YMCA Training College (today's Springfield College) instructor James Naismith invented basketball there in 1891. Naismith's account of the first basketball game indicates the optimism about personal and social improvement that has long undergirded American sports. For Leo Durocher, coiner of the taunt "Nice Guys Finish Last," baseball was a way out of the working-class confines of West Springfield.

Holyoke's experience also has had a prototypical quality. In this classic milltown, many of America's ethnic working-class dramas have been reenacted. Mary Doyle Curran's novel *The Parish and the Hill* recounts the struggles of three generations of Irish-Americans between the Civil War and the Great Depression. Tracy's Kidder's account of a year in the life of a fifth-grade public school class, *Among Schoolchildren*, describes the tensions between the established Irish and the Puerto Rican newcomers in Holyoke during the 1980s. For a perspective on the Polish-American experience, Mary Ellen Chase's *A Journey to Boston* tells a story of Polish farmers in Hadley, and Suzanne Strempek Shea, in her recent novel *Selling the Lite of Heaven*, deftly sketches Polish-American mores in her hometown of Bondsville.

An Abiding Sense of Place

What gives the Pioneer Valley cohesion is its beautiful landscape, conveying a strong "sense of place." Of the entire 400-mile stretch of the Connecticut River, the Massachusetts section of the Connecticut River is most like a valley, with broad flatlands surrounded by distant hills. It is a particularly American middle landscape, far from the coast, yet not the wilderness of Northern New England.

The area around Northampton, Mt. Tom, and Mt. Holyoke is particularly scenic. When "The Swedish Nightingale" Jenny Lind appeared in Northampton in 1851, she called it the "Paradise of America." During the nineteenth century, Mt. Holyoke was one of America's premier tourist attractions, drawing such visitors as Ralph Waldo Emerson, Charles Sumner, Washington Irving, and countless Britons. Henry James, in *Roderick Hudson* (1875) captured the idyllic quality of the area. Other novelists of the era, like Henry Ward Beecher, in *Norwood*, and Helen Hunt Jackson, in *Mercy Philbrick's Choice*, concurred in praising the pastoral beauty of the Valley.

The Connecticut Valley became a cultural icon. Painter Thomas Cole's masterwork "The Oxbow" (1836), presented Cole's ideal of human civilization existing in harmony with nature. This painting of the view from Mt. Holyoke profoundly influenced Romantic American landscape art, and the rise of the Hudson River School. Cole's "Essay on American Scenery" argued that the Connecticut and Hudson were America's preeminent scenic rivers:

> In the Connecticut we behold a river that differs widely from the Hudson. . . . The imagination can scarcely conceive Arcadian vales more lovely or more peaceful than the valley of the Connecticut — its villages are rural places where trees overspread every dwelling, and the fields upon its margin have the richest verdure.

In the mid-twentieth century, Mary Ellen Chase, in *A Journey to Boston*, called the Connecticut River Valley "one of the brightest lands in all the world. It is as bright as Florence, or as Fiesole, or as the brown hill towns of Umbria under the hot Italian sun."

In his *The Old Patagonian Express*, an account of his daunting trip through Latin America by train, Paul Theroux relished memories of the Pioneer Valley, especially in contrast to the strange places he visits. On the first leg of his trip, from Boston to Springfield, he reminisces about his college days at UMass:

> Not long afterward we were in Springfield. I had clear memories of the place, of getting off the train at that very station on a winter night and crossing the long bridge over the Connecticut

River to Route 91, to hitchhike the rest of the way to Amherst. There were ice floes on the river tonight, too, and the dark slopes of woods on the far side and the same knifing wind. Memories of school are always to me like memories of destitution, of inexperience, the joyless impatience I had suffered like poverty. I had some other sadnesses there, but the movement of travel is merciful. Before I could remember much — before this town and river could toss me a particular memory — it whistled and rushed me into the amnesia of night. We traveled west, the rumble of the train muffled by snow banks, through the forests of Massachusetts. But even in that darkness I recognized it. It was not the opaque night, the uninterrupted dark, of a foreign country's hinterland. It was the darkness that baffles only strangers. It was an average evening for this time of year in this place; and I knew all the ghosts here. It was the darkness of home.

Later, when he is on the Guatemala–El Salvador border, Theroux compares the idyllic scene there to the Pioneer Valley:

It was a shady road, circling around a hill, past a meadow and a glugging stream. What a transformation in landscapes! Earlier in the day I had thought I was going to wither and die in the wastes of the Motagua Valley, and here I was ambling through green humpy hills to the sound of birdsong. It was sunny late-afternoon as I walked from Guatemala into El Salvador, as fresh and breezy as a summer day in Massachusetts. The border crossing was as happy a hike as I have ever made and reminded me pleasantly of strolling down the Amherst Road into Shutesbury.

Despite its enduring beauty, the Pioneer Valley's "sense of place" has been subject to change. In more recent years, writers have been concerned about preserving the special qualities of the region's landscape. Mark Kramer's *Three Farms* worries about what would happen to farmland as dairying becomes uncompetitive. Archibald MacLeish issues a fervent plea against insensitive overdevelopment in "A Lay Sermon for the Hill Towns." Tony Hiss, in *The Experience of Place*, describes the efforts of UMass's Center for Rural Massachusetts to preserve the rural character of the Pioneer Valley, using them as a model for sensitive rural development. And Thomas Conuel tells the ironic environmental morality tale of the creation of the Quabbin Reservoir to provide Boston's water supply in *Quabbin: The Accidental Wilderness*.

The Pioneer Valley's Present Situation

Global technological and economic forces now impinge on the character of the Pioneer Valley. Distinct regional qualities and ways of doing things weaken. Commercial sprawl, cookie-cutter subdivisions, and expanding highways threaten to make the Valley look like Anyplace USA. Global economic forces erode local control of economic affairs. Yet people can live in the Pioneer Valley and do business elsewhere through the phone, fax, modem, and airplane.

The Pioneer Valley is a less provincial and more dynamic place. Since the 1960s and the transformation of the UMass into a major research university, the Upper Valley has grown into an increasingly attractive place to live. Northampton has become the liveliest New England college town outside of Cambridge. Artists, intellectuals, students, and seekers of every stripe enliven the region.

Springfield and Holyoke are enduring the socio-economic problems and the loss of confidence of many American urban centers. John Edgar Wideman's "Picking Up My Father at the Springfield Station" and Tracy Kidder's *Among Schoolchildren* chronicle these struggles perceptively.

Recent writings about the Pioneer Valley reflect an enduring appreciation of its qualities. Whether in the mainstream of American experience or on some far-flung tangent, the Valley maintains a special sense of place, grounded in its picturesque, inspirational landscape and its intellectual-reformist culture. The 100-plus writings gathered here testify to the persistent and vital tradition of this extraordinary region.

— James C. O'Connell

Acknowledgments

The Pioneer Valley is one of the least understood regions in New England. Many people outside the area lack a clear image of the Valley, and many locals take the place for granted.

Yet those in the know realize that the Pioneer Valley is one of the most scenic, historic, and culturally vital places in the country.

Historian Daniel Boorstin has described how modern communications and homogenized commercial development have "leveled times and places." As places have become more similar, many Americans celebrate the specific culture of particular regions and cities. To explain the sense of place, some writers have prepared anthologies of regional literature. Notable examples have included *The Berkshire Reader: Writings from New England's Secluded Paradise*; *A Place Apart: A Cape Cod Reader*; *The Maine Reader*; and *The Last Best Place: A Montana Anthology*. Each work is revealing about the rich traditions these unique places have engendered.

The Pioneer Valley has long inspired me. A Valley native, I have written *The Inside Guide to Springfield and the Pioneer Valley* (1986) and *Shaping an Urban Image: The History of Downtown Planning in Springfield, Massachusetts* (1990). Writing these books and living in the Pioneer Valley taught me much about the region, half-forming *The Pioneer Valley Reader* before I even realized it. I have been engrossed in writing about the Pioneer Valley both because of my rich experiences there and because of my feeling that the region's collective memory needs nourishing.

Now I live on Cape Cod, and it has been a trick to compile this anthology 150 miles from the Valley. The staff of the Sturgis Library, in Barnstable, has been superlative in helping obtain books through inter-library loan. Many people have suggested readings and provided insights about the Pioneer Valley. They have included David Glassberg, Joseph Carvalho, Guy McClain, Ed Lonergan, Frank Faulkner, Richard Todd, Richard Garvey, Lionel Delavigne, Dan Lombardo, and Elise Feeley. Louise Minks, of Greenfield Community College, was especially helpful in recommending several selections related to Franklin County. My wife Ann Marie was a helpful critic and a fellow enthusiast for the Pioneer Valley and its literature.

Finally, I extend grateful thanks to Ruth Owen Jones, who found the pictures for this book and wrote the informative captions, and to Jean Rousseau, publisher at Berkshire House, and his enthusiastic staff: my editor Sarah Novak, also Philip Rich, Madeleine Gruen, and Mary Osak.

I regret whatever readings I have missed or left out. This anthology has tried to feature the best writing about the Pioneer Valley. The book in no way has attempted to be a comprehensive reader of historical topics — that project awaits. This book is a highly personal collection of readings which convey the dialogue that has taken place about the Pioneer Valley. I look forward to discovering additional selections that describe some aspect of the Pioneer Valley experience.

The Connecticut River and the Valley

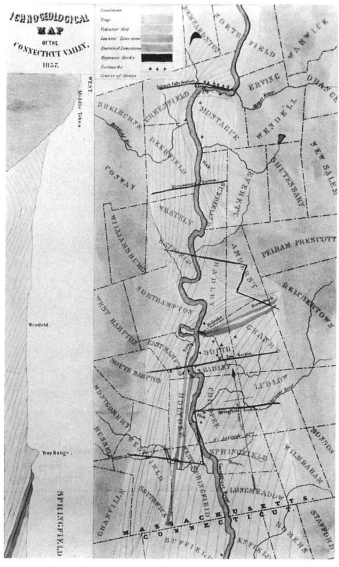

A 19th-century map showing the location of fossils and dinosaur footprints in the Connecticut Valley. From *Ichnology of New England* by Edward Hitchcock, 1857; courtesy of the Jones Library, Amherst.

GEORGE W. BAINE and HOWARD A. MEYERHOFF

George W. Baine was Professor of Geology at Amherst College. Howard A. Meyerhoff was Professor of Geology at the University of Pennsylvania. Their book, The Flow of Time in the Connecticut Valley: Geological Imprints, *first published in 1942, has long been a primer on Connecticut Valley geology. Besides describing the geological history and characteristics of the Connecticut River Valley, the book provides itineraries for exploring various geological landmarks and formations in the region.*

Geological Imprints

Throughout earth history, vulcanism and mountain-making have been spasmodic events; but so long as rain has fallen and water has run downhill to the sea, the unspectacular rivers have never relinquished their task of reducing the lands to the lowest grade on which water will flow. During all of the Jurassic and Cretaceous periods, and even into the Eocene epoch of the Tertiary, New England's rivers worked towards this end, and they came as close to attaining their goal as the restless earth has ever permitted them to do. The region from the Atlantic to the bases of the Green Mountains and the White Mountains was reduced to a broad, faintly terraced erosional plain. Not all of it was leveled, for Mount Wachusett, Mount Monadnock, the summits of Mount Greylock and Mount Ascutney resisted the wear and tear of the weather and of running water, and retained some of their original stature. At the headwaters of the streams the Green Mountain chain and the White Mountains also withstood reduction to the common level, forming the divide between St. Lawrence and Atlantic drainage. Such rivers as the Merrimack, the West, the Deerfield, and the Farmington followed somewhat different courses than they do today, for some of the drainage heading in the Western Upland of New England flowed straight across the red-rock valley to the sea.

In Middle Tertiary time renewed uplifts occurred, and ultimately the strathed surface was elevated 1,800 feet inland at the Green Mountain divide. Once more the rivers started busily cutting down; but in a protracted stillstand, while the New England upland still lacked 700 feet of its present elevation, the Atlantic Ocean planed off the hills in southern Connecticut as far north as Middletown, and the Farmington River adopted a more direct route across the marine plain to the sea. Before the West, Deerfield, and Westfield rivers could lower their channels to grade in the reinforced rocks of the Eastern Upland, a tributary of the Farmington worked headward along the poorly consolidated red rocks of the basin and diverted the waters of the northern streams into its own channel. This was the birth of the Connecticut River, and in late Tertiary time, the energies of the new-born stream were effectively expended widening the whole of the Triassic basin. Even some of its larger tributaries developed wide valley floors with steep walls in the hard crystalline rocks of the uplands. Only the lava flows and the buried old-rock mountains withstood planation in the red-rock basin. The flows form such trap ridges as Greenfield Ridge, the Mount Holyoke Range, the Mount Tom Range, the Hanging Hills of Meriden. Exhumed mountains are typified by Mount Warner.

All of northeastern North America was raised to great heights in late Pliocene time, and the Atlantic Ocean withdrew at least fifty miles southeastward from the present shoreline. The rejuvenated rivers deepened their valleys, forming narrow, sharply incised canyons like the gorges of the Hudson and the Saguenay; and the Connecticut made a deep groove in the lowland floor, cutting to depths which have been partly disclosed by drilling at the Calvin Coolidge Memorial Bridge and the Sunderland Bridge.

While the land stood in this high position, one winter's snow in the White Mountains failed to melt before the next began to fall. Snowfall accumulated upon snowfall, covering not only the White Mountains, but all of Canada and New England; and the Ice Age was here to stay more or less continuously for a million years. The ice piled up against the highest mountains and ultimately rose so far above them that it slid over their tops without attempting to detour around them. Its surface may have been 13,000 feet above sea level in northern New Hampshire, and its surface slope, which is estimated at 150 feet per mile, would give a thickness of 10,000 feet at Northampton. The continent yielded slowly under this great load, and it sank until all of the elevation gained in the Pliocene movement was wiped out, and more besides. The ice radiated from the centers of maximum accumulation — at first from the White Mountains, and then from northern Ontario, and finally from Labrador. The continental glacier crept southward to Long Island and Martha's Vineyard, where its front melted in the waters of the Atlantic as fast as new ice came up behind. It dragged and pushed and carried debris, only to dump it in a hummocky ridge, like a rampart, to mark its farthest advance.

At last the glaciers started to melt even faster than new masses moved down from the north, and the ice front began to recede 400 to 700 feet per year. The sea followed it, up the Hudson, up the St. Lawrence, in over the coastal lowlands for a short distance; and everywhere pounding waves made beaches at the water line. And in the path of its slow, deliberate retreat, the glacier left rock debris — boulders on the hills and in the valleys, boulders everywhere; all the landscape was marred and desolate.

The ice had weighed the pre-glacial valleys down more deeply in the north than in the south. One such valley was the Connecticut Lowland, in which water gathered to overflow-height at Middletown. Thus Lake Springfield came into being, and it spread northward as the ice front receded. North of the Holyoke Range another lake formed, and this northern body of water has been named Lake Hadley. Streams flowed off the ice, off the hills — flowed with unimpeded vigor, for there were no trees or grass to retard the run-off. Deltas grew out from the shores, and annual layers of clay settled on the lake bed.

The ice grew thinner, its area smaller, and its load lighter; and as Mother Earth lost her heavy burden, the land rose, more in the north than in the south. The differential rise decanted the water southward out of the lake basins, and the seas retired from the coastal lowlands. Old shores and sea beaches remained as flat terraces sloping gently southward. The rivers raced down the steep beach slopes to the old lake floors and sea bottom. They cut their channels deeply into the unconsolidated deltas and meandered back and forth over the flat, ungraded lacustrine plains, as if uncertain where to flow. They flooded the lands in the spring, leaving loose sand and silt for the winds to blow when the water was low. Sand dunes rose near the river banks at North Hadley, Sunderland, Hatfield, and South Deerfield; but the march of the dunes was arrested as post-glacial vegetation repossessed the land. It was at this point in the story that man found and settled the Connecticut Valley, becoming a witness to the geologic work of the river and an aid to the work of the wind as his plow bared the fertile soil to the elements.

From *The Flow of Time in the Connecticut Valley: Geological Imprints* by George W. Baine and Howard A. Meyerhoff. Connecticut Valley Historical Museum, 1963.

TIMOTHY DWIGHT

Timothy Dwight (1752-1817) provides the most reliable picture of Connecticut Valley towns during the early nineteenth century. While he was president of Yale College, from 1795 to 1817, Dwight traveled on summer vacation throughout the Northeast, writing descriptive letters that were published in 1821 as Travels in New England and New York. *A Northampton-born Congregational divine, the grandson of Jonathan Edwards and great-great grandson of "Pope" Solomon Stoddard (a prominent Puritan minister), Dwight's writings on the Connecticut Valley towns incorporated the received history of six generations living in the Valley.*

Dwight addressed his letters to an imaginary English gentleman explaining America to its critics. The Travels *traced the development of New England from wilderness to civilization and analyzed the Yankee character.*

Dwight was one of the first travelers to extol New England scenery, particularly that of the Valley's landscape. He also recognized and complimented the distinct character of the Valley's towns and inhabitants.

The Character of the Connecticut Valley

Dear Sir,

The inhabitants of this valley may be said in several respects to possess a common character, and in all the different states resemble each other more than their fellow citizens who live on the coast resemble them. This similarity is derived from their descent, their education, their local circumstances, and their mutual intercourse. In the older settlements most of the inhabitants are natives of this valley, and those who are not yield to the influence of a character which they continually see all around them. In the more recent settlements, where greater numbers, and often a majority, were not born in this tract, the same character has regularly gained ground, and in most of them is already evident to an observing traveler.

Education communicated by those who have a common character transmits its influence to those who are educated.

I have mentioned that their local situation contributed to the establishment of this similarity. They are so remote from a market as to be perfectly free from that sense of inferiority customarily felt by the body of people who live in the neighborhood of large cities. Hence a superior spirit of personal independence is generated and cherished.

At the same time, people who live on a pleasant surface and on a soil, fertile and easy of cultivation, usually possess softer dispositions and manners and feel themselves entitled to a higher character than those who from inhabiting rougher grounds acquire rougher minds and form coarser habits. Even the beauty of the scenery, scarcely found in the same degree elsewhere, becomes a source of pride as well as of enjoyment.

Here all the older settlements, and a greater part of the more recent ones, are formed in villages. The influence of this mode of settlement I have elsewhere exhibited. It is here realized in its fullest extent. Churches and suites of schools are built in them. Families have not only opportunity, but the most convenient opportunities, for being present at the public worship of GOD. Children also are sent universally at an early age to school, and begin their education almost as soon as they can speak. In consequence of these facts, the inhabitants are better educated and more orderly than in most other parts even of New England. There is no tract of the same size in which learning is more, or more uniformly encouraged, or where sobriety or decorum is more generally demanded or exhibited. Steadiness of character, softness of manners, a disposition to read, respect for the laws and magistrates, a strong sense of liberty, blended with an equally strong sense of the indispensable importance of energetic government, are all extensively predominant in this region.

The industry of these people is everywhere diffused, but less vigorous than among the inhabitants of the hills. In economy, hospitality, and charity, they are inferior to those of no other tract of equal extent.

The towns in this valley are not, like those along the Hudson, mere collections of houses and stores clustered round a landing, where nothing but mercantile and mechanical business is done; where the inhabitants appear to form no connections or habits besides those which naturally grow out of bargins and sales; where the position of the store determines that of the house, and that of the wharf often commands both; where beauty of situation is disregarded, and every convenience except that of trade is forgotten. On the contrary, they are villages destined for the reception of men busied in all the employments existing in this country, and usually contain a great part of the inhabitants in each township. The intention of settling in them is not merely to acquire property, but to sustain the relations, perform the duties, and contribute to the enjoyments of life. Equally, and to my eye happily, do they differ from most European villages. The villages on the other side of the Atlantic are exhibited as being generally clusters of houses standing contiguously on the street; built commonly of rough stone, clay, or earth, and roofed with thatch; without courtyards or enclosures; and of course incapable of admitting around each house the beautiful appendages of shrubs, trees, gardens, and meadows.

New England villages, and in a peculiar degree those of the tract under consideration, are built in the following manner.

The local situation is pitched on as a place in itself desirable, as a place where life may be passed through more pleasantly than in most others, as a place, not where trade compels, but where happiness invites to settle. Accordingly the position of these towns is usually beautiful. The mode of settlement is such as greatly to enhance the pleasure intended. The body of inhabitants is composed of farmers: and farmers nowhere within my knowledge of a superior character for intelligence and good manners. The mechanics, the class next in numbers, have their full share of this character, and usually aim at a higher degree of respectability than in most parts of the country. Of both sorts a considerable number merit the appellation of gentlemen. A more than common proportion of men liberally and politely educated reside in the towns of this valley, and the pleasures of intellectual and refined society are here enjoyed to a considerable extent.

To this character of the inhabitants, the manner of locating and building these towns is happily suited. The town plat is originally distributed into lots containing from two to ten acres. In a convenient spot on each of these, a house is erected at the bottom of the courtyard (often neatly enclosed) and is furnished universally with a barn and other convenient outbuildings. Near the house there is always a garden replenished with culinary vegetables, flowers, and fruits, and very often also prettily enclosed. The lot on which the house stands, universally styled the home lot, is almost of course a meadow, richly cultivated, covered during the pleasant season with verdure, and containing generally a thrifty orchard. It is hardly necessary to observe that these appendages spread a singular cheerfulness and beauty over a New England village, or that they contribute largely to render the house a delightful residence.

The towns in this valley, taken together, are better built than an equal number in any other part of the United States, unless perhaps on the eastern coast of Massachusetts where the wealth of the inhabitants is greatly superior. Most generally they are built of wood, and are neater, lighter, and pleasanter dwellings than those of brick or stone. As they stand at a distance from each other, they are little exposed to fire except from within, and accordingly are very rarely consumed. Both they and the public buildings are usually painted white. No single fact except the universal verdure and the interspersion of streams contributes equally to the sprightly, cheerful appearance of any country.

In this valley the principal commerce of the country within twenty miles of the river is carried on, and a great part of their mechanical business is done. Here the newspapers circulated throughout this region are printed, and the bookstores kept by which the inhabitants are supplied. Here also, the great body of information concerning this and other countries is first received and disseminated, and here fashions of all kinds are first adopted from abroad and diffused throughout the vicinity.

In this region poverty in its absolute sense is scarcely known. Those who are here styled poor possess usually both the necessaries and comforts of life. The paupers maintained by the public, compared with the whole number of inhabitants, are probably not more than one out of three or four hundred. Every man, with hardly an exception, lives on his own ground and in his own house. Every man, therefore, possesses an absolute, personal independence, derived from his earliest ancestor, and secured by the government under which he lives. It was born with him, and therefore sits upon him easily and naturally. The ancestor from whom he derived it, he respects. The government by which it is secured, he loves and venerates, and is ever ready to defend. Life here is therefore seen in all its pleasing, rural forms, and in these forms is seen with uncommon advantage.

A view north up the Connecticut River Valley from Mt. Holyoke; Mt. Sugarloaf and Mt. Toby are to the right of center in the distance. From American Scenery by Nathaniel P. Willis, 1838.

The intercourse of the inhabitants is invited and cherished by all the facts already mentioned. To these may be added the goodness of the roads and the inns, and the salubrity of the climate. The time has not been long passed since the roads on the hills were almost universally too rough to be traveled for pleasure. At that time the roads in this valley were generally good throughout a great extent. Hence the inhabitants were allured to a much more extensive intercourse with each other than those in any other part of New England except along the eastern coast. For the same reasons a multitude of strangers have at all times been induced to make this

valley the scene of their pleasurable traveling. The effects of this inter-
course on the minds and manners of the inhabitants I need not explain.

Beauty of landscape is an eminent characteristic of this valley. From
Hereford Mountain to Saybrook, it is almost a continued succession of
delightful scenery. No other tract within my knowledge, and from the
extensive information which I have received, I am persuaded that no
other tract within the United States of the same extent, can be compared
to it with respect to those objects which arrest the eye of the painter and
the poet. There are indeed dull, uninteresting spots in considerable num-
bers. These, however, are little more than the discords which are gener-
ally regarded as necessary to perfect the harmony. The beauty and the
grandeur are here more varied than elsewhere. They return oftener; they
are longer continued; they are finished by a hand operating in a superior
manner. A gentleman of great respectability, who had traveled in En-
gland, France and Spain, informed me that the prospects along the Con-
necticut excelled those on the beautiful rivers in these three counties in
two great particulars: the forests and the mountains (he might, I believe,
have added the intervals also), and fell short of them in nothing but
population and the productions of art. It is hardly necessary to observe
that both these are advancing with a rapid step (perhaps sufficiently
rapid) toward a strong resemblance to European improvement.

The first object, however, in the whole landscape is undoubtedly the
Connecticut itself. This stream may perhaps, with as much propriety as
any in the world, be named the beautiful river. From Stewart to the
Sound, it uniformly sustains this character. The purity, salubrity, and
sweetness of its waters; the frequency and elegance of its meanders; its
absolute freedom from all aquatic vegetables; the uncommon and univer-
sal beauty of its banks, here a smooth and winding beach, there covered
with rich verdure, now fringed with bushes, now crowned with lofty
trees, and now formed by the intruding hill, the rude bluff, and the
shaggy mountain, are objects which no traveler can thoroughly describe,
and no reader adequately imagine. When to these are added the numer-
ous towns, villages, and hamlets almost everywhere exhibiting marks of
prosperity and improvement, the rare appearance of decline, the numer-
ous churches lifting their spires in frequent succession, the neat school-
houses everywhere occupied, and the mills busied on such a multitude of
steams, it may be safely asserted that a pleasanter journey will rarely be
found than that which is made in the Connecticut Valley.

I am, Sir, yours, etc.

From *Travels in New England and New York* by Timothy Dwight, edited by Barbara Miller
Solomon. Harvard University Press, 1969.

BASIL HALL

During the 1820s and 1830s, many European travelers, including Alexis de Tocqueville, Harriet Martineau, and Frances Trollope, visited and wrote about the curious new nation across the seas. Captain Basil Hall (1788-1844) offered up one of the more positive accounts of the U.S.

Captain Hall, who had headed up several British Navy scientific expeditions of South America and the Orient, knew an attractive place when he saw it. He favorably compared the towns and landscape of New England with the ragged New York State he had just traversed. Hall enthused over ascending Mt. Holyoke and his account helped popularize the site as a tourist destination.

The View from Mt. Holyoke in 1827

The view from the summit of Mount Holyoke, which we visited on the 4th of October, is really splendid, and is otherwise most satisfactory for travellers, from bringing under their eyes a great extent of country. The top is 880 feet above the level of the river Connecticut, which winds about in the alluvial land below, in a very fantastic style. This pretty stream was visible in a northern direction, for many miles, in the gorges amongst the hills; but, on turning to the south, we could discover only a few touches of it here and there, which to the naked eye seemed merely patches of smoke; but when viewed through a pocket telescope, these glimpses looked like bits of some immense looking-glass shivered to pieces, and cast among the trees. As many of the hills and dales in this pleasing prospect had been long cleared of woods, the eye was not offended by that ragged appearance, so comfortless and hopeless-looking in most newly settled countries. Such spots, in this comparatively old part of the country, are laid out mostly in orchards, — but sometimes in meadow lands, or in wheat, or, more frequently still, in maize fields. The flourishing villages of Northampton, Hadley, and Amherst, lay almost at our feet. The planners of these, and indeed of most of the villages in that part of the United States, appear to have commenced by making a street, or unpaved avenue, of not less than eighty or a hundred yards in width, with a double row of trees on each side, and a walk between. The houses were almost invariably detached from one another, and stood back some ten or twelve yards from the broad and agreeably shaded walks lining the main street; the intervening space in front of the houses being generally railed in, and trimmed with shrubs, flowers, grass plots, and gravelled paths. Even the porches, and occasionally also the side of the windows and the ends of the houses, were

A view from Mt. Holyoke showing the oxbow south of Northampton. From *American Scenery* by Nathaniel P. Willis, 1837.

covered with creepers, in a very pleasing taste; and as most of these buildings were of wood, painted white, with dark green doors and folding shutters, made in the Venetian blind style, the effect of the whole was particularly striking.

Before stepping into the carriage, in which it appeared we might proceed about half way up Mount Holyoke, we consulted the people of the house as well as the guide-books, as to the facilities of the road; and I particularly asked the bar-keeper if he thought we might take the child. He laughed, and exclaimed, "O, no! you will never be able to get up if you take the infant; the road, I promise you, is very difficult and steep."

Travellers are an obstinate race, it is said; — but in truth, they seldom know rightly what to do till the excursion is over, and then their experience, like that of most people, comes rather late. As the habit of road-books and guides, for obvious reasons, is always to exaggerate things, so their object in this case was manifestly to make the mountain as high as possible. I therefore inferred, from nothing being said in the books of the difficulty of the ascent, that the patriotic bar-keeper was merely puffing off his favourite hill, by superadding an allowance of steepness. Accordingly, I decided upon carrying the whole party, notwithstanding the smile which I detected whisking about the lips of my informant as he closed the carriage door, and we moved off.

For the first mile and a half, our road lay through a flat alluvial meadow, covered with groups of haymakers, besides parties of men and women stripping overloaded apple-trees which lined the way, along which the fruit was piled into pyramids, ready for the waggons. After this, we crossed the Connecticut, a stream which gives its name to one of the eastern States, and soon afterwards began to clamber up a cleft in the hill, or what in fact was more like a South American Quebrada than any thing else — much steeper at all events than any road I ever saw attempted before in a wheeled carriage. At length the driver, declaring he could go no further, let us out, and pointed to a tolerably steep foot-path. We laughed to scorn this pygmy difficulty, and chuckled at the triumph over the bar-keeper and his predictions. By and by, however, the path took a bend, upon which the inclination became like that of a stair, with this material difference, that the steps on the mountain side were formed of loose stones, planted at such awkward distances from one another, that the effort necessary to establish a proper footing, was by no means trifling. Here I was, of course, obliged to hoist the young lady on my back, — and a weary tug we had of it!

The proverbial facility of descent, however, was any thing but easy in our case, and I really do not know how we should ever have got down again — with whole bones, at least — had we not met a gentleman and his son, an active boy, ramblers like ourselves, and such obliging persons, that we scrupled not to accept their aid in our difficulties.

The beauty of the prospect from the summit of this noble hill, by completely arresting our attention, had rendered us careless about sundry threatening squalls of rain, which stalked slowly over the landscape, like enormous giants with their heads thrust into the clouds, and adding much to the grandeur of the scenery, both by their own majestic and half mysterious appearance, and by the long belts of shadow which trailed behind them for many a league. In the course of time one of these drizzly monsters advanced upon Mount Holyoke, and after drenching the village of Northampton beneath us, and setting all our friends, the haymakers and apple-gatherers, to the right about, took possession of the high ground, so as to shut us completely out from the wide world we had been admiring.

As there was nothing more to be seen, and the night was falling fast, it became necessary to retrace our steps without delay. The path, however, up which we had laboriously climbed, looked twice as steep as before; the stones, moreover, were nearly as slippery from the shower, as so many blocks of ice, and consequently, the danger of tumbling far greater than in the first instance. A false step on the ascent would merely have brought our noses in contact with the ground, but a similar slip now might have pitched us headlong down the ravine. On reaching the inn at Northampton, the steps were let down by our friend the bar-keeper, who, as he lifted the exhausted little girl from the carriage, and observed the state of fatigue of the whole party, seemed half tempted to reproach us with our insensibility to his warning; but he managed his triumph with better taste, and merely smiled when I groaned out that he was the better prophet of the two.

From *Travels in North America in the Years 1827 and 1828* by Basil Hall. Cadell & Co., Edinburgh, 1829.

Paleo-Indians camouflaged to hunt caribou, which ranged south into the Valley around 8,000 BC. Drawing by Marie Litterer; courtesy of the Pratt Museum, Amherst College.

BEN BACHMAN

Ben Bachman, journalist and outdoorsman, wrote an account of traveling up the Connecticut River from Long Island Sound, mainly by canoe, after sewerage treatment facilities had cleaned up much of the river and its banks. Upstream: A Voyage on the Connecticut River *weaves together history, geology, and personal adventure. It is an account from the river's perspective, with cities and rail yards and neighborhoods observed just over the river banks.*
Bachman describes the stretch from Springfield past Holyoke to Mt. Sugarloaf.

Upstream from Springfield

Springfield eventually became the largest city in the valley, but its early development seems to have been retarded by the lack of ready access to the outside world. No large ships could pass Enfield Rapids, and overland transportation was primitive in the extreme. Flatboats were used for heavy cargo, but the upriver trip was slow and laborious, and it was not until the eve of the Industrial Revolution that Springfield's population exceeded 3,000 (less than half of that of Hartford, and less than that of many other river towns in Connecticut).

The coming of the railroad made the difference. Springfield was fortunate enough to be on one of the first railroads in New England, an east-west route between Boston and Albany that soon became, and still is, the most important line in the region (now owned by Conrail). Springfield matured as a manufacturing center during the nineteenth century, yet even now it seems a lesser city than Hartford, perhaps because Hartford is a state capital or because Springfield, like all cities in Massachusetts, pales in Boston's shadow. Boston has the glamour, Springfield the factories. But if Springfield's riverfront skyline is not so impressive as Hartford's, then neither does Springfield have Hartford's grinding poverty. Despite wealthy suburbs and an immense pool of insurance company capital, Hartford is the fourth poorest city in the United States, according to 1980 census data. Springfield may be a bit drab, but it is a hard-working, solid, kind of town.

Unfortunately, this is a matter of some practical concern to a canoeist. I would not consider leaving a car parked unattended at a boat ramp in Hartford. When I drove up to Springfield to launch the canoe on the third of June, I did not give vandalism a second thought. The parking lot by the ramp, which is actually in West Springfield, across the river from downtown, was crowded with cars and boat trailers. A white-haired old fellow with a fishing license pinned to his hat gave me a pretty good going-over as I carried the canoe down to the water. I looked up at him and said, "Nice morning."

"Yup," he said, and then clammed up. It *was* a nice morning, the third one in a row, clear and windless. A pale half moon hung low in the western sky. The river in Springfield did not appear to be any narrower than in Hartford; if anything, the Connecticut seemed wider now. It was exciting. It made me want to hurry. There is always a sense of expectancy when you glide out on the water, and now, as soon as I shoved off, I felt the pull of the current. The river was still high, but without the intense siltiness of the few days before. The water was more green than brown. It was slick and smooth, but not like a lake; it implied hidden power. The sun was hot. Just then a large fish jumped, frozen for an instant in a glittering arc of spray, standing on its tail before it struck the surface of the river with a loud, flat smack. I passed under two bridges: one of them the double-track railroad span by the signal tower, the other, a highway bridge whose heroic concrete arches turned out to be hollow inside; and then the Connecticut stretched out ahead of me, broad and reflective in the harsh urban light. A few grackles and a crow or two picked at flotsam cast up on the bank. I concentrated on paddling, on maintaining a steady rhythm, trying to put my whole body into it, not just the arms.

At some unidentifiable point I passed from Springfield to Chicopee. Springfield, Chicopee, and Holyoke long ago merged into an unbroken industrial-residential corridor, a continuous belt of two-family houses, apartment buildings, abbreviated front yards, madonnas in bathtubs, three-story brick high schools, liquor stores with grilles over the windows; a sprawl of neighborhoods, not downtown and not quite suburb either, the universal zone common to every city in the Northeast since shortly after the beginning of the Industrial Revolution. It was laid out, mainly from scratch, for wagons and trolley cars, then adapted, without complete success, to the automobile, and, like all such places in New England, it has absorbed peoples and cultures like a sponge. During the late nineteenth century, at least thirty different languages were spoken on the streets of Chicopee, with Polish, French, and Italian heard most often. Now Spanish has come on strong. For the last hundred and twenty-five years, neighborhoods like these have been the vital, pumping heart of industrial New England; they still are.

From the river you see the back of Chicopee: roofs through the trees, steeples and smokestacks rising higher, power lines, telephone poles, the blank gaze of abandoned factories, a pair of golden arches, the cinderblock backs of discount stores, big blue dumpsters, bald tires, and shopping carts pushed down a bank. And dikes. A big river is a dangerous and unpredictable neighbor, and men have learned to keep it at arm's length. There is an emotional distance, too, because the river is a thing apart, a thing of motion, a thing defined by motion. Like a freight train in the night, it is always passing through; it does not belong to any one place. But this train never stops. It never holds still. You cannot get a fix on it. It is always different — from one moment to the next — yet it is only doing now what it has always done, what it will always do. There is a raw, primal urgency in the flow, something that seems to hark back to an era when the earth was young, but in truth the river does not belong to any one time any more than it belongs to one place. Its essence, the majestic purposefulness of the flow, its honesty and awesome power, is incorruptible. It can be polluted or dammed, but it cannot be stopped. The river's will cannot be denied. It touches the human soul, and the heart, too, which is good reason to be suspicious of your feelings while out on the water, but I do know this: the reality of the river always surpasses the expectation. Perhaps it will not lead the canoeist to great truths or even to minor ones, but there is always something here to arrest the mind and the eye, and it will bring you back again and again.

By eleven-thirty I had arrived at the mouth of the Chicopee River, which empties into the Connecticut from the east. The Chicopee is the Connecticut's largest tributary, with a watershed of 720 square miles. Quabbin Reservoir, on one of the Chicopee's branches (the Swift River), supplies 40 percent of the drinking water consumed in Massachusetts, including most of Boston's. There seemed to be a goodly amount left over this morning, because the Chicopee was flooding its banks. The current was slack at first, then lively. (The name Chicopee means "rushing water.") About a half-mile in from the mouth, a five-story textile mill loomed beside a set of rapids.

Holyoke, Massachusetts. No other city in the Connecticut Valley gives so vivid a picture of nineteenth-century industrial America. Holyoke is pure New England mill town. For the best effect the view should be from the east, from the top of a bluff, on a raw morning when the scudding clouds are the color of an old Salvation Army overcoat. First there is the river, wide and full of rapids, swinging around a curve, and then the city itself, climbing the hills on the far bank. Holyoke is vast, dense, and somber. Cold black water races through the canals. Smokestacks and church spires reach into the sky. There are bricks, millions upon millions of dark, sooty bricks, and a wealth of detail: granite windowsills, brass weathervanes, copper-sheathed cupolas, bell towers, ornamental ironwork, heavy wooden doors, cobblestone alleys, stone steps worn smooth by millworkers' feet. Holyoke was built for the ages.

The mill buildings, even in abandonment, are awesome. The architecture was meant to intimidate. The winter wind never blows colder than it does down these bleak streets lined with rusting cars, three-decker wooden houses, and brick tenement blocks. The bars fill up at eight in the morning. The unemployment offices are crowded.

The Connecticut River was first dammed at the falls between South Hadley and Holyoke in 1828. A 1987 aerial view looking south shows the modern hydroelectric dam as well as the three levels of canals built in the 1840s for the city's textile mills. Courtesy of Holyoke Water Power.

The present Holyoke Water Power Company dam is a large, surprisingly graceful structure about a thousand feet long, but the first dam at this site was an embarrassing failure. It collapsed during the dedication ceremony in 1848, washing down the river before the astonished eyes of the assembled dignitaries. The dam was rebuilt, but twenty-four of the original twenty-five cotton mill sites beside the canal system remained vacant, and the Hadley Falls Company slid into bankruptcy. Holyoke's major product eventually turned out to be paper, not textiles. Now the Holyoke paper industry has faded, but the dam still generates electricity.

When I inspected the facility in April 1983, the powerhouse was being enlarged so that an additional set of turbines and generators could be installed. A pair of colossal penstocks — concrete pipes big enough to drive a dump truck through — led down from the dam, and one of them had been opened. There were men inside it, working.

I crossed over to the east side of the Connecticut and found a place to launch the canoe near a small bicentennial park that commemorates the old Hadley Falls navigation canal. A short section of the canal has been restored to an approximation of its nineteenth-century appearance. Despite the restraining influence of the dam, just a half-mile downstream, there was a substantial current running in the river, this being the peak of the runoff. There was a stiff wind also, blowing upstream for once. It raised a chop in the silty brown water, but with the wind at my back, the canoe was rock steady. Mount Tom loomed in the distance where the river made a turn to the right. According to the diagram on a brass plaque in the park, the old canal ended at about that point, and there was a low dam, like the one at Enfield, reaching all the way across to the opposite shore. It was just high enough to smooth out the last bit of whitewater.

The dam has been gone for years, and as I approached the bend under Mount Tom I felt the current accelerate. I could see it accelerate. The surface of the water had a tight, tense look to it, like metal subjected to extreme stress. Out in the middle of the river a large tree shot by, rolling over and over. I stayed close to the bank. Outside of an actual rapid, I do not believe I have ever seen a current this powerful. There was no way my little 2-horsepower motor could make any headway against it. If the current started to drive me down the river stern first or if the motor suddenly quit, the canoe would probably swing around broadside and swamp; I wasn't sure what to do. I deliberated for a bit and decided to set the bow at a forty-five-degree angle to the flow so that the force of the current pressing against the hull, combined with the forward thrust of the motor, would ferry the canoe across the river to the west shore. It worked perfectly, and once on the other side I found a convenient back current, just as I thought I might. It petered out all too soon, but the river was flooding the woods a little (something it hadn't been able to do on the east shore because of sheer rock banks), and the water among the trees was relatively quiet and shallow enough to use the setting pole. It was easy going. After a while I came to some broad ledges of dark red stone that jutted out into the main current, raising a formidable set of standing waves. I tied the canoe to a tree and got out to look for dinosaur tracks.

The ledges ran into the river on a slant, the rock laid down in thin, flat plates in dozens of layers, something like sheets of mica. Where the top layers had flaked away it revealed sets of wavy ripple marks that resembled the ripples in the mud of a shallow lake bottom, which is exactly what they were: fossilized ripples about 100 million years old. Fossil-bearing rocks such as these are prime territory for dinosaur tracks, and with that in mind, it becomes difficult to keep from seeing, or imagining that you see, them everywhere. Every irregularity in the rock begins to look like a track. The best tracks at this particular location, however, are a bit farther inland, on unweathered slabs exposed during highway construction.

From *Upstream: A Voyage on the Connecticut River* by Ben Bachman. Houghton Mifflin, 1985.

The Colonial Frontier

A recreation of an early 18th-century parlor in the Wells-Thorn House in Deerfield.
Photo by Amanda Merullo; courtesy of Historic Deerfield.

SAMUEL ELIOT MORISON

One of the seminal figures in the history of the Pioneer Valley was its original pioneer and the founder of Springfield, William Pynchon (1590?-1662). The settlement that he established in 1636 was significantly different from those he left around the Massachusetts Bay. Although Pynchon was no less pious than the Winthrops and Cottons he left behind, his settlement was not intended as a "city on a hill" but a post to trade with the Indians for furs and to cultivate the fertile Connecticut Valley. Anyone seeking the connection between Puritanism and capitalism need look no further than William Pynchon.

Pynchon strove to remain independent from political authority. Originally Pynchon's settlement was under the Connecticut colony, but Pynchon fell out with Connecticut founder Thomas Hooker over selling him corn at a discount and switched to the jurisdiction of Massachusetts. Yet he kept his distance from the colonial government in Boston. Not until 1647 did he attend the General Court as Western Massachusetts representative. Within five years, he ran afoul of Boston authorities for his heretical pamphlet "The Meritorious Price of Our Redemption." This work became one of the first books banned and burned in Boston. Pynchon returned to England rather than wrangle with his fellow Puritans.

The following passage describes how Springfield ended up in Massachusetts after starting out in Connecticut. The author, Samuel Eliot Morison (1887-1976), is a noted maritime historian. Here he explains how the interests of the Connecticut Valley were fundamentally different from those of the maritime coast.

How Springfield Left Connecticut

The town was the New England institution where democracy seeped in and leavened the rest; and although until 1647 only freemen of the colony were supposed to take part in town meetings, Springfield paid no attention to the requirement. All admitted inhabitants voted in town meeting and were fined one bushel of corn for failing to attend. Yet even at the earliest date Springfield was not a social democracy. William Pynchon paid about half the town taxes, and had the most land. He was the only trader. His son John, his sons-in-law Henry Smith and Elizur Holyoke, and his friend the minister formed with him a little local aristocracy of wealth, piety, and talents, commanding a weight of moral and material influence which would have made short shrift of a local opposition. And, most important, William Pynchon was the local magistrate and judge, invested with power to probate wills, hold petty sessions, and try all causes not involving loss of life or limb. In other words, the squire of Springfield in Essex had become the squire of Springfield in Massachusetts.

In the early years of the plantation it formed part of the same government as the River Towns, and might well have become permanently attached to the Colony of Connecticut, but for the failure of William Pynchon to get along with Thomas Hooker. The circumstances form quite an interesting little chapter in New England politics, diplomacy, and economic thought.

Agawam was first included with Windsor, Hartford, and Wethersfield under the governing commission of eight appointed by the General Court of Massachusetts on March 3, 1636; and William Pynchon was one of the commissioners. During the ensuing year the commissioners held several courts, or meetings, in the three River Towns; but only one of these was attended by the founder of Springfield. After the term of the commissioners expired on March 3, 1637, the people of the River Towns set up what amounted to an independent government by electing a new set of magistrates, including Pynchon, and sending "committees" of three deputies from each town to join with the magistrates in a General Court. It was the first court so composed which declared "offensiue warr against the Pequoitt." There was no one from Springfield at this court; and apparently the Connecticut authorities agreed that if the ten or twelve men at Springfield would take care of themselves, nothing more would be expected of them; Pynchon nevertheless was taxed for his Agawam property by Massachusetts Bay. His friend and fellow-magistrate Roger Ludlow wrote to him from Windsor on May 17, 1637, to be careful and watchful of the friendly Indians, to keep his powder dry, and trust in God, for however pressing the danger, it would be impossible for the River Towns to come to his assistance. Accordingly Pynchon and his little band of pioneers kept strict watch against surprise.

More serious trouble developed out of Pynchon's contract for supplying corn. The corn crop of the war summer, 1637, proved insufficient; and by the middle of a severe winter it was clear that if a supply were not imported, there would be a famine next spring in the River Towns. Here was a case when a monopoly was wise, as our recent war experience has proved. Free trade in corn with the Indians would have resulted in the natives being robbed and cheated, and the people being charged famine prices by speculators. Hence the General Court on March 8, 1638, "ordered with the consent of Mr. Pincheon" that he should purchase from the Indians and deliver to the three River Towns 500 bushels of corn at 5s. per bushel — or a penny or two more if he had to pay as much as "six sixes of Wampom a pecke." Private persons were forbidden to trade, unless in case of necessity and upon order of three magistrates. On returning a few days later to Agawam and finding the Indians determined either to get more than the contract price or to hold their corn for a rise, Pynchon wrote back to Hartford that he feared he could not carry out the contract at the price fixed. The Connecticut authorities, fearful at the approach of famine, lost no time in sending Captain John Mason up-river to procure the necessary corn. It was but a few months since Mason had earned the name of a mighty warrior by leading the devastating slaughter of Pequots at Mystic fort, and obviously sending out such a man on such an errand was disturbing, to say the least. The Indians at first refused to trade with Mason. A conference was held between him, Pynchon, Moxon the minister, and a Nonotuck Indian in Pynchon's house at Agawam. Here it appeared that Mason wished to pay the Indian in advance to go up to Woronoco and bring down corn. Pynchon advised him that it was fatal to pay Indians in advance, they always skipped to the woods with the wampum and never delivered the goods; and Moxon chimed in with a homely simile: "An Indian promise is noe more than to have a pigg by the taile." Mason finally agreed to pay no money until he saw the corn; but little or none was forthcoming for the price he offered; and the hot-tempered Captain returned down-river, convinced that Pynchon was thinking only of his own profit and prestige, and trying to hold up Connecticut for higher prices.

Within a month the Connecticut General Court summoned Pynchon to Hartford and placed him on trial for "unfaithfull dealing in the trade of corne" and for breach of his oath as a magistrate. The particular charges were that he had obstructed the Mason mission, both by forbidding the Indians to trade with the Captain, and by refusing to procure a canoe that they needed for transportation. In defense he alleged that he acted as Mason's interpreter and "took off the fears" of an Indian reluctant to do business with the warrior; that, when his own plantation was in dire necessity, when the beer had given out and he himself had less than half a bushel of corn on hand for his family; when the neighbors were begging him to raise the price so that the Indians would sell, he refused to exceed the maximum limit allowed by his instructions. In the matter of the canoe, it appears that there was only one in Agawam which the Indians would use; and the owner refused to lend it because he needed it for the planting season.

The court, before coming to a decision, sent for Masters Thomas Hooker and Samuel Stone, respectively pastor and teacher of the Hartford Church, to express an expert opinion on the ethical question involved. As usual it was Hooker who did all the talking. He accused Pynchon of holding off buying "that he should have all the trade to himselfe, and have all the corne in his owne hands, . . . and so rack the country at his pleasure." "He then delivered his judgment peremptorily that I had broken my oath," says Pynchon. "To this I was silent, being grieved at so hard an answer." Upon Hooker's opinion the Court fined Pynchon forty bushels of corn for "unfaithfulness." Two months later Captain Mason was sent north again, with a squad of soldiers and a threatening message to the Indians to deliver corn, or they would regret it. Even at that, Mason had to pay 12s. a bushel, more than double the price allowed Pynchon by the Court. This fact alone seems a complete justification of Pynchon's policy.

An engraving after a 1657 oil painting of William Pynchon, founder of Springfield. From *History of the Connecticut Valley in Massachusetts* by Louis H. Everts, 1879.

There was more to this case, it seems to me, than a personal dispute; it was really the clash of paternalism with *laissez faire*. Hooker doubtless believed in the same economic principles as did Cotton, Winthrop — and for that matter, St. Thomas Aquinas. That is to say he believed in the medieval figment of a "just price," of the unlawfulness of usury, or of raising prices to meet a brisk demand. Corn was scarce and Connecticut in danger of starving; *ergo*, argued Hooker and the General Court, the Indians should charge them even less for corn than in normal years. And if Pynchon did not see eye-to-eye with them, he must be a usurer, a profiteer, an evil person. Pynchon, on the contrary, represented the instinctive theory of the seventeenth-century business man, impatient of ecclesiastical and political trammels. Observe the conclusion of his letter to Ludlow: ". . . I cannot see how it can well stand with the public good and the liberty of free men to make a monopole of trade." Nor will he consent to "any man's hindrance when God doth not hinder them." Even the Indians had a more exact appreciation of economic laws than did the Reverend Thomas Hooker and the General Court; for they observed that having obtained "eight sixes" of wampum for a peck of corn the year before, when corn was plenty, they would certainly not sell it for "six sixes," when corn was in brisk demand.

Moreover, the Connecticut authorities followed up the case in a petty and persecuting manner, writing to the Church at Roxbury that Master Hooker regarded their distinguished brother Pynchon to be a profiteer and an oath-breaker, and that they ought to proceed against him "in a church way" — i.e., to censure or excommunicate him. Although the Roxbury church eventually gave Pynchon a clean bill of health, his defense cost him much trouble, journeying, and anxiety, and was not concluded for three years.

After this it is not surprising to find that Pynchon preferred to live under some other government than the "democratic" one at Hartford. Six weeks after he had been condemned and fined, he was appointed one of a Connecticut commission of three to treat with the Bay authorities about a confederation. During the conference Massachusetts claimed that Springfield came within her line. Pynchon readily accepted this claim as an excuse for seceding from Connecticut, "and that motion by Mr. Pincheon," declared Connecticut at a later date, "arose (as is verily conceived) from a present pange of discontent vpon a sensure hee then lay vnder by the Gouernment of Conectacutt."

Massachusetts refused to confederate unless Agawam were admitted to be hers. It is rather difficult to see why, if it were moral for Thomas Hooker and his congregation to secede from Massachusetts, it should be immoral for Springfield to secede back; but Master Hooker thought otherwise.

Massachusetts Bay was apparently willing to leave the question open pending a final agreement on the subject with Connecticut. It was not until 1642 that Pynchon was elected to his former chair in the Court of Assistants; and until 1649 Springfield was not represented in the General Court. Rival surveys of the boundary line were made by the two colonies, appeals to the King were threatened on both sides; and Connecticut attempted to prejudge the case by authorizing her then Governor, Edward Hopkins, to purchase Woronoco (Westfield) and erect a trading-house there. Connecticut attempted to tax exports down-river from Spring-field, and Massachusetts proposed to retaliate on imports from Connecticut. In 1650, the Commissioners of the United Colonies washed their hands of the question, declaring their "desire to bee spared in all further agitations concerning Sprinkfield." And from that time the incorporation of Springfield in Massachusetts was never seriously challenged.

Undeniably, with three days' marches of wilderness between him and the capital, it was much easier for Pynchon to do business under the Bay jurisdiction than under Connecticut. It was not that the Bay was any less paternalistic than the River, but that Boston was far away and Hartford only a short distance downstream.

From "William Pynchon: Founder of Springfield, Massachusetts" by Samuel Eliot Morison. *Massachusetts Historical Society Proceedings*, February 1931 (Vol. LXIV).

THOMAS PYNCHON

Thomas Pynchon, one of America's leading contemporary writers, is a direct descendant of Springfield's founder William Pynchon. In his novel Gravity's Rainbow *(1973), Thomas Pynchon interjects an exhilarating account of his ancestor, named "William Slothrop." Slothrop's Western Massachusetts is "the fork in the road America never took," a metaphor for the unconstrained experience of life that most people never know.*

Thomas Pynchon's connection to or knowledge of Western Massachusetts is unclear because he is a recluse, supposedly in Arizona. Even his publisher has not known his exact whereabouts for years. Pynchon is also the author of The Crying of Lot 49 *and* V.

William Pynchon and "The Road Not Taken"

William Slothrop was a peculiar bird. He took off from Boston, heading west in true Imperial style, in 1634 or -5, sick and tired of the Winthrop machine, convinced he could preach as well as anybody in the hierarchy even if he hadn't been officially ordained. The ramparts of the Berkshires stopped everybody else at the time, but not William. He just started climbing. He was one of the very first Europeans in. After they settled in Berkshire, he and his son John got a pig operation going — used to drive hogs right back down the great escarpment, back over the long pike to Boston, drive them just like sheep or cows. By the time they got to market those hogs were so skinny it was hardly worth it, but William wasn't really in it so much for the money as just for the trip itself. He enjoyed the road, the mobility, the chance encounters of the day — Indians, trappers, wenches, hill people — and most of all just being with those pigs. They were good company. Despite the folklore and the injunctions in his own Bible, William came to love their nobility and personal freedom, their gift for finding comfort in the mud on a hot day — pigs out on the road, in company together, were everything Boston wasn't, and you can imagine what the end of the journey, the weighing, slaughter and dreary pigless return back up into the hills must've been like for William. Of course he took it as a parable — knew that the squealing bloody horror at the end of the pike was in exact balance to all their happy sounds, their untroubled pink eyelashes and kind eyes, their smiles, their grace in cross-country movement. It was a little early for Isaac Newton, but feelings about action and reaction were in the air. William must've been waiting for the one pig that wouldn't die, that would validate all the ones who'd had to, all his Gadarene swine who'd rushed into extinction like lemmings, possessed not by demons but by trust for men, which the men kept betraying . . . possessed by innocence they couldn't lose . . . by faith in William as another variety of pig, at home with the Earth, sharing the same gift of life. . . .

He wrote a long tract about it presently, called *On Preterition*. It had to be published in England, and is among the first books to've been not only banned but also ceremonially burned in Boston. Nobody wanted to hear about all the Preterite, the many God passes over when he chooses a few for salvation. William argued holiness for these "second Sheep," without whom there'd be no elect. You can bet the Elect in Boston were pissed off about that. And it got worse. William felt that what Jesus was for the elect, Judas Iscariot was for the Preterite. Everything in the Creation has its equal and opposite counterpart. How can Jesus be an exception? Could we feel for him anything but horror in the face of the unnatural, the extracreational? Well, if he is the son of man, and if what we feel is not horror but love, then we have to love Judas too. Right? How William avoided being burned for heresy, nobody knows. He must've had connections. They did finally 86 him out of Massachusetts Bay Colony — he thought about Rhode Island for a while but decided he wasn't that keen on antinomians either. So finally he sailed back to Old England, not in disgrace so much as despondency, and that's where he died, among memories of the blue hills, green maizefields, get-togethers over hemp and tobacco with the Indians, young women in upper rooms with their aprons lifted, pretty faces, hair spilling on the wood floors while underneath in the stables horses kicked and drunks hollered, the starts in the very early mornings when the backs of his herd glowed like pearl, the long, stony and surprising road to Boston, the rain on the Connecticut River, the snuffling good-nights of a hundred pigs among the new stars and long grass still warm from the sun, settling down to sleep. . . .

Could he have been the fork in the road America never took, the singular point she jumped the wrong way from?

From *Gravity's Rainbow* by Thomas Pynchon. Viking Penguin, 1973.

JOHN PYNCHON

At the funeral of John Pynchon (1626-1703), "Pope" Solomon Stoddard eulogized him as "a father of the country." The son and heir of Springfield founder William Pynchon, John was a political leader and the richest citizen in the Connecticut Valley during the second half of the seventeenth century. His letters and account books provide an unmatched record of colonial social and economic history.

Pynchon's letter to Massachusetts governor John Leverett on the burning of Springfield in 1675 in King Philip's War describes what he and his fellow Puritan colonists considered to be the most perilous event in Springfield's brief history. This attack ushered in a period of more than thirty years of frontier fighting in the Valley between the English and Indians.

The Burning of Springfield

Honored Gentlemen,

I t is not for me to find fault with the Providence of God, or to blame in the least that strict order, that we should leave no soldiers in garrison, but call out all. In the day of it, it was my rule and a ground for my action, though very much against my mind, had I been left to myself. On the 4th of October I ordered the soldiers that were left to secure Springfield to march up to Hadley, as also some at Westfield to report to Northampton, who accordingly attended it. We had set our work to march the next day, having discovered a parcel of Indians; but in the night intelligence came from Hartford and also a post from Springfield that Springfield would be burnt by Indians that day, there being, as Indians had informed, 5000 of Philip's and other Indians lying against Springfield. This unexpected tidings diverted our going forth, and made us march to Springfield with about 200 men (the rest left to secure the towns above). When we came to Springfield we found the intelligence too true, it being well in the afternoon e'er we could get thither, when we saw most of the town in flames. At our approach the Indians drew off, so that we could not come to sight of them, only our scouts discovered seven. There are about 30 dwelling houses burnt down in Springfield and 24 or 25 barns, great destruction of men's corn and hay; many families having nothing to live on, all their corn being burnt, and many all their goods; nay some whose houses are standing had carried out their goods into neighbors' houses which they judged more likely than their own, and there had their goods burnt. Three persons we had slain and three or four more wounded, two whereof we much fear will hardly recover. What the

Lord will do with his wilderness people and chiefly them of this river, we know not; he seems to answer our prayers by terrible things in righteousness. I have made it our work since I came to Springfield to send out scouts to discover Indians, but can effect nothing, though we have reason by what we discover to judge they are about us or drawing down the river. It is the work of the soldiers here now, (having spent the day after we come in destroying the Indian wigwams, etc.) to secure and save what corn is remaining (if it be savable) for the inhabitants to live on, though many talk of going away. I would not have the place deserted nor give such advantage to the Indians if possible. But many families that have nothing at all left, and there being no mill to grind any corn, are discouraged exceedingly, for in these last flames my corn mill (as well as my sawmill) was burnt down, together with three houses more I had which tenants lived in as well as the barns belonging to them. Oh, that I may sensibly say with holy Job: naked came I and naked shall I return and blessed be the name of the Lord. There is no unrighteousness with God in this sharp dispensation; oh that we may be silent before him and not open our mouths, but lie at his foot yet as to duty be doing what he requests, and truly here our straits are what to do now. I am not for giving up this place to the enemy; it were as it were to quit the cause of God and the interest of his people (though for my own part I know not which way to have a subsistence here). But yet there can be no holding the place without many soldiers and it's hard now to maintain them here: bread being wanting, meal being not to be had because the mill is burnt, and we find already too great complaint of the soldiers, though they have flesh enough, for want of bread and want of comfortable lodging and housing. The neighbors having thronged up the houses that are standing so that we are greatly strained; and to send away the soldiers were to lose the place and expose all to ruin.

This Providence obstructs our going out, there being need of soldiers in all the towns to save them; which things I have formerly hinted, though they have not so much been regarded, except that Hartford Council did concur with me that there were needed 1000 men to deal with these Indians and secure our towns, which now to be sure cannot be had so nigh winter; yet I am ready to think winter will be the time to deal with the Indians. Now this day we have news from Hartford of the Indian enemy being supposed to be there, and Major Treat is sent for thither with a part of his soldiers, so that we are in no other capacity now but to preserve our towns, if that. It is reported 200 of Philip's men and others are not far from Wethersfield and trading with these Indians to poison them and make them false. The Lord be our support and help when the help of man fails, and preserve us from the rage and malice of our enemies. Surely he will revenge for their falsehood in his time and send defense to his people when it may make most for his glory and their good. To his grace I commend you who am, gentlemen,

Your most unworthy and most humble servant,

John Pynchon

From *The Pynchon Papers, Volume I: Letters of John Pynchon, 1654-1700*, edited by Carl Bridenbaugh. Colonial Society of Massachusetts, 1982.

JOHN WILLIAMS

One of America's earliest bestsellers was The Redeemed Captive, *published in 1707, by Deerfield minister John Williams (1664-1729). So fascinated were Americans with the story of Deerfield settlers taken into captivity by the French and Indians that the book went through six editions in the eighteenth century.* The Redeemed Captive *established the frontier story convention in which Indians were depicted as bloodthirsty slaughterers.*

Much of the drama in the story stems from the cultural clash between English and French and Indians, and between Protestants and Catholics. Reverend Williams wrote the book after being ransomed ("redeemed") from the French in Canada. He returned to resettle Deerfield, where he served as minister until his death.

The Redeemed Captive

On the twenty-ninth of February 1704, not long before break of day, the enemy came in like a flood upon us, our watch being unfaithful: an evil, whose awful effects in a surprisal of our fort, should bespeak all watchmen to avoid, as they would not bring the charge of blood upon themselves. They came to my house in the beginning of the onset and, by their violent endeavors to break open doors and windows with axes and hatchets, awakened me out of sleep; on which I leaped out of bed, and running toward the door, perceived the enemy making their entrance into the house. I called to awaken two soldiers in the chamber and returned towards my bedside for my arms. The enemy immediately broke into the room, I judge to the number of twenty, with painted faces and hideous acclamations. I reached up my hands to the bedtester for my pistol, uttering a short petition to God for everlasting mercies for me and mine on the account of the merits of our glorified redeemer, expecting a present passage through the Valley of the Shadow of Death, saying in myself as Isaiah 38:10-11: "I said in the cutting off my days, 'I shall go to the gates of the grave. I am deprived of the residue of my years.' I said, 'I shall not see the Lord, even the Lord in the land of the living. I shall behold man no more with the inhabitants of the world.'" Taking down my pistol, I cocked it and put it to the breast of the first Indian who came up, but my pistol missing fire, I was seized by three Indians who disarmed me and bound me naked, as I was in my shirt, and so I stood for near the space of an hour. Binding me, they told me they would carry me to Quebec. My pistol missing fire was an occasion of my life's being preserved, since which I have also found it profitable to be crossed in my own will. The judgment of God did not long slumber against one of the three which took me, who was a captain, for by sunrising he received a mortal shot from my neighbor's house, who opposed so great a number of French and Indians as three hundred and yet were no more than seven men in an ungarrisoned house.

I cannot relate the distressing care I had for my dear wife, who had lain-in but a few weeks before and for my poor children, family, and Christian neighbors. The enemy fell to rifling the house and entered in great numbers into the house. I begged of God to remember mercy in the midst of judgment, that He would so far restrain their wrath as to prevent their murdering of us, that we might have grace to glorify His name, whether in life or death, and, as I was able, committed our state to God. The enemies who entered the house were all of them Indians and Mohawks, insulted over me awhile, holding hatchets over my head threatening to burn all I had. But yet God beyond expectation made us in a great measure to be pitied, for though some were so cruel and barbarous as to take and carry to the door two of my children and murder them, as also a Negro woman, yet they gave me liberty to put on my clothes, keeping me bound with a cord on one arm, till I put on my clothes to the other, and then changing my cord, they let me dress myself and then pinioned me again. They gave liberty to my dear wife to dress herself and our children.

About sun an hour high we were all carried out of the house for a march and saw many of the houses of my neighbors in flames, perceiving the whole fort, one excepted, to be taken. Who can tell what sorrows pierced our souls when we saw ourselves carried away from God's sanctuary to go into a strange land exposed to so many trials, the journey being at least three hundred miles we were to travel, the snow up to the knees, and we never inured to such hardships and fatigues, the place we were to be carried to a popish country?

Upon my parting from the town, they fired my house and barn. We were carried over the river to the foot of the mountain, about a mile from my house, where we found a great number of our Christian neighbors, men, women, and children, to the number of a hundred, nineteen of which were afterward murdered by the way and two starved to death near Cowass in a time of great scarcity or famine the savages underwent there. When we came to the foot of our mountain, they took away our shoes and gave us, in the room of them, Indian shoes to prepare us for our travel. While we were there, the English beat out a company that remained in the town and pursued them to the river, killing and wounding many of them, but the body of the army, being alarmed, they repulsed those few English that pursued them.

A rare daguerreotype from 1848 of Deerfield's "Indian House." Built for John Sheldon between 1692 and 1698, the home withstood the Indian and French attack in 1704. The house was torn down shortly after the photograph was made; its front door with holes made by tomahawks is at the Memorial Hall Museum. Courtesy of the Pocumtuck Valley Historical Association, Memorial Hall Museum, Deerfield.

I am not able to give you an account of the number of the enemy slain, but I observed after this fight no great insulting mirth as I expected and saw many wounded persons, and for several days together they buried several of their party and one of chief note among the Mohawks. The governor of Canada told me his army had that success with the loss but of eleven men, three Frenchmen, one of which was the lieutenant of the army, five Mohawks, and three Indians; but after my arrival at Quebec I spoke with an Englishman, who was taken the last war and married there and of their religion, who told me they lost above forty and that many were wounded. I replied the governor of Canada said they lost but eleven men. He answered, "'Tis true that there were but eleven killed outright at the taking of the fort, but that many others were wounded, among who was the ensign of the French." But, said he, "They had a fight in the meadow, and that in both engagements they lost more than forty. Some of the soldiers, both French and Indians then present, told me so," said he, adding that, "The French always endeavor to conceal the number of their slain."

After this we went up the mountain and saw the smoke of the fires in the town and beheld the awful desolations of our town, and, before we marched any farther, they killed a sucking child of the English. There were slain by the enemy of the inhabitants of our town to the number of thirty-eight besides nine of the neighboring towns. We traveled not far the first day; God made the heathen so to pity our children that, though they had several wounded persons of their own to carry upon their shoulders for thirty miles before they came to the river, yet they carried our children, incapable of traveling, upon their shoulders and in their arms.

When we came to our lodging-place the first night, they dug away the snow and made some wigwams, cut down some of the small branches of spruce trees to lie down on, and gave the prisoners somewhat to eat, but we had but little appetite. I was pinioned and bound down that night, and so I was every night while I was with the army. Some of the enemy who brought drink with them from the town fell to drinking, and in their drunken fit they killed my Negro man, the only dead person I either saw at the town or on the way. In the night an Englishman made his escape; in the morning I was called for and ordered by the general to tell the English that, if any more made their escape, they would burn the rest of the prisoners.

He that took me was unwilling to let me speak with any of the prisoners as we marched; but on the morning of the second day, he being appointed to guard the rear, I was put into the hands of my other master who permitted me to speak to my wife when I overtook her and to walk with her to help her in her journey. On the way we discoursed of the happiness of them who had a right to a house not made with hands, eternal in the heavens and God for a father and a friend; as also that it was our reasonable duty quietly to submit to the will of God and to say the will of the Lord be done. My wife told me her strength of body began to fail and that I must expect to part with her, saying she hoped God would preserve my life and the lives of some, if not all of our children with us, and commended to me, under God, the care of them. She never spoke any discontented word as to what had befallen us, but with suitable expressions justified God in what had befallen us.

We soon made a halt in which time my chief surviving master came up, upon which I was put upon marching with the foremost, and so made to take my last farewell of my dear wife, the desire of my eyes, and companion in many mercies and afflictions. Upon our separation from each other we asked, for each other, grace sufficient for what God should call us to. After our being parted from one another, she spent the few remaining minutes of her stay in reading the holy Scriptures, which she was wont personally every day to delight her soul in reading, praying, meditating of and over, by herself in her closet, over and above what she heard out of them in our family worship.

I was made to wade over a small river and so were all the English, the water above knee-deep, the stream very swift; and after that to travel up a small mountain; my strength was almost spent before I came to the top of it. No sooner had I overcome the difficulty of that ascent, but I was permitted to sit down and be unburdened of my pack; I sat pitying those who were behind and entreated my master to let me go down and help up my wife, but he refused and would not let me stir from him. I asked each of the prisoners as they passed by me after her, and heard that in passing through the abovesaid river, she fell down and was plunged over head and ears in the water; after which she traveled not far, for at the foot of this mountain the cruel and bloodthirsty savage who took her, slew her with his hatchet at one stroke, the tidings of which were very awful; and yet such was the hard-heartedness of the adversary that my tears were reckoned to me as a reproach.

From *The Redeemed Captive* by John Williams, edited by Edward W. Clark. University of Massachusetts Press, 1976.

LUCY TERRY PRINCE

Lucy Terry Prince (1724?-1821) wrote the first published poem by an African-American. Born in Africa and brought over on a Rhode Island slave ship, she was a servant in Deerfield for many years, eventually moving to Vermont, where she lived out the rest of her long life.

The poem describes the last Indian attack on Deerfield, in 1746. It was probably a transcription of an oral composition, since Prince was renowned for her storytelling. (The title refers to the fence, or bar, between two common fields in the area where the settlers were attacked.)

The Bars Fight

August, 'twas the twenty-fifth,
Seventeen hundred forty-six,
The Indians did in ambush lay,
Some very valient men to slay,
The names of whom I'll not leave out:
Samuel Allen like a hero fout,
And though he was so brave and bold,
His face no more shall we behold.

Eleazer Hawks was killed outright,
Before he had time to fight, —
Before he did the Indians see,
Was shot and killed immediately.

Oliver Amsden he was slain,
Which caused his friends much grief and pain.
Simeon Amsden they found dead
Not many rods distant from his head.

Adonijah Gillett, we do hear
Did lose his life which was so dear.
John Sadler fled across the water,
And thus escaped the dreadful slaughter.

Eunice Allen see the Indians coming,
And hopes to save herself by running;
And had not her petticoats stopped her,
The awful creatures had not catched her,

nor tommy hawked her on the head,
And left her on the ground for dead.
Young Samuel Allen, Oh, lack-a-day!
Was taken and carried to Canada.

"The Bars Fight" by Lucy Terry Prince, 1746. Published in *A History of Deerfield, Massachusetts* by George Sheldon. Pocumtuck Valley Association, 1895.

A 1908 view of "The Street," Deerfield's mile-long main street.
Courtesy of Deerfield Academy.

CONRAD AIKEN

The WPA (Works Progress Administration) travel guides of the late 1930s
are considered masterpieces of travel literature and Americana. The Massa-
chusetts WPA Guide *includes a chapter on Deerfield by novelist and poet*
Conrad Aiken (1889-1973).

Deerfield: A Beautiful Ghost

If it is no exaggeration to say that Deerfield is not so much a town as
the ghost of a town, its dimness almost transparent, its quiet almost a
cessation, it is essential to add that it is probably quite the most
beautiful ghost of its kind, and with the deepest poetic and historic
significance to be found in America. Salem, with its somber echoes of the
witch hangings, of the brighter pages of the clipper-ship trade with the
East, New Bedford with its whale-ships, Concord with its bold patriotism
and its almost unexampled literary flowering — these all perhaps have a
greater 'importance.' But Deerfield has something to say which none of
these say, and says it perfectly. It is, and will probably always remain, the
perfect and beautiful statement of the tragic and creative moment when
one civilization is destroyed by another. And the wonderful ghostliness
of this mile-long 'Street' of grave and ancient houses, the strange air of
unreality which hangs over it, arises precisely from the fact that the little
town is really saying two things at once. It is saying, 'I dared to be
beautiful, even in the shadow of the wilderness'; but it is also saying,
'And the wilderness haunts me, the ghosts of a slain race are in my
doorways and clapboards, like a kind of death.'

The air of unreality, moreover, is simplified and heightened by the
fact that Deerfield is one of those towns which have literally and com-
pletely been forgotten by time: it has fallen asleep. To all intents, nothing
has happened there for two hundred years; and the whole history of its
greatness is crowded into the first three decades of its existence, the
violent and dreadful years from 1672 to 1704, when it was the northwest
frontier of New England, the spearhead of English civilization in an
unknown and hostile country. The town of Dedham having been awarded
a grant of land in 1663, the site of Deerfield was 'laid out' in the Pocumtuck
country just west of the Connecticut River in 1665. Not a single Dedham
man settled there until 1669, when Samuel Hinsdell of Dedham, a squat-
ter, began the cultivation of the fertile soil, where the Pocumtucks had
grown their corn and pumpkins and tobacco; and by 1672 Samson Frary
and others had joined him. After two expeditions to Boston, Hinsdell got

the consent of the General Court to form a township.

A minister was procured and the little town throve. In 1673 it had twenty families, and two years later its population numbered 125. But seeming peace and prosperity were to prove only an illusion: with the outbreak of King Philip's War began the interminable series of Indian and French attacks on Deerfield which for thirty years kept its inhabitants in constant terror. The two most famous of these — the Bloody Brook massacre of 1675 and the great Deerfield raid of 1704 — practically emptied the town: the first, in fact, wholly, and the second of all save its garrison. In 1675 the garrison was withdrawn, the families were scattered among the towns lower in the valley, and for seven years Deerfield's houses were empty.

Not to be discouraged, the survivors in 1678 presented a petition to the General Court asking leave to return. They had their way, the town was re-established in 1682, and in 1686 was held its first town meeting. John Williams, destined to become Deerfield's most famous citizen, came to take over the church in the same year, induced by the handsome offer of 'sixteen cow-commons of meadow-land,' a 'homelott,' and a house 'forty-two foot long, twenty foot wide, with a lentoo.' Of Williams's part in the great raid of 1704, during Queen Anne's War, when half the town was burned, 49 inhabitants killed, and Williams himself with 110 others taken captive to Canada, it is sufficient here to say that Williams's own account of it in 'The Redeemed Captive' remains the best.

With its slow rehabilitation after the great raid, Deerfield had really ended its active life, and began to become the long reminiscence which it seems destined to be. Agriculturally, its importance died with the opening of the West, though it still grows its tobacco and cucumbers; a development of handicrafts late in the eighteenth century was of short duration; and a revival of them again in the early part of the present century — needlework, hand-weaving, basket-making — is only now (1937) making headway. Actually, the town's chief industry is its schools. Deerfield Academy is one of the oldest boarding-schools in the country: this and Eaglebrook, a preparatory school for boys, and Bement, co-educational, add about five hundred to the town's population.

"Deerfield" by Conrad Aiken, in *Massachusetts: A Guide to its Places and People*, Federal Writer's Project of the Works Progress Administration. Houghton Mifflin, 1937.

Reform and Renewal

A depiction of John Brown organizing African-Americans in a secret league of Gileadites at Springfield in the early 1850s. From Springfield, 1636-1886 *by Mason A. Green, 1888.*

JONATHAN EDWARDS

*The towering thinker in colonial America was a Northampton minister —
the Reverend Jonathan Edwards (1703-1758). His importance to the Connecticut
Valley lay in his rejection of the reason-based Congregationalism predominat-
ing at Harvard College. The Valley had long bred singular thinkers. Edwards's
grandfather "Pope" Solomon Stoddard, a long-time Northampton minister,
had allowed his entire congregation to receive communion, contravening
traditional Puritan strictures about offering communion only to the "elect."
The remoteness of the Valley from Boston encouraged Edwards and others to
devise their own way.*

*Edwards initiated the Great Awakening, the emotional religious revival of
the 1730s and 1740s which encouraged increasing independence in thought
and feeling. His "Narrative of Surprising Conversions" (1735) relates the
beginnings of the Great Awakening in Northampton.*

*According to contemporary accounts, Edwards's 1741 sermon "Sinners in
the Hands of an Angry God" inspired fear and weeping among his listeners.*

Surprising Conversions in Northampton

My Letter to a Brother   May 30. 35.
Dear Sir

In answer to your Desire, I here send you a Particular account of the
Present Extraordinary circumstances of this Town, & the neighbouring
Towns with Respect to Religion. I have observed that the Town for
this several years have gradually been Reforming; There has appeared
Less & Less of a party spirit, & a contentious disposition, which before had
Prevail'd for many years between two Parties in the Town. The young
People also have been Reforming more and more; They by degrees Left
off their frolicking, and have been observably more decent in their
attendance on the Publick worship. The winter before Last there appeared
a strange flexibleness in the young People of the Town, and an unusual
disposition to Hearken to Counsel, on this Occasion; It had been their
manner of a Long Time, & for Ought I know, alwaies, to make sabbath
day nights & Lecture days, to be Especially Times of diversion, & Company
Keeping: I then Preach'd a sermon on the Sabbath before the Lecture, to
show them the unsuitableness, & Inconvenience of the Practice, & to
Perswade them to Reform it; & urged it on Heads of Families that It
should be a thing agreed among them to Govern their Families, & keep
them in at those times.

& There happen'd to be at my house the Evening after, men that belonged to the several parts of the Town, to whom I moved that they should desire the Heads of Families, in my name, to meet together in their several neighbourhoods, that they might Know Each others minds, and agree Every one to restrain his Family; which was done, & my motion Complied with throughout the Town; but the Parents found Little or no occasion for the Exercise of Government in the case; for the young People declared themselves convinced by what they had heard, and willing of themselves to Comply with the Counsel Given them; & I suppose it was almost universally complied with thenceforward.

After this there began to be a Remarkeable Religious Concern among some Farm Houses, at a Place Called Pascommuck, & five or six that I hoped were savingly wrought upon there. & in April there was a very sudden and awfull death of a young man in Town, in the very Bloom of his youth, who was violently siezed with a Pleurisy & taken Immediately out of his head, and died in two days; which much affected many young People in the Town. This was followed with another death of a young married woman, who was in Great Distress in the Beginning of her Illness, but was hopefully Converted before her death; so that she died full of Comfort, and in a most Earnest & moving manner, warning & counselling others, which I believe much contributed to the solemnizing of the spirits of the young People in the Town; and there began Evidently to appear more of a Religious concern upon Peoples minds.

In the Fall of the year I moved to the young People that they should set up Religious meetings, on Evenings after Lectures, which they complied with; this was followed with the death of an Elderly Person in the Town, which was attended with very unusual Circumstances, which much affected many People. about that Time began the Great noise that there was in this Part of the Countrey about Arminianism, which seemed strangely to be overruled for the Promoting of Religion; People seemed to be Put by it upon Enquiring, with concern & Engagedness of mind, what was the way of salvation, and what were the Terms of our acceptance with God; & what was said Publickly on that occasion; however found fault with by many Elsewhere, & Ridicul'd by some, was most Evidently attended with a very Remarkeable blessing of Heaven, to the souls of the People in this Town, to the Giving of them an universal satisfaction & Engaging their minds with Respect to the thing in Question, the more Earnestly to seek salvation in the way, that had been made Evident to them; & then, a Concern about the Great things of Religion began, about the Latter End of December, & the beginning of January, to Prevail abundantly in the Town, till in a very Little Time it became universal throughout the Town, among old and young, & from the highest to the Lowest; all seemed to be siezed with a deep concern about their Eternal salvation; all the Talk in all companies, & upon occasions was upon the things of Religion, and no other talk was anywhere Relished; & scarcely a single Person in the whole Town was Left unconcerned about the Great things of the Eternal World: Those that were wont to be the vainest, & Loosest Persons in Town seemed in General to be siezed with strong convictions: Those that were most disposed to contemn vital & Experimental Religion, & those that had the Greatest Conceit of their own Reason: the highest Families in the Town, & the oldest Persons in the Town, and many Little Children were affected Remarkeably; no one Family that I know of, & scarcely a Person has been Exempt & the Spirit of God went on in his saving Influences, to the appearance of all Human Reason & Charity, in a truly wonderfull and astonishing manner.

The news of it filled the neighbouring Towns with Talk, & there were many in them that scoffed and made a Ridicule of the Religion that appeared in Northampton; But it was observable that it was very frequent & Common that those of other Towns that came into this Town, & observed how it was here, were Greatly affected, and went home with wounded spirits, & were never more able to Shake off the Impression that it made upon them, till at Length there began to appear a General concern in several of the Towns in the County: in the month of march the People in new Hadley seemed to be siezed with a deep concern about their salvation, all as it were at once, which has Continued in a very Great degree Ever since: about the same time there began to appear the Like Concern in the west Part of Suffield, which has since spread into all Parts of the Town. It next began to appear at Sunderland, & soon became universal, & to a very Great Degree. about the same Time it began to appear in Part of Deerfield, Called Green River, & since has filled the Town. It began to appear also at a part of Hatfield, and after that the whole Town in the second week in April seemed to be siezed at once, & there is a Great & General concern there. and there Gradually Got in a Considerable degree of the same Concern into Hadley old society, & Mr Hopkins's Parish in Springfield, but it is nothing near so Great as in many other places.

Sinners in the Hands of an Angry God

Your wickedness makes you as it were heavy as lead, and to tend downwards with great weight and pressure towards hell; and if God should let you go, you would immediately sink and swiftly descend and plunge into the bottomless gulf, and your healthy constitution, and your own care and prudence, and best contrivance, and all your righteousness, would have no more influence to uphold you and keep you out of hell, than a spider's web would have to stop a fallen rock. Were it not for the sovereign pleasure of God, the earth would not bear you one moment; for you are a burden to it; the creation groans with you; the creature is made subject to the bondage of your corruption, not willingly; the sun does not willingly shine upon you to give you light to serve sin and Satan; the earth does not willingly yield her increase to satisfy your lusts; nor is it willingly a stage for your wickedness to be acted upon; the air does not willingly serve you for breath to maintain the flame of life in your vitals, while you spend your life in the service of God's enemies. God's creatures are good, and were made for men to serve God with, and do not willingly subserve to any other purpose, and groan when they are abused to purposes so directly contrary to their nature and end. And the world would spew you out, were it not for the sovereign hand of him who hath subjected it in hope. There are black clouds of God's wrath now hanging directly over your heads, full of the dreadful storm, and big with thunder; and were it not for the restraining hand of God, it would immediately burst forth upon you. The sovereign pleasure of God, for the present, stays his rough wind; otherwise it would come with fury, and your destruction would come like a whirlwind, and you would be like the chaff of the summer threshing floor.

The wrath of God is like great waters that are dammed for the present; they increase more and more, and rise higher and higher, till an outlet is given; and the longer the stream is stopped, the more rapid and mighty is its course, when once it is let loose. It is true, that judgment against your evil works has not been executed hitherto; the floods of God's vengeance have been withheld; but your guilt in the mean time is constantly increasing, and you are every day treasuring up more wrath; the waters are constantly rising, and waxing more and more mighty; and there is nothing but the mere pleasure of God, that holds the waters back, that are unwilling to be stopped, and press hard to go forward. If God should only withdraw his hand from the flood-gate, it would immediately fly open, and the fiery floods of the fierceness and wrath of God, would rush forth with inconceivable fury, and would come upon you with omnipotent power; and if your strength were ten thousand times greater than it is, yea, ten thousand times greater than the strength of the stoutest, sturdiest devil in hell, it would be nothing to withstand or endure it.

The bow of God's wrath is bent, and the arrow made ready on the string, and justice bends the arrow at your heart, and strains the bow, and it is nothing but the mere pleasure of God, and that of an angry God, without any promise or obligation at all, that keeps the arrow one moment from being made drunk with your blood. Thus all you that never passed under a great change of heart, by the mighty power of the Spirit of God upon your souls; all you that were never born again, and made new creatures, and raised from being dead in sin, to a state of new, and before altogether unexperienced light and life, are in the hands of an angry God. However you may have reformed your life in many things, and may have had religious affections, and may keep up a form of religion in your families and closets, and in the house of God, it is nothing but his mere pleasure that keeps you from being this moment swallowed up in everlasting destruction. However unconvinced you may now be of the truth of what you hear, by and by you will be fully convinced of it. Those that are gone from being in the like circumstances with you, see that it was so with them; for destruction came suddenly upon most of them; when they expected nothing of it, and while they were saying, Peace and safety: now they see, that those things on which they depended for peace and safety, were nothing but thin air and empty shadows.

The God that holds you over the pit of hell, much as one holds a spider, or some loathsome insect over the fire, abhors you, and is dreadfully provoked: his wrath towards you burns like fire; he looks upon you as worthy of nothing else, but to be cast into the fire; he is of purer eyes than to bear to have you in his sight; you are ten thousand times more abominable in his eyes, than the most hateful venomous serpent is in ours. You have offended him infinitely more than ever a stubborn rebel did his prince; and yet it is nothing but his hand that holds you from falling into the fire every moment. It is to be ascribed to nothing else, that you did not go to hell the last night; that you was suffered to awake again in this world, after you closed your eyes to sleep. And there is no other reason to be given, why you have not dropped into hell since you arose in the morning, but that God's hand has held you up. There is no other reason to be given why you have not gone to hell, since you have sat here in the house of God, provoking his pure eyes by your sinful wicked manner of attending his solemn worship. Yea, there is nothing else that is to be given as a reason why you do not this very moment drop down into hell.

O sinner! Consider the fearful danger you are in: it is a great furnace of wrath, a wide and bottomless pit, full of the fire of wrath, that you are held over in the hand of that God, whose wrath is provoked and incensed as much against you, as against many of the damned in hell. You hang by a slender thread, with the flames of divine wrath flashing about it, and ready every moment to singe it, and burn it asunder; and you have no interest in any Mediator, and nothing to lay hold of to save yourself, nothing to keep off the flames of wrath, nothing of your own, nothing that you ever have done, nothing that you can do, to induce God to spare you one moment.

From *Jonathan Edwards: Representative Selections*, edited by Clarence H. Faust and Thomas H. Johnson. Hill and Wang, 1962.

ROBERT LOWELL

Robert Lowell (1917-1977), one of America's great twentieth-century poets, wrote many poems on historical subjects, including his ancestor Jonathan Edwards. An old-line Boston Brahmin, Lowell was steeped in New England's history. He was fascinated by the Puritan notion of pervasive evil and explored its persistence in modern times. In "Jonathan Edwards in Western Massachusetts," Lowell journeys to Northampton to come to terms with his famous ancestor.

Jonathan Edwards in Western Massachusetts

E dwards' great millstone and rock
of hope has crumbled, but the square
white houses of his flock
stand in the open air,

out in the cold,
like sheep outside the fold.
Hope lives in doubt.
Faith is trying to do without

faith. In western Massachusetts,
I could almost feel the frontier
crack and disappear.
Edwards thought the world would end there.

We know how the world will end,
but where is paradise, each day farther
from the Pilgrim's blues for England
and the Promised Land.

*Was it some country house
that seemed as if it were
Whitehall, if the Lord were there?
so nobly did he live.*

*Gardens designed
that the breath of flowers in the wind,
or crushed underfoot,
came and went like warbling music?*

Bacon's great oak grove
he refused to sell,
when he fell,
saying, "Why should I sell my feathers?"

Ah paradise! Edwards,
I would be afraid
to meet you there as a shade.
We move in different circles.

As a boy, you built a booth
in a swamp for prayer;
lying on your back,
you saw the spiders fly,

basking at their ease,
swimming from tree to tree —
so high, they seemed tacked to the sky.
You knew they would die.

Poor country Berkeley at Yale,
you saw the world was soul,
the soul of God! The soul
of Sarah Pierrepont!

So filled with delight in the Great Being,
she hardly cared for anything —
walking the fields, sweetly singing,
conversing with some one invisible.

Then God's love shone in sun, moon and stars,
on earth, in the waters,
in the air, in the loose winds,
which used to greatly fix your mind.

Often she saw you come home from a ride
or a walk, your coat dotted with thoughts
you had pinned there
on slips of paper.

You gave
her Pompey, a Negro slave,

and eleven children.
Yet people were spiders

in your moment of glory,
at the Great Awakening — "Alas, how many
in this very meeting house are more than likely
to remember my discourse in hell!"

The meeting house remembered!
You stood on stilts in the air,
but you fell from your parish.
"All rising is by a winding stair."

On my pilgrimage to Northampton
I found no relic,
except the round slice of an oak
you are said to have planted.

It was flesh-colored, new,
and a common piece of kindling,
only fit for burning.
You too must have been green once.

White wig and black coat,
all cut from one cloth,
and designed
like your mind!

I love you faded,
old, exiled and afraid
to leave your last flock, a dozen
Houssatonic Indian children;

afraid to leave
all your writing, writing, writing,
denying the Freedom of the Will.
You were afraid to be president

of Princeton, and wrote:
"My deffects are well known;
I have a constitution
peculiarly unhappy:

flaccid solids,
vapid, sizzy, scarse fluids,
causing a childish weakness,
a low tide of spirits.

I am contemptible,
stiff and dull.

Why should I leave behind
my delight and entertainment,
those studies
that have swallowed up my mind?"

From *For The Union Dead* by Robert Lowell. Farrar, Straus & Giroux, 1964.

JAMES MACGREGOR BURNS

There is nothing like bad economic times to stimulate, in the words of Thomas Jefferson, "a little rebellion now and then." That was how the depression following the Revolution led to Shays's Rebellion in Western Massachusetts. In 1786-1787, debtor farmers of Western Massachusetts protested at being dispossessed of their property. The protests escalated into a pitched battle between thousands of disaffected farmers and the state militia at the Springfield Arsenal. Though the rebels were dispersed, the young nation's political leaders were motivated to draw up the Constitution to establish an orderly national governmental framework.

The author of the following account of Shays's Rebellion is James MacGregor Burns, Woodrow Wilson Professor of Government Emeritus at Williams College and political scientist.

Shays's Rebellion

Western Massachusetts, late January 1787. Down the long sloping shoulders of the Berkshire Mountains they headed west through the bitter night, stumbling over frozen ruts, picking their way around deep drifts of snow. Some carried muskets, others hickory clubs, others nothing. Many wore old Revolutionary War uniforms, now decked out with the sprig of hemlock that marked them as rebels. Careless and cocksure they had been, but now gall and despair hung over them as heavy as the enveloping night. They and hundreds like them were fleeing for their lives, looking for places to hide.

These men were rebels against ex-rebels. Only a few years before, they had been fighting the redcoats at Bunker Hill, joining General Stark in the rout of the enemy at Bennington, helping young Colonel Henry Knox's troops pull fifty tons of cannon and mortars, captured from the British at Ticonderoga, across these same frozen wastes. They had fought in comradeship with men from Boston and other towns in the populous east. All had been revolutionaries together, in a glorious and victorious cause. Now they were fighting their old comrades, dying before their cannon, hunting for cover like animals.

The trouble had been brewing for years. Life had been hard enough during the Revolution, but independence had first brought a flush of prosperity, then worse times than ever. The people and their governments alike struggled under crushing debts. Much of the Revolutionary specie was hopelessly irredeemable. People were still paying for the war through steep taxes. The farmers in central and western Massachusetts

A portrait of Daniel Shays from the Springfield Daily Republican *in 1877.* Courtesy of the Jones Library, Amherst.

felt they had suffered the most, for their farms, cattle, even their plows could be taken for unpaid debts. Some debtors had been thrown into jail and had languished there, while family and friends desperately scrounged for money that could not be found.

Out of the despair and suffering a deep hatred had welled in the broad farms along the Connecticut and the settlements in the Berkshires. Hatred for the sheriffs and other minions of the law who flung neighbors into jail. Hatred for the judges who could sign orders that might wipe out a man's entire property. Hatred for the scheming lawyers who connived in all this, and battened on it. Hatred above all for the rich people in Boston, the merchants and bankers who seemed to control the governor and the state legislature. No single leader mobilized this hatred. Farmers and laborers rallied around local men with names like Job Shattuck, Eli Parsons, Luke Day. Dan Shays emerged as the most visible leader, but the uprising was as natural and indigenous as any peasants' revolt in Europe. The malcontents could not know that history would call them members of "Shays's Rebellion." They called themselves Regulators.

Their tactic was simple: close up the courts. Time and again, during the late summer and early fall of 1786, roughhewn men by the hundreds crowded into or around courthouses, while judges and sheriffs stood by seething and helpless. The authorities feared to call out the local militia, knowing the men would desert in droves. Most of the occupations were peaceful, even jocular and festive, reaching a high point when debtors were turned out of jail. Most of these debtors were proud men, property owners, voters. They had served as soldiers and junior officers in the Revolution. They were seeking to redress grievances, not to topple governments. Some men of substance — doctors, deacons, even judges — backed the Regulators; many poor persons feared the uprisings. But in general, a man's property and source of income placed him on one side or the other. Hence the conflict divided town and country officials, neighbors, even families.

Then, as the weather turned bitter in the late fall, so did the mood of the combatants. The attitude of the authorities shifted from the implacable to the near-hysterical. Alarmists exaggerated the strength of the Regulators. Rumors flew about that Boston or some other eastern town would be attacked. A respectable Bostonian reported that "We are now in a State of anarchy and confusion bordering on a Civil War." Boston propagandists spread reports that British agents in Canada were secretly backing the rebels. So the Regulators were now treasonable as well as illegal. The state suspended habeas corpus and raised an army, but lacking public funds had to turn to local "gentlemen" for loans to finance it. An anonymous dissident responded in kind:

"This is to lett the gentellmen of Boston [know?] that wee Country men will not pay taxes, as the think," he wrote Governor Bowdoin in a crude, scrawling hand. "But Lett them send the Constabel to us and we'll nock him down for ofering to come near us. If you Dont lower the taxes we'll pull down the town house about you ears. It shall not stand long then or else they shall be blood spilt. We country men will not be imposed on. We fought of our Libery as well as you did. . . ."

Country people and city people had declared for independence a decade before. They had endorsed the ideals of liberty and equality proclaimed in the declaration signed by John Adams and others. But now, it seemed, these ideals were coming to stand for different things to different persons. Fundamental questions had been left unresolved by the Revolution. Who would settle them, and how?

In western Massachusetts, in January 1787, people were suffering through the worst snowstorms they could remember. But weather could not stop the insurrection. For months both government men and Regulators had been eyeing the arsenal at Springfield, with its stores of muskets and ammunition. Late in January, Captain Shays led one thousand or more of his men, in open columns by platoons, toward the arsenal. General William Shepard, commanding the "loyal" troops, sent his aide to warn the Regulators to stop. Shays's response was a loud laugh, followed by an order to his men, "March, God damn you, march!" March they did, their muskets still shouldered, straight into Shepard's artillery. A single heavy cannonade into the center of Shays's column left three men dead and another dying, the rest in panic. In a few seconds the rebels were breaking rank and fleeing for their lives.

What now? The Regulators were not quite done. Those who gathered in friendly Berkshire towns after the long flight west calculated that the mountain fastness to the north and the long ranges stretching south provided natural havens for guerrilla resistance. But they underrated the determination of the government to stamp out the last embers of rebellion. The well-armed militia ranged up and down the county, routing the rebels. Hundreds of insurgents escaped into New York and Vermont, whence they sent raiding parties into Berkshire towns.

One of these towns was Stockbridge, where people had been divided for months over the insurgency. For hours the rebels roamed through the town, pillaging the houses of prominent citizens and "arresting" their foes on the spot. At the house of Judge Theodore Sedgwick, an old adversary, they could not find the judge but they encountered Elizabeth Freeman, long known as "Mum Bett." Arming herself with the kitchen shovel, Mum let them search the house but forbade any wanton destruction of property, all the while jeering at their love for the bottle. She had hidden the family silver in a chest in her own room. When a rebel started to open it, she shamed him out of it, according to a local account, with the mocking cry, "Oh, you had better search that, an old nigger's chest! — the old nigger's as you call me."

Soon the raiders streamed out of town to the south. They had time to free some debtors from jail and celebrate in a tavern. Then the militiamen cornered them in the woods, killing or wounding over thirty of them.

The uprising was over. Some Regulators felt that they had gambled all and lost all. As it turned out, they had served as a catalyst in one of the decisive transformations in American history. Though their own rebellion had failed, they had succeeded in fomenting powerful insurrections in people's minds. Rising out of the grass roots of the day — out of the cornfields and pasturelands of an old commonwealth long whipped by religious and political conflict — they had challenged the "system" and had rekindled some burning issues of this revolutionary age.

From *The American Experiment: The Vineyard of Liberty* by James MacGregor Burns. Alfred A. Knopf, 1982.

FREDERICK DOUGLASS

Frederick Douglass (1818-1895) was the foremost African-American leader in nineteenth-century America. An escaped slave, Douglass became a noteworthy abolitionist advocate before the Civil War. One of his early abolitionist associates was John Brown, whom he met in Springfield for the first time in 1847. He describes the meeting in his 1893 autobiography, The Life and Times of Frederick Douglass, *relating the incident in confidential tones and not letting on who the prominent abolitionist is and where he met him until the end of the passage. Brown influenced Douglass to accept armed struggle as a necessary stage in the freeing of the slaves. Twelve years later, Brown attacked the federal arsenal at Harper's Ferry, Virginia, and Douglass fled to England to escape implication in the plot.*

Meeting John Brown

About the time I began my enterprise in Rochester I chanced to spend a night and a day under the roof of a man whose character and conversation, and whose objects and aims in life, made a very deep impression upon my mind and heart. His name had been mentioned to me by several prominent colored men, among whom were the Rev. Henry Highland Garnet and J.W. Loguen. In speaking of him their voices would drop to a whisper, and what they said of him made me very eager to see and to know him. Fortunately, I was invited to see him in his own house. At the time to which I now refer this man was a respectable merchant in a populous and thriving city, and our first place of meeting was at his store. This was a substantial brick building on a prominent, busy street. A glance at the interior, as well as at the massive walls without, gave me the impression that the owner must be a man of considerable wealth. My welcome was all that I could have asked. Every member of the family, young and old, seemed glad to see me, and I was made much at home in a very little while. I was, however, a little disappointed with the appearance of the house and its location. After seeing the fine store I was prepared to see a fine residence in an eligible locality, but this conclusion was completely dispelled by actual observation. In fact, the house was neither commodious nor elegant, nor its situation desirable. It was a small wooden building on a back street, in a neighborhood chiefly occupied by laboring men and mechanics; respectable enough, to be sure, but not quite the place, I thought, where one would look for the residence of a flourishing and successful merchant. Plain as was the outside of this man's house, the inside was plainer. Its furniture would have satisfied a Spartan. It would take longer to tell what was not in this house than what was in it. There was an air of plainness about it which almost suggested destitution. My first meal passed under the misnomer of tea, though there was nothing about it resembling the usual significance of that term. It consisted of beef-soup, cabbage, and potatoes — a meal such as a man might relish after following the plow all day or performing a forced march of a dozen miles over a rough road in frosty weather. Innocent of paint, veneering, varnish, or table-cloth, the table announced itself unmistakably of pine and of the plainest workmanship. There was no hired help visible. The mother, daughters, and sons did the serving, and did it well. They were evidently used to it, and had no thought of any impropriety or degradation in being their own servants. It is said that a house in some measure reflects the character of its occupants; this one certainly did. In it there were no disguises, no illusions, no make-believes. Everything implied stern truth, solid purpose, and rigid economy. I was not long in company with the master of this house before I discovered that he was indeed the master of it, and was likely to become mine too if I stayed long enough with him. He fulfilled St. Paul's idea of the head of the family. His wife believed in him, and his children observed him with reverence. Whenever he spoke his words commanded earnest attention. His arguments, which I ventured at some points to oppose, seemed to convince all; his appeals touched all, and his will impressed all. Certainly I never felt myself in the presence of a stronger religious influence than while in this man's house.

In person he was lean, strong, and sinewy, of the best New England mold, built for times of trouble and fitted to grapple with the flintiest hardships. Clad in plain American woolen, shod in boots of cowhide leather, and wearing a cravat of the same substantial material, under six feet high, less than 190 pounds in weight, aged about fifty, he presented a figure straight and symmetrical as a mountain pine. His bearing was singularly impressive. His head was not large, but compact and high. His hair was coarse, strong, slightly gray and closely trimmed, and grew low on his forehead. His face was smoothly shaved, and revealed a strong, square mouth, supported by a broad and prominent chin. His eyes were bluish-gray, and in conversation they were full of light and fire. When on the street, he moved with a long, springing, race-horse step, absorbed by his own reflections, neither seeking nor shunning observation. Such was the man whose name I had heard in whispers; such was the spirit of his house and family; such was the house in which he lived; and such was Captain John Brown, whose name had now passed into history, as that of one of the most marked characters and greatest heroes known to American fame.

After the strong meal already described, Captain Brown cautiously approached the subject which he wished to bring to my attention; for he seemed to apprehend opposition to his views. He denounced slavery in look and language fierce and bitter, thought that slaveholders had forfeited their right to live, that the slaves had the right to gain their liberty in any way they could, did not believe that moral suasion would ever liberate the slave, or that political action would abolish the system. He said that he had long had a plan which could accomplish this end, and he had invited me to his house to lay that plan before me. He said he had been for some time looking for colored men to whom he could safely reveal his secret, and at times he had almost despaired of finding such men; but that now he was encouraged, for he saw heads of such rising up in all directions. He had observed my course at home and abroad, and he wanted my coöperation. His plan as it then lay in his mind had much to commend it. It did not, as some suppose, contemplate a general rising among the slaves, and a general slaughter of the slave-masters. An insurrection, he thought, would only defeat the object; but his plan did contemplate the creating of an armed force which should act in the very heart of the South. He was not averse to the shedding of blood, and thought the practice of carrying arms would be a good one for the colored people to adopt, as it would give them a sense of their manhood. No people, he said, could have self-respect, or be respected, who would not fight for their freedom. He called my attention to a map of the United States, and pointed out to me the far-reaching Alleghanies, which stretch away from the borders of New York into Southern States. "These mountains," he said, "are the basis of my plan. God has given the strength of the hills to freedom; they were placed here for the emancipation of the negro race; they are full of natural forts, where one man for defense will be equal to a hundred for attack; they are full also of good hiding-places, where large numbers of brave men could be concealed, and baffle and elude pursuit for a long time. I know these mountains well, and could take a body of men into them and keep them there despite of all the efforts of Virginia to dislodge them. The true object to be sought is first of all to destroy the money value of slave property; and that can only be done by rendering such property insecure. My plan, then, is to take at first about twenty-five picked men, and begin on a small scale; supply them with arms and ammunition and post them in squads of fives on a line of twenty-five miles. The most persuasive and judicious of these shall go down to the fields from time to time, as opportunity offers, and induce the slaves to join them, seeking and selecting the most restless and daring."

He saw that in this part of the work the utmost care must be used to avoid treachery and disclosure. Only the most conscientious and skillful should be sent on this perilous duty. With care and enterprise he thought he could soon gather a force of one hundred hardy men, men who would be content to lead the free and adventurous life to which he proposed to train them; when these were properly drilled, and each man had found the place for which he was best suited, they would begin work in earnest; they would run off the slaves in large numbers, retain the brave and strong ones in the mountains, and send the weak and timid to the north by the underground railroad. His operations would be enlarged with increasing numbers and would not be confined to one locality.

When I asked him how he would support these men, he said emphatically that he would subsist them upon the enemy. Slavery was a state of war, and the slave had a right to anything necessary to his freedom. "But," said I, "suppose you succeed in running off a few slaves, and thus impress the Virginia slaveholders with a sense of insecurity in their slaves, the effect will be only to make them sell their slaves further south." "That," said he, "will be what I want first to do; then I would follow them up. If we could drive slavery out of *one county*, it would be a great gain; it would weaken the system throughout the State." "But they would employ bloodhounds to hunt you out of the mountains." "That they might attempt," said he, "but the chances are, we should whip them, and when we should have whipped one squad, they would be careful how they pursued." "But you might be surrounded and cut off from your provisions or means of subsistence." He thought that this could not be done so they could not cut their way out, but even if the worst came he could but be killed, and he had not better use for his life than to lay it down in the cause of the slave. When I suggested that we might convert the slaveholders, he became much excited, and said that could never be, "he knew their proud hearts and that they would never be induced to give up their slaves, until they felt a big stick about their heads." He observed that I might have noticed the simple manner in which he lived, adding that he had adopted this method in order to save money to carry out his purposes. This was said in no boastful tone, for he felt that he had delayed already too long, and had no room to boast either his zeal or his self-denial. Had some men made such display of rigid virtue, I should have rejected it, as affected, false, and hypocritical, but in John Brown, I felt it to be real as iron or granite. From this night spent with John Brown in Springfield, Mass., 1847, while I continued to write and speak against slavery, I became all the same less hopeful of its peaceful abolition. My utterances became more and more tinged by the color of this man's strong impressions. Speaking at an anti-slavery convention in Salem, Ohio, I expressed this apprehension that slavery could only be destroyed by blood-shed, when I was suddenly and sharply interrupted by my good old friend Sojourner Truth with the question, "Frederick, is God dead?" "No," I answered, "and because God is not dead slavery can only end in blood." My quaint older sister was of the Garrison school of non-resistants, and was shocked at my sanguinary doctrine, but she too became an advocate of the sword, when the war for the maintenance of the Union was declared.

From *Life and Times of Frederick Douglass* by Frederick Douglass. The Library of America, 1994.

OLIVE GILBERT

The Connecticut Valley was a center of abolitionist sentiment with stations on the Underground Railroad. In 1843, former slave Sojourner Truth (c. 1797-1883) came from New York to Springfield, then moved on to Northampton, speaking at camp meetings and to small groups about achieving freedom for the slaves. The Narrative of Sojourner Truth, *written by a white friend Olive Gilbert in 1850, publicized her struggle and demonstrated her integrity.*

This excerpt from the Narrative *depicts her visit to Springfield and life at the utopian Northampton Association of Education and Industry. The Northampton Association was a transcendentalist and socialist community that operated a silk factory in Florence. The utopian Northampton Association hosted frequent talks by such reformers and abolitionists as William Lloyd Garrison, Lydia Maria Child, and Wendell Phillips, which influenced Sojourner Truth and attracted Frederick Douglass.*

Sojourner Truth: Stirrings of Abolition

At this meeting, she received the address of different persons, residing in various places, with an invitation to visit them. She promised to go soon to Cabotville, and started, shaping her course for that place. She arrived at Springfield one evening at six o'clock, and immediately began to search for a lodging for the night. She walked from six till past nine, and was then on the road from Springfield to Cabotville, before she found any one sufficiently hospitable to give her a night's shelter under their roof. Then a man gave her twenty-five cents, and bade her go to a tavern and stay all night. She did so, returning in the morning to thank him, assuring him she had put his money to its legitimate use. She found a number of the friends she had seen at Windsor when she reached the manufacturing of Cabotville, (which has lately taken the name of Chicopee,) and with them she spent a pleasant week or more; after which, she left them to visit the Shaker village in Enfield. She now began to think of finding a resting place, at least, for a season; for she had performed quite a long journey, considering she had walked most of the way; and she had a mind to look in upon the Shakers, and see how things were there, and whether there was any opening there for her. But on her way back to Springfield, she called at a house and asked for a piece of bread; her request was granted, and she was kindly invited to tarry all night, as it was getting late, and she would not be able to stay at every house in that vicinity, which invitation she cheerfully accepted. When the man of the house came in, he recollected having seen her at the camp-meeting, and

Sojourner Truth lived for a time at the Northampton Association, a utopian community. Everyone was expected to help with the work of the group; Truth took it upon herself to do the laundry. Drawn in 1867 by Charles C. Burleigh, Jr.; courtesy of Historic Northampton.

repeated some conversations, by which she recognized him again. He soon proposed having a meeting that evening, went out and notified his friends and neighbors, who came together, and she once more held forth to them in her peculiar style. Through the agency of this meeting, she became acquainted with several people residing in Springfield, to whose houses she was cordially invited, and with whom she spent some pleasant time.

One of these friends, writing of her arrival there, speaks as follows. After saying that she and her people belonged to that class of persons who believed in the second advent doctrines; and that this class, believing also in freedom of speech and action, often found at their meetings many singular people, who did not agree with them in their principal doctrine; and that, being thus prepared to hear new and strange things, 'They listened eagerly to Sojourner, and drank in all she said;' — and also, that she 'soon became a favorite among them; that when she arose to speak in their assemblies, her commanding figure and dignified manner hushed every trifler into silence, and her singular and sometimes uncouth modes of expression never provoked a laugh, but often were the whole audience melted into tears by her touching stories.' She also adds, 'Many were the lessons of wisdom and faith I have delighted to learn from her.' . . . 'She continued a great favorite in our meetings, both on account of her re-markable gift in prayer, and still more remarkable talent for singing, . . . and the aptness and point of her remarks, frequently illustrated by figures the most original and expressive.

'As we were walking the other day, she said she had often thought what a beautiful world this would be, when we should see every thing right side up. Now, we see every thing topsy-turvy, and all is confusion.' For a person who knows nothing of this fact in the science of optics, this seemed quite a remarkable idea.

'We also loved her for her sincere and ardent piety, her unwavering faith in God, and her contempt of what the world calls fashion, and what we call folly.

'She was in search of a quiet place, where a way-worn traveller might rest. She had heard of Fruitlands, and was inclined to go there; but the friends she found here thought it best for her to visit Northampton. She passed her time, while with us, working wherever her work was needed, and talking where work was not needed.

'She would not receive money for her work, saying she worked for the Lord; and if her wants were supplied, she received it as from the Lord.

'She remained with us till far into winter, when we introduced her at the Northampton Association.' . . . 'She wrote to me from hence, that she had found the quiet resting place she had so long desired. And she has remained there ever since.'

She did not fall in love at first sight with the Northampton Associa-tion, for she arrived there at a time when appearances did not correspond with the ideas of associationists, as they had been spread out in their writings; for their phalanx was a factory, and they were wanting in means to carry out their ideas of beauty and elegance, as they would have done in different circumstances. But she thought she would make an effort to tarry with them one night, though that seemed to her no desirable affair. But as soon as she saw that accomplished, literary and refined persons were living in that plain and simple manner, and submitting to the labors and privations incident to such an infant institution, she said, 'Well, if these can live here, *I* can.' Afterwards, she gradually became pleased with, and attached to, the place and the people, as well she might; for it must have been no small thing to have found a home in a 'Community composed of some of the choicest spirits of the age,' where all was characterized by an equality of feeling, a liberty of thought and speech, and a largeness of soul, she could not have before met with, to the same extent, in any of her wanderings.

Our first knowledge of her was derived from a friend who had resided for a time in the 'Community,' and who, after describing her, and singing one of her hymns, wished that we might see her. But we little thought, at that time, that we should ever pen these 'simple annals' of this child of nature.

When we first saw her, she was working with a hearty good will; saying she would not be induced to take regular wages, believing, as once before, that now Providence had provided her with a never-failing fount, from which her every want might be perpetually supplied through her mortal life. In this, she had calculated too fast. For the Associationists found, that, taking every thing into consideration, they would find it most expedient to act individually; and again, the subject of this sketch found her dreams unreal, and herself flung back upon her own resources for the supply of her needs. This she might have found more inconvenient at her time of life — for labor, exposure and hardship had made sad inroads upon her iron constitution, by inducing chronic disease and premature old age — had she not remained under the shadow of one, who never wearies in doing good, giving to the needy, and supplying the wants of the destitute. She has now set her heart upon having a little home of her own, even at this late hour of life, where she may feel a greater freedom than she can in the house of another, and where she can repose a little, after her day of action has passed by. And for such a 'home' she is now dependent on the charities of the benevolent, and to them we appeal with confidence.

From *Narrative of Sojourner Truth* by Olive Gilbert, 1875 edition.

WASHINGTON GLADDEN

During the 1870s, the poverty and deplorable working conditions of much of industrial America spurred the infamous labor violence of 1877 and subsequent efforts of social reform. In Springfield, the Reverend Washington Gladden (1836-1918), pastor of the North Congregational Church from 1874 until 1882, advocated applying Christian principles to the solution of the "social question," in keeping with the movement known as the Social Gospel. One of his earliest works, Working Men and Their Employers *(1876), argued that employers had a Christian responsibility to treat their workers justly. He was a national reform figure for more than a quarter century.*

Gladden had several Western Massachusetts connections. He attended Williams College and served as a pastor in North Adams. In Springfield, he renewed an acquaintance with Springfield Republican *editor Samuel Bowles II. In his* Recollections *(1909), Gladden described the influence of the* Republican *and outlined his views on the "social question."*

Samuel Bowles II

Springfield was the natural capital of the four western counties of Massachusetts, and the cluster of large towns by which it was surrounded, Chicopee, Holyoke, Northampton, and Westfield, with Hartford, the capital of Connecticut, only half an hour distant on the south, made it a centre of considerable influence. What counted for much in this respect was the Springfield "Republican," a newspaper whose weight and force as an organ of public opinion has long been wholly out of proportion to the size of the community in which it circulates. It is doubtful whether the field of any newspaper was ever better cultivated than this of the Springfield "Republican." In every hamlet of these four western counties a correspondent gathered up the local news and forwarded it to Springfield, and these reports, generally crude, were skillfully edited and condensed in the office, so that a picture of the life of western Massachusetts, complete in its detail, was spread before the readers of the "Republican" every morning. By this means a community of interest and feeling was cultivated; in matters social and political the people could coöperate intelligently. Not that the lead of the "Republican" was always followed in such matters; often there was wide dissent from its positions, and loud complaints against the excesses of its independency; but the people had come to rely upon its truthfulness and its courage, and its influence was felt in every part of its field.

How pervasive and salutary this influence has been, the people of that community may not fully realize. Over all their affairs this guardian has always been watching sleeplessly; no conspiracy against the public welfare could escape its vigilance, and no corrupt consideration could muzzle its utterance. Municipal or political irregularities of all sorts were sure to be discovered and dragged into the light; graft and extravagance were held in check by its presence. I think that the municipalities of western Massachusetts will be found to be singularly free from civic and financial abuses. Springfield has expended money freely for public buildings and improvements, but its debt is small, its tax rate is low, and no scandals that I remember have appeared in its City Hall. The capitalization of its public service companies has always been very moderate — least this was so until a recent day; what may have happened since the great New England railroad monopoly has been absorbing the electric lines of the cities, I do not know. But for all this social and civic health and vigor western Massachusetts is indebted, in no small degree, to the Springfield "Republican." It is not, of course, the only influence; other good newspapers and other moral agencies have been at work in this field, but there has been no other influence so salutary and so persistent as that of this leading newspaper. If newspapers of the type of the Springfield "Republican" could be planted all over this country at intervals of not more than one hundred miles, the foundation would be laid for a great improvement in social and political morality.

For all this large result the community was made indebted to Samuel Bowles. He was the second editor of the name. The "Weekly Republican" was founded by his father, in 1824; it was changed to a daily, in 1844, at the urgent instance of the younger Samuel, who was then but eighteen years old; the upbuilding and development of this paper had been his life-work. He had had good collaborators, chief of whom was Dr. Holland, whose wholesome and homely social essays had added greatly to the popularity of the journal. But the life and soul of the "Republican" had always been Samuel Bowles. For thirty years he had been pouring all his energies into it, and better than most men he worked out his ideals. On the literary side they were distinct and sensible. He wanted no fine writing, but the news should be told and the comment presented in clear, crisp, idiomatic English, with no surplus verbiage. The paper must tell the truth; correspondents were encouraged to state the thing as it appeared to them; not seldom the editorial columns and the correspondence columns were openly at war. Readers were made sure that the facts would not be concealed from them, and that they were likely to get all sides of a controverted question. Over the staff of reporters and editors the influence of the chief was potent. "He was a man," says one of his old associates, "of notable presence, tall, spare, nervous, with keen cavalier face, full brown beard and dark brown hair that was neither of Indian stiffness nor of effeminate curl, but between the two; a rich brown-red complexion, a strong nose, and brilliant and divining eyes before which no falsehood could stand. . . . He was often severe, and sometimes the young apprentice would feel that he was cruel; but he was generous in praise as stern in censure, and a word of approval from the chief coupled with one of his wonderful smiles was worth a hundred flatteries beside. The personal aura which surrounded him in social intercourse was nowhere more potent than among the young men in the office, when he criticised and inspired them."

Samuel Bowles, editor of the
Springfield Republican.
From *History of the Connecticut*
Valley in Massachusetts
by Louis H. Everts, 1879.

When I first knew Mr. Bowles, during my college days, and afterward in North Adams, he was very modest about his ability as a writer. Of the management of a newspaper he knew that he was master, but he was diffident respecting his literary skill. Indeed, his earlier writing was by no means brilliant; it was clear, intelligent, businesslike, but it had little sparkle or color. All this came to him late in life. During the last ten years he developed a degree of skill as a writer which was a surprise to those who knew him in his earlier days. The blossoming of his art seems to have come on the occasion of his visit to California, in 1865; the letters which he wrote to the "Republican" on that journey, which are collected in his volume "Across the Continent," are full of piquant, fresh, poetical English. And the letters of all this period, which are gathered up in Mr. Merriam's admirable biography, are delightful examples of the epistolary art.

When I took up my home in Springfield in 1875, Mr. Bowles was fifty-one years of age, and ought to have had twenty-five years of good work ahead of him, but it was easy to see that his work was nearly done; the symptoms of nervous breakdown were manifest. I saw him not often; his strength was consumed by his daily duties, and he had not much left for social pleasures. He had been most cordial in his appreciation of my journalistic experience. " I hope," he had written me three months before, "you will not leave journalism. The harvest is large and the laborers are few. It is bigger than the pulpit. I won't be so conceited as to say that it is better." But when I became, so to speak, a member of his parish once more, he gave me a warm welcome, and showed a kindly interest in my work. Now and then I had the honor of a seat at his table, at those rather informal dinner parties which he sometimes gave to a few gentlemen, when guests of distinction were visiting him. Over all the questions of national politics we used to talk freely when we met; in the Hayes-Tilden campaign he was disposed to favor Tilden, but he asked me to give the "Republican" my reasons for the opposite preference, and printed it conspicuously, with a cordial word, on the editorial page. His fear was that Hayes was a man of putty, and could be manipulated by the worst elements of the Republican Party; he was sure, after Hayes was con-firmed in his seat, that the Cabinet would be composed of rotten timber. About this he was quite pessimistic. On the day when the Cabinet was announced, I saw the bulletin, with the names of Evarts and Schurz and Sherman and Devens, — the strongest Cabinet for many years, and nobody representing the reactionary wing of the party, — and I climbed to the editorial rooms of the "Republican." "How now?" I demanded. "Well," he said, "it's too good to believe. I didn't think they would let him do it. The fact is, parson, there's one element these fellows never count on, and that is God." It was no irreverence; it was his way of saying that the machinations of the politicians had been divinely overruled. He was very chary of expressions like that, but I think that he meant it, that day.

Several years before his death they made him a Trustee of Amherst College. Free lance in theology as he notoriously was, his appointment as custodian of the interests of that very conservative institution was regarded as somewhat extraordinary. But he proved to be a most valuable member of the Board, nor were his religious views ever suffered to embarrass, in any way, the administration. One day I expressed to him my gratification at the appointment, and jocularly ventured the hope that he might do something to brace up the orthodoxy of the institution. "Well, no, parson," he said; "I don't go much on theology; but now and then a question of morals in the financial management comes up, and then I shine out!"

During the last year of his life he stirred up the people of Springfield to undertake a more efficient organization of their local charities. The "Republican," at his instigation, kept the matter before the public until a meeting was called and steps were taken to form an association for the care of the poor. It was my privilege to prepare the report and to draft the form of organization of which the Union Relief Association of Springfield was constituted, in which service I was brought into frequent conferences with Mr. Bowles. It was the last opportunity I had of talking much with him, and I gratefully treasure the memory of those interviews. As soon as the Association was organized, he himself took out a subscription paper, and raised the money necessary for putting the machinery into operation. It was almost his last public service.

Six months later came the fatal stroke which prostrated him, and left him but a few weeks of lingering suffering. I saw him once, after that; he asked for me. The great brown eyes were full of wistful friendliness; there were a few cheerful and courageous words. It was not many days later that we carried him away to his resting-place in the beautiful cemetery, near his home.

The "Social Question"

When my work began in Springfield, in the spring of 1875, the industries of the country had not yet recovered from the collapse of 1873. It was a season of industrial depression; large numbers of men were out of work, and the outlook for a multitude of industrious and capable men was gloomy. Meetings of the unemployed were held in the Police Court room at the City Hall, and various schemes were suggested by which the city might offer relief to those in want. Those who attended these meetings were not, as a rule, the soberest and most capable workingmen, but the more restless and turbulent of the laboring class. Their leader was an Irishman, of an impulsive and reckless temper, whose talk to the crowd had sometimes been of an inflammatory character. One day he came to me with an urgent request that I go down to the meeting that night, and speak to the multitude. I accepted the invitation, and found myself confronted with a company of laborers who were evidently not in a complacent mood. What I had to say to them did not fully harmonize with their ruling idea, for I expressed doubt as to whether it would be possible for the city to furnish work for them, and exhorted them to be ready to do any kind of work that might be offered, at merely nominal wages, rather than beg or be idle. It was not, as I am able now to recall it, a speech which was calculated to conciliate that audience; I fear it did not recognize so clearly as it ought to have done the responsibility of the community for the relief of such conditions. I am sure that I should put the case a little differently to-day, if I were speaking to such a company.

The men listened to me, however, respectfully, and at the close of my address I said to them: "I have told you what I think is the sensible thing for you to do; next Sunday night I am going to talk to your employers, to the people who are in the habit of hiring labor, and wish you would come to the church and hear what I shall say to them." Quite a number of them accepted the invitation. In that sermon I urged upon my congregation the duty of furnishing work, wherever it was possible, to the unemployed; I suggested that building and repairing could be very cheaply done, in the existing conditions of the labor market; and that those who had any surplus funds could probably use them productively, just then, in the employment of labor. That sermon was one of the most effective I ever preached; it started two or three of my parishioners to building houses; it set quite a number of people to repairing and remodeling their premises; it resulted in organizing one or two small businesses which gave employment to several people. If one could only get such results as these quite frequently, preaching would seem to be better worth while.

Those of the workingmen who heard what I had to say to the employing class seemed to be satisfied that the pulpit was not prejudiced against them, and my friend, the Irish agitator, continued, after that time, regularly to attend my church, with which he afterward united, becoming one of my most loyal parishioners.

From *Recollections* by Washington Gladden. Houghton Mifflin, 1909.

EDWARD BELLAMY

Edward Bellamy (1850-1898) is one of the most influential authors to hail from the Pioneer Valley. Bellamy's utopian novel Looking Backward *(1888), which depicted a society free from the injustices of private capitalism, was one of the great bestsellers of its era and was translated into more than twenty languages.*

Bellamy, a Chicopee Falls native, worked as a journalist for the Springfield Union *and joined his brother Charles in establishing the* Springfield Penny (Daily) News *in 1880. He wrote book reviews and essays, many of them of a philosophical turn, for the Springfield newspapers.*

If the reader peruses Bellamy's articles, letters, and diary entries to discover how his experience in Chicopee Falls and Springfield influenced Looking Backward, *one would find virtually nothing about his home area. Bellamy indicates that he originally became outraged at the inequalities of the capitalist system after witnessing European poverty.*

How I Wrote "Looking Backward"

U p to the age of eighteen I had lived almost continuously in a thriving village of New England [Chicopee Falls], where there were no very rich and few very poor, and everybody who was willing to work was sure of a fair living. At that time I visited Europe and spent a year there in travel and study. It was in the great cities of England, Europe and among the hovels of the peasantry that my eyes were first fully opened to the extent and consequences of man's inhumanity to man. . . . Although it had required the sights of Europe to startle me to a vivid realization of the inferno of poverty beneath our civilization, my eyes having once been opened I had no difficulty in recognizing in America and even in my own comparatively prosperous village, the same conditions in course of progressive development. . . .

Since I came across this echo of my youth and recalled the half-forgotten exercises of mind it testifies to, I have been wondering not why I wrote "Looking Backward," but why I did not write it, or try to, twenty years ago.

Like most men, however, I was under the sordid and selfish necessity of solving the economic problem in its personal bearings before I could give much time to the case of society in general. I had, like others, to fight my way to a place at the world's work-bench where I could make a living. For a dozen or fifteen years I followed journalism, doing in a desultory way, as opportunity offered, a good deal of magazine and book writing.

In none of the writings of this period did I touch on the social question but not the less all the while it was in my mind, as a problem not by any means given up, how poverty might be abolished and the economic equality of all citizens of the republic be made as much a matter of course as their political equality. I had always the purpose, some time when I had sufficient leisure, to give myself earnestly to the examination of this great problem, but meanwhile kept postponing it, giving my time and thoughts to easier tasks.

Possibly I never should have mustered up courage for an undertaking so difficult, and indeed so presumptuous, but for events which gave the problem of life a new and more solemn meaning to me. I refer to the birth of my children.

"How I Wrote 'Looking Backward'" by Edward Bellamy. *The Ladies Home Journal*, April 1894.

Chicopee in 1856, with the factories of Ames Co., sword and light artillery manufacturers.
Courtesy of Chicopee Public Library.

CORINNE MCLAUGHLIN and GORDON DAVIDSON

The Upper Pioneer Valley has been known for alternative cultural groups since the 1960s. Some have been political or peace groups, while others have been independent communities, or communes, such as The Farm (Montague), Fare-Thee-Well Community (Worthington), Temenos (Shutesbury), and Renaissance Community (Gill). The Sirius Community, active in Shutesbury since 1978, has been one of the most successful with its emphasis on spiritual life, consensus governance, and worker-owned cooperatives.

Sirius Community leaders Corinne McLaughlin and Gordon Davidson chronicled their community's development as well as those of others across Western Massachusetts and the country in Builders of the Dawn: Community Lifestyles in a Changing World *(1985).*

The Sirius Community

Sirius, the community we founded in 1978 near Amherst, Massachusetts, is organized as a non-profit educational corporation to offer classes, retreats, and educational materials for the public and to help people with their spiritual growth. We are committed to being good custodians for our eighty-six acres of land, once held sacred to three tribes of Native Americans. We honor the oneness of all life and are learning to work in harmony with the forces of nature in our garden and forest to create a healing of the earth.

We respect the presence of God within each person and see everyday life as our spiritual teacher, mirroring back to us our own internal state, showing us where we're stuck and need to grow in love. We have a sanctuary for group meditation and emphasize contacting our own inner source of Divinity for guidance, rather than relying on outer teachers. Members are free to follow whatever spiritual disciplines are most inspirational and helpful to them.

We have an egalitarian governing process using group meditation and consensus decision-making. Weekly "personal sharing" meetings are held to share inspiration, resolve interpersonal problems, and decide business issues. Community tasks such as gardening, cooking, carpentry, and maintenance are shared by both men and women. Work is seen as "joyful productivity," an opportunity to put love in action. Work begins with a moment of silence, an "attunement," to affirm our oneness with God, each other, and the plants and tools with which we are working. We value both nature and technology in the community, as we have gardens as well as computers. We grow much of our own food organically, can and freeze goods for the winter, and heat all our houses with wood from our land. All new buildings have been built with an energy-efficient solar design to conserve the earth's resources. We use a variety of wholistic health practices for preventative health care.

As a small community, we've had the opportunity to experiment with designing different economic systems to find which would meet our needs most effectively. In the process of applying our ideals to real life situations, we've learned a great deal about the positive and negative aspects of these systems and their spiritual value, both for us and for society.

Because we observed so much over-consumption, greed, waste, and inequality in the private enterprise system operating in this country, we assumed that a socialist system of total sharing of income and resources, more akin to the early Christian monasteries, would be a more spiritually oriented economic system for our community. So we began our community in this way. Our income for the first couple of years came mainly from donations, our education programs, and later from a construction business. We pooled all our income and paid all expenses — mortgage, food, utilities, entertainment, clothes, doctors — out of this central pot.

This arrangement created economic equality and a feeling of mutual support among us. For several years the system supported eight adults and four children in the community. It taught us a high level of cooperation and sharing, as everything that any one of us spent money on affected everyone else, and members were very conscientious about spending the group's money. It taught us how interconnected we are, both in the community and as members of the human family in general. It also helped us see more clearly the challenges of economics on a national and planetary level.

However, we also began to notice a certain lack of freedom with this system, in that everyone had to have the same lifestyle for it to work harmoniously. Or at least, everyone had to be extremely tolerant of differences, as it's difficult to work hard to provide someone else with goods or services that one does not value. In making decisions about spending community money, we had to get involved in the details of each other's personal life, which was very time-consuming and seemed unnecessary.

It was also difficult to have everyone producing an equal amount of income, as not only do people have different levels of income-producing ability on the job market, but also everyone preferred working inside the community rather than at outside jobs to bring in money. Since work in the community (in the garden, kitchen, office, or construction) was always very needed, no one was ever forced to get an outside job if s/he didn't feel "attuned to it on a soul level," didn't feel the rightness of it. But this work in the community did not always produce the cash we needed to meet our bills easily. So we worked fervently on improving our faith in God and the abundance of the Universe, praying that if we were doing the right thing, the money we needed to pay all our bills would be available. And it always was — though just barely at times, and usually with nothing left over to really expand and build the community. We seemed to only have faith in getting the bare minimum. There were perhaps deep-seated feelings of unworthiness about receiving greater abundance.

From this experience we realized that a workable communal (or socialist) system depends on having very structured rules and requirements, with a system of authority to force people to work outside and bring in money when needed. We weren't willing to do this, as we felt it limited the individual freedom that is necessary for a person's growth in different ways. We also began to recognize that spiritual values are inherent in an individual or free enterprise system, as well as in a socialist system, although they are different. Freedom is important in allowing each individual to choose her/his own lifestyle and develop in her/his own way, learning the particular lessons offered by these choices. Individual responsibility and dependability is another spiritual value fostered in the private system. Often people want to skip over this value and be part of a group, but, in fact, we found that groups only work if they're composed of people who are able to be deeply individually responsible. Another problem with communal economy, we learned, is that when things aren't flowing financially as well as they should, it's difficult to know who or what is responsible. There's no clear one-to-one feedback system, as there is for an individual, about negative attitudes (lack of faith) or lack of practical work that is limiting the financial flow.

The opportunity for individual creativity and initiative was also limited in our economic system. Community members had started several independent businesses, as a form of service for bringing spiritual values into the world, and they needed the financial independence and flexibility to build the business.

So we decided to change our economic system and create a blend of private and communal systems, including what seemed to be the spiritual aspects of both. We have a communal system for the areas of our life that we mutually value and share: the land, tools, machinery, food, and community buildings. Each Full Member of Sirius contributes an equal share towards these expenses (after donations are subtracted) and works a minimum of eight hours a week on community projects. The Full Members, who are staff for the educational center, can then build their own house or shared houses on the land, and some have begun to do so. We still buy our food together in bulk as a co-op and share evening and weekend meals together. This sharing of resources is continuing to build the sense of cooperation and mutual responsibility and support that we had experienced in our communal economy At the same time, each individual or family is providing for their own living expenses and choosing their own lifestyle. This allows greater freedom with finances, business, and personal development, and it develops personal accountability.

Interestingly enough, since we created this new system we have experienced more income both as individuals and as a community, with increased donations for new projects. Two new businesses were started by members when the system was changed, so it seems to have encouraged individual initiative and creativity in our situation. (For further information: Sirius Community, Baker Road, Shutesbury, MA 01072; 413-259-1251.)

From *Builders of the Dawn: Community Lifestyles in a Changing World* by Corinne McLaughlin and Gordon Davidson. Stillpoint Publishing, 1985.

JOYCE HOLLYDAY

One of the most dramatic Western Massachusetts political stories of recent years has been the tax protest against the American militarism waged by Randy Kehler and Betsy Corner. The Colrain couple's refusal to pay their income tax led the Internal Revenue Service to seize their house and evict them. The subsequent story of community solidarity with Kehler and Corner reflects the strong radical political strain in the Upper Pioneer Valley. (Five years later, Kehler and Corner had lost their house, but they are still living in the area.)

Tax Revolt in Franklin County

I t's a winter Saturday morning like many others in western Massachusetts. The snow outside is deep, but the sun beats in through the picture window and warms the dining room, aided by the heat of a wood-burning stove.

Betsy Corner serves ginger tea and keeps plates heaped high with hot pancakes, topped with canned peaches that came from the trees in the yard in a warmer season. Her husband, Randy Kehler, is battling the flu. Their 10-year old daughter, Lillian, eats quickly and takes off on her bike to see the lamb just born on the neighboring property.

It is January 20, 1990. If there is any fear or apprehension here, it isn't perceptible. But, as of midnight the night before, Betsy, Randy, and Lillian could be put out of their home at any moment.

They live in Colrain, Massachusetts (population 1,595). The town is tucked in a valley spread with apple orchards and maple trees, tapped this time of year for their sweet sap. A cluster of a few dozen homes at Colrain's center is marked by a diamond-shaped, yellow road sign proclaiming "THICKLY SETTLED."

The homes are mostly clapboard, and all three of Colrain's churches have standard New England-fare white steeples. Among the town's residents are many hard-working laborers and a few artists, trustworthy dairy farmers "in the best of the Old Yankee tradition" (according to Randy) and — during the summer — Richard Nixon's former ambassador to South Vietnam (owner of the only tennis courts in Colrain).

A cotton mill that specialized in hospital bandages stands silent, its business moved south. An old covered bridge crosses the frozen North River, and a small graveyard on the side of Colrain Mountain has headstones dating back to the mid-1700s.

This is an area rich in history. Perhaps most notable of local events was Shays's Rebellion. In 1786, as a result of an act of wealthy legislators in Boston, homesteading farmers in western Massachusetts found it impossible to pay off their debts and taxes; most had fought in the Revolutionary War and had been sent home from battle without any pay. Consequently, some farmers had their cattle and land seized, while others were sent off to desolate debtors' prisons. Daniel Shays organized hundreds of armed farmers, including a few from Colrain. Their rebellion was short-lived; but before it was over, they won the right to pay some of their taxes in goods instead of money.

This state's problems with taxes began even before the founding of the republic, when the Boston Tea Party made famous the rallying cry "No taxation without representation." In 1846 Massachusetts citizen Henry David Thoreau spent a night in jail for his refusal to pay taxes that supported the Mexican War, claiming the war was unjust and had been undertaken to extend slavery. Today, a century and a half later, there is a new tax revolt in the making in western Massachusetts, founded on principles that would make Daniel Shays and Henry David Thoreau proud.

"The federal government's policies regarding nuclear weaponry and military interventions contradict our deepest moral and spiritual values." Thus begins a statement by Betsy Corner and Randy Kehler, written on March 15, 1989, two weeks after the Internal Revenue Service officially seized their home.

Their statement continues: "We struggle to accept and live by the proposition that we are all children of God. . . . For us, this applies especially to the poor, including our sisters and brothers in Central America who are suffering and dying as a result of U.S. policies and U.S. arms, and our sisters and brothers here in our own country who are hungry and homeless while our government pours billions of dollars into an insane nuclear arms race that threatens to kill us all.

"How can we willingly give money to the federal government when we know that it will be used to cause, or threaten, so much harm to other members of our human family? Our answer is that we can't."

Randy and Betsy are convinced that our government's policies are not only immoral, but also illegal: "The Nuremburg Principles that resulted from the trials of Nazi war criminals, and which were subsequently ratified by the U.S. government, hold that individual citizens who commit *or collaborate with* 'crimes against humanity' must be held responsible for their actions. . . . We believe that preparing for nuclear war, and waging actual war against people in countries such as Nicaragua and El Salvador, are both crimes against humanity — and that helping to pay for them is a form of collaboration."

The first year after they were married, in 1977, Randy and Betsy's federal income tax bill came to exactly $32. Through the years, that bill has accumulated to $26,917.11, including some $6,000 in penalties and interest. They will not pay it to the federal government. Instead, they have donated half of that sum to local human service groups and the other half to victims of U.S. policy abroad.

In the fall of 1987, they donated $5,000 to Walk in Peace, a Georgia-based project that raises money for people in Nicaragua who have lost arms and legs as a result of contra land mines and attacks. Walk in Peace coordinator Don Mosley wrote to them: "Your contribution all by itself is nearly enough to finance the complete rehabilitation (including the making of artificial limbs) of five people. I hope you can grasp that in human terms."

Betsy and Randy ended their March 15 statement this way: "For us, that's what it all comes down to: human terms. And that's what keeps us going."

Betsy has lived in this county for 21 years. She is a landscape architect and sees nuclear weapons as a threat to the environment as well as to humanity. She hopes that someday federal funds will be channeled toward remedies for acid rain and ozone depletion rather than toward preparations for the destruction of the Earth.

Randy is a founder of the Traprock Peace Center in Deerfield, Massachusetts, and works with the Study Group on Electoral Democracy, committed to electoral reform in this country. He helped to found the Nuclear Weapons Freeze Campaign and served as its first national coordinator from 1981 to 1984.

Randy was jailed for 22 months during the Vietnam War for resisting the military draft. Just before going to prison in 1969, he delivered a speech that was heard by Daniel Ellsberg, then a consultant with the Rand Corp. who worked with the Pentagon on national security and nuclear war planning. Ellsberg was so moved by Randy's courage that he asked himself, "What could I do to help shorten the war if I were ready to go to prison for it?" Later he released the Pentagon Papers, which exposed the government's lies, crimes, and secret escalations and eventually led to an early end to the war and the resignation of President Richard Nixon. "Randy changed my life by his example," says Ellsberg. And many other lives were changed as a result.

The publicity around her parents' war tax resistance has brought attention upon the family that Lillian prefers to avoid. She has found a way to live a very normal 10-year-old existence in the middle of the controversy. Her schoolmates say little to her about it — although her friend Rachel bravely volunteered to chain herself to Lillian's house if the IRS should try to evict her family.

Betsy was pregnant with Lillian when the family moved into their home on June 1, 1979. Less than a year later, an olive green car pulled up one afternoon, and the men inside told Betsy they were from the Internal Revenue Service. It was not a good time to talk about taxes — Betsy was holding infant Lillian, and a neighbor's brush fire had gone out of control and was sweeping toward their home. Surveying the nearby field — filled with fire trucks, as well as curious and concerned Colrain citizens — the IRS officials decided their business could wait.

Since that time, Randy and Betsy have received piles of letters and levies. They became self-employed to avoid having wages garnished. The $743 they had in their bank account was seized. For a while they parked their two aging cars behind a nearby sand pit to hide them at night. It turned out that the effort was unnecessary; when Randy recently asked a local agent why the IRS had never seized the cars, the agent just smiled and said, "We've seen your cars."

On February 23, 1989, as Betsy was about to go off to work, the phone rang. William Gorcyzca, from the local IRS office in Greenfield, was calling to say that the IRS was going to seize their house. The day before, Betsy had received a letter from a friend with Witness for Peace in Nicaragua, describing how she had come across a contra land-mine explosion that had killed four people and found the lower half of a good friend.

"So I had this image in my mind when the IRS called," Betsy says, adding, "How can you back down when this is where the money goes?" Randy was away at a conference in Milwaukee, and when she called to tell him the news, he said, "I have a feeling this is going to change our lives dramatically."

Betsy scheduled a meeting for the evening Randy was expected back. His plane was delayed by snow. He walked into his living room late in the evening and found 50 people just ending their gathering. "There was an incredible sense of solidarity and excitement," Randy remembers, "as well as apprehension." As his friends filed past him out the door, one smiled and said, "Don't worry about it — we've got it all taken care of."

IRS officials announced July 19 as the date for a sealed-bid auction on Randy and Betsy's home, publicizing it widely. They set the minimum bid at an astoundingly low $5,100 (the house had recently been assessed at $45,000), justifying the low minimum by the fact that the land on which their home sits belongs to the Valley Community Land Trust and cannot be sold with the house.

Randy and Betsy's community of support prepared for the day. They ran ads next to the IRS' auction announcements, asking that no one make a monetary bid on Randy and Betsy's home. In-kind bids were collected at the town dump on Saturday mornings. Families went out and bought food. On the day of the auction, a huge pile of baby food and peanut butter, rice and dried beans, cereal, canned vegetables, and spaghetti was loaded on the sidewalk in front of the Greenfield IRS office, site of the auction.

Inside, on the other side of a glass window, three IRS agents opened a stack of 86 sealed bids, one by one. In the envelopes were folded-paper peace cranes, offers of home-baked blueberry pies, and a bid of 12 pints of blood to be donated to the Red Cross. One man bid 10 toilet seats, which, he explained, if priced according to Pentagon procurement standards, would far exceed the $5,100 minimum.

The only monetary bid received was 100 Nicaraguan cordobas, offered on this 10th anniversary of the Nicaraguan people's triumph. In all, the "in-kinder-and-gentler bid" by supporters came to 4,411 hours of community service — ranging from carpentry work at a women's shelter to massage and psychotherapy "for IRS agents experiencing on-the-job stress" — calculated at minimum wage to be worth nearly $30,000. Coupled with more than $6,000 worth of groceries, their bid was seven times the minimum required. But the IRS insisted on accepting only cash.

About half an hour after the auction began, an IRS agent walked out into the hall and quietly announced to Betsy and Randy's 500 supporters, "The property has been purchased by the United States government for the minimum bid of $5,100." The crowd broke into exuberant cheers and applause. A home may have been lost — that result was inevitable — but an astounding moral victory had been won.

Randy handed Betsy a bouquet of pink roses, and the two walked arm in arm outside, tears in their eyes, while jubilant supporters sang "We Shall Not Be Moved." In front of a swarm of TV cameras, Randy announced with great emotion, "They received not one monetary bid on our home."

Betsy offered her heartfelt thanks to all their supporters. Her voice cracked as she thanked her parents, who had come to the auction, her father watching the morning's proceedings from a lawn chair. She invited everyone to their home for a party, as the strains of "Amazing Grace" drifted over the crowd from a bagpipe.

Betsy and Randy now have two thick files full of letters from all over the country — and even other parts of the world. The letters are from acquaintances and strangers, from an old family friend who knew Randy as a child, from a man Randy met on a train once. Some include poems and prayers, others donations.

One is addressed simply "Betsy Corner and Randy Kehler (Patriots), Colrain, Mass." A class of junior-high students discussed their situation and sent a letter. A young man who as a teen-ager was the groundskeeper at the Bush summer home in Kennebunkport, Maine, wrote to say he had sent Barbara Bush a letter on their behalf. By far, the overwhelming sentiment in the letters is, "I wish I were as brave as you. . . ."

Responses in conservative Colrain and the surrounding towns were a bit more mixed. Randy and Betsy's tax resistance spawned a barrage of letters-to-the-editor in the local newspapers. Some suggested that they leave the country, or that Randy step down from his elected position with the Colrain School Committee.

But support also came, particularly in the form of offers of a place to stay if the family should be put out. A Guatemalan refugee couple gave a $20 bill to a friend and said, "Give it to that couple about to lose their home." School teachers and supermarket clerks offered words of encouragement, and the mail carrier smiled and said of the IRS, "I think you've got 'em over a barrel."

At Christmas the pastor of the conservative Colrain Community Church invited Randy to organize a brass ensemble to accompany the choir as it went caroling. In the living room of some conservative mainstays of the community, the husband said to his wife, "This is Randy Kehler. . . . You've heard of Randy Kehler." His wife smiled, offered Randy some hot chocolate, and said, "Oh, yes, I have — and I'm sure it's not *all* bad."

Some town skeptics turned around when they discovered that Betsy and Randy pay all their state and local taxes and had donated a portion of their federal tax money to the local veterans' center. And many found it compelling when Randy pointed out that in one year alone, Colrain residents paid $1.7 million in federal taxes to the Pentagon, yet suffer with an outgrown and substandard elementary school, with no auditorium or gymnasium and its library and cafeteria in a windowless basement. The school children are bused for gym classes to Colrain's Memorial Hall, which was recently repainted when the Colrain branch of the Kehler/Corner Support Committee and the Colrain Veterans of Foreign Wars worked side by side for three Saturdays on the project.

Even one local IRS agent admitted to Randy and Betsy, "We're not wholly unsympathetic to what you're doing." Perhaps most surprising of all, an officer of the local National Guard near Springfield invited Randy to come and talk to the recruits about nonviolent civil disobedience. The first sergeant apologized for the fact that all the men were holding their guns — they were in the midst of cleaning them for an inspection and couldn't leave them out of sight.

A very animated discussion ensued, with the recruits acknowledging that Randy and Betsy's actions were part of a long tradition that included the civil rights struggle and union organizing. One recruit said to Randy when it was over, "If they order this unit up to your house, I won't go." When Randy thanked him, he said, "Hey, there are some things you just don't do."

The IRS granted Betsy and Randy a 180-day "redemption period" from the time of the auction to pay their back taxes and buy back their house. They chose to redeem neither themselves nor their home. As far as they are concerned, it is still theirs.

A month after the January 19 deadline for redemption, they are still in their home. Betsy nods at two shoeboxes filled with photographs, sitting by the piano. "This is my effort at packing," she says.

Although the temperature is plummeting close to zero at night, daffodils and morning glories have begun to bloom in the greenhouse. It is time to start seedlings for the tomatoes, broccoli, and peppers that will cover the garden in the summer. "If you start thinking 'I'm not going to be here,' you stop doing these things," says Betsy.

An ice storm has hit the valley, spreading a bright glaze over the deep snow. In an effort to embarrass negligent residents, the Greenfield Recorder has published the addresses where sidewalks haven't been cleared. Betsy looks at their half-shoveled driveway and says, "I got too busy to finish it." She grins. "But the IRS is responsible — they own the house now." And jokes are made about how much money they could get from the federal government if someone would just be willing to go out and break a leg.

The Internal Revenue Service's ownership of the house is complicated by the reality of the land trust, established by Randy, Betsy, and others to limit land speculation and keep housing affordable. The land trust's lease "requires occupancy of the leasehold premises as the primary residence of the lessee," and residents must "share the philosophy, spirit, and goals of the organization." Otherwise, the Valley Community Land Trust can terminate the lease at any time.

The legal technicalities are complicated, but members of the land trust are entertaining the thought that, if the IRS should put Randy, Betsy, and Lillian out of their home, this group of people who believe housing should be a right rather than a profit-making commodity (many of whom practice war tax resistance) would be put in the position of landlord over the IRS — with the power to evict. Furthermore, a federal provision states that any unoccupied federal property shall be used to house homeless people — which at that point would include Betsy, Randy, and Lillian.

No one is sure what will happen next. In the last few months, more than 150 supporters have received nonviolence training and organized themselves into groups in preparation for a series of occupations of the house if Betsy, Randy, and Lillian are evicted.

All the publicity around the case makes it difficult for the IRS to back down — or to evict. Randy and Betsy never thought it would go this far. They never asked for the publicity, never considered war tax resistance a strategy or even a major part of their life. "It was an act of conscience," says Betsy. Paraphrasing the monk Thomas Merton, Randy adds, "In the end, all we can really do is the best we can, and let God make something good of it."

On a snowy Saturday evening, Randy and Betsy, with their friends Pat and Bob, Wally and Juanita, and Tom are gathered around the Kehler-Corner dining room table. Discussion is animated around a topic that is dear to all of their hearts.

One opinion acknowledges that not many people in this country are willing to risk their jobs or their homes in order to stop paying for the killing our government carries out, and therefore less risky options have to be encouraged if the idea of war tax resistance is going to take hold more broadly. Another side says that the important thing is for those with strong convictions to keep all their money out of the hands of the federal government and be willing to pay the consequences. "It's the most important thing a patriot can do in this day and age," comments Tom. "Someone who's absolutely saying no — that's the thing they fear the most."

"The IRS thinks everybody has a breaking point," adds Juanita. "If you don't give up, that gives courage to others." Indeed, the actions of this handful of people in western Massachusetts gathered around the dining room table are giving others courage. And they are just one part of a movement; estimates of people practicing war tax resistance in this country range from thousands to tens of thousands.

Randy observes, "Changes elsewhere in the world are causing us to imagine large, previously unthinkable changes here; it makes what we're doing seem more plausible. With a formerly imprisoned playwright as president of Czechoslovakia, the time is ripe to stir people's imaginings of what is possible if they are willing to step outside their normal attachments and fears."

Will their brand of tax revolt sweep the country? The people around the dining room table are humble enough to acknowledge that they are simply following their consciences; the rest is out of their hands.

But wouldn't it be nice?

From "'We Shall Not be Moved'" by Joyce Hollyday. *Sojourners*, May 1990.

Famous Visitors

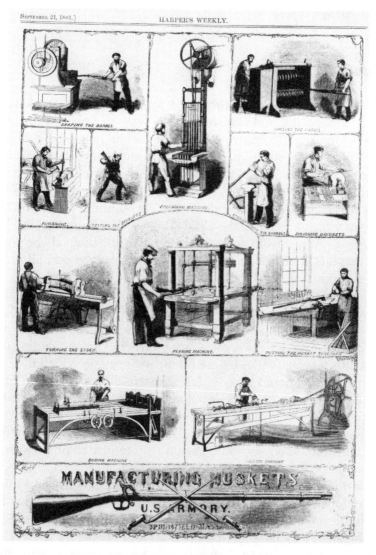

The United States Armory was established in Springfield in 1794; President George Washington visited its forerunner, the Continental Stores, in 1789. From Harper's Weekly, *Sept. 21, 1861; courtesy of the Connecticut Valley Historical Museum, Springfield.*

GEORGE WASHINGTON

The famous claim "George Washington slept here" includes Parson's Tavern in Springfield, in 1789 (on the site of today's Court Square). Washington (1732-1799) was taking a triumphal journey through New England after his inauguration as president. His one-day visit at Springfield included the Continental Stores, the forerunner of the Springfield Armory that Washington established five years later. This selection also describes the landscape between Hartford and Springfield.

Washington Slept Here

Wednesday, 21st. By promise I was to have Breakfasted at Mr. Ellsworths at Windsor on my way to Springfield, but the Morning proving very wet, and the rain not ceasing till past 10 Oclock I did not set out till half after that hour; I called however on Mr. Ellsworth and stay'd there near an hour. Reached Springfield by 4 Oclock, and while dinner was getting, examined the Continental Stores at this place which I found in very good order at the buildings (on the hill above the Town) which belong to the United States. The Barracks (also public property) are going fast to destruction and in a little time will be no more, without repairs. The Elaboratory, wch. seems to be a good building is in tolerable good repair and the Powder Magazine which is of Brick seems to be in excellent order and the Powder in it very dry. A Colo. Worthington, Colo. Williams (Adjutant General of the State of Massachusetts), Genl. Shepherd, Mr. Lyman and many other Gentlemen sat an hour or two with me in the evening at Parson's Tavern where I lodged and which is a good House. About 6 Miles before I came to Springfield I left the State of Connecticut and entered that of Massachusetts. The Distance from Hartford to Springfield is 28 Miles — both on Connecticut River. At the latter the River is crossed in Scows, set over with Poles and is about 80 rod wide. Between the two places is a fall and ten miles above Springfield is another fall, and others above that again — notwithstanding which much use is made of the Navigation for transportation in flats of about five tonns burthen. Seven miles on this side Hartford is Windsor a tolerable pleasant but not a large Village. Between Windsor and Suffield you pass through a level, barren & uncultivated plain for several Miles. Suffield stands high & pleasant — the Lds. good. From hence you descend again into another plain, where the Lands being good are much better cultivated. The whole Road from Hartford to Springfield is level & good, except being too Sandy in places & the Fields enclosed with Posts & Rails generally their not being much Stone. The Crops of Corn, except on the Interval Lands on the River are more indifferent (tho' not bad) in the Eastern than we found them in the Western part of the State of Connecticut.

There is a great equality in the People of this State — Few or no oppulent Men and no poor — great similatude in their buildings — the general fashion of which is a Chimney (always of Stone or Brick) and door in the middle, with a stair case fronting the latter, running up by the side of the former — two flush Stories with a very good shew of Sash & glass Windows. The size generally is from 30 to 50 feet in length and from 20 to 30 in width exclusive of a back shed which seems to be added as the family encreases. The farms by the contiguity of the Houses are small not averaging more than 100 Acres. These are worked chiefly by Oxen (which have no other feed than Hay) with a horse & sometimes two before them both in Plow and Cart. In their light Lands and in their sleighs they work Horses, but find them much more expensive than Oxen. Springfield is on the East side of Connecticut River; before you come to which a large branch of it called Agawam is crossed by a Bridge. It stands under the Hill on the interval Land, and has only one Meeting house — 28 Miles from Hartfd.

Thursday, 22d. Set out at 7 Oclock; and for the first 8 miles rid over an almost uninhabited Pine plain; much mixed with Sand. Then a little before the road descends to Chicabi River it is hilly, Rocky & Steep, & continues so for several Miles; the Country being Stony and Barren; with a mixture of Pine and Oak till we came to Palmer, at the House of one Scott where we breakfasted and where the Land, though far from good, began to mend, to this is called 15 Miles. Among these Pines are Ponds of fresh Water.

From *The Diaries of George Washington, Volume V, July 1786–December 1789*, edited by Donald Jackson and Dorothy Twohig. University Press of Virginia, 1979.

RALPH WALDO EMERSON

In 1823, young Harvard graduate Ralph Waldo Emerson (1803-1882) set out on a summer walking tour from Boston to the Connecticut River. His Journal *records visits to Amherst, Mt. Holyoke, Northampton, and Greenfield. These early thoughts on nature and human nature suggest the grand old man of American letters he was to become, as transcendentalist poet and philosopher.*

Walk to the Connecticut

Thursday, August 4

Tuesday Morning I engaged Mr Bartlett to bring me to Mrs Shepard's and I think the worthy man returned with some complacent recollections of the instructions & remarks he had dropped on the way for the stranger's edification. Our wagon ride was somewhat uneasy from below but its ups & downs were amply compensated by the richness & grandeur visible above & around. Hampshire County rides in wagons. In this pleasant land I found a house-full of friends, a noble house — very good friends. In the afternoon I went to the College. The infant college is an Infant Hercules. Never was so much striving, outstretching, & advancing in a literary cause as is exhibited here. The students all feel a personal responsibility in the support & defence of their young Alma Mater against all antagonists, and as long as this battle abroad shall continue, the Government, unlike all other Governments, will not be compelled to fight with its students within. The opposition of other towns & counties produces moreover a correspondent friendship & kindness from the people in Amherst, and there is a daily exhibition of affectionate feeling between the inhabitants & the scholars, which is the more pleasant as it is so uncommon. They attended the Declamation & Commencement with the interest which parents usually shew at the exhibitions of schools where their own children are engaged. I believe the affair was first moved, about three years ago, by the Trustees of the Academy. When the corner stone of the South College was laid, the Institution did not own a dollar. A cartload of stones was brought by a farmer in Pelham, to begin the foundation; and now they have two large brick edifices, a President's house, & considerable funds. Dr Moore has left them six or seven thousand dollars. A poor one-legged man died last week in Pelham, who was not known to have any property, & left them 4000 dollars to be appropriated to the building of a Chapel, over whose door is to be inscribed his name, Adams Johnson. Wm Phillips gave a thousand & Wm Eustis a hundred dollars and great expectations are entertained from some rich men, friends to the Seminary who will die without children.

They have wisely systematized this spirit of opposition which they have found so lucrative, & the students are all divided into thriving opposition societies which gather libraries, laboratories, mineral cabinets, &c, with an indefatigable spirit, which nothing but rivalry could inspire. Upon this impulse, they write, speak, & study in a sort of fury, which, I think, promises a harvest of attainments. The Commencement was plainly that of a young college, but had strength and eloquence mixed with the apparent 'vestigia ruris.' And the scholar who gained the prize for declamation the evening before, would have a first prize at any Cambridge competition. The College is supposed to be worth net 85000 dollars.

After spending three days very pleasantly at Mrs Shepard's, among orators, botanists, mineralogists, & above all, Ministers, I set off on Friday Morning with Thos Greenough & another little cousin in a chaise to visit Mount Holyoke. How high the hill may be, I know not; for, different accounts make it 8, 12 & 16 hundred feet from the river. The prospect repays the ascent and although the day was hot & hazy so as to preclude a distant prospect, yet all the broad meadows in the immediate vicinity of the mountain through which the Connecticutt winds, make a beautiful picture seldom rivalled. After adding our names in the books to the long list of strangers whom curiosity has attracted to this hill we descended in safety without encountering rattlesnake or viper that have given so bad fame to the place. We were informed that about 40 people ascend the mountain every fair day during the summer. After passing through Hadley meadows, I took leave of my companions at Northampton bridge, and crossed for the first time the far famed Yankee river.

From the Hotel in Northampton I visited Mr. Theodore Strong, where I have been spending a couple of days of great pleasure. His five beautiful daughters & son make one of the finest families I ever saw. In the afternoon, I went on horse back (oh Hercules!) with Allen Strong to Round Hill, the beautiful site of the Gymnasium, & to Shepherd's Factory about 4 miles from the centre of the town. Saturday Morning we went in a chaise in pursuit of a lead mine said to lie about five miles off which we found after great & indefatigable search. We tied our horse & descended, by direction, into a somewhat steep glen at the bottom of which we found the covered entrance of a little canal about 5 ft. wide. Into this artificial cavern we fired a gun to call out the miner from within. The report was long & loudly echoed & after a weary interval we discerned a boat with lamps lighted in its sides issuing from this dreary abode. We welcomed the Miner to the light of the Sun and leaving our hats without, & binding our heads we lay down in the boat and were immediately introduced to a

A vista from the east ridge of Greenfield at "Poet's Seat" looking south down the Connecticut River to the point where the Deerfield River joins it. Montague is on the east or left side. From *History of the Connecticut Valley in Massachusetts* by Louis H. Everts, 1879.

cave varying in height from 4 to 6 & 8 feet, hollowed in a pretty soft sandstone through which the water continually drops. When we lost the light of the entrance & saw only this gloomy passage by the light of lamps it required no effort of imagination to believe we were leaving the world, & our smutty ferryman was a true Charon. After sailing a few hundred feet the vault grew higher & wider overhead & there was a considerable trickling of water on our left; this was the ventilator of the mine & reaches up to the surface of the earth. We continued to advance in this manner for 900 feet & then got out of the boat & walked on planks a little way to the end of this excavation. Here we expected to find the lead vein, & the operations of the subterranean man, but were sadly disappointed. He had been digging through this stone for 12 years, & has not yet discovered any lead at all. Indications of lead at the surface led some Boston gentleman to set this man at work in the expectation that after cutting his dark canal for 1000 feet, he would reach the vein, & the canal would then draw off the water which prevented them from digging from above. As yet, he has found no lead but, as he gravely observed 'has reached some *excellent granite.*' In this part of the work he has 40 dollars for every foot he advances and it occupies him ten days to earn this. He has advanced 975 feet & spends his days, winter & summer, alone in this damp & silent tomb. He says the place is excellent for meditation, & that he sees no goblins. Many visiters come to his dark residence, & pay him a shilling apiece for the sight. A young man, he said, came the day before us, who after going in a little way was taken with terrors & said he felt faint, & returned. Said Miner is a brawny personage & discreet withal; has a wife, & lives near the hole. All his excavations are performed by successive blastings.

In the afternoon I set out on my way to Greenfield intending to pass the Sabbath with George Ripley. Mr Strong insisted on carrying me to Hatfield, & thence I passed chiefly on foot through Whately & Deerfield over sands & pinebarrens, & across Green River to Greenfield, and did not arrive there till after ten o'clock & found both taverns shut up. I should have staid in Deerfield if Mr S. had not ridiculed the idea of getting to Greenfield that night. In the morning I called at Mr Ripley's, & was sorely disappointed to learn that his son was at Cambridge. The family were exceedingly hospitable, and I listened with no great pleasure to a sermon from Rev. Mr Perkins of Amherst in the morng & in the afternoon rode over to the other parish with Mr R. to hear Rev Lincoln Ripley. After service Mr L. R returned with us, and in the evening we heard another sermon from Mr Perkins which pleased me abundantly better than his matins. He is a loudvoiced scripture-read divine, & his compositions have the elements of a potent eloquence, but he lacks taste. By the light of the Evening star, I walked with my reverend uncle, a man, who well sustains the character of an aged missionary. It is a new thing to him, he said, to *correspond* with his wife, and he attends the mail regularly every Monday morng. to send or recieve a letter.

After a dreamless night, & a most hospitable entertainment I parted from Greenfield & through an unusually fine country, crossed the Connecticut (shrunk to a rivulet in this place somewhere in Montagu). My solitary way grew somewhat more dreary, as I drew nearer Wendell and the only relief to hot sandy roads & a barren monotonous region was one fine forest with many straight clean pinetrees upwards of a hundred feet high 'fit for the mast of some great Admiral.' All that day was a thoughtless heavy pilgrimage and Fortune deemed that such a crowded week of pleasure demanded a reaction of pain. At night I was quartered in the meanest caravansera which has contained my person since the tour began. Traveller! weary & jaded, who regardest the repose of thine earthly tenement; Traveller, hungry & athirst whose heart warms to the hope of animal gratification; Traveller of seven or seventy years beware, beware, I beseech you of Mr Haven's Inn in New Salem. Already he is laying a snare for your kindness or credulity in fencing in a mineral spring for your infirmities. Beware —

From *The Journals and Miscellaneous Notebooks of Ralph Waldo Emerson*, edited by William H. Gilman et al. Harvard University Press, 1961.

NATHANIEL HAWTHORNE

Many literary figures of the nineteenth century made their way through Western Massachusetts. Nathaniel Hawthorne (1804-1864) especially enjoyed the Berkshires and, in the early 1850s, he stayed at "Tanglewood" in Lenox, where he befriended Herman Melville.

On a summer visit to North Adams in 1838, Hawthorne took a short excursion over what would be considered today's "Mohawk Trail," then down the Deerfield River Valley to Shelburne Falls. This tour is recounted in The American Notebooks.

Hawthorne's works include the novels The Scarlet Letter, The House of the Seven Gables, *and* The Blithedale Romance, *and several short stories.*

Down the Deerfield River

Leaving the tavern, we rode a mile or two further to the eastern brow of the mountain, whence we had a view over the tops of a multitude of heights, into the intersecting vallies of which we were to plunge, — and beyond them the blue and indistinctive scene extended, to the east and north, to the distance of at least sixty miles. Beyond the hills, it looked almost as if the blue ocean might be seen. Monadnock was visible, like a blue cloud against the sky. Descending the mountain, we by and bye got a view of the Deerfield river, which makes a bend in its course from about north and south to about east and west, coming out from one defile among the mountains, and flowing through another. The scenery on the eastern side of the Green Mountain is incomparably more striking than on the western, where the long swells and ridges have a flatness of effect; and even Graylock heaves itself so gradually that it does not much strike the beholder. But on the eastern side, peaks a thousand or two feet high rush up on either side of the river, in ranges, thrusting out the shoulders side by side; they are almost precipitous, clothed in woods, through which the naked rock thrusts itself forth to view. Sometimes the peak is bald, while the forest shags the body of the hill; and the baldness gives it an indescribably stern effect. Sometimes the precipice rises with abruptness from the immediate side of the river; sometimes there is a cultivated vally on either side, cultivated long, and with all the smoothness and antique rurality of a farm near cities; this gentle picture strangely set off by the wild mountain frame around it. Often it would seem a wonder how our road was to continue, the mountains rose so abruptly on either side, and stood so direct a wall across our onward course; while, looking behind, it would be an equal mystery how we had got thither, through the huge base of the mountain that seemed to have reared itself erect after our passage. But passing onward, a narrow defile would give us egress into a scene where new mountains would still seem to bar us. Our road was much of it level, but scooped out among mountains. The river was a brawling stream, shallow, and roughened by rocks; now we rode on a level with it; now there was a sheer descent down from the roadside upon it, often unguarded by any kind of a fence, except by the trees that contrived to grow on the headlong interval. Between the mountains there were gorges and defiles, that led the imagination away into new scenes of wildness. I have never ridden through such romantic scenery, where there was such variety and boldness of mountain-shapes as this; and though it was a broad sunny day, the mountains diversified the scene with sunshine and shadow, and glory, and gloom.

The geological potholes described by Hawthorne can still be seen just south of the Bridge of Flowers and Salmon Falls at Shelburne Falls. Photo by Geoffrey Bluh.

In Charlemont (I think) after passing a bridge, we saw a very curious rock, on the shore of the river, down about twenty feet from the roadside. Clambering down the bank, we found it a complete arch, hollowed out of the solid rock, and as high as the arched entrance of an ancient church, which it might be taken to be, though considerably dilapidated and weatherworn. The water flows through it; though the rock afforded standing room, beside the pillars. It was really like the archway of an enchanted palace, all of which has vanished but the entrance into nothingness and empty space. We climbed to the top of the arch, in which the traces of water having eddied are very perceptible. This curiosity occurs in a wild part of the river's course, and in a solitude of mountains.

Farther down, the river becoming deeper, broader and more placid, little boats were seen moored along it, for the convenience of crossing. Sometimes, too, the well-beaten track of wheels and hoofs passed down to its verge, then vanished, and appeared on the other side, indicating a ford. We saw one house, a pretty, small, house, with green blinds, and much quietness in its environments, on the other side of the river, with a flat-bottomed boat for communication. It was a pleasant idea, that the world was kept off by the river.

Proceeding onward, we reached Shelburne Falls. Here the river, in the distance of a few hundred yards, makes a descent of about 150 feet, over a prodigious bed of rock. Formerly, it doubtless flowed unbroken over the rock, merely creating a rapid; and traces of water having raged over it is visible in portions of the rock that now lie high and dry. At present, the river rages and roars through a channel which it has worn in the rock, leaping down in two or three distinct falls, and rushing downward, as from flight to flight of a broken and irregular staircase. The mist rises from the highest of these cataracts, and forms a pleasant object in the sunshine. The best view, I think, is to stand on the verge of the upper and largest fall, and look down through the whole rapid descent of the river, as it hurries foaming downward through its rock-worn path — the rocks seeming to have been hewn away, as when mortals make a road. These falls are the largest in this state, and have a very peculiar character; it seems as if water had more power at some former period than now, to hew and tear its passage through such an immense ledge of rock as here withstood it. In this rock, or parts of it now far beyond the reach of the water, it has worn what are called pot-holes; being circular hollows in the rock, where for ages stones have been whirled round and round by the eddies of the water; so that the interior of the pot is as circular and as smooth as it could have been made by art. Often, the mouth of the pot is the narrowest part — the interior being deeply scooped out. Water is contained in most of these potholes; sometimes so deep that a man might drown himself therein, and lie undetected at the bottom. Some of them are of a convenient size for cooking, which might be practicable by putting in hot stones.

The tavern at Shelburne Falls was about the worst I ever saw — hardly anything being to be had to eat — at least not of the meat kind. There was a party of students from the Rensalaer school, at Troy, spent the night there — a rough set of urchins from sixteen to twenty years old; accompanied by a wagon-driver, a short, stubbed little fellow, who walked about with great independence, tucking his hands into his breeches pockets, beneath his frock. The queerness was, such a figures being associated with classic youths. They were on an excursion which is yearly made from that school, in search of minerals; they seemed under rather better moral habits than students used to be in my time, but wild spirited, rude, and unpolished, somewhat like German students — which resemblance one or two of them increased by smoking pipes. In the morning, my breakfast being set in a corner of the same room with theirs, I saw their breakfast table with a huge wash-bowl of milk in the centre, and a bowl and spoon set for each guest.

From *The American Notebooks* by Nathaniel Hawthorne, edited by Claude Simpson. Ohio State University Press, 1972.

CHARLES DICKENS

Charles Dickens's (1812-1870) account of his first trip to the United States in American Notes *in 1842 was resented by many Americans who did not appreciate his caustic criticism of their country. His description of a trip on the Connecticut River was also uncomplimentary.*

From Springfield to Hartford

We went on next morning, still by railroad, to Springfield. From that place to Hartford, whither we were bound, is a distance of only five-and-twenty miles, but at that time of the year the roads were so bad that the journey would probably have occupied ten or twelve hours. Fortunately, however, the winter having been unusually mild, the Connecticut River was "open," or, in other words, not frozen. The captain of a small steamboat was going to make his first trip for the season that day (the second February trip, I believe, within the memory of man), and only waited for us to go on board. Accordingly, we went on board, with as little delay as might be. He was as good as his word, and started directly.

It certainly was not called a small steamboat without reason. I omitted to ask the question, but I should think it must have been of about half a pony power. Mr. Paap, the celebrated Dwarf, might have lived and died happily in the cabin, which was fitted with common sash-windows like an ordinary dwelling-house. These windows had bright red curtains, too, hung on slack strings across the lower panes; so that it looked like the parlour of a Lilliputian public-house, which had got afloat in a flood or some other water accident, and was drifting nobody knew where. But even in this chamber there was a rocking-chair. It would be impossible to get on anywhere, in America, without a rocking-chair.

I am afraid to tell how many feet short this vessel was, or how many feet narrow: to apply the words length and width to such measurement would be a contradiction in terms. But I may state that we all kept the middle of the deck, lest the boat should unexpectedly tip over; and that the machinery, by some surprising process of condensation, worked between it and the keel: the whole forming a warm sandwich, about three feet thick.

It rained all day as I once thought it never did rain anywhere, but in the Highlands of Scotland. The river was full of floating blocks of ice, which were constantly crunching and cracking under us; and the depth of water, in the course we took to avoid the larger masses, carried down the middle of the river by the current, did not exceed a few inches. Nevertheless, we moved onward, dexterously; and being well wrapped up, bade defiance to the weather, and enjoyed the journey. The Connecticut River is a fine stream; and the banks in summer-time are, I have no doubt, beautiful: at all events, I was told so by a young lady in the cabin; and she should be a judge of beauty, if the possession of a quality include the appreciation of it, for a more beautiful creature I never looked upon.

After two hours and a half of this odd travelling (including a stoppage at a small town, where we were saluted by a gun considerably bigger than our own chimney), we reached Hartford, and straightway repaired to an extremely comfortable hotel: except, as usual, in the article of bedrooms, which, in almost every place we visited, were very conducive to early rising.

From *American Notes* by Charles Dickens. Macmillan, 1893.

HENRY WADSWORTH LONGFELLOW

Idealism has been an element of Massachusetts culture since the Puritans attempted to build a "city upon a hill" in the seventeenth century. Brahmin poet laureate Henry Wadsworth Longfellow (1807-1882) expressed his anti-war ideals when he visited the Springfield Armory on his honeymoon in 1843. Inspired by the latent horror of the massed rifles, Longfellow penned "The Arsenal at Springfield." The poem, the favorite of his wife Frances Appleton, became widely popular. Visitors to the Springfield Armory National Historic Site can still view the "organ" of "burnished arms" that affected Longfellow.

The Arsenal at Springfield

This is the Arsenal. From floor to ceiling,
    Like a huge organ, rise the burnished arms;
But from their silent pipes no anthem pealing
    Startles the villages with strange alarms.

Ah! what a sound will rise, how wild and dreary,
    When the death-angel touches those swift keys!
What loud lament and dismal Miserere
    Will mingle with their awful symphonies!

I hear even now the infinite fierce chorus,
    The cries of agony, the endless groan,
Which, through the ages that have gone before us,
    In long reverberations reach our own.

On helm and harness rings the Saxon hammer,
    Through Cimbric forest roars the Norseman's song,
And loud, amid the universal clamor,
    O'er distant deserts sounds the Tartar gong.

I hear the Florentine, who from his palace
    Wheels out his battle-bell with dreadful din,
And Aztec priests upon their teocallis
    Beat the wild war-drums made of serpent's skin;

The tumult of each sacked and burning village;
    The shout that every prayer for mercy drowns;
The soldiers' revels in the midst of pillage;
    The wail of famine in beleaguered towns;

The bursting shell, the gateway wrenched asunder,
    The rattling musketry, the clashing blade;
And ever and anon, in tones of thunder
    The diapason of the cannonade.

Is it, O man, with such discordant noises,
    With such accursed instruments as these,
Thou drownest Nature's sweet and kindly voices,
    And jarrest the celestial harmonies?

Were half the power that fills the world with terror,
    Were half the wealth bestowed on camps and courts,
Given to redeem the human mind from error,
    There were no need of arsenals or forts:

The warrior's name would be a name abhorrèd!
    And every nation, that should lift again
Its hand against a brother, on its forehead
    Would wear forevermore the curse of Cain!

Down the dark future, through long generations,
    The echoing sounds grow fainter and then cease;
And like a bell, with solemn, sweet vibrations,
    I hear once more the voice of Christ say, "Peace!"

Peace! and no longer from its brazen portals
    The blast of War's great organ shakes the skies!
But beautiful as songs of the immortals,
    The holy melodies of love arise.

From *The Complete Works of Henry Wadsworth Longfellow*. Houghton Mifflin, 1893.

The Inspiration of Poets

The only known photograph of Emily Dickinson is this ca. 1846 daguerreotype taken when she was about sixteen. Courtesy of Amherst College Library.

EDWARD TAYLOR

Edward Taylor (1642-1729), a staunch Puritan divine who served as Westfield minister from 1671 until 1725, is considered the finest poet in colonial America. Like Emily Dickinson, he did not write for publication. His poems, in fact, were not published until 1937.

Taylor's poems were deeply spiritual. His masterpiece Preparatory Meditations *was a series of almost 200 meditations based on scriptural passages. Taylor's work is compared to the English devotional metaphysical poets John Donne, George Herbert, and Henry Vaughn. Virtually nothing in his poetry touches on life in frontier Westfield. What does stand out in his poetry is an intense devotion to God and conviction that divine providence permeates worldly events — even the death of his children or catastrophic weather.*

Upon Wedlock, and Death of Children

A Curious Knot God made in Paradise,
    And drew it out inamled neatly Fresh.
It was the True-Love Knot, more sweet than spice
    And set with all the flowres of Graces dress.
    Its Weddens Knot, that ne're can be unti'de.
    No Alexanders Sword can it divide.

The slips here planted, gay and glorious grow:
    Unless an Hellish breath do sindge their Plumes.
Here Primrose, Cowslips, Roses, Lilies blow
    With Violets and Pinkes that voide perfumes.
    Whose beautious leaves ore laid with Hony Dew.
    And Chanting birds Cherp out sweet Musick true.

When in this Knot I planted was, my Stock
    Soon knotted, and a manly flower out brake.
And after it my branch again did knot
    Brought out another Flowre its sweet breathd mate.
    One knot gave one tother the tothers place.
    Whence Checkling smiles fought in each others face.

But oh! a glorious hand from glory came
    Guarded with Angells, soon did Crop this flowre
Which almost tore the root up of the same
    At that unlookt for, Dolesome, darksome houre.

In Pray're to Christ perfum'de it did ascend,
And Angells bright did it to heaven tend.

But pausing on't, this sweet perfum'd my thought,
    Christ would in Glory have a Flowre, Choice, Prime,
And having Choice, chose this my branch forth brought.
    Lord take't. I thanke thee, thou takst ought of mine,
    It is my pledg in glory, part of mee
    Is now in it, Lord, glorifi'de with thee.

But praying ore my branch, my branch did sprout
    And bore another manly flower, and gay
And after that another, sweet brake out,
    The which the former hand soon got away.
    But oh! the tortures, Vomit, screechings, groans,
    And six weeks Fever would pierce hearts like stones.

Griefe o're doth flow: and nature fault would finde
    Were not thy Will, my Spell Charm, Joy, and Gem:
That as I said, I say, take, Lord, they're thine.
    I piecemeale pass to Glory bright in them.
    I joy, may I sweet Flowers for Glory breed,
    Whether thou getst them green, or lets them seed.

Upon the Sweeping Flood Aug: 13.14. 1683

Oh! that Id had a tear to've quencht that flame
    Which did dissolve the Heavens above
    Into those liquid drops that Came
        To drown our Carnall love.
Our cheeks were dry and eyes refusde to weep.
Tears bursting out ran down the skies dark Cheek.

Were th'Heavens sick? must wee their Doctors bee
    And physick them with pills, our sin?
    To make them purg and Vomit, see,
        And Excrements out fling?
We've griev'd them by such Physick that they shed
Their Excrements upon our lofty heads.

From *The Poems of Edward Taylor* edited by Donald E. Stanford. Yale University Press, 1963.

WILLIAM CULLEN BRYANT

William Cullen Bryant (1794-1878) was America's first poet of international stature. He hailed from Cummington, attended Williams College, and became an editor of the highly regarded New York Evening Post. *Bryant was a major force in national politics, first as a Jackson Democrat and later as a Lincoln Republican.*

Bryant wrote his greatest poems early in his twenties, when he still lived in Western Massachusetts. His poems were inspired by the nature observed round about Cummington. His masterpiece "Thanatopsis" (1817) was a meditation upon death conceived during his "solitary rambles in the woods." "Inscription for the Entrance to a Wood" (1818) finds God embodied in Nature.

Thanatopsis

To him who in the love of nature holds
Communion with her visible forms, she speaks
A various language; for his gayer hours
She has a voice of gladness, and a smile
And eloquence of beauty, and she glides
Into his darker musings, with a mild
And healing sympathy, that steals away
Their sharpness, ere he is aware. When thoughts
Of the last bitter hour come like a blight
Over thy spirit, and sad images
Of the stern agony, and shroud, and pall,
And breathless darkness, and the narrow house,
Make thee to shudder, and grow sick at heart; —
Go forth, under the open sky, and list
To Nature's teachings, while from all around —
Earth and her waters, and the depths of air, —
Comes a still voice —

              Yet a few days, and thee
The all-beholding sun shall see no more
In all his course; nor yet in the cold ground,
Where thy pale form was laid, with many tears,
Nor in the embrace of ocean, shall exist
Thy image. Earth, that nourished thee, shall claim
Thy growth, to be resolved to earth again,
And, lost each human trace, surrendering up

Thine individual being, shalt thou go
To mix forever with the elements,
To be a brother to the insensible rock
And to the sluggish clod, which the rude swain
Turns with his share, and treads upon. The oak
Shall send his roots abroad, and pierce thy mould.
Yet not to thine eternal resting-place
Shalt thou retire alone — nor couldst thou wish
Couch more magnificent. Thou shalt lie down
With patriarchs of the infant world — with kings,
The powerful of the earth — the wise, the good,
Fair forms, and hoary seers of ages past,
All in one mighty sepulchre. — The hills
Rock-ribbed and ancient as the sun, — the vales
Stretching in pensive quietness between;
The venerable woods — rivers that move
In majesty, and the complaining brooks
That make the meadows green; and, poured round all,
Old ocean's gray and melancholy waste, —
Are but the solemn decorations all
Of the great tomb of man. The golden sun,
The planets, all the infinite host of heaven,
Are shining on the sad abodes of death,
Through the still lapse of ages. All that tread
The globe are but a handful to the tribes
That slumber in its bosom. — Take the wings
Of morning — and the Barcan desert pierce,
Or lose thyself in the continuous woods
Where rolls the Oregan, and hears no sound,
Save his own dashings — yet — the dead are there;
And millions in those solitudes, since first
The flight of years began, have laid them down
In their last sleep — the dead reign there alone.
So shalt thou rest — and what if thou withdraw
Unheeded by the living — and no friend
Take note of thy departure? All that breathe
Will share thy destiny. The gay will laugh
When thou art gone, the solemn brood of care
Plod on, and each one as before will chase
His favorite phantom; yet all these shall leave
Their mirth and their employments, and shall come,
And make their bed with thee. As the long train

Of ages glide away, the sons of men,
The youth in life's green spring, and he who goes
In the full strength of years, matron, and maid,
And the sweet babe, and the gray-headed man, —
Shall one by one be gathered to thy side,
By those, who in their turn shall follow them.

So live, that when thy summons comes to join
The innumerable caravan, that moves
To that mysterious realm, where each shall take
His chamber in the silent halls of death,
Thou go not, like the quarry-slave at night,
Scourged to his dungeon, but, sustained and soothed
By an unfaltering trust, approach thy grave,
Like one who wraps the drapery of his couch
About him, and lies down to pleasant dreams.

Inscription for the Entrance to a Wood

Stranger, if thou hast learned a truth which needs
No school of long experience, that the world
Is full of guilt and misery, and hast seen
Enough of all its sorrows, crimes, and cares,
To tire thee of it, enter this wild wood
And view the haunts of Nature. The calm shade
Shall bring a kindred calm, and the sweet breeze
That makes the green leaves dance, shall waft a balm
To thy sick heart. Thou wilt find nothing here
Of all that pained thee in the haunts of men,
And made thee loathe thy life. The primal curse
Fell, it is true, upon the unsinning earth,
But not in vengeance. God hath yoked to guilt
Her pale tormentor, misery. Hence, these shades
Are still the abodes of gladness; the thick roof
Of green and stirring branches is alive
And musical with birds, that sing and sport
In wantonness of spirit; while below
The squirrel, with raised paws and form erect,
Chirps merrily. Throngs of insects in the shade
Try their thin wings and dance in the warm beam
That waked them into life. Even the green trees
Partake the deep contentment; as they bend

To the soft winds, the sun from the blue sky
Looks in and sheds a blessing on the scene.
Scarce less the cleft-born wild-flower seems to enjoy
Existence, than the wingèd plunderer
That sucks its sweets. The mossy rocks themselves
And the old and ponderous trunks of prostrate trees
That lead from knoll to knoll a causey rude
Or bridge the sunken brook, and their dark roots,
With all their earth upon them, twisting high,
Breathe fixed tranquillity. The rivulet
Sends forth glad sounds, and tripping o'er its bed
Of pebbly sands, or leaping down the rocks,
Seems, with continuous laughter, to rejoice
In its own being. Softly tread the marge,
Lest from her midway perch thou scare the wren
That dips her bill in water. The cool wind,
That stirs the stream in play, shall come to thee,
Like one that loves thee nor will let thee pass
Ungreeted, and shall give its light embrace.

From *Poetical Works* by William Cullen Bryant. Thomas Y. Crowell, 1893.

EMILY DICKINSON

Literature lovers would accord Emily Dickinson (1830-1886) highest place among the august company of Pioneer Valley writers. Critic Alfred Kazin called Dickinson "the first modern writer to come out of New England."

Emily Dickinson cultivated her modern consciousness in the Dickinson family homestead at 280 Main Street in Amherst. She hailed from a prosperous old Amherst family — her father Edward was a congressman. Her most creative spurt came during the Civil War, when she wrote 800 of her nearly 1800 poems. Dickinson published only seven poems in her lifetime, five in the Springfield Republican.

Emily Dickinson did not write expressly about the Pioneer Valley. Her poems have an abstract quality. She generally stayed at home, so she has little specific to say about the natural and social world around her in Amherst. Yet, Alfred Kazin wrote, "She is its [Amherst's] great reflector, perhaps because she never intended to 'do' Amherst itself. Amherst was the whole of America and the cycle of life." The nature, climate, and landscape of the Pioneer Valley inform her poetry profoundly.

Poems

SPRING

A Light exists in Spring
    Not present on the Year
    At any other period —
When March is scarcely here

A Color stands abroad
On Solitary Fields
That Science cannot overtake
But Human Nature feels.

It waits upon the Lawn,
It shows the furthest Tree
Upon the furthest Slope you know
It almost speaks to you.

Then as Horizons step
Or Noons report away
Without the Formula of sound
It passes and we stay —

A quality of loss
Affecting our Content
As Trade had suddenly encroached
Upon a Sacrament.

SUNRISE

The Fingers of the Light
Tapped soft upon the Town
With "I am great and cannot wait
So therefore let me in."

"You're soon," the Town replied,
My Faces are asleep —
But swear, and I will let you by,
You will not wake them up."

The easy Guest complied
But once within the Town
The transport of His Countenance
Awakened Maid and Man

The Neighbor in the Pool
Upon His Hip elate
Made loud obeisance and the Gnat
Held up His Cup for Light.

SUNSET

The largest Fire ever known
Occurs each Afternoon —
Discovered is without surprise
Proceeds without concern —
Consumes and no report to men
An Occidental Town,
Rebuilt another morning
To be burned down again

STORM

The Clouds their Backs together laid
The North begun to push
The Forests galloped till they fell
The Lightning played like mice

The Thunder crumbled like a stuff
How good to be in Tombs
Where Nature's Temper cannot reach
Nor missile ever comes

SUMMER

Summer begins to have the look
Peruser of enchanting Book
Reluctantly but sure perceives
A gain upon the backward leaves —

Autumn begins to be inferred
By millinery of the cloud
Or deeper color in the shawl
That wraps the everlasting hill.

The eye begins its avarice
A meditation chastens speech
Some Dyer of a distant tree
Resumes his gaudy industry.

Conclusion is the course of All
At *most* to be perennial
And then elude stability
Recalls to immortality.

From *The Poems of Emily Dickinson*, edited by Thomas H. Johnson. Harvard University Press, 1983.

JANE LANGTON

Emily Dickinson is a cult heroine in Amherst. Pilgrims from around the world commemorate the date of her death — May 15, 1886 — each year at her gravesite in Amherst's West Cemetery. Jane Langton's Emily Dickinson Is Dead, *a well-told mystery, does a deft turn on the cottage industry that Emily Dickinson has spawned. Boston-based mystery writer Jane Langton has proven herself masterful at local settings in* Dark Nantucket Noon, God in Concord, *and* The Memorial Hall Murder.

The Cult of Emily Dickinson

I n Amherst, Massachusetts, almost everyone laid claim to Emily Dickinson. She was like a colonial plantation, a piece of ephemeral real estate.

At Main Street, Owen swooped left and pumped to the top of the steep little hill. At the crest he stopped beside the Dickinson house and dragged the bike up the granite steps. THE DICKINSON HOMESTEAD, BY APPOINTMENT ONLY, said the sign at the front walk.

Owen didn't want an appointment. Owen knew every square inch of the public rooms. He glanced up now at the windows of the bedroom in which Emily Dickinson had written nearly two thousand poems, the room that had been a haven from intrusion by fools, a place of retreat from the polite people of the town. She was still retreating, decided Owen. In death she had removed to the family plot under the white ash tree in West Cemetery. She had withdrawn to her narrow white coffin, six feet under the ground. But she could escape no farther. Any bunch of idiots could claw at the grass growing on her grave and hold up chunks of turf and claim them for their own.

Moving down the sidewalk, Owen gazed through the hemlock hedge at the sloping Dickinson garden. The grass was wet. In the oak tree a bird hopped from branch to branch. Owen stared through the hedge, wondering who really owned Emily Dickinson. If anybody in Amherst could be said to possess the woman in this ninety-ninth year after her death, who would it be?

Oh, Lord, there were so many claimants! In all the five colleges of the Connecticut River Valley there were professors who regarded the poet as property — not to mention the fifty thousand students swarming on the streets of the local towns, Amherst and Northampton and South Hadley. Was there any other place in the world where one literary deity was worshipped so universally? Well, there was Stratford-on-Avon, and Concord, Massachusetts. Did everybody in Stratford own Shakespeare? Did everyone in Concord lay claim to Henry Thoreau? Here in Amherst even a piece of paper whipping down South Pleasant Street was apt to be a title deed, a page from *The Complete Poems*, unstuck from the paperback edition, fluttering out of somebody's motorcycle saddlebag. Impulsively, Owen covered his ears as he thought of the sounds of righteous Dickinson ownership, the rattle of a thousand typewriters, the battering of chalk on a hundred classroom blackboards.

Then he smiled. It wasn't just people, after all. Even that commonplace bird in the oak tree, there in the Dickinson garden, even that sassy robin who was whistling, head up, chirping a succession of phrases, spattering the whole side yard with cheerful melody, even that small bird could make a claim of its own upon Emily Dickinson. Maybe it was descended from the poet's own *Gabriel In humble circumstances* and owned the whole green lawn.

From *Emily Dickinson Is Dead* by Jane Langton. St. Martin's Press, 1984.

The Dickinson homestead was built in 1813 for Emily Dickinson's grandparents. Now a National Register house, it is open to visitors by appointment; about five thousand people from all over the world visited in 1994. Courtesy of Amherst College.

HELEN HUNT JACKSON

Helen Hunt Jackson (1830-1885) was considered in her day the great woman poet from Amherst. She wrote for publication, while her lifelong friend Emily Dickinson (they were born the same year) did not. Boston editor Thomas Wentworth Higginson befriended both women. He persuaded Jackson to begin writing and advised Emily Dickinson that her poems were not for publication within her lifetime. Helen Hunt Jackson even wrote a novel based on a sensitive poet resembling Emily Dickinson, Mercy Philbrick's Choice *(1876).*

Helen Hunt Jackson's oeuvre included poems, travel pieces, fiction, and children's stories. The poems "March" and "October" are from a series of "month" poems that capture the New England seasons.

October

The month of carnival of all the year,
  When Nature lets the wild earth go its way,
  And spend whole seasons on a single day.
The spring-time holds her white and purple dear;
October, lavish, flaunts then far and near;
The summer charily her reds doth lay
Like jewels on her costliest array;
October, scornful, burns them on a bier.
The winter hoards his pearls of frost in sign
Of kingdom: whiter pearls than winter knew,
Or Empress wore, in Egypt's ancient line,
October, feasting 'neath her dome of blue,
Drinks at a single draught, slow filtered through
Sunshiny air, as in a tingling wine!

March

Beneath the sheltering walls the thin snow clings, —
  Dead winter's skeleton, left bleaching, white,
  Disjointed, crumbling, on unfriendly fields.
The inky pools surrender tardily
At noon, to patient herds, a frosty drink
From jagged rims of ice; a subtle red
Of life is kindling every twig and stalk
Of lowly meadow growths; the willows wrap
Their stems in furry white; the pines grow gray

A little in the biting wind; midday
Brings tiny burrowed creatures, peeping out
Alert for sun.
                    Ah March! we know thou art
Kind-hearted, spite of ugly looks and threats,
And, out of sight, art nursing April's violets!

From *Verses* by Helen Hunt Jackson. Roberts Brothers, 1888.

Helen Hunt Jackson, shown here about 1865, enjoyed great popularity in the 19th century.
Courtesy of the Jones Library, Amherst.

FREDERICK GODDARD TUCKERMAN

Frederick G. Tuckerman (1821-1873), the son of a wealthy Boston merchant and a Harvard graduate, left his law practice in Boston at the age of twenty-six for a life of secluded study in Greenfield. He took a keen interest in literature, botany, and astronomy. Although not many of Tuckerman's poems explicitly mention the Greenfield area, several refer to the "River," which resembles the Connecticut.

Tuckerman's Poems *(1860 and later editions) attracted favorable attention from Emerson and Hawthorne. Some were published in* Atlantic Monthly *and* Putnam's. *Critic N. Scott Momaday wrote that Frederick G. Tuckerman, with Emily Dickinson and Jones Very, was "one of the three most remarkable American poets of the nineteenth century." Edmund Wilson wrote: "He was one of the few fine original poets of the later nineteenth century in the United States."*

Hymn Written for the Dedication of a Cemetery

Beside the River's dark green flow,
    Here, where the pinetrees weep,
Red Autumn's winds will coldly blow
    Above their dreamless sleep:

Their sleep, for whom with prayerful breath
    We've put apart today
This spot, for shadowed walks of Death,
    And gardens of decay.

This crumbling bank with Autumn crowned,
    These pining woodland ways,
Seem now no longer common ground;
    But each in turn conveys

A saddened sense of something more:
    Is it the dying year?
Or a dim shadow, sent before,
    Of the next gathering here?

Is it that He, the silent Power,
    Has now assumed the place
And drunk the light of morning's hour,
    The life of Nature's grace?

Not so — the spot is beautiful,
>And holy is the sod;
'Tis we are faint, our eyes are dull;
>All else is fair in God.

So let them lie, their graves bedecked,
>Whose bones these shades invest,
Nor grief deny, nor fear suspect,
>The beauty of their rest.

Ode: For the Greenfield Soldiers Monument

This slender spire of glossy stone,
>A nation's emblem poised above,
Speaks it to bleeding hearts alone?
>Ensign of sorrow and of love?

Or here, upon this village green,
>In half-light of the autumn day,
Meet we to mourn for what has been,
>A tale, a triumph passed away?

Yes, more: our gift is generous
>As theirs who gave their lifeblood free;
Not to the dead alone, to us
>Ourselves, and ours that yet shall be

We consecrate for distant years —
>No idle rite, our deep hearts stirred,
And tenderly, with prayers and tears —
>The gleaming shaft! the Eagle bird!

From *The Complete Poems of Frederick Goddard Tuckerman* edited by N. Scott Momaday. Oxford University Press, 1965.

ROBERT FROST

Robert Frost (1874-1963) originated the role of writer-in-residence, teaching at Amherst College between 1917 and 1963. In later years, the four-time Pulitzer Prize winner was required to appear only a few weeks a year and deliver special lectures. His base of operations was the Lord Jeffery Inn. Upon his death, the college memorialized Frost by naming its new library after him.

Frost's poetry evokes rural New England in general. None of Frost's poems refers overtly to Amherst and the Connecticut Valley, although several, including "Fire and Ice," were written there. Frost was noted as a no-nonsense conserva-tive, ready to cast a jaundiced eye upon faddish progressivism. He expressed his political skepticism and his inclination toward "form" in a letter to The Amherst Student, *written in response to the paper's good wishes on his sixtieth birthday.*

Fire and Ice

Some say the world will end in fire,
Some say in ice.
From what I've tasted of desire
I hold with those who favor fire.
But if it had to perish twice,
I think I know enough of hate
To say that for destruction ice
Is also great
And would suffice.

Letter to The Amherst Student, *March 25, 1935*

It is very, very kind of the *Student* to be showing sympathy with me for my age. But sixty is only a pretty good age. It is not advanced enough. The great thing is to be advanced. Now ninety would be really well along and something to be given credit for.

But speaking of ages, you will often hear it said that the age of the world we live in is particularly bad. I am impatient of such talk. We have no way of knowing that this age is one of the worst in the world's history. Arnold claimed the honor for the age before this. Wordsworth claimed it for the last but one. And so on back through literature. I say they claimed the honor for their ages. They claimed it rather for themselves. It is immodest of a man to think of himself as going down before the worst forces ever mobilized by God.

All ages of the world are bad — a great deal worse anyway than Heaven. If they weren't the world might just as well be Heaven at once and have it over with. One can safely say after from six to thirty thousand years of experience that the evident design is a situation here in which it will always be about equally hard to save your soul. Whatever progress may be taken to mean, it can't mean making the world any easier a place in which to save your soul — or if you dislike hearing your soul mentioned in open meeting, say your decency, your integrity.

Robert Frost in a photo from a 1950s U.S. Information Agency filmed interview showing Frost with students at Amherst College. Courtesy of the Jones Library, Amherst.

Ages may vary a little. One may be a little worse than another. But it is not possible to get outside the age you are in to judge it exactly. Indeed it is as dangerous to try to get outside of anything as large as an age as it would be to engorge a donkey. Witness the many who in the attempt have suffered a dilation from which the tissues and the muscles of the mind have never been able to recover natural shape. They can't pick up anything delicate or small any more. They can't use a pen. They have to use a typewriter. And they gape in agony. They can write huge shapeless novels, huge gobs of raw sincerity bellowing with pain and that's all that they can write.

Fortunately we don't need to know how bad the age is. There is something we can always be doing without reference to how good or how bad the age is. There is at least so much good in the world that it admits of form and the making of form. And not only admits of it, but calls for it. We people are thrust forward out of the suggestions of form in the rolling clouds of nature. In us nature reaches its height of form and through us exceeds itself. When in doubt there is always form for us to go on with. Anyone who has achieved the least form to be sure of it, is lost to the larger excruciations. I think it must stroke faith the right way. The artist, the poet, might be expected to be the most aware of such assurance. But it is really everybody's sanity to feel it and live by it. Fortunately, too, no forms are more engrossing, gratifying, comforting, staying than those lesser ones we throw off, like vortex rings of smoke, all our individual enterprise and needing nobody's co-operation; a basket, a letter, a garden, a room, an idea, a picture, a poem. For these we haven't to get a team together before we can play.

The background in hugeness and confusion shading away from where we stand into black and utter chaos; and against the background any small man-made figure of order and concentration. What pleasanter than that this should be so? Unless we are novelists or economists we don't worry about this confusion; we look out on it with an instrument or tackle it to reduce it. It is partly because we are afraid it might prove too much for us and our blend of democratic-republican-socialist-communist-anarchist party. But it is more because we like it, we were born to it, born used to it and have practical reasons for wanting it there. To me any little form I assert upon it is velvet, as the saying is, and to be considered for how much more it is than nothing. If I were a Platonist I should have to consider it, I suppose, for how much less it is than everything.

From *Robert Frost: Poetry and Prose* edited by Edward Connery Lathem and Lawrance Thompson. Holt, Rinehart & Winston, 1972.

ROBERT FRANCIS

Besides being one of the great poets of the Pioneer Valley (Robert Frost called him "the best neglected poet"), Robert Francis (1901-1987) led one of the region's exemplary lives. In the vein of Thoreau, he lived a life of simplicity — by himself, a vegetarian, with no occupation save that of a poet. His autobiography, The Trouble with Francis, *portrays a wry, modest man concerned above all with writing poetry.*

Francis moved to Amherst in 1926 and stayed the rest of his life. He lived three-and-a-half miles from Amherst center in a modest house he named Fort Juniper. Francis wrote several volumes of poetry, including Stand With Me Here *and* The Orb Weaver, *and such works of criticism as* The Satirical Rogue on Poetry. *Some of his journal entries are collected in* Travelling in Amherst, A Poet's Journal, 1930-1950.

Besides his own importance as a poet, Francis was also known as a friend and interlocutor of Robert Frost. Francis's Frost: A Time to Talk, Conversations & Indiscretions Recorded by Robert Francis *(1972) profiles Frost and indicates how the great man influenced him.*

The selections from Francis's autobiography describe meeting Robert Frost and living on a poet's meager income. The poem "Two Ghosts" is a dialogue between Emily Dickinson and Robert Frost.

Knowing Robert Frost

Amherst in 1932 was as peaceful a town as it had been in 1926 when I first saw it. The Agricultural College, to be sure, had just become the State College; but it still sold milk, butter, and buttermilk over the counter to townspeople. Melvin Graves in his great blue coat with brass buttons still presided at the central intersection: a father figure. Along Merchants Row — as shown in a photo several years later — only one car is moving, while at a safe distance, one pedestrian is crossing the street. What is today Louis' Supermarket was then a little box of a store, and where the big parking lot now extends along North Prospect Street were several quiet dwellings, one white house in particular seeming to catch and hold the sunlight. The second floor was occupied by Miss Minnie Dana, a retired teacher of sewing in the public schools. Short, erect, with hair piled in a pyramid, she seemed from a little distance a white-haired doll.

Though her living quarters took up most of the second floor, there were two extra rooms at the head of the front stairs which were reached without entering her apartment. The larger one, in the northwest corner, with all the winds of winter assaulting it, became mine. I paid partly in money, partly in labor, the amount of both small. My labor was chiefly taking out and down the ashes from the kitchen stove each morning, and bringing up the coal for the day. There was also some rug cleaning, but I forget what else. Kitchen privileges were included from the first and kept expanding until I was getting all my meals in Miss Dana's kitchen. Though our food was kept separate, we cooked side by side, ate together at a little kitchen table, then together did the dishes, she washing, I wiping. I say we cooked side by side, though I can't imagine my doing anything very substantial in those circumstances. A boiled egg or a baked potato must have been frequent.

Thus I spent the winter and spring of 1933. The Depression was at its lowest, but I hardly felt it. How could I fall when I was already on the floor? More important to me than Roosevelt's entry into the White House was Robert Frost's buying a home in Amherst. A full-time or part-time resident of the town for many years, he was now a homeowner and so, I felt, here for good. I wrote a little poem to celebrate the event and it was printed in the *Springfield Republican*. Then, on January 24, I met the man. I wrote in my journal: "Today I started a savings account with a ten-dollar deposit; and I met Robert Frost."

That I had lived over six years in the town of Amherst without meeting Frost, without being introduced to him by anybody or bumping into him by chance, is evidence of several things: my obscurity, my timidity, my caution, and my pride. I was unwilling to face him with nothing to bring, nothing to show. I could endure well enough being a nobody, but not when confronting so much of a somebody.

What led me finally and half-unsuspectingly to the Frost door was the extraordinary Mrs. Hopkins — Mrs. Arthur John Hopkins, Margaret Sutton Briscoe Hopkins. She was a born entrepreneur and for a year or more I had been familiar with her invitations and summonses, her consultations and expeditions. On the aforementioned evening she told me she had an errand somewhere in town and asked me to chauffeur her. We drove down to Sunset Avenue and stopped in front of a Victorian sort of house standing well back from the street. Leaving me behind, she went up to the door and disappeared. Within a few moments Robert Frost came out on the porch, peered down at me through the darkness, and beckoned me to come up and in. I remember how white his hair looked under the bright porch light. He was then not quite fifty-nine. When I went in with him, I found that Mrs. Hopkins had shown him my little tribute of a poem.

If I ask myself what it was in Frost that impressed, attracted, and fascinated me most in the years before I met him as well as in the years afterwards, the answer is power. He was a poet and he had power; the combination was striking. According to popular notion at least, a poet, however good he may be in his poetry, is otherwise generally ineffectual and inadequate. But here was a poet to whom the stock jokes couldn't be applied. He was a match for any man he ran into on the street, and usually more than a match. He could speak to any man in that man's language and on that man's terms, be he banker, merchant, farmer, senator, college president, or U.S. President. You had only to catch a glimpse of him anywhere to sense his solidarity, his weight, his sanity. And his power was not in spite of his being a poet but because of it. Everything had come first from the poems, poems that in themselves could speak to any man or so it seemed. They were poems no one could dismiss or laugh aside. They had a sureness, a balance, a relevance that was like a fact of nature. But though the poems were the basis of his ascendancy, the man himself kept increasing and enriching that ascendancy. Unlike some poets he always seemed more than his poems, inexhaustible. What he said was fresher and terser than what others said. Like a boxer his mind stood on tiptoe for the next parry and thrust. People listened because they were too fascinated not to. Yet no matter how playful and teasing his words, his face kept its Newfoundland gravity, its Great Dane sadness. What made Frost's power the more impressive was, of course, its effortlessness. Celebrity? A plain man, rather bulky, white-haired, going about his business.

As for me, power, any kind of power, was notably what I didn't have and never had had, even the most commonplace kinds: a boy's power of fist, a youth's athletic prowess, and later, position, money, wife, children. Even in my poetry I felt myself so little the poet that I didn't want to be called one. I suppose that if I hadn't felt so deficient my contact with Frost could not have been so exhilarating. It was tonic, life-enhancing, like high-pressure weather and country air.

Frost never smiled in greeting me at the door. He simply looked me in the eye gravely, candidly, mildly, then led the way to his study. It was not so much his not smiling that struck me — after all he was not given to much smiling — as it was that cool, level glance, that utter absence of mask or role. It set the tone of our friendship. And, of course, it contrasted with other Frosts, especially the platform Frost so conscious of his audience and of himself. When he came to the door and merely looked at me, I felt I was confronting the essential man.

If I had brought some of my new poems, he would slump down in his big leather chair and go through them broodingly, mumbling them to himself. I had the uncanny feeling that he was inside my poems and that anything he said about them would be said from inside. What he said was brief and unforgettable.

I have already described Frost's conversation. Everything he touched on was so interesting that one didn't question just why he should be touching on it. He could start anywhere and end anywhere. Like a Roman fountain he just kept on flowing. He talked easily about himself and just as easily about his contemporaries, his fellow poets. He knew them all. Sometimes with a bit of malice, but often indulgently and even fondly, he would pick on their foibles and poke fun. No one was spared, not even his acknowledged friends. At a later time I would take this delicious gossip with some reservations, especially after I saw how thin-skinned Frost was himself. But at the time it did me good like a tonic. The poetry world which had seemed so remote and formidable and glittering was reduced in size to a matter of pygmies and puppets which one could pick up and set down as in a game of chess.

My visits were generally in fall or spring, for the Frosts, like migratory birds, were wintering to the south and summering to the north. Seasonally when I thought it time for their Amherst arrival I would go round to Sunset Avenue after dark to see if there was a light in a window.

One thing that made me feel rich was knowing Robert Frost and talking with him in my home from time to time. Luckily he never called when I was in hiding. His first visit here was on May 21, 1950, when Fort Juniper was nearly ten years old. His delay in coming was partly due, no doubt, to the fact that my house was built at a time when he was not associated with Amherst College (1938-1946) and was coming to town less often and more briefly than either before or later.

If he came first partly out of curiosity, he continued to come because Fort Juniper proved the best possible place for uninterrupted conversation. Perhaps he had a special reason to feel at home here since my house was comparable to his cabin in Ripton, Vermont. I think he liked to think that he and I lived in much the same way, whereas some young poets he knew might talk about doing something like this but never did.

There were three Frosts I knew. First was the Frost of the poems, the man in or behind the poems. This Frost I met years before I met the poet himself face to face. Second was the platform Frost, the mischievous, teasing, sparkling entertainer. And not on the platform only but at any evening gathering where he sat in a comfortable chair and did all the talking and sparkled from first to last. The third Frost was the man I sat across from when there were just the two of us (with at most one other) in the room. Completely relaxed, no effort to shine now, the tone kindly rather than teasing, yet always a trace of teasing still. He did most of the talking and he talked mostly about himself, yet this always seemed the most natural thing in the world for him to do (as indeed it was) and equally natural for any hearer to want to listen to.

When he praised my work, I never for an instant questioned his sincerity, yet I couldn't help wondering why he and practically nobody else rated me as he did. Two of his letters to Louis Untermeyer speak of me. Untermeyer takes this as evidence that Frost, contrary to what some people were saying, could praise a younger poet. Another view that one hears today is that Frost's praise was only of those poets he didn't consider potential rivals.

One thing I know is that what he said to me about my work was immensely encouraging, and I believe his criticism and appreciation of other younger poets must have been equally sensitive and generous.

After he had been here I would usually try to recapture in my journal the gist of what he had said even to his wording if possible. On the basis of these records I think he came to Fort Juniper nine times between 1950 and 1959, twice with Armour Craig, twice with Charles Green, twice with Hyde Cox, and twice with Samuel French Morse. Once he came and went by taxi.

This taxi visit occurred on October 30, 1956. The weather was mild enough for us to sit outdoors for a while, but as a precaution I put around Mr. Frost a big sheet of cardboard as a screen against the light breeze. He said it reminded him of a time long past when he and Ezra Pound had been in a London restaurant together. Pound had spouted poetry so loudly that a waiter came and put a screen around them.

When we went indoors I made a fire in the fireplace and Frost sat on the couch opposite. He had mentioned *The Faber Book of Modern American Verse*, edited by Auden and published in England (later brought out in America as *The Criterion Book of Modern American Verse)*, but he had not yet seen a copy. I happened to have one, since Rebecca Richmond had just bought one in London and sent it to me. Sitting beside Frost on the couch I had the pleasure of pointing out how his poem, "The Gift Outright," had been presented by Auden as a sort of theme poem. Frost was pleased, and pleased with the selection of other poems of his.

Then we turned to the three short poems of mine. "Walls" and "Swimmer" were on one page, and "Apple Peeler" on the next.

APPLE PEELER

Why the unbroken spiral, Virtuoso,
Like a trick sonnet in one long versatile sentence?

Is it a pastime merely, this perfection,
For an old man, sharp knife, long night, long winter?

Or do your careful fingers move at the stir
Of unadmitted immemorial magic?

Solitaire. The ticking clock. The apple
Turning, turning as the round earth turns.

When he caught sight of it, Frost said, "Oh! *this* poem," and he looked around at me with such a smile as I had never seen on his face before. It was as if he had caught me redhanded and was amused to have done so.

At first I hadn't the faintest notion of what it was all about. But as he continued to smile at me mockingly but without any hostility, and to make various hints, I came to understand that he thought the poem referred to himself, for whom the writing of poetry was now merely a pastime, a virtuoso stunt. The trouble was that line: "Like a trick sonnet in one long, versatile sentence." He was under the impression that his sonnet, "The Silken Tent," was the only sonnet in one sentence in the English language. And for him a "trick" poem was a false one, whereas I had used the word with no sense of disparagement. I told him my poem did not refer to him and that he had not been in my mind when I wrote it, though I doubtless did think of "The Silken Tent" among other things. But I could see he was not wholly convinced. So I added that as for writing sonnets in one sentence, David Morton had done it again and again.

"Oh, has he?" said Frost surprised. "Then that makes it all right."

He had fallen into the very error that he took other people to task for: reading into a poem what was not there and failing to see what was. My poem was not about an old poet but about an old apple peeler, and the person responsible for the image was no other than old Mrs. Boynton, the Mrs. Bemis of *We Fly Away.*

Of all the memorable things I heard Robert Frost say, two have stuck in my mind most persistently and have continued to tease me. Sitting in my home on the evening of December 10, 1950, he remarked casually that he had never lifted a finger to advance his career and that what had come to him had just come to him.

I thought how magnificent it was that success, recognition, and high honor could come to a man without his seeking them, indeed, could come all the more because he had not sought them. At the same time I was asking myself how this policy might apply to me. If I lifted not a finger to advance my career, what would happen? Precisely nothing. My problem was not whether or not to lift a finger but how to lift it. I felt there were appropriate ways and inappropriate ways for me to exert myself, and I had faith that the appropriate ways had the better chance of being effective.

After Frost's death when his letters to Louis Untermeyer were published I discovered a Frost I had never known, a fourth Robert Frost, shall we say? What I had taken him to mean by not having lifted a finger was evidently not what he meant.

The other thing I keep thinking about is a question he asked me (on October 23, 1952). "What do you do when you're not actually writing?"

That he could ask such a question made me feel helpless to answer it. But he scarcely waited for an answer. "You can't just lie on your back," he added. And then he spoke of something he had learned to do to fill up his time, something both useful and recreational: sharpening the cutterbar of the mowing machine.

Robert Francis in his Fort Juniper doorway. He built his small cottage home in 1940 on land he bought for $75. Today the house is given by the year to visiting writers-in-residence. Courtesy of the Jones Library, Amherst.

I had a quick vision of the things that filled up my time and that would have easily filled up a hundred times the time I had, the things I tried desperately to crowd into the day that was never never long enough. What did I do when I was not actually writing? What could I say? Where begin?

Frost may have thought that he and I lived in much the same way, but how vastly different our daily lives were! His life was all laissez-faire except for the poetry. He gave himself to that and let everything else take care of itself. There was always somebody to do the needed things that he hadn't done or had only half done. He puttered about his farm. Now and then he prepared a meal.

But if I didn't prepare my meals, I wouldn't be eating. Marketing, cooking, dish-washing. Washing, ironing, mending, bed-making, floor-mopping. Gardening, grass-cutting, leaf-raking, snow-shoveling. Storm windows off and screens on, screens off and storm windows on. And then the letters to answer and the books to get from the libraries and return on time. The entertaining of friends, the refreshments to serve that wouldn't be served if I didn't do it, and always the dishes. If I wanted flower wine to offer my guests, I had to gather the blossoms and go through the whole procedure myself; and if I wanted wild grape jelly to sweeten the coming winter, I had to find and gather the wild grapes and do everything to the pouring of the hot wax. To say nothing of music: violin, piano, recordings. Yes, to say nothing of many things.

Yet it was not a chance acquaintance who asked the question but a friend who had known me for years and was genuinely interested in me and sympathetic to my way of life. If *he* could ask what I did to keep from being bored and lazy, then what did *anybody* know about me?

I knew I couldn't make my situation intelligible, and, what is more, I didn't altogether want to. I was not proud of my incessant busyness. I could have envied the miraculous sense of leisure that Robert Frost carried around with him at all times. If anyone had reason or excuse to be incessantly busy about important things, it was he. And it was I who should have found the infinite leisure to sit out under some tree like Buddha or any meditative toad.

Living on a Poet's Income

Finally, the economic question: how do you earn your living? A man can live without a job, can live without a wife, can live without God, but he can't live without money.

There are people, I venture, whose possible curiosity about me would be satisfied if they knew the answer to this question. How do I live? That is, how do I keep alive? Since I do keep alive and have kept alive these many years, obviously I must have some income other than my earnings. Did someone die and leave me enough to take care of me? Have I investments or annuities? Where are the ravens of Elijah in my life? One man who knows me fairly well asked me point-blank some time ago if I were still getting my unemployment insurance. When I told him that I had never received unemployment compensation and was not eligible for it since I was never unemployed, I could see that he wasn't altogether convinced.

On the other hand if I really have no subsidy, then I must be poor indeed, living from hand to mouth, always on the edge of destitution.

That no poet can live on (from or off) his poetry is a truism endlessly repeated and seemingly never challenged. I have never heard anyone define what living on one's poetry might consist of. Just what could legitimately be included? Sales of poems to magazines, of course, and royalties on books of poems, and reprint fees from anthologies. Would writing books not of poetry but about poetry be included? How about fees for poetry readings? Or for lectures on poetry or poets? Or for a three-day visit to a college or university where the poet in addition to a reading meets with students and perhaps does a little classroom teaching? How about book reviewing, either of poetry or of books about poetry? And how about a fellowship or grant given to a poet because he is a poet? Would this qualify as one way of living on poetry? Precisely where do we draw the line?

But this is only half the story. Along with the question of how much a poet can earn from his poetry is the question of how much or little he needs to spend. If he earns little but spends little, why can't he be said to live on his poetry?

My specialty has been not to earn much but to spend little. Ever since I began to live alone I have done practically all my housework indoors and out. I have bought like a Scotchman and often I haven't bought at all. Some of the things I have sometimes got along without I was happier to do without anyway.

The telephone, for example. Whatever convenience it has been to me it has generally been a greater inconvenience. The convenience was largely for other people, the inconvenience for me. Incoming calls were mostly requests or invitations, which I could have declined gracefully by letter; or if the caller has called in person, I could have softened the impact of a no with a cup of coffee and some home baking. But the telephone is peremptory. It rings and you jump. Once you lift the receiver and say hello, you are on the spot. Possibly worse than the actual ringing of the telephone bell is the incessant threat of its ringing any hour of day or night. For me it is a privilege and a luxury to have lived without a telephone the past dozen years.

And I would put barbers in the same class with phones. Since 1953 I have done my own barbering and thus have been able to cut my hair as often as I pleased and in the way I pleased, without paying anybody, to say nothing of tips. At one stroke I have escaped all barbershop conversation and the public display of myself as if I were up for auction. I do not sit and wait my turn nor is my shop ever closed after hours or on Sundays or holidays. Until a couple of years ago I kept this matter a secret, lest the Barbers of the United States United might get wind of it and pillory me as a public enemy. But now that so many young men are cutting their own hair or letting it go uncut, I have lost my timidity.

Another thing that I am especially glad to save on is the meat I don't eat, my chief motive being humanitarian and philosophic, however, rather than economic.

I have also gone without some things I wanted and needed until such time as I could afford them and could find the right article. I lived without a refrigerator until the Little Giant came to my notice. (Emphasize the "little" rather than the "giant.") For ten years now it has fitted snugly into my very small kitchen, taking up no unnecessary space and consuming no unnecessary electricity. Even so, I do not use it the year round. During the cool half of the year I transfer to a simple coldbox that fastens to the outside of a kitchen window. What a satisfaction to put to good use a little of the vast amount of coldness that nature gives away each year.

If I have been thrifty, I have sometimes been lucky. It was luck that Fort Juniper was built at a time when costs were low after the Depression, and when native pine lumber was cheap because of the hurricane of 1938. Luck also that there was a water main along Market Hill Road in front of my house, so that I didn't have to take the expensive gamble of digging a well; and that electricity could be brought to the house without need of an extra pole.

The summer of 1954 marked a turning point in my finances. From three weeks of teaching and lecturing at Chautauqua I earned $724, whereas my total income for 1953 had been $502.23. From 1954 on I could count on some sort of backlog earned each summer which, even if all else failed, would support me throughout the year. Later, after the publication of *The Orb Weaver*, and still later following *Come Out Into the Sun*, I began to receive invitations for brief visits to colleges and universities. For a three-day visit I was paid at a considerably higher rate than for teaching in writers' workshops. For a one-day visit (perhaps just a reading) the rate was still higher. The shorter the stay the better the pay. It was not that I could command a fee, but rather that my fellow poets were commanding fees and I profited by being one of them. Even so, my usual honorarium was at the lower rates, I suppose.

My stipend the year I lived in Rome was $3500, and I didn't spend it all but had something in the neighborhood of a thousand dollars to cheer the future with. My stipend from the Amy Lowell Scholarship was $4000. These have been my only considerable subsidies.

After coming home from Italy in 1968 I became aware of a new state of affairs. My bank balances which had always tended to dwindle now kept their level, like the Widow's Cruse of Oil, or even increased. Twice this past year I have drawn out $1000 from my checking account to add to my savings account.

God knows I have no reason to feel proud of this mild upswing in my fortunes, any more than I have reason to feel proud of my thrift which is only a little common sense with a dash of the sportive. In this I am different from Thoreau who boasted of his financial accomplishments in the first chapter of *Walden*. But Thoreau had a much bigger story to tell than I, since he had a much smaller budget to live on.

From The Trouble with Francis: An Autobiography *by Robert Francis. University of Massachusetts Press, 1971.*

Two Ghosts

Amherst. Dark hemlocks conspiring at the First Church midway between the Mansion on Main Street and the back entrance (the escape door) of the Lord Jeffery Inn. Between one and two after midnight.

R   Someone is here. Angelic? Or demonic?
E   Someone less than someone.
R   Emily?
E   How could you divine me?
R   An easy guess, you who were ghost while living
    and haunting us ever since.
E   A ghost to catch a ghost?
R   A poet to catch a poet.
E   And you — you must be the Robert who said:
    "The petal of the rose it was that stung."
    Or did *I* say it?
R   We both have said it now.
E   Sweet the bee — but rose is sweeter —
    Quick his sting — but rose stings deeper —
    Bee will heal — rose petal — never
R   You talk of bees who were yourself white moth.
E   Seldom flitting so far from home.
    Oftener the other way to touch my stone.
    Have you seen it?
R   *Called Back?*
E   The stone keeps calling me back.
R   I would have cut a different epitaph.
    Called on. Called ahead.
E   But on and back are both one now, aren't they?

R   My stone is not a stone but a heap, a pile
E   Why should immortality be so stony?
R   — a mass, a mausoleum, a mock mountain
    over there. Have you seen?
E   Oh, I took *that* for a factory or fort.
R   Fort of learning, factory of scholars.
    And my name cut deep in granite. Have you seen?
E   I never dared to go so far — so near.
R   "Less than someone," you said. I say,
    "More than someone." You are a name now, Emily.
E   Why do they hunt me so?
R   The scholar-scavengers?
E   Once I could hide but now
    they try my mind, they pry
    apart my heart.
R   We were both hiders. You
    in your father's house. I
    in the big buzzing world.
    I craved to be understood
    but feared being wholly known.
E   You said, "Anything more than the truth
    would have seemed too weak."
R   And you, "Truth like ancestors' brocades
    can stand alone." I should say truth
    is not the dress but the naked lady.
E   Or naked gentleman.
R   Have it as you will.

(A tower clock strikes two)

R   There's truth for you.
    To tell the truth
    Is all a clock can do.
E   But clocks are human — like us all —
    they err — grow ill — and finally fail.
R   They never lie intentionally.
E   Why did you say, "Nature's first green is gold?"
    Some buds, yes, but the buds of beech are cinnamon,
    and the swamp maple — but need I tell you?
R   And why — why did you say:
    "Nature rarer uses yellow than another hue?"
    Think of the dandelions, Emily, the fields

of solid yellow. Think of the forsythias
and buttercups. The sugar maple's pendant blooms,
the cowslips, cinquefoil, golden Alexanders,
the marigolds and all the goldenrods.
Witch-hazel and October trees: beech, elm,
maple, popple, apple!

E   Why did Emerson, your Emerson, my Emerson, say,
"Succory to match the sky?" Imagine!

R   Your lines that haunt me most —

E   What are they?

R   "After great pain a formal feeling comes.
The nerves sit ceremonious like tombs."

E   Oh! Oh!

R   "After great pain — "

E   And that line of yours:
"Weep for what little things could make them glad."

R   I was writing of children.

E   We are all children.

R   Laugh at what little things could make them weep.

E   Can make us all weep. Were you a believer?

R   I took the dare to believe. I made myself
believe I believed. And you?

E   Two angels strove like wrestlers in my mind:
one belief, one disbelief.

R   "After great pain — "

E   Oh!

R   Emily? Emily!

———————————

From *Robert Francis: Collected Poems*, 1936-1976. University of Massachusetts Press, 1976.

SYLVIA PLATH

Sylvia Plath (1932-1963) attended Smith College between 1950 and 1955 and taught there from 1957 to 1958. During her year teaching at Smith, while her husband British poet Ted Hughes taught at the University of Massachusetts, they lived on Elm Street opposite Child's Park. Her love of the park inspired "Child's Park Stones" (1958). She wrote: "I have just written a good syllabic poem on the Child's Park Stones as juxtaposed to the ephemeral orange and fuchsia azaleas and feel the park is my favorite place in America." Other poems Plath wrote about the region during this year included "Above the Oxbow" and "In Midas' Country."

Sylvia Plath is regarded for her poems, letters, and her novel The Bell Jar, based on her breakdown when she tried to commit suicide after her junior year at Smith.

Above the Oxbow

Here in this valley of discreet academies
We have not mountains, but mounts, truncated hillocks
To the Adirondacks, to northern Monadnock,
Themselves mere rocky hillocks to an Everest.
Still, they're our best mustering of height: by
Comparison with the sunken silver-grizzled
Back of the Connecticut, the river-level
Flats of Hadley farms, they're lofty enough
Elevations to be called something more than hills.
Green, wholly green, they stand their knobby spine
Against our sky: they are what we look southward to
Up Pleasant Street at Main. Poising their shapes
Between the snuff and red tar-paper apartments,
They mound a summer coolness in our view.

To people who live in the bottom of valleys
A rise in the landscape, hummock or hogback, looks
To be meant for climbing. A peculiar logic
In going up for the coming down if the post
We start at's the same post we finish by,
But it's the clear conversion at the top can hold
Us to the oblique road, in spite of a fitful
Wish for even ground, and it's the last cliff
Ledge will dislodge our cramped concept of space, unwall

Sylvia Plath, center, made the pages of the Springfield Republican *as an undergraduate at Smith in 1954. At Smith, Plath also worked as a correspondent for the* Daily Hampshire Gazette. Photo by D.I. Crossley; courtesy of the Smith College Archives.

Horizons beyond vision, spill vision
After the horizons, stretching the narrowed eye
To full capacity. We climb in hopes
Of such seeing up the leaf-shuttered escarpments,
Blindered by green, under a green-grained sky

Into the blue. Tops define themselves as places
Where nothing higher's to be looked to. Downward looks
Follow the black arrow-backs of swifts on their track
Of the air eddies' loop and arc though air's at rest
To us, since we see no leaf edge stir high
Here on a mount overlaid with leaves. The paint-peeled
Hundred-year-old hotel sustains its ramshackle
Four-way veranda, view-keeping above
The fallen timbers of its once remarkable
Funicular railway, witness to gone
Time, and to graces gone with the time. A state view-
Keeper collects half-dollars for the slopes
Of state scenery, sells soda, shows off viewpoints.
A ruddy skylight paints the gray oxbow

And paints the river's pale circumfluent stillness
As roses broach their carmine in a mirror. Flux

Of the desultory currents — all that unique
Stipple of shifting wave-tips is ironed out, lost
In the simplified orderings of sky-
Lorded perspectives. Maplike, the far fields are ruled
By correct green lines and no seedy free-for-all
Of asparagus heads. Cars run their suave
Colored beads on the strung roads, and the people stroll
Straightforwardly across the springing green.
All's peace and discipline down there. Till lately we
Lived under the shadow of hot rooftops
And never saw how coolly we might move. For once
A high hush quietens the crickets' cry.

In Midas' Country

M eadows of gold dust. The silver
Currents of the Connecticut fan
And meander in bland pleatings under
River-verge farms where rye-heads whiten.
All's polished to a dull luster

In the sulfurous noon. We move
With the languor of idols below
The sky's great bell glass and briefly engrave
Our limbs' image on a field of straw
And goldenrod as on gold leaf.

It might be heaven, this static
Plenitude: apples gold on the bough,
Goldfinch, goldfish, golden tiger cat stock-
Still in one gigantic tapestry —
And lovers affable, dovelike.

But now the water-skiers race,
Bracing their knees. On unseen towlines
They cleave the river's greening patinas;
The mirror quivers to smithereens.
They stunt like clowns in the circus.

So we are hauled, though we would stop
On this amber bank where grasses bleach.
Already the farmer's after his crop,

August gives over its Midas touch,
Wind bares a flintier landscape.

Child's Park Stones

In sunless air, under pines
    Green to the point of blackness, some
        Founding father set these lobed, warped stones
    To loom in the leaf-filtered gloom
Black as the charred knuckle-bones

Of a giant or extinct
    Animal, come from another
        Age, another planet surely. Flanked
    By the orange and fuchsia bonfire
Of azaleas, sacrosanct

These stones guard a dark repose
    And keep their shapes intact while sun
        Alters shadows of rose and iris —
    Long, short, long — in the lit garden
And kindles a day's-end blaze

Colored to dull the pigment
    Of the azaleas, yet burnt out
        Quick as they. To follow the light's tint
    And intensity by midnight
By noon and throughout the brunt

Of various weathers is
    To know the still heart of the stones:
        Stones that take the whole summer to lose
    Their dream of the winter's cold; stones
Warming at core only as

Frost forms. No man's crowbar could
    Uproot them: their beards are ever-
        Green. Nor do they, once in a hundred
    Years, go down to drink the river:
No thirst disturbs a stone's bed.

From *The Collected Poems of Sylvia Plath* edited by Ted Hughes. Harper & Row, 1981.

ADRIENNE RICH

Adrienne Rich has been known not only for her poetry, but also for her vigorous critical and political essays. Rich moved from New York City to Western Massachusetts in 1979 and lived in the area for several years.

"Mourning Picture" (1965) was inspired by the painting of the same name by Edwin Romanzo Elmer (1850-1923), a remembrance of his deceased daughter Effie. It is now at the Smith College Museum of Art.

Besides sixteen volumes of poetry, Rich has written the prose works Of Woman Born; Blood, Bread & Poetry; What is Found There: Notebooks on Poetry and Politics; *and* On Lies, Secrets, and Silence. *She has taught at City College of New York, Cornell, Douglass College at Rutgers, San Jose State University, and Stanford, and has won a MacArthur Fellowship.*

Mourning Picture

They have carried the mahogany chair and the cane rocker
out under the lilac bush,
and my father and mother darkly sit there, in black clothes.
Our clapboard house stands fast on its hill,
my doll lies in her wicker pram
gazing at western Massachusetts.
This was our world.
I could remake each shaft of grass
feeling its rasp on my fingers,
draw out the map of every lilac leaf
or the net of veins on my father's
grief-tranced hand.

Out of my head, half-bursting,
still filling, the dream condenses —
shadows, crystals, ceilings, meadows, globes of dew.
Under the dull green of the lilacs, out in the light
carving each spoke of the pram, the turned porch-pillars,
under high early-summer clouds,
I am Effie, visible and invisible,
remembering and remembered.

They will move from the house,
give the toys and pets away.
Mute and rigid with loss my mother

will ride the train to Baptist Corner,
the silk-spool will run bare.
I tell you, the thread that bound us lies
faint as a web in the dew.
Should I make you, world, again,
could I give back the leaf its skeleton, the air
its early-summer cloud, the house
its noonday presence, shadowless,
and leave *this* out? I am Effie, you were my dream.

From *The Fact of a Doorframe: Poems Selected and New, 1950-1984* by Adrienne Rich. W.W. Norton & Company, 1984.

"*Mourning Picture,*" *an oil on canvas by Edwin Romanzo Elmer of Ashfield, was painted in 1890.* Courtesy of Smith College Museum of Art.

JOSEPH BRODSKY

Joseph Brodsky, a native of Leningrad, emigrated to the United States in 1972. While teaching at Mount Holyoke College, the Russian poet won the Nobel Prize for Literature. His noted collections of poetry include A Part of Speech *and* Watermark. Less Than One: Selected Essays *examines his life in Leningrad and Russian culture and literature. Brodsky was U.S. Poet Laureate in 1991.*

"The Hawk's Cry in Autumn" (1975), written early during Brodsky's stay in America, captures late autumn in the Connecticut Valley.

The Hawk's Cry in Autumn

W ind from the northwestern quarter is lifting him high above
      the dove-gray, crimson, umber, brown
      Connecticut Valley. Far beneath,
chickens daintily pause and move
unseen in the yard of the tumbledown
farmstead, chipmunks blend with the heath.

Now adrift on the airflow, unfurled, alone,
all that he glimpses — the hills' lofty, ragged
ridges, the silver stream that threads
quivering like a living bone
of steel, badly notched with rapids,
the townships like strings of beads

strewn across New England. Having slid down to nil
thermometers — those household gods in niches —
freeze, inhibiting thus the fire
of leaves and churches' spires. Still,
no churches for him. In the windy reaches,
undreamt of by the most righteous choir,

he soars in a cobalt-blue ocean, his beak clamped shut,
his talons clutched tight into his belly
— claws balled up like a sunken fist —
sensing in each wisp of down the thrust
from below, glinting back the berry
of his eyeball, heading south-southeast

to the Rio Grande, the Delta, the beech groves and farther still:
to a nest hidden in the mighty groundswell

of grass whose edges no fingers trust,
sunk amid forest's odors, filled
with splinters of red-speckled eggshell,
with a brother or a sister's ghost.

The heart overgrown with flesh, down, feather, wing,
pulsing at feverish rate, nonstopping,
Propelled by internal heat and sense,
the bird goes slashing and scissoring
the autumnal blue, yet by the same swift token,
enlarging it at the expense

of its brownish speck, barely registering on the eye,
a dot, sliding far above the lofty
pine tree; at the expense of the empty look
of that child, arching up at the sky,
that couple that left the car and lifted
their heads, that woman on the stoop.

But the uprush of air is still lifting him
higher and higher. His belly feathers
feel the nibbling cold. Casting a downward gaze,
he sees the horizon growing dim,
he sees, as it were, the features
of the first thirteen colonies whose

chimneys all puff out smoke. Yet it's their total within his sight
that tells the bird of his elevation,
of what altitude he's reached this trip.
What am I doing at such a height?
He senses a mixture of trepidation
and pride. Heeling over a tip

of wing, he plummets down. But the resilient air
bounces him back, winging up to glory,
to the colorless icy plane.
His yellow pupil darts a sudden glare
of rage, that is, a mix of fury
and terror. So once again

he turns and plunges down. But as walls return
rubber balls, as sins send a sinner to faith, or near,
he's driven upward this time as well!
He! whose innards are still so warm!

Still higher! Into some blasted ionosphere!
That astronomically objective hell

of birds that lacks oxygen, and where the milling stars
play millet served from a plate or a crescent.
What, for the bipeds, has always meant
height, for the feathered is the reverse.
Not with his puny brain but with shriveled air sacs
he guesses the truth of it: it's the end.

And at this point he screams. From the hooklike beak
there tears free of him and flies *ad luminem*
the sound Erinyes make to rend
souls: a mechanical, intolerable shriek,
the shriek of steel that devours aluminum;
"mechanical," for it's meant

for nobody, for no living ears:
not man's, not yelping foxes',
not squirrels' hurrying to the ground
from branches; not for tiny field mice whose tears
can't be avenged this way, which forces
them into their burrows. And only hounds

lift up their muzzles. A piercing, high-pitched squeal,
more nightmarish than the D-sharp grinding
of the diamond cutting glass,
slashes the whole sky across. And the world seems to reel
for an instant, shuddering from this rending.
For the warmth burns space in the highest as

badly as some iron fence down here
brands incautious gloveless fingers.
We, standing where we are, exclaim
"There!" and see far above the tear
that is a hawk, and hear the sound that lingers
in wavelets, a spider skein

swelling notes in ripples across the blue vault of space
whose lack of echo spells, especially in October,
an apotheosis of pure sound.
And caught in this heavenly patterned lace,
starlike, spangled with hoarfrost powder,
silver-clad, crystal-bound,

the bird sails to the zenith, to the dark-blue high
of azure. Through binoculars we foretoken
him, a glittering dot, a pearl.
We hear something ring out in the sky,
like some family crockery being broken,
slowly falling aswirl,

yet its shards, as they reach our palms, don't hurt
but melt when handled. And in a twinkling
once more one makes out curls, eyelets, strings,
rainbowlike, multicolored, blurred
commas, ellipses, spirals, linking
heads of barley, concentric rings —

the bright doodling pattern the feather once possessed,
a map, now a mere heap of flying
pale flakes that make a green slope appear
white. And the children, laughing and brightly dressed,
swarm out of doors to catch them, crying
with a loud shout in English, "Winter's here!"

From *To Urania* by Joseph Brodsky. "The Hawk's Cry in Autumn," 1975, translated by
Alan Myers and the author. Farrar, Straus & Giroux, 1988.

*An October 1992 aerial photograph down the Connecticut River from north of Mount Sugarloaf
showing Montague, Sunderland, and East Deerfield farmland with the Holyoke Range on the
horizon.* Photo by Richard W. Wilkie.

ARCHIBALD MACLEISH

Archibald MacLeish (1892-1982) had a second home in Conway dating back to 1927. The Pulitzer Prize winner, who lived in the Boston area when he taught at Harvard, recognized that the Hilltowns were quite a different place in his poem "New England Weather" (1976). MacLeish's "Conway Burying Ground" (1976) meditates upon aging and the knowledge of death.

New England Weather

Hay-time when the Boston forecast
calls for haying weather, hot and fair,
Conway people stick to garden chores
and nod toward nightfall at the cemetery:

that's where Sumner Boyden's lying now
and Sumner always told the town, if Boston
promised shine you'd better count on showers
'long toward evening with your hay crop lost.

He meant, no man can tell the weather
anywhere but where he's from:
you have to have the whole of it together,
bred in your bones — the way the wind-shifts come,

how dust feels on a hayfork handle
days when there'll be thunder up for sure,
and how the swallows skim, the cattle stand,
when blue stays blue and even clover cures.

He knew the Conway signs and when the Boston
forecast didn't, team went back to stalls
and chances were, by half-past four at most
we'd hear the thunder up toward Shelburne Falls.

It wasn't luck. New England weather
breeds New Englanders: that changing sky
is part of being born and drawing breath
and dying, maybe, where you're meant to die.

A view west from Shelburne Falls in spring, with a fast-moving weather front approaching.
Photo by Geoffrey Bluh.

Conway Burying Ground

They set up stones to show where time has ended
  first for one man, then another, on and on:
  stones in rows where time has run,
run out, run out for Jane, for Mary's Joe,
but what time is, they do not know.

Only the old know time: they feel it flow
like water through their fingers when the light
ebbs from the pasture and they wade in night.
It frightens them.

Time to the old is world, is will,
turning world, unswerving will,
interval

           until

From *New and Collected Poems 1917-1982* by Archibald MacLeish. Houghton Mifflin, 1985.

RICHARD WILBUR

Poet Richard Wilbur has enjoyed a connection to the Connecticut Valley dating back to his student days at Amherst College (class of '42). He taught at Wesleyan University in Connecticut from 1957 until 1977 and at Smith College as writer-in-residence from 1977 to 1986. Wilbur's honors have included the Pulitzer Prize, Bollingen Prize, and National Book Award. In 1987, he became the second U.S. Poet Laureate.

Wilbur is also noted for his translations of Molière and his libretto for Leonard Bernstein's Candide.

A resident of Cummington, Wilbur has written several poems on the natural world encountered in the Connecticut Valley and the Berkshire hills.

Orchard Trees, January

It's not the case, though some might wish it so
Who from a window watch the blizzard blow

White riot through their branches vague and stark,
That they keep snug beneath their pelted bark.

They take affliction in until it jells
To crystal ice between their frozen cells,

And each of them is inwardly a vault
Of jewels rigorous and free of fault.

Unglimpsed by us until in May it bears
A sudden crop of green-pronged solitaires.

Fern-Beds in Hampshire County

Although from them
Steep stands of beech and sugar-maple stem,
Varied with birch, or ash, or basswood trees
Which spring will throng with bees,
While intervening thickets grow complex
With flower, seed, and variance of sex,
And the whole wood conspires, by change of kind,
To break the purchase of the gathering mind,
The ferns are as they were.

Let but a trifling stir
Of air traverse their pools or touchy beds
And some will dip their heads,
Some switch a moment like a scribbling quill
And then be still,
Sporadic as in guarded bays
The rockweed slaps a bit, or sways.
Then let the wind grow bluff, and though
The sea lies far to eastward, far below,
These fluent spines, with whipped pale underside,
Will climb through timber as a smoking tide
Through pier-stakes, beat their sprays about the base
Of every boulder, scale its creviced face
And, wave on wave, like some green infantry,
Storm all the slope as high as eye can see.
Whatever at the heart
Of creatures makes them branch and burst apart,
Or at the core of star or tree may burn
At last to turn
And make an end of time,
These airy plants, tenacious of their prime,
Dwell in the swept recurrence of
An ancient conquest, shaken by first love
As when they answered to the boomed command
That the sea's green rise up and take the land.

"Orchard Trees, January" from *New and Collected Poems* by Richard Wilbur. Harcourt Brace Jovanovich, 1988.

"Fern-Beds in Hampshire County" from *Walking to Sleep: New Poems and Translations.* Harcourt Brace & Company, 1967.

PAUL MARIANI

Paul Mariani has taught English at the University of Massachusetts since the late 1960s. He has published several volumes of poetry, including Crossing Cocytus *(1982) and* Prime Mover *(1985). Mariani is also known as the biographer of William Carlos Williams. His poem "A Break in the Weather" (1985) describes an epiphanic moment on the bridge over the Connecticut at Sunderland.*

A Break in the Weather

D one in and travelling west yesterday
down over the WPA bridge connecting
Sunderland and South Deerfield, on my way
to see the dentist (a tedious half-

terrifying way to spend a morning:
the horse needle filled with novocaine,
the droning highspeed drill, the boring
ride alone) half-past nine and warm enough

to nudge a crocus out of its benumbing
winter sleep, grey swales of greysplotched
grey on grey, erratic windswept drizzle,
the swish swash of milk- and oiltrucks slashed

across my trenchslit vision when, all at once,
out there standing on the midspan of the bridge:
a young man wrapped in a forsythia-yellow poncho
and bearded as some scholar of the Talmud.

Before the Mack truck lumbered splashing
into view, I got to see this place for once —
saw it through another with his eyes shut,
arms bent upward at the elbow, hands cupped up

and rain streaming down his face. There,
just there behind him: the world opening south
to the horizon, unfolding like some giant crocus,
as the clouds swirled stippled grey and white

in bold strokes above the southward
crowding river, as once atop Mount Washington
I remember with winds whipping the glacial scars
and once as I suppose it must have been

those years ago, when horned with radiance,
Moses stood talking with his God. Pilgrim,
stranger, whatever you care to call yourself,
you who stood there above the waters

spelling the Connecticut, my thanks for waking me
to such splendid weather before the traffic
crashed back over us again in torrents
and I lost you in the slanting rearview mirror.

From *Prime Mover: Poems 1981-1985* by Paul Mariani. Grove Press, 1985.

Politics

Pioneer Valley political buttons. Courtesy of Barbara K. Jones; photo by Jean Lafond.

CALVIN COOLIDGE

*How does one rise from the Northampton Common Council to the White
House? That is the question answered in Calvin Coolidge's* Autobiography.

*Coolidge (1872-1933) was a Vermonter who came to Northampton via
Amherst College. In 1896, he started studying for the bar exam at a local law
firm. Within two years he was elected to the Common Council and went on to
serve as city solicitor, clerk of courts, mayor, state representative, state senator,
lieutenant governor, governor, vice president, president, and retiree at The
Beeches in Northampton. His* Autobiography *is related in a matter-of-fact,
somewhat naive way. There seems little struggle. Politics for Coolidge is simply
like getting a promotion.*

Climbing the Greasy Pole in Northampton

W hen I decided to enter the law it was only natural, therefore,
that I should consider it the highest of the professions. If I had
not held that opinion it would have been a measure of intellec-
tual dishonesty for me to take it for a life work. Others may be hampered
by circumstances in making their choice, but I was free, and I went where
I felt the duties would be congenial and the opportunities for service
large. Those who follow other vocations ought to feel the same about
them, and I hope they do.

My opinion had been formed by the high estimation in which the
Bench and Bar were held by the people in my boyhood home in Vermont.
It was confirmed by my more intimate intercourse with the members of
the profession with whom I soon came in contact in Massachusetts after I
went there to study law in the autumn of 1895. When I was admitted to
practice two years later the law still occupied the high position of a
profession. It had not then assumed any of its later aspects of a trade.

The ethics of the Northampton Bar were high. It was made up of men
who had, and were entitled to have, the confidence and respect of their
neighbors who knew them best. They put the interests of their clients
above their own, and the public interests above them both. They were
courteous and tolerant toward each other and respectful to the Court.
This attitude was fostered by the appreciation of the uprightness and
learning of the Judges.

Because of the short time I had spent in preparation I remained in the
office of Hammond and Field about seven months after I was admitted to
the Bar. I was looking about for a place to locate but found none that
seemed better than Northampton. A new block called the Masonic Build-

ing was under construction on lower Main Street, and when it was ready for occupancy I opened an office there February 1, 1898. I had two rooms, where I was to continue to practice law for twenty-one years, until I became Governor of Massachusetts in 1919. For my office furniture and a good working library I paid about $800 from some money I had saved and inherited from my grandfather Moor. My rent was $200 per year. I began to be self-sustaining except as to the cost of my table board, which was paid by my father until September, but thereafter all my expenses I paid from the fees I received.

I was alone. While I had many acquaintances that I might call friends I had no influential supporters who were desirous to see me advanced and were sending business to me. I was dependent on the general public; what I had, came from them. My earnings for the first year were a little over $500.

My interest in public affairs had already caused me to become a member of the Republican City Committee, and in December, 1898, I was elected one of the three members of the Common Council from Ward Two. The office was without salary and not important, but the contacts were helpful. When the local military company returned that summer from the Cuban Campaign I did my best to get an armory built for them. I was not successful at that time but my proposal was adopted a little later. This was the beginning of an interest in military preparation which I have never relinquished.

During 1899 I began to get more business. The Nonotuck Savings Bank was started early that year, and I became its counsel. Its growth was slow but steady. In later years I was its President, a purely honorary place without salary but no small honor. There was legal work about the county which came to my office, so that my fees rose to $1,400 for the second year.

I did not seek reelection to the City Council, as I knew the City Solicitor was to retire and I wanted that place. The salary was $600, which was not unimportant to me. But my whole thought was on my profession. I wanted to be City Solicitor because I believed it would make me a better lawyer. I was elected and held the office until March, 1902. It gave me a start in the law which I was ever after able to hold.

The office was not burdensome and went along with my private practice. It took me into Court some. In a jury trial I lost two trifling cases in an action of damages against the city for taking a small strip of land to widen a highway. I felt I should have won these cases on the claim that the land in question already belonged to the highway. But I prevailed in an unimportant case in the Supreme Court against my old preceptor Mr. Hammond. It is unnecessary to say that usually my cases with him were decided in his favor. The training in this office gave me a good grasp of municipal law, that later brought some important cases to me.

I worked hard during this early period. The matters on which I was engaged were numerous but did not involve large amounts of money and the fees were small. For three years I did not take the time to visit my old home in Vermont, but when I did go I was City Solicitor. My father began to see his hopes realized and felt that his efforts to give me an education were beginning to be rewarded.

What I always felt was the greatest compliment ever paid to my professional ability came in 1903. In the late spring of that year William H. Clapp, who had been for many years the Clerk of the Courts for Hampshire County died. His ability, learning and painstaking industry made him rank very high as a lawyer. The position he held was of the first importance, for it involved keeping all the civil and criminal records of the Superior Court and the Supreme Judicial Court for the County. The Justices of the Supreme Judicial Court appointed me to fill the vacancy. I always felt this was a judgment by the highest Court in the Commonwealth on my professional qualifications. Had I been willing to accept the place permanently I should have been elected to it in the following November. The salary was then $2,300, and the position was one of great dignity, but I preferred to remain at the Bar, which might be more precarious, but also had more possibilities. Later events now known enable any one to pass judgment on my decision. Had I decided otherwise I could have had much more peace of mind in the last twenty-five years.

As the Clerk of the Courts I learned much relating to Massachusetts practice, so that ever after I knew what to do with all the documents in a trial, which would have been of much value to me if I had not been called on to give so much time to political affairs. These took up a large amount of my attention in 1904 after I went back to my office, so that my income diminished during that year. I had been chosen Chairman of the Republican City Committee. It was a time of perpetual motion in Massachusetts politics. The state elections came yearly in November, and the city elections followed in December. This was presidential year. While I elected the Representatives to the General Court by a comfortable margin at the state election I was not so successful in the city campaign. Our Mayor had served three terms, which had always been the extreme limit in Northampton, but he was nominated for a fourth time. He was defeated by about eighty votes. We made the mistake of talking too much about the deficiencies of our opponents and not enough about the merits of our own candidates. I have never again fallen into that error. Feeling one year was all I could give to the chairmanship I did not accept a reelection but still remained on the committee.

My earnings had been such that I was able to make some small savings. My prospects appeared to be good. I had many friends and few enemies. There was a little more time for me to give to the amenities of life. I took my meals at Rahar's Inn where there was much agreeable company consisting of professional and business men of the town and some of the professors of Smith College. I had my rooms on Round Hill with the steward of the Clarke School for the Deaf. While these relations were most agreeable and entertaining I suppose I began to want a home of my own.

From *The Autobiography of Calvin Coolidge*. Cosmopolitan Book Corporation, 1929.

Calvin Coolidge and Grace, his wife, received the news that he had won the governor's seat in 1918 at his Massasoit Street duplex apartment in Northampton. Courtesy of Calvin Coolidge Memorial Room, Forbes Library, Northampton.

JOHN FOSTER (FOSTER FURCOLO)

Foster Furcolo (1917-1995) was the last citizen of Western Massachusetts to hold statewide office in the Commonwealth. He was governor between 1957 and 1961. Before that he had served as Edward Boland's predecessor in Congress, from 1949-1953. Furcolo liked to analyze the art of politics, as he deduced it from local experience, and wrote Ballots Anyone? How to Run for Office and Win.

In 1957, while governor, Furcolo penned the satirical political novel Let George Do It! A Comedy About America Politics *under the* nom de plume *of John Foster. It is a tale of mischievous ward politics in an unnamed medium-sized Massachusetts city. Furcolo claimed that this novel was supposed to outrage the public toward ward politics. He closed with the lines: "Politics is your business. Don't Let George Do It." Rather than an expose, the novel reads more as a celebration of "The Last Hurrah" era. Furcolo tells the story of ward heeler George Clancy putting up neophyte Peter Martin for state representative. They engage in such political scams as pretending to have differ-ent ethnic identities to appeal to each ethnic group.*

Let George Do It! *avoided depicting specific figures and scrambled up many of the city's locations, but there is a strong flavor of Springfield throughout.*

Election Rituals

I guess political cards are the most important thing in a campaign because, like George says, a candidate should always have them with him. No matter where you are or who you meet, as you leave you hand him a card and say, "Give me a thought on September fifteenth" or "If you don't have anyone else in mind, will you give me your vote?" — or anything else that gets the idea across. If the guy says "No" you should not argue with him. However, most people won't tell you "No" even if they are with somebody else. If he says he is pledged to somebody else — and once in a while they do — then you got to say that his man is a great fellow and you hope he wins if you don't. "Say it even if he's a louse," George told me. "Then that makes you a good fellow. You got to be a good fellow — understand?" Usually whoever you gave the card to would say "Sure" and often they would ask for more cards. I used to give out lots of cards to one person until George stopped me. "The more they tell you they're going to do, the less they do," he used to say. "The fellow who's going to help you wants only one card. He keeps that in his pocket and shows it to everybody. When you give anybody a bunch of them, it's a sure sign he won't do nothing for you. He'll throw them away."

I was always kind of self-conscious about handing out the cards, but not George. He would stand in the back of a crowded hall and, as the people were going out, he would be there with a stack of cards, handing them left and right and saying, almost like a man selling hot dogs: "Here you are, folks. Your next Representative, Peter Martin. Be with a winner, friend." That "Be with a winner" was his favorite sentence, I think. Anytime somebody would tell him they were voting for one of my opponents, George would tell him not to waste his vote. "So-and-So's a good fellow," he would say, "and I'd be with him if he had a chance, but he hasn't got a show." Then he'd go on to name the Mayor, the District Attorney, the Congressman, and all the big Democrats. "They're all with Peter Martin," he'd whisper very confidentially. "How can he lose with that kind of backing?" Then he'd hand the person one of my cards and say, "Be with a winner, friend; be with a winner." I have never yet heard any politician talk about any candidate's platform or ability or anything except "who was with him." And the ones they name as being "with him" — even when they really are — never do anything to help him. The only ones who help a candidate, as near as I can tell, are his own friends, like Eddie and Joe and fellows like that.

But, as I was saying, George was very strong for cards and before the campaign was over I had cards printed in French, Polish, and Italian. There were sections of the city with big foreign votes and we wanted to get them. We also had a card printed for the colored people. He mailed three thousand of them out two days before election — one to every voter in the colored section. It was George's idea. He had everything on it just like on my regular card except, instead of my picture, he had a picture of a colored fellow, and underneath the picture it said in very small letters, "Vote for Peter Martin, a friend of the colored." George said that we meant the colored man on the card to be saying that. "We don't mean you're the colored man," he told me, "and it's not our fault if the colored people think you're colored and vote for you because they think that. That colored fellow on the card is just a voter who's telling his friends to vote for you." Eddie and Joe finally agreed it was all right to send them out because nobody was going to get them but colored people anyway. "And," Joe pointed out, "before anybody finds out about it the election'll be over anyhow."

"And anyhow," George pointed out, "we can say one of your opponents sent them out. Dirty politics against you. Something like that skunk Mason would pull." He was quiet for a long time after that and then he wanted to send postcards to the Irish and Italian section — postcards saying my opponent Murphy was a great guy and signed by the President of the Planned Parenthood League. "If the Irish think all the birth control people are for Murphy," George argued, "they'll be for anybody but Murphy."

I guess it was a good idea but we finally didn't do it because it would have cost too much money to print and mail out enough government postcards to do any good. Besides that, as we decided after talking it over, there was no guarantee that I'd get the votes of those who decided not to vote for Murphy. Like George finally said, by the law of averages I'd probably get only about ten per cent of the votes Murphy would lose and yet I'd be standing the whole expense of taking the votes away from him. "We ain't going to stand no hundred per cent of the cost just to get ten per cent of the votes," George says. It taught me two good political lessons: first, get full value for the money you spend in a campaign; and second, while you may want their votes, there are some people you don't want to let the public know are with you.

The cards printed about me in the foreign languages were very good, I thought. The Italian cards had me as Pietro Martin, the French as Pierre Martin, and on the Polish it was Petrovich Martin. Joe thought "Petrovich" was Russian, but it was the closest we could come to a Polish name, so we used it. I began to wonder what my nationality really was supposed to be. If it was a Polish rally, George would be saying: "The only Polish candidate, friends. Don't go back on your own kind." Then he'd say "Nashtrovia," which is a Polish word meaning "Good luck" or something friendly like that.

If it was an Italian rally he would be saying to the people as they went in or out: "Pietro Martino, folks. The printer forgot to put the 'o' on, but he's your pisan, friends. Only Italian candidate running."

Eddie suggested that we make the name "Pietro Martino" on the card itself. George refused. "We can get away with the 'Pietro,' all right," he explained. "After all, that's just the Italian of 'Peter.' But making it 'Martino' in print would be just laying it on too thick. And it couldn't be a mistake, either." That was how it was with George — if it could have been a reasonable mistake, it was all right. Otherwise, it was no go.

The French cards were the hardest for George. He had to say "Pierre Martin," pronouncing the Martin as though he had a cold in his head and saying it as though it was spelled "Mar-Tehn." The way he said it was good and you would have thought it was a regular pea-soup talking.

George was always very particular about cards at clambakes or picnics. All the candidates would be there with their own cards, of course, and George always waited until they had made the rounds handing them out. Then he would go around with mine, take the other cards away from those people who would let him, and give them mine instead. "Be with a winner, friend," he would say, taking away the card of one of my opponents. "Don't waste your vote."

Usually the people didn't object, but once in a while George would bump into someone who would not give up the card he already had. When that happened, if there was any unpleasantness, George would never give that person my card. Instead, he would back away saying, "Well, I don't care who you vote for as long as it ain't for Peter Martin. I wouldn't give that guy Peter Martin the time of day. He's no friend of mine." He afterwards explained to me that he would try to get the other person so mad at him that they would vote for whoever George said was the candidate he liked the least.

I got to know a lot about clambakes and picnics and outings. There was always a bar or something and the candidate would be expected to buy drinks for whoever was there. Usually the same bunch would hang around the bar and they would drink with every candidate and tell him what a great guy he was and how they were with him and all their friends would vote for him.

The womenfolks, for the most part, never went near the bar. They would sit along the sidelines talking and laughing and when two strangers came in wearing jackets, while almost everyone else was in shirt sleeves or aprons, they would nudge each other and the word "politician" would go up and down the line. The men at the bar would be drinking beer until the politician ordered a round for everybody — and then the bartenders would automatically give everyone "a shot and a beer." I never saw any barflies drink anything else as long as a candidate was paying for it. Sometimes one of the fellows would order another drink and then tell the bartender it was "on Mr. Martin, the Representative." There was nothing to do then except pay for it or look like a piker. So, the windup was that you were marked down either as a sucker or a cheap skate. I often think that the best thing for a candidate to do is not to go to those things. It's impossible to go and not end up at the bar because someone will take you there.

At the Polish outings you would have to talk about what a great guy Woodrow Wilson was and how the Russians were cutthroats and the Germans were worse. That is all right except once in a while you will be telling that to a Russian because, if you are like me, you cannot tell a Russian from a Pole. And that is not so good.

At the Italian picnics you would not get stuck much for drinks, but how you would get hit for tickets! Everybody you met was selling tickets to this dinner or that picnic or something else.

George also told me the best thing to do when I saw anyone I had met before at some Italian affair was to call out: "Ehi, comba." That meant that I was his friend and that I wished he was my godfather or best man or something like that. I think the Italians must have trouble remembering names themselves because everybody called everybody else "comba" —

and they couldn't all be godfathers and best men.

"Always tell them Italy is a great place and that the Italians don't get enough representation over here," said George.

I don't think most groups really gave a darn about politics or offices but they liked to talk about it. They were never getting enough "recognition," whatever that was — but, whatever it was, they would get it when I got elected. As George said one time: "You are a racial candidate. That is what we've got to sell them. They're a racial group and you're a racial candidate." George's idea was always to be as vague as possible about just where I got my French blood . . . or my Italian . . . or my Polish . . . or whatever it was. Then if someone really pinned me down, to say a great-grandparent. "That's far enough back," he used to say, "and it's hard to trace. After all, there are eight great-grandparents."

The way he had it figured out we had as good a chance of getting the racial vote as any candidate and we were going to try hard for it. With the Polish and Italian groups it was not too hard to know what to do because both those groups would follow their own leaders and if we had the key men, we could be fairly sure of getting a fair vote. With the French it was different — they were all leaders and no candidate could tell whether he was coming or going with them.

Anyway, what with the political cards and my getting around to picnics and weddings and stag parties and rallies and all, things were beginning to look pretty good. It looked like the racial vote was mine. George had seen to that!

———————————

From *Let George Do It! A Comedy About America Politics* by John Foster (Foster Furcolo). Harcourt, Brace & Company, 1957.

LAWRENCE F. O'BRIEN

*Good, clean machine politics, that's what Larry O'Brien (1917-1990)
developed and then codified in Springfield. He started his career meeting
politicians at his father's cafe near Court Square. O'Brien broke in managing
the congressional campaigns of Foster Furcolo. In 1952, O'Brien made the
fateful step of becoming Western Massachusetts coordinator for John F.
Kennedy's first U.S. Senate run.*

*O'Brien managed Kennedy's 1960 presidential run as well as Hubert
Humphrey's and George McGovern's. He was chief congressional liaison for
Kennedy and Johnson, postmaster general, and chairman of the Democratic
National Committee during the fateful Watergate days of 1972. Life called him
the "resident professor of politics."*

O'Brien is also known for two books — No Final Victories, *his political
memoirs and account of Watergate, and the "O'Brien Manual." The "O'Brien
Manual" started as mimeographed pages of basic political advice prepared for
Foster Furcolo's first congressional race. It became a Bible in Kennedy cam-
paigns and was printed as an official National Democratic Party handbook for
the presidential campaigns of 1960, 1964, and 1968.*

In this selection from No Final Victories, *O'Brien recounts Jack
Kennedy's introduction to Springfield in the 1952 U.S. Senate race.*

JFK Comes to Springfield

Early in 1951, not long after my return to Springfield, a fellow I
knew in the Elks Club came into our cafe and asked if I knew
Congressman Kennedy.

"I know him," I said, "but not intimately."

My friend explained that the Elks hoped Kennedy might address a
large outdoor gathering they would be having in the spring and won-
dered if I might extend the invitation. I said I would be glad to and I
wrote Kennedy and explained why this would be a good speaking en-
gagement for him — it was nonpartisan, there would be a big crowd, and
so on. I knew Kennedy well enough to suspect he would jump at the
chance to address a large audience in western Massachusetts, where he
was not so well known.

I had first met Jack Kennedy back in 1947, when he was serving his
first term in Congress. I had been talking with my good friend Eddie
Boland, who was then the registrar of deeds in Springfield, when Eddie
reminded me that young Congressman Kennedy was speaking that after-
noon to a labor convention at the Springfield Auditorium, just across

Court Square from Eddie's office.

"Have you heard about this guy?" Eddie asked me.

"Yeah, I've read about him," I said.

"He's a real comer," Eddie said. "He could be President someday. Let's go take a look at him."

I agreed and we left Eddie's office and walked to the auditorium. I was curious. I didn't know much about the young congressman, but I knew about the Kennedy family, for it was the most prominent Irish-Catholic family in Massachusetts. The Kennedys were known not only for their wealth and for their generous contributions to charities and to the Church, but also because Joseph P. Kennedy had been Roosevelt's ambassador to England. We all had read about Joe, Jr.'s death during the war and Jack Kennedy's heroism when his PT boat was sunk, and we knew there were other brothers and sisters whose pictures appeared in the society pages from time to time. The Kennedys were a Massachusetts legend even then, and if Jack Kennedy was speaking in Springfield, I thought I'd better have a look at him.

His speech struck me as routine. The important fact was not what Kennedy said but simply that already, as a young first-term congressman, his name brought him speaking invitations all over the state. After the speech, Eddie Boland and I went up and Eddie introduced me. Kennedy had to hurry off to a radio station, but he asked Eddie and me to meet him for a drink after his interview. We met at the Kimball Hotel — our drinks were Cokes, I recall — and talked for an hour or so before he drove back to Boston. Nothing memorable was said, but he was pleasant and likable. Certainly he made a favorable impression on us, which was what he intended. Even then he knew it was worth an hour of his time to cultivate a couple of local politicians who might someday be useful to him.

When I arrived on Capitol Hill in 1949, I looked Kennedy up and we had lunch at Mike Palm's Restaurant a couple of times. At first I was trying to advance Furcolo's interests, trying to persuade Kennedy to co-sponsor this or that bill of Furcolo's. But Kennedy wanted as little as possible to do with Furcolo. He had rejected our request that he campaign for Furcolo in 1948 and he wasn't interested in sponsoring Kennedy-Furcolo bills. I assumed that he regarded the ambitious Furcolo as a potential rival for state-wide office.

I had no luck helping Furcolo with Kennedy, but we remained friendly. We were almost exactly the same age — he was born about six weeks before I was born in 1917 — and we shared an interest in politics. He was very young and casual in those days. I recall his wearing sneakers and khaki pants one day when we lunched on Capitol Hill, and he was considered rather offbeat by congressional standards. For his part,

Kennedy was bored by the House and was often conspicuous by his non-participation in its affairs. You sensed, without his telling you, that he would not be making a career of the House, yet you did not have to be a genius to see that he had a real future in politics.

I liked Kennedy and enjoyed his company, but when I left Capitol Hill and returned to Springfield I had no reason to think I'd ever be seeing him again. Then, a few weeks after I wrote him about the Elks Club speaking invitation, I got a call from Frank Morrissey, who was an aide to the congressman and later a judge in Massachusetts. Morrissey said Kennedy would be in the Springfield area soon and would like to talk with me. I said that would be fine, and on a Sunday in March we had dinner at Kelly's Lobster House in nearby Holyoke. Kennedy was not long in getting to the point.

"Larry, I'm not going to stay in the House," he told me. "I'm not challenged there. It's up or out for me. I'm definitely going to run for state-wide office next year. I don't know many people in western Massachusetts and I'd like your help."

"What are you running for?" I asked.

"I don't know yet," he admitted. "I want to run against Lodge, but if Dever makes that race I'll run for governor."

His reply and his uncertainty reflected his status in the state's politics at that point. Henry Cabot Lodge, the respected Republican senator, was up for re-election in 1952 and was widely viewed as unbeatable. Paul Dever, the aging "boy wonder" of Massachusetts politics, was the state's Democratic governor. If Dever wanted to run against Lodge, the Democratic nomination was his for the asking. Only if Dever decided to play it safe, and run for re-election as governor, could Kennedy make the race against Lodge.

I admired Kennedy's audacity, for here was a fellow in his mid-thirties who was eagerly seeking a race against one of the most popular senators in Massachusetts history. But I discouraged any thought that I might be involved in his campaign. The memories were still fresh from my Washington experience and my break with my friend Furcolo.

"I need your help, Larry," Kennedy kept saying. "You did some terrific organizational work for Foster and I don't have anybody who can do that."

"Thanks but no thanks," I told him emphatically. "I'm out of politics. For good."

Kennedy was a hard man to say no to. He thanked me for telling him about the Elks Club speech and asked if I'd let him know about other good speaking engagements in my area. I said I would. Then, as a follow-up to our talk, Frank Morrissey sent me some Kennedy literature and asked if I'd pass it on to people who might be interested. I kept the material in my cafe, where some of the town's Democrats would have a chance to look at it. Later in the spring Kennedy called me.

"Larry, I want to talk to you," he said in that distinctive Boston accent of his. "Do you ever come to Boston?"

"Not often," I said. "I might be in to see the Red Sox this spring. I'll call you if I am."

As it turned out, I went to Boston for a Memorial Day double-header between the Red Sox and the Yankees. I called Kennedy in advance and we agreed to meet for dinner at the Ritz-Carlton Hotel after the game. We had a long and pleasant talk, which essentially covered the same ground as our talk in March — Kennedy was still planning to run for either senator or governor the next year and he still wanted my help. For my part, I said again that I was definitely out of politics.

"Larry, I want to meet the party workers in western Massachusetts," he said. "You can at least help me there, can't you?"

It seemed like a modest request, so I said yes, I could probably help in that regard.

"How should we do it?" he pressed. He knew that the kind of gathering he would hold in his highly political district in Boston might not be appropriate for the lower-keyed politics of Springfield.

"I'd suggest an informal reception early in the evening," I said. "Just coffee and sandwiches, no drinks. You meet everyone personally, shake their hand, and make brief, informal remarks."

"Terrific," Kennedy replied. He was leaning forward over the table, eagerly taking in everything I said. This was politics — this was progress. "Where will we have it?"

"I'd suggest Blake's Restaurant." I told him. "They've got an upstairs room that will hold several hundred people."

"What about the invitations?"

"I can take care of them," I said. "I've got lists of all the people you ought to meet."

Kennedy was beaming when we left the Ritz-Carlton. Then a few weeks later, after I'd sent out the invitations to the reception, which was in June, I received an unexpected call from Kennedy.

"Larry," he said, "your friend Furcolo just called me and said he was really bulled off about my coming into his district without clearing it with him. It doesn't bother me, but I thought you ought to know."

"It doesn't bother me," I assured him.

I understood Furcolo's anger, of course. It's traditional that if one congressman is visiting another congressman's district he "clears" the visit, or at least gives advance notice. That way the host congressman won't be embarrassed by having some constituent or reporter break the news of the visit to him. He can always say, "Why, yes, of course, I told my distinguished colleague he was welcome to visit our district."

Kennedy could play by the rules when he chose to, but he didn't choose to with Furcolo and he wasn't about to clear anything with him.

But that wasn't the end of it. The day before the reception, Kennedy called again, this time from New York. I took the call in the phone booth in the cafe.

"Larry," he began. "Foster called again."

"Yeah?"

"He says I should cancel our reception."

"For any particular reason?" I asked. This whole thing was getting absurd.

"Yeah," Kennedy replied. "He said he hated to tell me this, but I should cancel because O'Brien was in trouble and might have some legal problems."

I couldn't believe what I was hearing. I had no legal problems, none whatsoever. I could only assume that Furcolo was so anxious to keep Kennedy from association with me that he had fabricated the story as a desperate ploy to scare Kennedy into canceling the trip. I was stunned, then increasingly angry. I had thought I was out of politics, but here I was in the middle of the worst kind of political back-stabbing.

I bit my lip and cursed silently, until finally Kennedy said, "Well, what do you think of that?"

"I haven't any comment on it," I said.

"What's your advice?"

"My advice, if you're worried about it, is to forget the meeting tomorrow. It doesn't matter to me, one way or the other."

Kennedy paused a minute, then said: "Where am I supposed to meet you and what time?"

"At noon outside Howard Johnson's Restaurant," I told him.

"I'll see you there," he said and hung up.

In the dozen years ahead, when I was impatient or angry with Kennedy, I would sometimes think back to that time when he had to make a quick judgment between Furcolo and me. Furcolo was a member of Congress; I was a cafe owner whom Kennedy knew precious little about. The easy thing, the safe thing would have been to plead illness and cancel the reception. Why risk involvement with some local pol who might be in some sort of trouble? But Kennedy chose to trust me rather than Furcolo, and I would have to say that I don't know another man in politics who would have made the same decision.

I met Kennedy at noon the next day. He had driven from Boston with

Morrissey and with Bob Morey, his regular driver in those days. We went to lunch, then went to my mother's apartment to talk until it was time to go to the reception. My father had died the previous year and he, to my knowledge, had never met Kennedy, but Kennedy and my mother became friendly. She was a woman of great poise and self-assurance and Kennedy was intrigued by her.

"Mrs. O'Brien," he said with a twinkle in his eye, "why don't you have more of a brogue?"

She laughed and explained that in the part of Ireland she and her husband had come from, many people didn't have pronounced brogues. She went on to say, "But in fact I have a sister who has acquired a brogue since she came here." They moved into a conversation about local politics, for if my mother was not an activist she nonetheless had acquired a good deal of political know-how. She certainly knew aspects of Springfield politics that Kennedy didn't know, and he was fascinated to hear her views.

Kennedy's curiosity was one of his most striking qualities. He had led a life, somewhat sheltered from the workaday world that most of us know, and so he moved through life with an insatiable curiosity about many things that most of us take for granted. Once he came to my cafe and tried his hand at drawing beer from the taps. I had probably drawn my first glass of beer at age fifteen and several thousand more after that, but it was an entirely new experience to Kennedy. Next he wanted to know where the beer came from.

"For Pete's sake, Jack," I protested. "It comes from barrels down in the cellar."

"Let's take a look," he insisted, and nothing would do but that we go down for a guided tour of the walk-in cooler where we kept our barrels of beer. This led, finally, to a detailed discussion of the profit margin on each glass of beer sold.

Finally, that June afternoon, we left my mother's apartment and proceeded to the reception at Blake's Restaurant. We arrived early, when the big hall was empty except for the refreshments and the red, white, and blue bunting we had put up for decoration. Slowly, the party workers began to file in and I stood with Kennedy near the door to make the introductions. Each guest, before he or she reached Kennedy, was asked by a hostess to sign a guest book — it seemed like a "social" touch, but in truth I wanted all the names for follow-up mailings.

Kennedy was warm and gracious to the people who filed past him. He had the ability to focus exclusively on each person for a few seconds, establishing real human contact, making the person feel that he would remember and treasure those few seconds of conversation.

In political situations, such as a receiving line, a politician often has about ten seconds to give an impression that may last a lifetime. In Kennedy's case, because of his youth and his wealth, many people would be ready to dislike him if he appeared standoffish. Although he was reserved, Kennedy had a genuine interest in people. I could literally see this reflected in the faces of the people who filed through that receiving line to meet him — nervous or hesitant as they approached him, loosening up as he took their hand, and finally beaming with pleasure as they walked away from their first encounter with one of the famous Kennedys.

His remarks were low-key. He was pleased to be in Springfield, pleased to meet all of them, and he hoped to come back again, perhaps someday — this said lightly — as a candidate for office.

As we left the reception, Kennedy knew it had gone well. "God, what a great meeting," he kept saying. Then, as we drove away, his mood changed.

"Let me ask you something, Larry. What would you have done if I had called off this reception because of what Furcolo said?"

"That's very simple," I told him. "I'd have gone to the meeting and told them exactly what happened."

"Do you mean you would have told them I canceled because Furcolo said you might be in legal difficulties?"

"That's absolutely right. And the papers would have picked it up — it would have made an interesting story."

"You'd really have done that?"

"Why not? What would you suggest I do with several hundred of my friends gathered there at my invitation?"

Kennedy shook his head in bewilderment. "Politics," he muttered. "What a business."

The next day I mailed him the guest book and he wrote everyone a note of thanks. He loved that guest-book idea, and it became a fixture of his later campaigns.

One result of the reception at Blake's Restaurant was Kennedy's determination to have me on his campaign team. And, in retrospect, it's clear that my resolve to stay out of politics was weakening. Part of it was my long-time love of politics, but more of it was my growing affection and respect for Jack Kennedy. He represented something new in Massachusetts politics.

From *No Final Victories: A Life in Politics from John F. Kennedy to Watergate* by Lawrence F. O'Brien. Doubleday, 1974.

JOSEPH NAPOLITAN

One of Larry O'Brien's protégés was Joseph Napolitan. Napolitan was one of the pioneering political consultants in America, developing television advertising and polling into sophisticated campaign techniques. Napolitan started by managing the campaigns of Springfield mayors Thomas J. O'Connor and Charles V. Ryan during the late 1950s and early 1960s. He went on to serve as a political consultant for presidential candidates John F. Kennedy, Hubert H. Humphrey, Alaska Senator Mike Gravel, Congressman Richard Neal, French President Giscard D'Estaing, and several Latin American politicians. Napolitan founded the American Association of Political Consultants.

Napolitan's The Election Game and How to Win It *was written as a Democratic strategy for beating Richard Nixon in 1972. The main anecdotes about Springfield recount Mayor Thomas O'Connor's first television commercial and District Attorney Matthew Ryan's first campaign.*

Election Anecdotes

The first television spot I ever conceived in a political campaign was in 1957. It was my first campaign, and my candidate was a young man named Tom O'Connor, who was running for mayor of Springfield, Massachusetts, against an incumbent who had served six consecutive two-year terms and was considered unbeatable.

The spot featured an exploding bomb like the ones they always draw in cartoons, a black ball with a long fuse, that blows up and the pieces form the words "New Leadership — Tom O'Connor." (God, can you imagine a candidate today using an exploding bomb in a mayoral election? Environments change.) We made the spot in a local film studio, sticking a wick on a bowling ball and filming it as the fuse fizzed. The studio added a little razz-ma-tazz, and there was our ten-second spot.

I doubt that that commercial had much to do with Tom O'Connor's victory (he defeated his opponent in the Democratic primary in every one of the city's sixty-four precincts), but it was the first of many experiments I was to make with television as a medium to elect candidates to office.

(Four years I ran a campaign against O'Connor with another candidate, and we beat him. That's when I began to believe that maybe the campaign manager really did have something to do with winning elections. And fourteen years later O'Connor turned up in my office again, wanting to run for mayor, which he was prevented from doing by a legal technicality.)

One of the best campaigns I've ever handled, very early in my career, was for district attorney in the western district of Massachusetts. My candidate, who is one of my closest friends, was Matthew Ryan, and we were faced with a nine-man primary. One of the jobs of a manager or a consultant is to innovate, to capitalize, to turn apparent liabilities into assets. During that primary, in the early fall of 1958, the Springfield newspapers had a blackout on political news. They apparently wanted some outrageous change in a tax bill that would have brought them enormous benefits, and when neither Senator Leverett Saltonstall nor Senator John F. Kennedy nor Congressman Edward P. Boland would intervene, they reacted childishly and declared that henceforth there would be no political statements carried in either the morning or the evening newspaper, which were the only papers in town. Hardly a realistic or mature approach, but that's what they did and it's on the record.

You don't have a lot of money to spend in a primary for DA in the western part of Massachusetts, so you try to use a little ingenuity. A thought struck me one night at home; I called Ryan and he agreed to try it.

The next morning I telephoned the advertising department of the newspapers and asked if there were any restriction on the style of type we could use in an ad. There was a puzzled silence, and I was told no, none at all.

"Fine," I replied. "I want to reserve a full page for next Sunday." (Two days before the primary.)

"Okay."

"Now tell me the deadline for getting the copy in for the Sunday ad."

"Noon on Friday."

"Right."

Having been a reporter and makeup editor on those newspapers, I was familiar with the type and headline styles of the Sunday Republican. So I promptly proceeded to write and assemble a full page of copy, photographs, even a cartoon. The package was delivered to the newspaper at ten minutes to twelve on Friday. The page looked just like any other page in the Republican that Sunday — except that every item was about Matthew Ryan, including a lead article with the headline Ryan Rated Best-Qualified Candidate for District Attorney.

We had the legal disclaimer, of course — in small type at the top of the page — and a legal signature in the lower right-hand corner. You might have to look hard to find them, but they were there.

This might have worked all right even if the papers were carrying political news, but with the political blackout that had been in force, the full page about Matty Ryan struck like a bombshell. A harassed advertising executive called me at my home on Sunday noon to tell me that by eleven o'clock Sunday morning he had received calls from every one of the other eight candidates or their managers, and from most of the executives on the newspaper. The next day the paper passed a rule banning type styles in advertisements similar to those used in their news columns.

On Tuesday Ryan won the primary by sixteen hundred votes, was elected district attorney two months later, and has served ever since without opposition in either primary or general elections.

Here, again, every candidate had the same opportunity to utilize an existing situation, and most of them did run full-page ads that Sunday, but none had the impact ours did. (I don't always get the bright ideas; I've had people on the other side in other elections come up with equally effective concepts that have helped torpedo or seriously bruise my candidate.)

From *The Election Game and How to Win It* by Joseph Napolitan. Doubleday, 1972.

Springfield,
"City of Homes"

Court Square in Springfield in 1839. From *Historical Collections . . . History and Antiquities of Every Town in Massachusetts* by John W. Barber, 1839.

JONATHAN DANIELS

*In 1939, journalist and ex-FDR press secretary Jonathan Daniels (1902-1981)
took a swing through New England to learn "what New England meant to
itself and to America." Daniels recounted his observations in* A Southerner
Discovers New England *(1940). In Springfield, he visited the home of the
Merriam-Webster Dictionary. Daniels extolled the Merriam-Webster
Dictionary as a quintessential Yankee product based on achieving the highest
quality. Today, Merriam-Webster is still serving as linguistic arbiter of
American English from 47 Federal Street in Springfield.*

Noah's Book

I thought that language, even in Springfield, had been moving since
Webster died and went to the lexicographers' heaven long ago. But
his book lived and grew. I think I like the men who keep it in wise
commerce as an educational institution not much, if any, inferior to
Harvard, better than I should have liked the old man who wrote it or at
least let his name to be put on the front of it. The last Southern traveler
who described him — Anne Royall, who wrote in 1826 before his big
American Dictionary of the English Language appeared — did not like him
at all:

"I knocked at the door with more than common enthusiasm," wrote
Mrs. Royall, who was noted for her sharp tongue, "for though we back-
woods folks are not learned ourselves, we have a warm liking for learn-
ing. In a few minutes a low, chubby man, with a haughty air, stepped into
the room; his race was round and red, and by no means literary looking.
He was dressed in black broadcloth, in dandy style; in short, he comes
nearer the description of a London cockney than any character I can think
of; he eyed me with ineffable scorn, and scarcely deigned to speak at all.
I am sorry for his sake I ever saw the man, as it gave me infinite pain to
rescind an opinion I had long entertained of him."

If the lady scorned didn't like him, some millions of others since have
nevertheless revered his name — which must be the most valuable name
in the whole history of the written and printed word in America. I don't
think the Merriams ever saw him; I am sure the Bakers never did. But
when the young Merriams, booksellers of Springfield, bought for $3,000
in 1843 the publishers' remainders of his big book and the right to reprint
his books, including the famous *Speller*, they bought a bargain and began
a business which, beyond every difficulty and the millions it has made,
still remains rich and enriching in Massachusetts. Of course, the process

was not so simple as that sounds nor quite so cheap. They later paid the Webster family a quarter of a million for copyright renewal.

Before the company grew to its present safety in its big book's present preeminence, it had to fight the War of the Dictionaries, Webster *vs.* Worcester. Old Noah said before he died at the beginning of the fifty years' fight that Joseph Emerson Worcester was a plagiarist, but there were plenty of the fastidious who preferred Worcester's book. Today the Merriam Company may report that in those days the Merriams, grateful for the competition which made them produce a better and better book, used to get down on their knees and "Thank God for Worcester!" Maybe so. I suspect that the victor counting his spoils can get more satisfaction out of saying his prayers.

I came to the old Myrick Building on Broadway, where Noah's erudite and profitable tradition persists, over the short pleasant road from Hartford. The road led past the Fuller Brush factory — and I remembered that it had not been many years since Fuller Brushes were as well-known for the foot-in-the-door persistence of their salesmen as for the excellence of their products. A Connecticut countryman who had sold all but one of the Boston terrier pups he advertised had pinned a piece of brown paper over the s on "pups." There was tobacco growing under its tented shade and beautiful lettuce and tomatoes in the fields. The drought did not seem quite as dire as it had been described. Beside the road an R.F.D. carrier was conversing with the proprietor of a farm which advertised duck eggs. A girl in shorts was helping her mother and father pick vegetables in Suffield. Florists and tobacco buyers were in business close to the highway. A hitch-hiker wanting a ride undertook to make himself momentarily and almost indecently attractive like a grimacing prostitute. Men like ants were laboring on levees to keep back the floods which too often come up out of the long and beautiful Connecticut.

The Myrick Building on Broadway was a worn, even weary-looking, old building in which to expect alert specialists to be catching the precise meanings of the last words for people everywhere. An old-fashioned elevator in it took me up to the floor where, beyond cases full of Websteriana — from copies of Noah's *Speller* which sold 70,000,000 copies to the last and richest full leather, seal grain, India paper copy of the *New International Dictionary* — a switchboard girl let me into the office of Robert C. Munroe.

At fifty-nine President Munroe had been with the Merriam Company for more than forty years. He had come from birth in Holyoke and high school in Springfield to a clerkship among the dictionaries when he was eighteen years old. He had never been far from the trade in definitions since. At twenty-four he was the company's advertising manager. Before

AN

AMERICAN DICTIONARY

OF THE

ENGLISH LANGUAGE;

CONTAINING

THE WHOLE VOCABULARY OF THE FIRST EDITION IN TWO VOLUMES QUARTO; THE ENTIRE CORREC-
TIONS AND IMPROVEMENTS OF THE SECOND EDITION IN TWO VOLUMES ROYAL OCTAVO;

TO WHICH IS PREFIXED

AN INTRODUCTORY DISSERTATION

ON THE

ORIGIN, HISTORY, AND CONNECTION, OF THE LANGUAGES OF WESTERN ASIA AND EUROPE,

WITH AN EXPLANATION

OF THE PRINCIPLES ON WHICH LANGUAGES ARE FORMED.

BY NOAH WEBSTER, LL. D.,

*Member of the American Philosophical Society in Philadelphia; Fellow of the American Academy of Arts and Sciences in Massachusetts;
Member of the Connecticut Academy of Arts and Sciences; Fellow of the Royal Society of Northern Antiquaries in Co-
penhagen; Member of the Connecticut Historical Society; Corresponding Member of the Historical Societies
in Massachusetts, New York, and Georgia; of the Academy of Medicine in Philadel-
phia, and of the Columbian Institute in Washington; and Honorary
Member of the Michigan Historical Society.*

GENERAL SUBJECTS OF THIS WORK.

I.—ETYMOLOGIES OF ENGLISH WORDS, DEDUCED FROM AN EXAMINATION AND COMPARISON OF WORDS OF CORRESPONDING
ELEMENTS IN TWENTY LANGUAGES OF ASIA AND EUROPE.
II.—THE TRUE ORTHOGRAPHY OF WORDS, AS CORRECTED BY THEIR ETYMOLOGIES.
III.—PRONUNCIATION EXHIBITED AND MADE OBVIOUS BY THE DIVISION OF WORDS INTO SYLLABLES, BY ACCENTUATION, BY
MARKING THE SOUNDS OF THE ACCENTED VOWELS, WHEN NECESSARY, OR BY GENERAL RULES.
IV.—ACCURATE AND DISCRIMINATING DEFINITIONS, ILLUSTRATED, WHEN DOUBTFUL OR OBSCURE, BY EXAMPLES OF THEIR
USE, SELECTED FROM RESPECTABLE AUTHORS, OR BY FAMILIAR PHRASES OF UNDISPUTED AUTHORITY.

REVISED AND ENLARGED,

BY CHAUNCEY A. GOODRICH,

PROFESSOR IN YALE COLLEGE.

WITH PRONOUNCING VOCABULARIES OF SCRIPTURE, CLASSICAL, AND GEOGRAPHICAL NAMES.

SPRINGFIELD, MASS.

PUBLISHED BY GEORGE AND CHARLES MERRIAM,

CORNER OF MAIN AND STATE STREETS.

1848.

*A title page from the 1848 edition of the Merriam-Webster dictionary. George and Charles
Merriam began publishing Noah Webster's dictionary after they bought the rights in 1843.
Courtesy of the Jones Library, Amherst.*

he was forty he was a director and the clerk of the company — which is
the New England equivalent of the secretary of the corporation. He had
become president in 1934. Man with a long nose and sharp eyes, he

looked, I thought, as a city Yankee ought to look back of the British-tailored influence of Boston in the cities in the country and not on the sea.

He talked with dry humor and practical philosophy. He contemplated the New England past and future with calmness but not without pride and not without hope. He was a rooted man, and chain stores did not please him. He was, I felt, typical of his place and position without being tagged with it. He lived in suburban Longmeadow, which is a rich man's town (82 per cent of the inhabitants own their homes, 202 people out of a thousand file income-tax returns, the highest in both cases in New England). He was not only the expected Congregationalist, Republican, Rotarian, he had also been president of the Longmeadow Historical Society which has filled the old Storrs parsonage with a fine collection of colonial furniture. In the Merriam Company, he stood on his own hard heels as president, not being connected with either the tribe of the three Merriam brothers, or the newer tribe of the three Baker generations.

Mr. Munroe, who had been expecting me, took me into an old-fashioned paneled board room. There under a portrait of the over-all-presiding Noah (another, better picture had been sent to a world's fair), he introduced me to Ingham C. Baker and Lewis L. McShane. By Merriam hundred-year standards Mr. McShane, a well upholstered pleasant gentleman, is a newcomer from Kansas — out of education, I think — into the book-building tradition which has extended from Webster to Dr. William Allan Neilson, president of Smith College and editor-in-chief of the newest big dictionary. Baker is, like Mr. Munroe, on the book selling side. He is the grandson of that Orlando M. Baker who came from the West to enter the company in the 1870's (president, 1904-19), and the son of Asa George Baker (president, 1922-34) who is now chairman of the board. He has a cousin, Harris W. Baker, also grandson of Orlando, who is now clerk of the corporation. There is not a Merriam in the company now; there never was a Webster. But some of the Merriam descendants still own stock.

We talked about the business, its history, its size. The main thing I felt about its strength was the belief in the book. They turn out books by the thousands and deal in words by the hundred thousand. But there is a sense of responsibility about each word and a determination to assume that responsibility cost what it may in technical specialists, in scholars, in the search for citations. Printing and so publishing may be the true grandparent of mass production. But the quality of the product, about which more and more New Englanders are talking in a competitively difficult mass production age, is nowhere in New England given greater emphasis nor more profound faith than I found in the old Myrick Building in Springfield.

Today Webster is a name and not very much more. From it Merriam provided the productive continuity in understanding that no product is ever perfect. When they called in Chauncey Goodrich to supervise the first Merriam-Webster Dictionary — which appeared in 1847, four years after Webster died — he was not merely Webster's son-in-law. Even so early in New England, businesses were probably suffering from the presence in them of men who were just sons-in-law. Goodrich was a scholar in his own head. Dr. Noah Porter, who made the book better after him, was scholar, too, sufficiently able to be called to the Presidency of Yale. The procession of scholars, who have steadily built new and better dictionaries under Webster's name, down to Dr. William Allan Neilson and all the specialists in diverse fields who helped make the latest dictionary, were called by men of commerce who realized from the beginning that the best business was the best book. Such men may be more important than the scholars in New England. At a time when the pressures in many industries are for cheaper, cheaper goods, rather than better, better ones, success in the commerce of the dictionary may be at least a symbol.

Of course, it is simpler as well as wiser for a company with a product that is an accepted standard to keep its quality high and higher than it is for a maker of textiles or shoes or anything else in a fierce industrial competition related chiefly to price. It is all right to talk about quality, but if the chain stores demand price in purchases the quality has got to come down or the plant will have to shut down. Ralph Waldo Emerson, whom the Merriam Company likes to quote about the world beating a road to the house of a man who made better chairs or knives, crucibles or church organs, had never seen a chain store. Sadder or better, in recent years the world has been going to cluttered counters which sell cheaper chairs or knives, crucibles or church organs. Drugstores have been selling a good part of them between the prescription counter and the soda fountain. But quality remains in New England factories as well as in the dictionary offices where scholarship is steadily spurred to make a better product for a world-wide sale.

Not only does quality remain: Around it also in New England there persists the character which is the basis of quality.

From *A Southerner Discovers New England* by Jonathan Daniels. Macmillan, 1940.

TIMOTHY LEARY

Classical High School, Springfield's late renowned college prep high school, had its share of famous graduates. In his memoirs Flashbacks, *graduate Timothy Leary, the Harvard professor who became known as the "high priest" of lysergic acid diethylamide, recounts his troubles with aristocratic principal William C. Hill. Leary's rebellious disposition got him into hot water even before the 1960s when he advised young people to "turn on, tune in, and drop out."*

Flashbacks

My desire to fashion new educational methods based on the imprinting capacities of the brain was undoubtedly due to my own unfortunate educational experiences in high school and my first two colleges.

In 1935, Classical High School was an imposing institution, reputed to be one of the best "college prep" schools in New England. Approaching the wide stairs one expected to see Plato, Aristotle, Andrew Carnegie and Herbert Hoover, all of them dressed in togas, bearing the tablets of wisdom. To me, this Protestant Mind Factory was a bewildering place populated with superior creatures. Girls in bobby sox, saddle shoes, and bulging soft sweaters dazzled me with their Episcopalian glamour. The older boys were all huge swaggering jocks being groomed for Harvard, Princeton, Dartmouth. I was intimidated.

The principal of Classical High, William C. Hill, was a towering man with a Supreme Court justice shock of white hair. It was his custom to assemble incoming freshmen classes and explain the motto of the school — the Kantian Categorical Imperative — "No one has a right to do that which if everyone did would destroy society." When escorting adult visitors the principal would stop students in the hallway to have us parrot this totalitarian doctrine.

For two years I was withdrawn socially and confused academically. I commuted from outlying Indian Orchard, carrying my peasant paperbag lunch. I studied diligently but without comprehension, especially in Latin class, where I was alternately aroused and irritated by hotshot goody-goody girls from snooty Longmeadow suburbs who could decline nouns with precision. I tried out for athletic teams, but my scrawny body and pipestem limbs proved inadequate. In my eagerness to excel I joined the debating team, the traffic squad, the glee club, and the school paper. But it was all kid stuff.

Then I encountered a gene-pool that was to play a central role in my future life. I started hanging out with a group of Jewish students. Before high school I had never known anyone Jewish. In the New England of the 1930s one's friends came from one's own religious and economic grouping.

I was delighted to encounter these strange kids, so different from WASPs and Catholics, smart, brash, funny, worldly, earthy, and playful. Probably because I admired and liked them for the right reasons, they adopted me as the only Christian in their set. We played poker and tennis and discussed sports and girls. They showed me that the world was bigger, wilder and more delightfully varied than my insular background had led me to believe. From them I learned to look beyond the conventional.

My sexual immaturity was glaringly obvious to my new friends. I listened in awe to their tales of the female anatomy. We were all obsessed with fleetingly seen breasts and flashing thighs. "Her dress was up to her neck and I could see what she had for breakfast" was a phrase used at least three times a day

My new friends contributed further to my education by lending me dirty comic books, in which Jiggs turned Maggie from nagging wife to enraptured concubine with his three-foot-long member and Olive Oyl threw silken panties to the wind, screaming with pleasure at the ministrations of the equally endowed Popeye.

At sixteen I obtained a driver's license. With it came a job as a delivery boy for Uncle Arthur's boutique. I had mobility, I had money — and sitting at the desk in front of mine was Rosalind, the wildest sexiest girl in the school. After classes I would walk to the store, package dresses to be home-delivered, pick up Rosalind at her house, and zoom around the exclusive sections of the city, stopping on deserted streets to smooch with my sophisticated girlfriend.

One night she led me into her family's sun porch, lay down on the couch, and held her arms out to me. I lay on top of her. We kissed madly. Rosalind moved her hips and guided me into my first fuck.

With my hormones activated, I changed from a shy, reserved youth to a brash, confident extrovert. Rosalind and I became high school steadies and popular stars in the adolescent social life. Within six months I became president of the school senate and editor of the paper.

Rosalind's sophistication gave me a worldly perspective that made high school activities seem childishly simple. We shared that delicious sense of sexual complicity that gave us courage to innovate. Rosalind brought a playful style to the school paper, contributing to a racy, funny gossip column full of innuendoes that the kids loved and the teachers puzzled over. We ran several comical exposes. We put out a special program issue for the big football game with *Tech*. At year's end our paper swept the competition and was named the outstanding high school publication in western Massachusetts.

But in spite of our success I got in deep trouble with Principal Hill. I was called into his office after writing a particularly fiery editorial suggesting that the Categorical Imperative was totalitarian and un-American in glorifying the welfare of the state over the rights of the individual.

Mr. Hill stood stiffly behind his desk holding in his hand my attendance record, incontrovertible evidence that I had been playing hooky with some regularity. "Do you realize that you have skipped school more than any other student in your class? I suppose your absences were caused by your editorial duties?"

"There's a lot of running around involved in the job, sir."

Mr. Hill turned his back on me and looked out the window onto State Street and St. Michael's Cathedral.

"I could and I should expel you," he said, "but I won't. I have known your family for a long time and I know how this would crush them."

"Thank you, sir," I said.

"One final thing. Are you considering asking me to write you a letter of recommendation for college entrance?"

I nodded.

"My advice to you is: don't. Do you understand?"

"Yes sir," I said.

From *Flashbacks: An Autobiography* by Timothy Leary. Jeremy P. Tarcher, 1983.

DAVID BLACK

David Black, of Springfield and Amherst College, has written The Plague Years: A Chronicle of AIDS, Murder at the Met, *and* Medicine Man: A Young Doctor on the Brink of the Twenty-First Century. *Black's autobiographical novel about growing up in Springfield,* Like Father *(1978), recounts his relationship with his offbeat father. This selection relates a fictional account of the father's run-in with the FBI for organizing a teachers union. His real-life father Henry Black taught at Springfield's Classical High School in the 1950s and 1960s.*

Like Father

Some years after he moved to Springfield, he started agitating for a teachers' union. The union that existed was — he claimed — a company union, which never disagreed with the School Committee. It was called the Springfield Educational Association, the SEA, which to the naive eye and ear of a child spelled *sea*, so I always imagined the SEA to be an oceanic force, which my father — like King Canute on the beach — was trying to stop. He seemed heroic, but even his heroism seemed a little foolish.

To call attention to the demands he thought a real union should make — better wages, better retirement and medical benefits, a better life insurance plan — my father launched a strike all by himself. It was a curiously gentle strike. My father did not want to deprive his students of an education, an education he felt he was best equipped to give them, so he limited his picketing to after-school hours.

When the final bell rang, he would take off his suit jacket and put on a heavy plaid wool shirt, the kind construction workers wore; and he would march up and down in front of the high school where he taught, carrying a sign that listed his grievances. He crunched through the drifts of dried leaves. He called to the people looking sideways out the windows of their cars, which they slowed as they passed him. He stood, bouncing from one foot to the other — like a boxer in training — to keep warm; and he argued with the hecklers who surrounded and baited him. A few of his students, unsure whether to jeer or defer to him, paused to watch and listen; and my father with quick impatient gestures waved them closer and, trying to be fair, explained, not only his position, but the antagonistic position of the SEA and the School Committee. The boys, their blue notebooks held stiff-armed close to their thighs, and the girls, their notebooks pressed like shields against their breasts, asked no questions of him, but snickered and murmured to each other while my father lectured.

I was eleven, and I begged to be allowed to picket with him. He made a sandwich board for me out of shirt cardboards taped together, which said: "Teachers have families to support too" on one side and "Support the AFT" — the American Federation of Teachers, the local branch of which my father was trying to start — on the other. While my father harangued the crowd, I stood beside him, glancing from one unfriendly face to another. We stayed out until twilight. As we walked home together, our placards rolled under our arms, the streetlamps came on, very yellow in the dusk. I used the excuse of a chill to turn up my jacket collar as hoodlums did. My father, as silent with me as he was voluble with his students and the crowd of curiosity seekers, hunched his shoulders against the cold, which gave his shadow humps on each side of his head, making it look like the shadow of a large bird with folded wings. When we reached our house, which was at the top of a hill, my father stopped and turned, looking down at the city cupped in the river valley below us; and, breaking his silence, he gestured down the slope and asked, "Think you can beat me to the end of the block?"

We sprinted the few hundred feet to the curb. The lights of the city and, beyond the city, the bridges over the wide Connecticut River and, on the other shore, West Springfield glimmered in the autumn dark. The smell of the night was as clear, as chilly, and as sharp as glass needles in the nostrils, painfully pure. The race — which we often ran after coming home from picketing — became our ritual, a moment shared before we went inside to the bright, supper-smelling house. Despite his limp, my father could run fast. He always beat me, always said, as we huffed back up the block home, that he was getting old and it wouldn't be too long before I beat him.

Two or three times a week, after supper, my father's cronies stopped by the house to play jazz and argue politics. Frank Polishook, a Polish science teacher, was as short as my father, but bulkier. He had grown up on a farm outside Springfield and still had a tough farm boy's muscles, which bulged on his forearms and upper arms like wet twisted towels. Polishook was an anarchist, who had hewed a bomb shelter out of the granite bedrock on which he had built his house. The shelter, a damp dim chamber that smelled like stagnant pond water, had a table, a few kerosene lanterns, and dozens of cartons of canned goods. When my father took me to visit Polishook and see the shelter, we sat, listening to the breeze blow across the door with the low whistle of someone blowing across the top of a soda bottle, while Polishook described the improvements he intended to make: air filter, generator, paneling, wooden floor, chemical toilet. The room was twelve feet by fourteen feet.

"I'd rather blow up," my father said.

"I'm going to put a chess board down here," Polishook said. "And books."

By the end of the fifties, Polishook had become a John Birchite, his anarchism leading him down an alley of self-interest. His shelter, which had been enlarged and elaborated, looked like a den. It had knotty-pine walls, an oak floor, acoustical tiles on the ceiling, a bar, a generator-powered refrigerator in which he kept bottles of Polish vodka mixed with sweet raspberry syrup, a pool table, a rack of rifles, and — as he had promised my father — a chess set and a library, which included *The Encyclopaedia Britannica*, *The Book of Knowledge*, *The Harvard Classics*, and bound back issues of *Popular Mechanics*, *Popular Science*, and *Field & Stream*. He had installed a wood-burning furnace and painted it to look like the whale in Walt Disney's cartoon film *Pinocchio*. Little by little, he had bought all the land surrounding his house, so finally he owned an entire mountain of five hundred acres, on which he hunted deer. On weekends, he lived in his bomb shelter and cooked his venison on a propane stove while listening to his shortwave radio.

Johnny Butter, a history teacher, who wore knickerbockers and drove a Packard, also stopped at our house after supper. He was a Trotskyite, whose ancestors had followed William Pynchon from Roxbury, Massachusetts, to Springfield in 1636. He lived on Crescent Hill in a Victorian mansion that was always dark because he refused to use any but forty-watt bulbs in his light fixtures. He thought brighter bulbs were wasteful. Very thin and very tall, he habitually stooped, his body forming a question mark, and his expression was puzzled, as though the question he punctuated could not be answered. He claimed to be physiologically unable to cry; his tear ducts did not function normally. As a result, whenever he was sad enough to weep, he would suffer extreme pain. During the twenty years my father knew him, Butter spent a great deal of time and money going to specialists who promised to cure his ailment, to let him cry.

Polishook and Butter, like the others who visited — the Henry Wallace Democrats, the Stalinists, the DeLeon and Norman Thomas Socialists, the old Wobblies — refused at first to support my father's efforts to start a union until it was decided what politics the union would adhere to. My father, a pluralist, wanted to include every political sect, Republicans as well as pro-Soviets. He did not believe in any kind of closed shop. He did not even want the union, if it became successful, to have a stranglehold on the teaching community.

The teachers would drink and rant at each other, while my mother herded my sister and me into my father's study upstairs on the second floor. Halfway through the evening, when the arguing devolved into personal attacks, or, occasionally, thrown punches and broken furniture, my father would take out his trumpet and start playing one of the old jazz tunes he knew. Polishook sat at the piano, the stool pushed far back, his arms straight out as though he were about to swan-dive into the keys, his fingers amazingly nimble. Butter dragged his drums from the trunk of his car and, having set them up in front of the fireplace, played leaning far forward, his head turned, his ear next to the skins, his eyes closed. The other teachers retrieved their instruments from the front hall where they left them when they came in, or sat — the ones who didn't play instruments — tapping their feet and humming or singing along. My sister and I would slip downstairs to sprawl on the floor, eating pretzels and gulping beer from forgotten opened bottles.

Of the leftists who congregated at my parents house, Polishook and Butter were the first to overcome their objections to the new union; and they joined out of affection for my father, not because they agreed with his tactics or politics. But Polishook and Butter — local characters — were popular at their schools, and they were obstinate. They dogged their co-workers through the halls and hounded them at faculty meetings. One by one, they signed them up. The union grew, and although it was still small compared to the SEA, the School Committee became nervous.

To discredit my father and destroy his union, the School Committee asked the F.B.I. to investigate him. The F.B.I., grandstanding in order to disgrace my father in front of his students — who, they were afraid, might have been politically infected by his radical ideas — came to my father's class during school hours to ask him to go with them for questioning.

When the agents arrived in his classroom, my father was dressed in a shoulder-length white wig, spirit-gummed mustache and beard, and a ratty gray caftan. His face was made up as sallow as a bruise, and he had puttied his large nose to make it larger. As was his custom, my father was acting out a scene from Shakespeare, trying to demonstrate to his students that the plays were stories to watch, not merely texts to read. He was, that day, teaching *The Merchant of Venice*; he was disguised as Shylock.

The F.B.I. agents took my father to an office across from the City Hall and next door to the Court Square Theater, which alternated movies with vaudeville. "As they questioned me," my father told us, "I looked out the window at the alley where someone was walking greyhounds from an act. He'd come out the door with a greyhound on a leash, stroll up and down a few times, and then go back in. A few minutes later, he'd come out the door again with, I assume, another greyhound on a leash, walk him up and down, and go back in. A few minutes later, he'd come out with another dog, walk him, and go back in. This went on for the hour I was in the office. I don't know why he didn't walk them all at once."

The F.B.I. questioning was designed simply to give the School Committee an excuse to fire my father. This was during the early McCarthy years. My father sued the School Committee for reinstatement, arguing in open letters to the city's two newspapers that anyone who understood politics knew that the socialist party to which he belonged was more anti-Soviet than the House Un-American Activities Committee. Russia had betrayed the Revolution. He couldn't forgive that. He demanded that J. Edgar Hoover run a real investigation on him and make the findings public. He had nothing to be afraid or ashamed of in his past.

Having noticed how disarmed the F.B.I. agents had been by his Shylock costume when they arrested him (my father had refused to take the disguise off; he had classes to teach all day and it would have taken him too long to get back in costume after the questioning), my father found a lawyer who agreed to put him on the stand dressed as Marx, Engels, Lenin, Trotsky, and Stalin, and to let my father expound upon the differences among the various socialist and communist dogmas. My father wanted publicity because he saw the trial as a chance to educate the public politically. He had faith in his neighbors.

The judge, a man named Conor with a red raised birthmark disfiguring half his face, was a Catholic. Having been educated by the Jesuits, he admired my father's logical mind as much as he deplored his politics. He allowed the trial to run its flamboyant course, patiently allowing my father to make his case, while he sat with his elbow on his chair arm and his birthmarked cheek resting, hidden, in his upraised hand.

The last day of the trial was the first day it snowed that year. My father stopped in the middle of his speech and, crossing to the window, said simply, "Look, it's snowing. It's too beautiful a day to talk any more politics."

It was a beautiful day. The snow, caught against the mullions of the high windows, spread across the glass, making the room darker. The radiators hissed, thin filaments of steam spraying from the valves. The courtroom seemed more closed, cozier. Sounds — spectators' coughs, the rustle of papers as lawyers shuffled their notes — seemed louder. My father thanked the court, the jury, and the visitors for bearing with him and sat down abruptly. He was not in costume. It was his day to address the jury as himself. But he fingered his cheek as though he were trying to tug off some final mask of flesh, as though the teacher who was fighting for his job was as much a disguise as the radical leaders he had been impersonating.

The judge cleared his throat in the quiet, sat up straight in his squeaking chair, and said, "Yes, it is a beautiful day outside." He called a lunch recess.

Later, after the trial was over, one of the jurors admitted to a friend that she had been charmed by my father's sudden interruption of his speech to comment on the weather. That had decided her to vote in his favor. The rumor piggybacked its way on one conversation after another until it reached my father, who said, "I thought so. When Emily Dickinson was at Mount Holyoke College, she once wrote on a test paper that it was too beautiful a day to be in class and left. She got an 'A.'"

The jury found for my father. The judge, after the trial was over, paused in the doorway of his chambers and, getting my father's attention with a crook of his finger, quoted St. Augustine: "Bear with me, my God, while I say something of my wit, Thy gift, and on what dotage I wasted it."

My father, who had not memorized any St. Augustine, but, after eleven years in college, had memorized some Horace, responded in Latin: "*Adhuc sub judice lis est*," which means "The proceedings are still in front of the judge" or, more colloquially, "The jury's still out on that." My father did not believe he was wasting his intelligence on unworthy doctrines.

From *Like Father* by David Black. Red Dembner Enterprises, 1978.

MAX EHRLICH

Max Ehrlich was a Springfield native who moved to Southern California,
where he wrote television and film screenplays and the novels The Big Eye *and*
The Cult. *In* The Reincarnation of Peter Proud *(1974), Ehrlich tells the*
semi-autobiographical story of a UCLA professor who gradually discovers he
led a previous life in 1940s "Riverside" (aka Springfield). The book became a
bestseller.

The book conveys the hazy memories of Springfield that anyone might have
who had moved away in the late 1940s and returned to the city after urban
renewal twenty-five years later. Protagonist Peter Proud fails to recognize
much of the demolished downtown, but does recall the view of the city from the
Connecticut River and from the Campanile. He also encounters Springfield's
iconic statue "The Puritan" (called "Cotton Mather" in Peter Proud*).*

The Reincarnation of Peter Proud *became a movie starring Michael*
Sarrazin, Jennifer O'Neil, and Margot Kidder. The movie has some standing in
Springfield as one of the few Hollywood movies filmed there.

The Reincarnation of Peter Proud

It was a hot spring day. The broiling highway slipped under the
wheels of his car, an endless strip of shining white concrete. He was
tooling along at a steady seventy. The sound of the motor and the
singing of the tires mesmerized him into a kind of stupor. He had to fight
to keep his eyes open. On the right of the turnpike, the great green
roadsigns loomed up and then whooshed by, their bold white letters
shimmering in the heat haze. There were still a hundred miles to go
before he reached Boston. Once on the plane, he would sleep.

A big river appeared on the left. He had not been in this particular
area before, but he knew it was the Connecticut River. At the moment
it lay supine, a broad gray snake dozing in a bath of faint mist, its shiny
skin rippling and glinting a little in the sun. Beyond, on the other bank,
was a city.

Suddenly he was wide awake.

He stared at the river. Here, from this elevation, he could see that it
had a peculiar reverse-S curve. And beyond it, the city.

It looked like any of the other cities he had seen. Yet, it did not. There
was something about it, something in its contour, the way it was de-
signed. The way the hills rose beyond the city. Farther down, three
bridges spanned the river. One, an automobile bridge, white in color.
Another a railroad trestle. And the third, an old steel bridge, its girders

painted red.

In the dream, the river in the distance had this same reverse-S curve. Still, that wasn't particularly unusual — the river probably made a lot of similar curves as it meandered down toward the ocean from the north. Yet this particular reverse-S was near the city.

In the dream there had been two bridges, not three. But the white bridge looked comparatively new. He seemed to remember the trestle, and the bridge with the red girders. But maybe he was simply reading them into the dreams.

He looked for the tower, the tall, delicate Florentine rectangle towering over a public square. The one with the spectator's balcony where he had stood, in his hallucination, and looked out over the city and down on the square itself.

But there was no tower. And without the tower, it wasn't the town. Yet — yet — there was something about the place. He saw the big turnpike sign rushing up on his right: Riverside. Exit One Mile.

Riverside. It meant nothing to him. It jogged no memory. It was just another name. The smart thing was to go right by it, and get on to Boston. And from there, home.

But he found himself easing down his speed and moving over to the right lane and toward the exit ramp. Almost as though his head were saying one thing, his hands another.

He crossed the big white bridge and drove into the city. Bridge Street. River Street. Columbus Avenue. The names on the street signs meant nothing to him. There were the usual gas stations, used-car lots, wholesale houses, cafeterias, and drugstores. The usual crowds on the streets, the usual buses, the usual traffic. Just another town.

But again, there was something about it. He saw an occasional building that seemed to look familiar. The curve of a street. The way the river and the opposite bank looked from here. The factories on the other side, smoke eddying from their chimneys. They seemed familiar, and yet they did not. And he thought again, Take it easy. This isn't the place. It can't be. You want to see something badly enough, you can see it.

He was hungry. He decided he'd have a bite and push on. Parking the car on what seemed to be a main street, he remembered that he had run out of cash. He'd have to cash some traveler's checks. There was a bank just across the street. The sign said: Puritan Bank and Trust. He walked inside.

And then Peter saw him. *Cotton Mather.*

The big Puritan stood on a pedestal at the rear of the bank. He was a huge effigy, larger than life size, perhaps ten feet tall. He looked exactly as he had in the dream. Dark red tunic, caught at the waist with a leather band. Over this, a sleeveless jacket of dull gray. A doublet and leather

Springfield's campanile in the 1920s. From the Clifton Johnson Collection; courtesy of the Jones Library, Amherst.

hose lined with oilskin. A large conical broadbrim hat. Broad white collar of linen. The face hard and stern. The eyes cold and dead.

Well, old friend, thought Peter, it's you at last. We have finally met. . . .

He walked toward the rear of the bank, toward the effigy. He heard his steps echoing on the floor. Dimly, he was aware of the business of the bank going on around him — the people standing in lines to complete their transactions, the cashiers behind the glass wall, the buzz and hum of voices. The area in which the Puritan stood on his pedestal had been roped off. Peter looked up at the effigy. The old Puritan towered above him, gigantic, frightening. Exactly as he had in the dream. The cold eyes seemed to be looking down, glaring at him.

"Everything all right, sir?"

Peter whirled around. A uniformed bank guard was staring at him curiously. Peter was shaking. He tried to pull himself together. Finally he managed a smile.

"That figure up there. I've never seen anything like it before. It's very — impressive."

The guard smiled. "That's one word for it. A lot of people around here think it's just plain ugly. The directors of the bank have been talking about getting rid of it. But I don't know — people in town are used to seeing it here. You know — it's part of the bank, tradition, and all that. Some of 'em would miss old Cotton if they took him away. Looks real lifelike, doesn't he?

"Yes, he does." He stared at the guard. "Is that what everybody calls him — Cotton?"

"Yes, sir. After Cotton Mather. It's kind of a nickname, I guess."

"How long has he — it — been here?"

"Well, of course, it's a kind of trademark for the bank, you might say. Been here ever since the bank has. That would be about forty years. I'll tell you this much. Old Cotton up there is a real dust collector. About every five years we have to throw away his clothes and get him a new set."

"I see." He wanted to turn again and take another long look at the effigy. It wasn't every day you could stare at a dream come true. He knew the Puritan's eyes were only glass, but he had the curious feeling that they were alive and boring into him. He was in the aftermath of shock now. He could feel the gooseflesh all over his body, and he knew he was still shivering. The guard stood there, watching him.

"Where can I cash some traveler's checks?"

"Over there, sir. Any one of those windows." He walked toward one of the windows. He did not look back; he didn't dare. Sweat broke out on his forehead. He knew there couldn't be another figure like that anywhere else in the world. And he had found it. Or had it found him?

This, he thought, was the place where I lived. Before I died. No doubt about it now. Riverside, Massachusetts.

The clerk behind the glass partition cashed Peter's check.

"Noticed you staring at the old witchburner."

"Yes."

The clerk grinned. "Every stranger who walks in here usually stops to take a good look. Catches your eye, if you know what I mean. A great attention-getter." He smiled ruefully. "But how would you like to have that ugly devil staring you in the face every day? The way I have to." The clerk shook his head in distaste.

Peter walked out of the bank and onto the street. He got into the car and started to drive north. Somehow he knew there was a curve just ahead, and then beyond that the intersection of two main avenues. Now he knew he had been here before. Some of the buildings, the older buildings, seemed familiar to him. He drove around the curve, paused for a traffic light, and then without hesitation took the street to the left. State Street, the sign read.

Another turn, this one to the right. And then he saw it. The arched railroad bridge spanning the street just ahead. It was made of gray granite and supported by a small turret-like structure at each end. Just as he had seen it in the dream. Except that now it seemed much grayer than he remembered it.

He drove under the arch and, without hesitation, took the next left. Chestnut Street. It was strange, he thought. He could remember the name of no street in his dreams. Yet, now that he was here, he seemed to know exactly where to go. And he knew precisely what would appear when he turned right on Chestnut.

The public square was there, just as he expected. There was the same green lawn. The same green park benches lining the diagonal walk. The same two statues. The sign said: Court Square.

But there was no tower.

He parked the car and walked into the square. On the site where he had seen the tower, there was now another building. It looked fairly new and was modern in design. Functional, all stainless steel and glass. He saw that it was the town's municipal building. It housed the Superior Court, the Riverside Police Department, the City Clerk's Office, the Department of Parks.

His immediate reaction was one of anger. He had wanted to find that tower there; he had expected it. It had been one of the artifacts in the museum of his memory. Now they had destroyed it, and it seemed like some kind of desecration.

An old man was sitting on a bench reading a newspaper. He wore bifocals and was neatly dressed. Peter walked up to him.

"Excuse me, sir."

The man put down the paper and stared up at him with rheumy blue eyes.

"Yes?"

"Wasn't there a tower here a few years ago?"

"Sure was. They used to call it the Municipal Tower."

"When did they tear it down?"

"Oh, along about 1950. Or maybe it was '51."

"I see."

"They had another name for it, too. The Campanile. Designed it after some tower in Italy. Florence, Venice, somewhere like that. You could see it for miles around. But it was pretty old. The engineers figured it was unsafe, so they tore it down."

"Wasn't there some kind of observation balcony at the top?"

"Yep. Sure was. Great view from there, too. Used to take my grandchildren up there. Personally, I think it was a damned shame they tore it down. The tower looked pretty, standing there. I mean, it made the town. But then, what can you do? The stupid bastards are always tearing down something beautiful and putting up something ugly. Said they had to do it in the name of progress. The real estate was too valuable." The old man snorted. "The same old story. When a fast buck is involved, nobody respects anything."

The man went back to his newspaper. Peter found an empty bench and sat down. He felt faint, giddy. His heart was pounding violently. He thought, all right, let's try to put it together now. Let's try to put it all together.

This is where I lived before I died. Riverside, Massachusetts.

But who was I?

From *The Reincarnation of Peter Proud* by Max Ehrlich. Simon & Schuster, 1974.

DANIEL OKRENT

Daniel Okrent, a former Worthington resident, was the founder and editor of New England Monthly. *One of his projects at the magazine was relating how New England changed since the late 1940s. The following* New England Monthly *article became a photograph book,* The Way We Were: New England Then, New England Now *(1989). The book's photographs depict New England before suburbanization, highways, and television and feature Springfield before urban renewal. Urban renewal is a story that turned out badly in scores of American cities. Okrent conveys a sense of what was lost in Springfield.*

Okrent also is known for his interest in baseball, and has written Nine Innings *(1985), edited* The Ultimate Baseball Book *(1981), and appeared in Ken Burns's "Baseball." He is the editor of* Life.

What Was Lost to Urban Renewal

In some ways, what obliterated Ryan Drug, the neighborhood pharmacy in Springfield, Massachusetts, was an earlier time's taste, so different from what prevails today. Inside Ryan's was a marble and mahogany soda fountain stretching along one wall, a pressed tin ceiling hovering over the glass and wood library cases that harbored the drugstore's stock. When I visited the neighborhood last fall, Donald Ryan, whose grandfather started in 1895 what is now a chain of five stores, presided at the branch that is now just up Main Street from the original store. "I remember when we tore out the soda fountain, replaced the library cases with open gondolas, and put in a dropped acoustical ceiling," Ryan told me. "In the early fifties, those things were old-fashioned, and there was nothing worse than being old-fashioned." He smiled. "Boy, what you'd have to pay for those today!"

Back then, they could have been had for their scrap value. The forties occupied the last moment when what we now value as antique, charming, or quaint still surrounded us. After the war, the newly stoked engines of production remade nearly every commonplace item America knew. The physical manifestations of the past became objects of derision and neglect. But, even more than the soda fountain and the tin ceiling, what really affronted the taste of the fifties was the neighborhood that Ryan Drug served. The North End had long been Springfield's immigrant quarter, and by World War II it had become a largely black enclave. It was a thickly populated neighborhood, "full of life," Ryan recalled, but, by the perceptions of the time, hopelessly ill-suited to the people who lived there.

Of course, the act of perception is shaped as much by the baggage carried by the perceiver as by the evidence that sits before him. The sensibility that could see no value in a marble soda fountain was likely to be blind to anything that wasn't modern. "Plastic" had not yet become an epithet; boxes of brick and glass were admired for their sleekness, their *new*ness.

Consequently, when the nation looked at its inner-city neighborhoods, it was sensibility as much as sympathy that brought in the bulldozers. "Urban renewal" meant urban destruction; Americans were so obsessed with newness that, according to the federal criteria that determined whether housing was substandard, residential buildings of a certain age were *by legal definition* suspect. Neighborhoods such as the North End, where the vast majority of homes were turn-of-the-century antiques, were doomed. Springfield still calls itself The City of Homes; by the mid-sixties, though, it had used federal and state funds to destroy 1,300 of them, along with 355 business establishments, including Ryan Drug.

A step behind the bulldozers came the construction teams. The 105-acre renewal site saw low-rise, low-density government offices and private businesses rise on the rubble that once housed such people as David Rankin, a newsboy. Rankin lived at home with his widowed mother on Tenth Street in the North End, in a two-story wooden house with a picket fence in front. Then renewal wiped out the house — wiped out Tenth Street, in fact. Rankin, a black man who had sold his papers at the corner of Main and Bridge streets for nearly two decades, disappeared. Peter Slepchuk, who with his brother Walter has owned a pinball arcade-turned-video game parlor on Main Street for forty-two years, remembers Rankin as a sweet-natured, slightly dull-witted soul who quite likely wouldn't have been able to cope with the wrench of forced change. "I guess he just died," Slepchuk told me.

Had he not, Rankin would probably have been installed in one of the five towers of the publicly assisted Riverview Apartments, along with the rest of the North Enders who didn't know better than to live in older homes that did not meet the era's standards of taste. There, he would have found no bus service to get him to his downtown street corner, no grocery store in which to shop. The neighborhood stores of the North End didn't reopen at Riverview: the few blocks' walk to Rankin's downtown corner now belong to IBM, to faceless medical offices, and to the new plant of Springfield Newspapers, the company — now owned by a chain, of course — that made the papers he sold each day.

The newspaper firm, as it happened, put up its dull loaf of a building on precisely the spot where Ryan Drug had once stood. Don Ryan relocated on another treeless block of Main Street. You know the store — there's one like it everywhere: An asphalt parking lot fronts Ryan Drug and the other establishments in its ugly little mall. Inside the drugstore, fluorescent lights and electronic antitheft devices gaze upon anonymous rows of packaged products. But there's another expression of modern American emblazoned in Ryan's window: a sign proclaiming that the prescription department accepts Medex 3, Medicaid, Master Health Plus, Health New England, Healthy Start, and seven other reimbursement plans.

On my next stop I'd learn that the same social impulse that in time would have provided David Rankin with subsidized medicines might have saved the North End from the bulldozers. The final fruits of a broadening democracy are empowerment and entitlement. Back when the North End demolition was proposed, public hearings in Springfield's Municipal Auditorium brought forth the testimony of 106 speakers — only two of whom spoke out against the program. The postwar impulse toward newness ignited the entire idea of urban renewal, but it was fueled by an abiding willingness to concede to government and to the business community the shaping prerogatives of our culture. Then, in a few years, this part of the social contract would be ripped up and re-drafted. As it turned out, the two lonely dissidents at the Municipal Auditorium were heralds of a great cultural shift.

From "The Way We Were" by Daniel Okrent. *New England Monthly*, October 1988.

GEORGE V. HIGGINS

George V. Higgins, best-selling author of more than two dozen books, including The Friends of Eddie Coyle, Outlaws, *and* Bomber's Law: A Novel, *started his career as a journalist in Springfield in the mid-1960s. While serving as Associated Press bureau chief in Springfield and attending Boston College Law School, Higgins wrote a paper under the guidance of Dean Father Robert Drinan on the racial tensions in Springfield during the summer of 1965. The opening of this unpublished account describes the incident at the Octagon Lounge that led to charges of police brutality, demonstrations, and community upheaval.*

The Hot Summer of '65

I t was a still, warm, peaceful night in the City of Homes, and some of the citizens went out for a glass of beer or a tall cold drink and a little entertainment, a few hours of not thinking about being tired, or the things that bothered them. In the morning the problems would still be there to be faced, but in the morning it would be Saturday and you could sleep late and catch a ballgame in the afternoon, or play a round of golf, if you got up early. It was Friday night. It was time to relax a little, and catch your breath.

But relaxation in Springfield resembles relaxation in other communities where the people come in two or more colors: it is done pretty much along ethnic lines.

There are about 170,000 people living in Springfield. About 17,000 of them are Negroes. The white people are distributed geographically throughout the city, mostly on economic lines. The Negroes, ninety per cent of them, live within one square mile in the east-southeastern sector of the community. The Springfield Urban League reported recently that sixty per cent of the housing occupied by non-white persons is substandard in Springfield. Eighteen percent of that occupied by white is substandard. And one effort to cure the situation, the Riverview Housing project, has created another black ghetto. Thirty per cent of the city's non-white families live in what the Office of Economic Opportunity in Washington defines as poverty.

The people from the one square mile don't relax in the same places as the white people. They live with Negroes, and their children attend one of the seven elementary schools in Springfield with more than fifty-one per cent of its enrollment Negro. The Buckingham Junior High School is in that square mile — it's more than ninety per cent Negro. When the people from that area go out on Friday nights, they go to Negro bars.

On the night of July 16th, 1965, the Octagon Lounge at 146 Rifle Street was such a bar.

Rifle Street cuts off Allen Street right in front of the Springfield Armory, Water Shops, Ordnance Corps Plant. You go west down Rifle past the four-story grey-painted stone apartment building known as Lincoln Hall. The Mill River Cafe and Delahanty's Drugs are located on the ground floor. Next door there's a Humble Oil gas station, and next to that, right at the intersection of Rifle heading west and Central Street running roughly north and south, is the building that used to be the Octagon Lounge. Across Rifle Street there's a low fence, and the ground slopes away to the brook. The land rises steeply on the other side of the water to a long building used by the armory.

The Octagon Lounge and Cafe is now Ciriaco's Lounge and Steak Room. It occupies the ground floor of what apparently started out as a two-story brick house, with another half-story of wooden superstructure added later. The house itself is painted white. The facing of the lounge and restaurant is red brick. There are two billboards on top of the building, facing east toward the Water Shops.

If you go in the Rifle Street entrance, there is a bowling machine on your left and a substantial bar on your right. The floor is black and white linoleum. The paneling is light birch and the chairs are upholstered in green plastic.

Beyond the bar is the restaurant section, also accessible from the outside by a door opening on Central Street. The paneling in the restaurant is light birch and the chairs and benches are covered with green plastic. The room is divided up with birch partitions about as high as the third button on the shirt of a man who is standing up.

If you go out the Central Street door of Ciriaco's, you find yourself across the way from Lee Pulsifer's heating business, run in a one-and-one-half story grey building. North of the restaurant is a driveway wide enough for two cars. There's a cyclone fence set into a concrete base, and on the other side is the grey three-story wooden tenement numbered 508 and 510 Central Street, where Stewart Weldon lived on the night of July 16th, 1965.

There was a good crowd at the Octagon that night. Jimmie Ray and the Four Sharps were on the bandstand and the doorman, Lester E. (Skippy) Williams Jr., had a turnaway crowd on his hands by ten-thirty. There were people waiting outside on the narrow sidewalk to pay the ninety-nine cents admission into the lounge for dancing. Those who wanted to get into the bar were accommodated as they came.

That meant there were about 150 people in the Octagon just before midnight. There's no indication that they were unruly or more than normally noisy. Almost all of them were Negro.

Just before midnight, a cruiser operated by the Springfield Police Department came down Rifle Street. The men in the cruiser were Patrolmen Thomas Sheehan and Michael Shumway. They are white.

The cruiser stopped near the Octagon and Sheehan got out. He began to write out a parking ticket. There was a car parked partly on the sidewalk on Central Street, which is narrow, and Sheehan intended to tag it.

The car belonged to Albert Lee. On the night of July 16th he was 23 years old. He lived at 175 Walnut Street in Springfield. He had just arrived at the Octagon Lounge with a friend. He is Negro. The friend was Stewart Weldon. He lived next door at 510 Central Street. He was 24 years old. He is a Negro.

Someone in the Octagon Lounge told Albert Lee and Stewart Weldon that the police were outside tagging Lee's car. Lee and Weldon went outside to see what was happening.

By 1:00 a.m. on July 17th, 1965, eighteen persons had been arrested in the area around the Octagon Lounge. Policemen commanded that night by Det. Sgt. James F. Williams, would testify that between 200 and 400 persons had raged about in the street, shouting curses and hurling bottles and rocks at the officers, resisting and breaking arrest, and necessitating the summoning of every available prowl car and policeman in the City of Homes to the intersection of Rifle and Central Streets to handle a disturbance that approached if it did not constitute, a riot.

Seventeen of those arrested were Negroes. They and other civilians present charged that the policemen had set upon them without provocation, beaten them with clubs, abused them and shouted racial insults at them, threatened them with bodily harm and death, and in general employed the most shocking brutality to injure inoffensive people who had given no reason for the police to bother them.

An uncivilized, unlawful, dangerous disturbance, said the police. A vicious display of lawless police savagery, said the civilians. At 1:00 a.m. on July 17th the summer of 1965 was not over in Springfield. There would be more warm, still nights for movie-going and shopping. There was as yet no trouble in the community as a whole, whatever bad feeling there was between the police and the people they had arrested. But trouble was available. It was ready for the asking.

From *The Five-Month Summer* by George V. Higgins. 1966.

JOHN EDGAR WIDEMAN

John Edgar Wideman, one of many nationally known writers to have taught at the University of Massachusetts, was a finalist in non-fiction for the National Book Award for his memoirs about his family, Fatheralong. *Wideman's final chapter, "Picking Up My Father at the Springfield Station," treats the currents of racist feeling in the Pioneer Valley. Wideman takes a harsh look at the underside of Springfield off Interstate 91, around the Amtrak station at 1:30 a.m. For Wideman, Springfield is an example of what has gone wrong with America, a sentiment shared by many north of the Mount Holyoke Notch.*

Wideman has won a MacArthur grant and two PEN Faulkner Awards and has written several books which have received wide acclaim.

Picking Up My Father at the Springfield Station

After the exit ramp on I-91 East, to reach the Springfield railroad station you keep bearing right through anonymous arteries of street and road in various stages of finish. No people here, only concrete and emptiness, blowing crap. You could be on the wrong side of a backdrop whose face is painted to seem like a city. You see braces, scaffolding, steel beams, and wires jerryrigged to support the illusion of city, stuff the audience isn't supposed to notice from their seats out front. Filth and grit accumulating for years because no one cleans backstage or paints, no one needs to pretend this abandoned, litter-strewn approach to the city is anything but what it is. The scale of your surroundings is intimidatingly massive expressway overpasses, vast, unpaved stretches of no-man's-land where streets and roads dissolve, hulking buttresses and piers of the interstate, strung with cables thick as trees. The whine, clatter, thump of wildly varying road surfaces under your tires increase the feeling of being out of control, being lost, stuck somewhere you shouldn't be, behind zebra-striped barriers or yellow police tape, a restricted zone that just might be dangerous for you or your vehicle but you missed the warning signs. Not only are you in jeopardy, but maybe you're about to crash through the façade, knock down some crucial stick propping up the immense, haphazard ugliness pretending to be a city.

Picturing myself in my car again on the way to pick up my father for the wedding, my route through the outskirts of Springfield brings me down and around to the city proper, a long, straight street in another country, with homemade shop signs in Spanish, blocks of Third World decay, citizens of many colors draped in windows, doorways, on corners, in parked cars, often with a look in their eyes that asks what you're asking

— Is this the right place, how in the hell did I wind up here?

A kind of scoured openness on all sides when you reach the broad streets intersecting at the Peter Pan bus depot. The sense of claustrophobia, of being an intruder abruptly ceases. No, you aren't lost, this is the way, you didn't detour and trespass into someone else's country, these wide streets, bland, commercial buildings assure you you're still in a Massachusetts town. Through a series of lights, an underpass, then the street narrows again, the marquee of the Roxy or Imperial or Palace advertises ancient coming attractions and you signal a left turn, across oncoming traffic.

I go effortlessly to the station, imagining a daytime ride, though it was night when I picked up my father, the route perfectly reproduced except for a tiny blank spot where the name of a street I can't recall should be printed on a sign stuck to a building across the intersection where I turn to parallel on my left a high wall of sooty-faced stone blocks rising to the plateau upon which trains cross the city. The bare, white shield of sign teases me. The street name precious because it's not there.

When I turn onto this unidentifiable street, cut off from the city by a looming stone wall, it's night again. Two-thirds of the way down the long block, cabs cluster at the double glass doors of the Springfield station. Cars occupy all the metered spaces on the station side of this one-way street and stretch in an unbroken row along the side marked no parking. Cars ahead of me and cars behind, a bright-eyed parade snaking along at 1:30 in the morning. A cop car, roof light pulsing, stalls traffic till it climbs the curb at the entrance to the station. Once past this commotion, I notice red taillights of a parked car wink on. I brake. Wait for a tan compact to maneuver away from the curb, signaling the driver behind me to stay put, so I can pull up and back in, hoping I won't have to hurt, kill, or be killed for this vacant slot.

As I lock up, I check out the station entrance. A man's leading two cops through the doors. In a big hurry. White-helmeted cops brandishing nightsticks. Half past one in the morning. Someone, somewhere in the station behaving badly. Somebody hurt or about to be hurt.

The night warm. I'd noticed bare arms and legs inside parked cars. At least an hour before my father's train due. Cabbies milling around the door are discussing the likelihood of being robbed. Who has been, who hasn't, a guy who got hit three times who's giving up night work even though it's the least-hassled driving and good tips.

The cops exit, casual and cocky, no civilian in tow. Their car, strobe spinning, shrugs off the sidewalk into snarled traffic, plowing a lane where there didn't seem room for one. The bright door of the station at this hour a bit like the threshold of a nightclub. A stage. A gauntlet. I hang at the periphery of the cabbies' talk, where the glow framing the entrance begins to merge with shadow. Play the game of being a regular, not only in this world, but of it. Check out the cruising cars while their occupants check me out. Let people wonder who I might be, what my job is on this street busy as high noon in the middle of the night.

When a woman wearing six-inch spike heels and a black miniskirt clatters down the sidewalk from the dark end of the street and turns, all hip-length, bouncing red pony-tail and lean, long bare legs, into the train station, I ride her wake through the doors, far enough behind to watch the cabdrivers watch her. Though none of the men close to blocking her way, each backs off a fraction of an inch as she trots by.

An elderly, brown-skinned guy with a ring of keys and a broom sits on a bench fastened to the floor just inside the door. He clears his throat and glances at another guy in coveralls, slouching nearby. Both give the young woman a swift, concentrated, head-to-toe exam. Yes, they see her. Yes, they are quite aware her Lycra top is more like a paint job with very thin paint than a piece of clothing, and yes they're aware she's nearly naked from the waist down and young and slinky sexy enough to turn most men's heads, turn most men's dicks hard if they let their dicks get hard every time some hustling ho' all skinny legs and hair and bubble of butt with most of her booty showing comes around. The men look — looking's free, ain't it? — quickly find each other's eyes again, and exchange a nod. Uh-huh. Yeah. So what, girl. Don't mean a thing. Ain't nothing to me.

The woman plugs coins into a coffee machine and gets no satisfaction. Slaps it a couple of times, turns to the man with the broom, flashes a half-frown, half-question at him. He shrugs. On duty but none of his business. She digs into her shoulder bag, finds more change, and plinks it in. Machine delivers second go-round. She bends to draw out the paper cup of coffee. Calves flex, a little quiver of thigh. Bends miraculously so she exposes no more of her behind than's already on display. Lets you know she knows you're looking, and she's in charge of what's free and what ain't. She's the show and knows that, too. Pouts at the vending machine, puckers her purple lips, blows on the cup and gingerly takes a sip. No satisfaction. She wrinkles her nose. With her free hand she pats and smoothes the nothing she's wearing, tosses the rope of fake red hair over one shoulder, pumps up on spike heels, and in a tap-tappety-tap volley she's back out on the street.

No sign of a disturbance the brace of cops and civilian had been chasing. Nowhere for anybody to hide in the tiny waiting room. One door straight ahead, another to the left, lead to the tracks, to stairways and tunnels you must negotiate to reach the platform overhead where trains arrive and depart. Vending machines flank the entrance. On one wall a locked rest room, a ticket booth behind metal screening and dirty glass. Along the opposite wall a bank of rental lockers with and without doors, two benches bolted into the floor that might seat a total of six, if the six were small and very fond of one another. A narrow counter in front of the booth, a few posters and notices on the wall, and that was about it. Unsubtly as a prison cell this place embodies its opinion of you, shouts its message of unwelcome with every corner cut, each unlovely detail, every stain, crack, drip, hole, missing or mutilated feature.

Though I had strolled in at what seemed to be street level, the waiting room is situated underground. A cave in a hillside. Bad light, bad air, the weight of tracks, trains, earth, sky pressing down. Black earth leaching through the thin skin of ceiling and walls, every sweating seam and gritty crack a hole in the dike.

Caves, tunnels, cellars, tenements, back alleys, and backyards, the deserted, seedy, out-of-order back doors of the city, greeting my father and his father, generations of young black men arriving, from South to North, country to town. Would this always be the common ground where we'd meet? Sons and fathers. Fathers and sons.

Train stations, bus stations, the servants' entrance, where you were supposed to slip in and do your grubby business without disturbing the folks moving about in clean, well-lit rooms of the big house.

Who decided things should be this way? Who decreed, and worse, who went along with the program? Clearly the front-door people benefited from such an arrangement — back doors, front doors, privileged access limited to a few. Why wouldn't they dream it up, demand it if they could get away with demanding. Why wouldn't they fight to hold on if somehow they contrived to seize a monopoly on the front door. But the others, the ones who outnumbered front-door people many, many times over, why were they a party to arrangements keeping them hat in hand, cooling their heels while they tapped gently at the back door. Generation after generation adrift in bus stations, train stations, hitching the highways, foot-slogging through moats of industrial wasteland belting the city's heart.

From *Fatheralong* by John Edgar Wideman. Random House, 1994.

Sports

James Naismith of Springfield invented the game of basketball in this gymnasium in 1891. He hung a peach basket on each end below the overhead running track. Courtesy of Naismith Memorial Basketball Hall of Fame, Springfield.

JAMES NAISMITH

There are few sports that can trace their lineage back to a specific date and place. Basketball is one of them. Springfield YMCA College (today, Springfield College) instructor James Naismith (1861-1939) was assigned the task of developing a game comparable to football that could be played indoors. In 1891, after some trial and error, Naismith came up with a game in which a player scored goals by tossing a soccer ball into a peach basket. Naismith's account of his invention is a must-read for aficionados of the game. Note the rowdiness of the YMCA College students when Naismith tried to entice them into trying a new sport. Anyone interested in the further development of the game should visit the Basketball Hall of Fame in Springfield.

(Volleyball also was invented in the Pioneer Valley, two years later — by a Holyoke YMCA instructor, William G. Morgan.)

The First Basketball Game

During the summer of 1891, the need for some new game became imperative. From many different states the young men had gathered for the summer term of the Springfield training school. No matter where they came from, these directors complained that the members of the gymnasium classes were losing interest in the type of work that had been introduced by R.J. Roberts, at one time a circus performer. Tired of the spectacular stunts, Roberts had inaugurated a system of exercise that he had termed body-building work, intended largely to develop physique, health, and vigor, with little thought for the interest of the participant. Body-building work consisted of light and heavy apparatus exercise based on the German system, but excluded many of the stunts that were performed by the expert gymnast. Those directors who had been trained under Roberts' leadership found it difficult to attract young men to their classes.

In the late seventies, college students had begun to take an interest in intercollegiate sports, especially track and football. These games had become firmly established, and many of the more active students took part in them. When the men who engaged in these sports went to the city to enter business and found that they had leisure time, it was only natural that they should look for some kind of athletic diversion. In an effort to find it, they joined the athletic clubs, the bicycle clubs, the Y.M.C.A., and other organizations of this type. During the winter season these clubs had nothing to offer in the way of athletics, but tried to interest the men in gymnastics.

The former college men were natural leaders in their communities. When they compared the thrills of football with those of mass and squad gymnastics, they were frankly discontented. The expert gymnast got all the excitement from a perfect performance of a daring stunt and the football player from winning an intercollegiate contest. What this new generation wanted was pleasure and thrill rather than physical benefits. The summer school students freely discussed these conditions. No one, however, seemed to be able to offer a solution to the problem.

When I had decided how I would start the game, I felt that I would have little trouble. I knew that there would be questions to be met; but I had the fundamental principles of a game, and I was more than willing to try to meet these problems. I continued with my day's work, and it was late in the evening before I again had a chance to think of my new scheme. I believe that I am the first person who ever played basketball; and although I used the bed for a court, I certainly played a hard game that night.

The following morning I went into my office, thinking of the new game. I had not yet decided what ball I should use. Side by side on the floor lay two balls, one a football and the other a soccer ball.

I noticed the lines of the football and realized that it was shaped so that it might be carried in the arms. There was to be no carrying of the ball in this new game, so I walked over, picked up the soccer ball, and started in search of a goal.

As I walked down the hall, I met Mr. Stebbins, the superintendent of buildings. I asked him if he had two boxes about eighteen inches square. Stebbins thought a minute, and then said:

"No, I haven't any boxes, but I'll tell you what I do have. I have two old peach baskets down in the store room, if they will do you any good."

I told him to bring them up, and a few minutes later he appeared with the two baskets tucked under his arm. They were round and somewhat larger at the top than at the bottom. I found a hammer and some nails and tacked the baskets to the lower rail of the balcony, one at either end of the gym.

I was almost ready to try the new game, but I felt that I needed a set of rules, in order that the men would have some guide. I went to my office, pulled out a scratch pad, and set to work. The rules were so clear in my mind that in less than an hour I took my copy to Miss Lyons, our stenographer, who typed the set of thirteen rules.

When Miss Lyons finished typing the rules, it was almost class time, and I was anxious to get down to the gym. I took the rules and made my way down the stairs. Just inside the door there was a bulletin board for notices. With thumb tacks I fastened the rules to this board and then walked across the gym. I was sure in my own mind that the game was good, but it needed a real test. I felt that its success or failure depended largely on the way that the class received it.

The first member of the class to arrive was Frank Mahan. He was a southerner from North Carolina, had played tackle on the football team, and was the ringleader of the group. He saw me standing with a ball in my hand and perhaps surmised that another experiment was to be tried. He looked up at the basket on one end of the gallery, and then his eyes turned to me. He gazed at me for an instant, and then looked toward the other end of the gym. Perhaps I was nervous, because his exclamation sounded like a death knell as he said,

"Huh! another new game!"

When the class arrived, I called the roll and told them that I had another game, which I felt sure would be good. I promised them that if this was a failure, I would not try any more experiments. I then read the rules from the bulletin board and proceeded to organize the game.

There were eighteen men in the class; I selected two captains and had them choose sides. When the teams were chosen, I placed the men on the floor. There were three forwards, three centers, and three backs on each team. I chose two of the center men to jump, then threw the ball between them. It was the start of the first basketball game and the finish of the trouble with that class.

As was to be expected, they made a great many fouls at first; and as a foul was penalized by putting the offender on the side lines until the next goal was made, sometimes half of a team would be in the penalty area. It was simply a case of no one knowing just what to do. There was no team work, but each man did his best. The forwards tried to make goals and the backs tried to keep the opponents from making them. The team was large, and the floor was small. Any man on the field was close enough to the basket to throw for goal, and most of them were anxious to score. We tried, however, to develop team work by having the guards pass the ball to the forwards.

The game was a success from the time that the first ball was tossed up. The players were interested and seemed to enjoy the game. Word soon got around that they were having fun in Naismith's gym class, and only a few days after the first game we began to have a gallery.

The class met at eleven-thirty in the morning, and the game was in full swing by twelve o'clock. Some teachers from the Buckingham Grade School were passing the gym one day, and hearing the noise, decided to investigate. They could enter the gallery through a door that led to the street. Each day after that, they stopped to watch the game, sometimes becoming so interested that they would not have time to get their lunch. These teachers came to me one day and asked me why girls could not play that game. I told them that I saw no reason why they should not, and this group organized the first girls' basketball team.

It is little wonder that the crowd enjoyed the game. If we could see it today as it was played then, we would laugh too. The players were all mature men; most of them had mustaches, and one or two had full beards. Their pants were long, and their shirts had short sleeves. Sometimes when a player received the ball, he would poise with it over his head to make sure that he would make the goal. About the time that he was ready to throw, someone would reach up from behind and take the ball out of his hands. This occurred frequently and was a never-ending source of amusement. No matter how often a player lost the ball in this manner, he would always look around with a surprised expression that would plainly say, "Who did that?" His embarrassment only added to the laughter of the crowd.

It was shortly after the first game that Frank Mahan came to me before class hour and said:

"You remember the rules that were put on the bulletin board?"

"Yes, I do," I answered.

"They disappeared," he said.

"I know it," I replied.

"Well, I took them," Frank said. "I knew that this game would be a success, and I took them as a souvenir, but I think now that you should have them."

Mahan told me that the rules were in his trunk and that he would bring them down later. That afternoon he entered my office and handed me the two typewritten sheets. I still have them, and they are one of my prized possessions.

At the Christmas vacation a number of the students went home and some of them started the game in their local Y.M.C.A.'s. There were no printed rules at that time, and each student played the game as he remembered it. It was not until January, 1892, that the school paper, called the *Triangle*, first printed the rules under the heading, "A New Game."

One day after the students returned from their vacation, the same Frank Mahan came to me and asked me what I was going to call the game. I told him that I had not thought of the matter but was interested only in getting it started. Frank insisted that it must have a name and suggested the name of Naismith ball. I laughed and told him that I thought that name would kill any game. Frank then said:

"Why not call it basketball?"

"We have a basket and a ball, and it seems to me that would be a good name for it," I replied. It was in this way that basketball was named.

When the first game had ended, I felt that I could now go to Doctor Gulick and tell him that I had accomplished the two seemingly impossible tasks that he had assigned to me: namely, to interest the class in physical exercise and to invent a new game.

From *Basketball: Its Origin and Development* by James Naismith. Association Press, 1941.

LEO DUROCHER

Tough, industrial, sports-crazy — that's how feisty baseball manager Leo Durocher described his hometown of West Springfield in the 1920s. Durocher's working-class community may have been where he first decided that "nice guys finished last."

Leo "The Lip" relates how he learned hard-nosed play from Rabbit Maranville, Springfield's Hall of Fame shortstop. The accuracy of Durocher's recollections must be wondered at when he mentions skating on the frozen Connecticut River one hundred miles up to Boston and back. Durocher, who led the Dodgers, Giants, Cubs, and Astros, is the sixth-winningest manager in baseball history.

Nice Guys Finish Last

I was born on the kitchen table on the top floor of a three-decker wooden house on Merrick Street in West Springfield, Massachusetts. Two days later, my mother was back at her work. That's the way it was done in that kind of neighborhood, at that time.

I was the youngest of four sons, spaced two years apart. My brothers, in order of their age, were Clarence, Raymond and Armand. Not very long after I was born my father, who had been an engineer for the Boston and Albany railroad, suffered a heart attack. Not serious enough to completely disable him but enough to wipe out whatever small savings he might have had and to limit his activities.

And so my earliest memory is quite probably of my mother leaving the house to work as a maid in a downtown Springfield hotel.

We were so poor, I sometimes say, that we didn't live on the wrong side of the track, we lived in the middle of the track. A joke which has a certain bite to it, in our case, because my father had gone back to work for the railroad. His job was to go from locomotive to locomotive and make sure the fires were properly banked.

We never had a Christmas tree; I remember that particularly. Christmas was always held on the linoleum floor in the kitchen in front of the old iron stove. When I was five or six, I wanted a drum. Oh, Lord, how I wanted that drum. More than anything I have ever wanted before or since. When I went to bed on Christmas Eve, I remember my mother and dad saying, "Well, you've been a pretty good boy; not the best but pretty good. Santa Claus may stop by."

When I woke the next morning there was a drum right there along-side me on the bed. Well, let me tell you, no rich kid ever got a Mercedes-

Benz that meant so much to him as that drum meant to me. That's something poor people have on rich people. Anything my parents gave me I knew they were giving me out of sacrifice and sweat and love.

Not, as you may have guessed, that I didn't give them immediate cause to regret it. I started banging on that drum as soon as I woke up, and I never stopped. For three days, I went marching around the neighborhood with the drum hanging from around my neck, whacking away at it. At night I went marching around the house. The three-decker houses that were so common in those days had two apartments to each floor, six families in all. After a couple of days, five families in our house and twelve families in the adjoining houses were screaming to shut that kid up.

The shouts were in French, because it was a neighborhood of French Catholics. My mother, whose maiden name was Clara Provost, was born in a little town just outside Montreal. My father, George, came from the little French community of Cohoes, in upper New York. He was a small man, possibly five feet four inches. My mother was barely over five feet. Nothing except French was spoken in our home, or, except for the Latin liturgy, in church. I didn't know one word of English when I started public school. Until I began to play professional baseball, my name was always pronounced the French way; not De-*roach*-er but Doo-roe-*shay*. When I began to mix more with the other kids in town, socially and in athletics, their nickname for me was Swamper. After a while it was, anyway. It developed something like this: Frog . . . Bullfrog . . . Swamp . . . Swamper. Jeez, do you know the last time I heard that name? I was sent to Atlanta in the Southern Association in my second year of organized baseball, and we were playing the inmates at the Atlanta prison. I hit a ground ball and was running to first when I heard some guy in the stands holler out, "Hey, Swamper." One of my classmates had got out of Springfield the hard way.

My mother ran the house, there was never any doubt about that. As far as I can remember, my father hit me only once. When I was about ten or eleven. He had been transferred to Cambridge, Mass., a few months earlier, but we were living in the same kind of a house, the top floor of a three-decker, almost directly across from the streetcar barn. One Sunday after church, I thought it would be a good idea to hide behind the car barn and smoke a cigarette. To show how smart I was, I had picked a spot that was visible from our kitchen window. In those days, a beating meant that the old man took off his belt and let you have it. I was one of that kind of kid who couldn't be made to cry. The more he hit me, the madder I got. I just kept looking over my shoulder at him, as if to say, *Go on, hit me harder; I dare you!*

The beating I knew I had coming to me, but when my mother told me to go to bed without supper that night I went running out of the house and was gone all night. All night they looked for me. Know where I was? I had sneaked back into the house and was hiding under the second-floor staircase. At five in the morning, my father finally found me huddled there, half asleep, and picked me up and carried me up the stairs, kind of nuzzling me and sneaking in a kiss here and there. I suppose I knew from that time on that there was nothing I could do wrong as far as my father was concerned.

After a year in Cambridge we moved back to a big house on Elm Street, on the other side of Springfield. It was like moving into a whole new world. The boys were beginning to contribute toward the house by then, but mostly my mother was able to swing it by taking in boarders. For the rest of the time that I was at home, we'd all sit down together, family and boarders, and the food would be passed around on steaming platters.

I always worked at something or other. It was expected. All the usual things that kids did; I had a paper route; I was right there knocking on doors with my shovel when it snowed. I mowed lawns. I worked in an ice-cream parlor. Springfield was really a small city within a rural setting. There was farmland all around us. When I was in high school, I'd work the tobacco fields in Agawam, the town just to the south of us. During the harvest season, we'd work from seven in the morning until six at night. They'd roll back the cheesecloth that had been protecting the field from the frost and, goddam, you'd go up and down those rows as fast as you could. On a good day you could make yourself maybe $3.50.

There was no organized activity for kids. We were on our own, and we did everything. Crazy things. As soon as the Connecticut River would freeze over, eight or ten of us would put on our racing skates and skate all the way up to Boston. A hundred miles back and forth. We'd start out early in the morning, staying close to the shore where the ice was safe, and when we'd get to the Harvard Rowing Club, we'd just turn around and head back.

Almost all the kids could ride horses, because horses were all around us. I myself learned how to ride — are you ready for this? — by playing polo. Springfield College had a polo team, I knew a couple of the guys from high school, and after I had got to where I could sit a horse, I'd go galloping around the grounds whacking away at the hard little ball.

Through it all, I had one steady job. By the time I was twelve or thirteen, I was already very concerned about my grooming. Although you wouldn't think it to look at me now, I used to have a great mop of blondish hair. My hair was so thick that I couldn't run a comb through it, I had to put my head under the faucet and smooth it back with a towel. The local barber happened to have three pool tables in his back room, and so I made a deal with him. I would wait for him to open every Saturday morning, he would cut my hair for me and then I would go back and sweep the floor, clean the tables and set out the chalk in preparation for the big Saturday afternoon crowd. Well, the poolroom didn't open until one o'clock and I would be finished by noon. That gave me an hour to practice. At the beginning, I was so small that I had to stand on a box to reach the balls. By the time I was in high school I was so good that I was the "house man." I'd come in after school and go to work racking balls, and if anybody wanted a game, either for "time" or for a side bet I would take them on. When any hustler breezed into town looking for a game, the older guys would back me, sometimes for as much as $100. With the money on the line, I didn't lose.

When I began to make some money, hustling pool, I'd save up $75 for a custom-made suit (easily the equivalent of $500 today). I don't know what it was that made me so clothes-conscious; nobody else in my family was, certainly. We were the kind of family where my mother washed all the clothes, shirts included, and hung them on the line in the kitchen to dry overnight. My shirts she had to starch: I can still see my mother, God rest her soul, dipping the collars and cuffs of my shirts in a little can of starch, letting them dry for a few minutes, ironing them out and hanging them up on a hanger. Leo wouldn't stand for any wrinkles.

There was one other athlete in the family. My oldest brother, Clarence. Clarence was a wonderful center fielder and, something I never was, a hitter. I used to think of him when I'd see that little Albie Pearson who played for the California Angels in the early sixties. Clarence was just about Pearson's size, he could field every bit as good and he had a lot more power. Enormous power for a little man. But Clarence was also a brilliant student, and he had the sense of responsibility that you find in oldest sons. He studied business administration at Springfield College, went to work at the bottom rung of one of the biggest manufacturing companies in Springfield and ended up as executive vice president.

I can't say that Clarence was my first hero, though. When we moved to Elm Street, we were living only two blocks from Rabbit Maranville, the shortstop for the Boston Braves. Rabbit was not only the great hero of all of Springfield, he was a fellow Frenchman — and my father knew him. Actually could go up to him and talk to him. The Rabbit was a little fellow, that's how he got his nickname, but he was smart and he was colorful. My father took me to Boston a couple of times to see him play, and everybody would wait for a high pop fly to be hit in his general direction so they could see his "vest-pocket" catch. Sheer logic tells you that the best way to catch a fly ball is up over the eyes so that you are watching it all the way. Rabbit would catch it beneath his belt buckle.

Plop! Followed by laughter. Followed by applause.

The guy I will never forget, though, was Heinie Groh, the third baseman for Cincinnati. Groh had the oddest batting stance I have ever seen. The best way for you to visualize it — and I have never seen it described quite right — is to picture a soldier standing at present arms. That was Groh. He would stand there facing the pitcher head-on, with his feet together and the bat held straight up in front of him. To complete the picture, just in case you couldn't recognize him, you know, he used what was always referred to as "Heinie Groh's bottle bat," the shortest, thickest bat I have ever seen. By the time the ball was at the plate, of course, he had swung around and was in a normal hitting stance — and the sonofabuck could really hit.

Although Rabbit Maranville never had a chance to see me play, my father was quick to tell him I was the best young player in town, and a shortstop at that, and he took a certain amount of interest in me. What that meant was that I was getting tips about playing shortstop from the man who was going to become the first shortstop to be elected to the Hall of Fame, and I was getting them at a time when I was eager to learn. Know the hitters, he would say. Study them. Anticipate where the ball was going to be hit. Get rid of the ball quick. Rabbit didn't have the best arm in baseball, but he was known for being able to get the ball away faster than anybody in the game. I became faster. Ask anybody who saw me play and they will tell you that it looked as if I was throwing the ball before I caught it. Pee Wee Reese tried to imitate me when he first came up, and for four or five games he was throwing the ball all over the place. What you can learn at thirteen or fourteen, you just can't learn at nineteen and twenty. "Do it your way," I'd tell him. "Not mine. I was doing it this way when I was just a baby, and it's part of me. With your arm, you don't have to get the ball away that fast."

We little guys had to make up in brains and toughness what we lacked in size, Rabbit would tell me. "Never take a backward step out there. The first backward step a little man takes is the one that's going to kill him."

He gave me something more tangible than advice, too. A brand-new glove. And then he took a big scissors and cut a hole right in the middle of it, just the way he did with his own glove. You were catching the ball really against the bare skin. It stung like hell at first, but it was surprising how quickly my hand hardened. In a very short time, I felt nothing at all except when I'd catch a hot line drive. (The gloves in those days were so much smaller than they are today that you can't really call them the same thing. In those days; the player had to make the play, not the glove.)

I used Rabbit Maranville's glove on through the minors and during my first couple of years with the Yankees. I kept it until it was such a rag that I could fold it up and stuff it in my pocket. When the time finally came when I had to get myself a new one I picked up a scissors and got ready to cut out another hole. And then I asked myself why. I was doing it because Maranville did it, and that was no reason at all. Instead of cutting a hole in the glove, I slit the inside, took out all the padding, and kept a layer of leather between the ball and my hand. That one was in tatters by the time I was through; it was practically falling apart. But I held onto it to the end of my career. They were the only two gloves I ever had.

Maranville was playing for the St. Louis Cardinals the first year I went to spring training with the Yankees, and by coincidence both clubs trained in St. Petersburg and we played each other often. The first time Rabbit saw me play, he said to me, "You do things backwards right now better than a lot of guys that have been here for years." Boy, that was praise from on high. I considered myself the Rabbit's protégé, and I waited for him to tell me how well I had learned my lessons. Instead, he said, "Where did you learn to get the ball away like that?"

Where did I — ? *From you, Rabbit! From you!* That's how I came to understand that all the time I had looked upon myself as his protege, he had looked on me as a neighborhood kid who was always being brought around by his father. *And who would have thought the kid was actually going to make it?* One of those things.

By another coincidence, I was on the field when Rabbit played his final game. I was with the Cardinals myself then and Rabbit, at the age of forty-five, was making a comeback with the Boston Braves. It may very well have been the first exhibition game of the spring season. I know it was at St. Petersburg, and Rabbit was being thrown out at the plate. Exhibition game or not, forty-five years old or not, the Rabbit came barreling into the catcher and you could hear the ankle crack. He was lying there in agony, with the ankle twisted completely around. The batter on deck for the Braves was Shanty Hogan, their big catcher. "Don't stand there looking at me," the Rabbit rasped at him, "Knock me out.

And just as quick as that, Hogan whacked him on the chin and knocked him out cold. That was my teacher, Rabbit Maranville, one hell of a little guy.

From *Nice Guys Finish Last* by Leo Durocher. Simon & Schuster, 1976.

JOHN MCPHEE

After reading about the two-fisted brand of baseball practiced by Springfield's Leo Durocher, let us move up to Deerfield Academy, where headmaster Frank Boyden elevated sportsmanship to the highest pinnacle. Every student at Deerfield played something and gained some competency and self-confidence while he was at it.

This piece is by New Yorker *writer John McPhee, who attended Deerfield in the 1940s. McPhee has written more than twenty books, including* Oranges, The Pine Barrens, *and* Coming Into the Country, *about Alaska. An additional selection from McPhee's profile of Frank L. Boyden is in the section "Educational Life."*

Good Sportsmanship at Deerfield

Boyden's principle of athletics for all has remained one of the main elements of the school's program, and Deerfield is unmatched in this respect today. Where once he did not have enough boys for even one team, he now has teams for all five hundred. When a boy at Deerfield chooses a sport, he automatically makes a team that has a full schedule of games with other schools. For example, Deerfield usually has at least eight basketball teams, each with game uniforms, away games, and all the other incidentals of the sport on the varsity level. This is true in soccer, baseball, football, tennis, lacrosse, hockey, squash, swimming, skiing, track, and cross-country as well. With few exceptions, every boy at Deerfield is required to take part in three sports a year. There is no set number of teams in any sport. According to the boys' choices, there may be a few more football teams one year and a few more soccer teams the next. Deerfield has sent on a share of athletic stars — football players such as Mutt Ray to Dartmouth and Archie Roberts to Columbia, for instance — but Deerfield is not really an atmosphere in which a great athlete is likely to develop. The headmaster's belief in sport is exceeded by his belief that everything has its place and time. Deerfield athletes are given no time for extra practice, nor are they permitted to practice any sport out of season. In the fall and the spring, the basketball courts are locked, and baskets are actually removed from the backboards.

In the early days, having the headmaster as a player produced some disadvantages for Deerfield teams. Once, in a pick-off situation in baseball, when he caught the throw from the pitcher and put his glove down, the opposing player slid safely under him. "Out," said the umpire. Any other baseball player would have congratulated himself on his luck, but the headmaster had to tell the umpire that the fellow had in fact been safe. From the start, he had been preaching sportsmanship to his boys. People who remember those days say that he was the first person in that part of the country to stress courtesy in athletics. "We may wish they were interested in other things," he said at the time, "but we must meet existing conditions, and since they will have athletic sports anyway, let us control them and make them a moral force." No matter how able a Deerfield player was or how close a game had become, if he showed anger he was benched. If a basketball player said anything the least bit antagonistic to the man he was guarding — even something as mild as "Go ahead and shoot" — a substitute would go into the game. Athletics was one of the ways in which Deerfield became known, and from the beginning the headmaster wanted his teams to be smartly dressed and thoroughly equipped. In the early years, he often spent at least a third of his salary on athletic equipment, and when a woman of the town offered a contribution to the school, he asked if he might use it for baseball uniforms. "Something has lifted the spirit of this community," she said to him. "Go and buy the best uniforms you can find, but don't tell anyone I gave the money for it."

The headmaster played on Deerfield teams until he was about thirty-five, and he was head coach of football, basketball, and baseball until he was nearly eighty. "I can't go to a funeral anywhere from Athol to Northampton without an elderly man's coming up and reminding me of a baseball game we once played against one another," he says. His sense of football has always been vague but imaginative. His blocking assignments were not precise. During his years as player-coach, he put straps on the belts of his linemen so that the backs — himself included — could hang on and be pulled forward for short gains. In baseball, he followed a simple strategy. "If you can put your glove on a fast ball, there is no reason you can't put your bat on it," he has said for sixty-four years. "Anyone can learn to bunt." Deerfield teams use the squeeze play as if there were no alternative in the sport. He continued to hit fungoes to his baseball teams until he was seventy-five years old. It was a high point of any Deerfield baseball day to watch him hit precise grounders to his scrambling infield. Toward the end of his coaching years, the headmaster found that he could not hit the ball with quite as much snap as he liked to give it. He complained that the ground was getting softer. His main talent as a coach was that he always seemed to know what a boy could do and then expected no more of him. He knew, somehow, when a pitcher was almost through. If his assistant coaches happened to prevail on him to leave a pitcher in a game, disaster usually followed. What he did not know about football he made up through his knowledge of boys, and he could win a game with the right remark. He once did so — in the early nineteen-twenties — by taking his quarterback aside and saying to him, "You're just like a race horse. Sometimes you're too tense to do your job. Take it easy. You'll run faster."

Visitors today sometimes think that the headmaster is a little theatrical when he walks up and down the sidelines — eighty-six years old, and wearing a player's duffel coat that almost reaches the ground — and acts as if he were on the verge of jumping into the game. Something they may not be able to imagine is what it must mean to him to remember the games against small local schools when he himself was in the backfield and there were fifteen or twenty boys in the academy, and now, more than sixty years later, to be watching his team make one touchdown after another until the final score is Deerfield 28, Exeter 0. As a semi-retired coach, the headmaster still gives the same pre-game talks he has always given. In a way that is desperate, unyielding, and total, he wants to win, but he wants to win with grace. "The consequence of poor sportsmanship is that you lose, somewhere along the line," he says. "Remember, it's better to lose in a sportsmanlike way than to win and gloat over it." And he goes along in that vein for a while, until he has satisfied the requirements of his conscience. Then he says, "Now, boys, let's not let up on them for a minute. Let's win this one, if possible, by forty points."

From *The Headmaster: Frank L. Boyden of Deerfield* by John McPhee. Farrar, Straus & Giroux, 1966.

Frank Boyden at Deerfield Academy in the 1950s hitting grounders to his boys in the infield. Courtesy of Deerfield Academy.

MADELEINE BLAIS

Madeleine Blais's account of the 1992-1993 Amherst High School Girls Basketball team traces the Hurricanes' ascent to the state championship. It describes the rise of women's sports and the self-awareness that has accompanied it. Blais, a Springfield native, wrote for the Boston Globe *and* Miami Herald. *She teaches journalism at the University of Massachusetts. Some of her pieces are collected in* The Heart Is an Instrument: Portraits in Journalism.

Amherst High Girls Basketball Championship

By the time the Western Mass Regional Finals were held on March 5 at the Civic Center in Springfield, hundreds of Amherst fans proceeded down Interstate 91 in weather-weary vehicles, paralleling the progress of the Hurricanes' thin metal bus past dark clumps of mountains and the Soldiers' Home with its name spelled out in big letters on a hillside.

Coach Moyer sat in front on the aisle so that his legs could extend out. This was it, the long shadow on the lawn that haunted every season, the game at season's end that Amherst had lost five years in a row.

The bus deposited them at the entrance for players and performers. It was a short walk in the slush and over the mounds of snow.

The Hurricanes usually counted on Jen and Jamila for the pregame invocation, those talismanic words that would goad them to victory. It was important that they say something special beyond whatever remarks Coach had to offer.

Tonight in the tense private moments as a team just before the game in the washed-out light of the locker room, it was Kristin Marvin who stepped forward. Both Ron Moyer and Trish Lea, the junior varsity coach who had moved up in the postseason to lend her skills, waited outside in a dingy corridor. This was the team's time to commune with itself. Kristin, who sometimes liked to act as if life were just a party, one huge Big Mac fully loaded with pickles and ketchup and onions, had the look this evening of zeal as she commandeered the floor. The intensity of Kristin's expression was mirrored in the way she gripped a scroll of thin white computer paper; her face glowed from the inside out. The words spilled out, quick and interlocking, like pieces of a jigsaw puzzle still stuck together, as she read from a document she had composed during a bout of insomnia two nights before:

"I'm sitting here on Thursday night, thinking that the possibility of sleep is about four hours away. Watching our hockey team lose by one point tonight got me so pumped and hyper for Saturday's game that I've been pacing my house and hyperventilating. I've watched so many of our teams become 'almosts.' Almost win Western Mass, almost be good enough, almost have *it*. And as I stood there and watched the tears roll down Kunk's face, I swore I would not let that kind of sorrow hurt any one of us right here.

"I know that the one obstacle that stands in the path of a Western Mass Championship is inside us. Kathleen said to me tonight she felt she wasn't pumped enough. She didn't feel the "fire." I feel it now, and I want to record the intensity that it's causing. I don't need to whine about losing to Hamp two years in a row, or mention Lauren Demski, or remind you of what total bitches the team is now. You all know that. And that gets your mind pumped, and it makes you want to be angry and intense, but it doesn't provide that indescribable rush of adrenaline and emotion that makes us go out and kick ass.

"I'm not gonna ask any of you to win the game, or try to win the game tonight. That's Coach's job. What I ask of you is, every time you see a loose ball, lunge for it. Every rebound, reach for it as if it were rightfully yours — 'cause it is. Concentrate on every shot like it's your last. Push and hurt your player a little harder each time. Everyone box out like you're Lucia. And most of all, feel the love of the game and the love for each other every second you're on the floor or on the bench. That kind of passion, which I know we have, if we play with it tonight, Hamp is gonna be out in the first four minutes. They know it too — they know as well as us what we have is unstoppable, and they're scared. They should be. I want Hamp blood, we all do. I want to see their cowardly, prejudiced, pathetic, selfish pride squirming and dying on the floor by the end of the game."

The Hurricanes were ensnared; the very language of Kristin's speech was a kind of contraband, especially to the younger girls, who were at the point of trying on vocabulary as if it were a daring garment. It resounded in the dank utilitarian room, a renegade trumpet.

"Okay, I've gone on enough. I just couldn't do this without putting my two cents in. I was gonna write a petition, but I was afraid Jen wouldn't sign it."

There was a brief pause, a momentary inward gasp as every one wondered how Jen would react to this acknowledgment of the tensions that sometimes existed between the two friends. Jen hated petitions, the way they preened with the often false promise of due process. Under most circumstances, she believed it was better to "suck it up," teenage slang for "grin and bear it." Would Jen flinch or smile, look askance or raise a fist? Jen gave Kristin an approving look: "You go, girl."

"Let me just say, this could very well be the last time in my life that I put on a uniform and play in a real game of basketball. Last time. It could also be the last time we all play together as a team. Just think about that. It's a pretty intimidating thought. So I just ask that you all pretend tonight as if this were the last game of basketball that you could ever play, and put that much heart into it. But I don't really need to. I know you'll all do it. I hope you all feel that fire, because tonight we all need each other to be here. You are my sisters, and I honestly love every one of you that much. Thank you for providing the most rewarding, special experience of my life. I will never forget any of you. No matter what happens tonight, I want you to remember Hoop Phi and know we're the best.

Amherst Regional winners celebrated the Western Massachusetts Regional Girls' Basketball Championship on March 5, 1993, at the Springfield Civic Center. Left to right: Jennifer Gallante, manager; Meghan Carpenter, manager; Emily Shore, Jennifer Pariseau, Jamila Wideman, Kristin Marvin (behind arm), Sophie King, and Jessi Denis. They went on to win the state title. Courtesy of Ron Moyer, Amherst Regional coach.

"We have more heart than the whole fucking town of Northampton, so let's prove it."

And then Kristin paused, and with all the dignity of a priest who recites a sacred phrase and all the feistiness of a drill sergeant who expects the troops to hop to, she shouted her most rousing rendition ever of "Hoop," to which the crowd of girls huddled in their circle, arms entwined, fired back, as in a fusillade:

"Phi!"

Coach Moyer knew they would win.

Two of Northampton's strongest players plowed down Kathleen just as she took the first shot of the game, a successful two-pointer on a fearless drive down the middle. He was terrified she'd landed on her ankle. But she scurried up from her momentary spread-eagled pose on the floor, and at the foul line where she had the chance to make another point for a threepoint play, she situated herself square to the basket.

As the tension grew, and the contradictory cries from fans on both sides filled the air, she hoisted the ball with strong arms and, using her entire body, propelled it upward in a clean curve.

Another nifty point.

Bob Pariseau was struck by the difference between Kathleen a year ago and Kathleen on this evening. In all his time of watching sporting events, he could not name another transformation, amateur or professional, on such a sweeping scale.

Kathleen herself could hardly believe that it had been at the exact same point in the season a year ago that she'd collapsed in a sniveling heap outside the gym at Cathedral. She had bottomed out, and that plunge downward had triggered a transition in her head, a psychological transformation as slow and subtle as water and air and light on the smallest seed.

She thought about last year's final game:

After such embarrassment, you kick yourself. You kick hard and it hurts. But after that, you get pissed. You realize that in all the Mr.-Nice-Guy, "Nah, I'm not good" games, you've been pushed around. You start to feel used and manipulated. All this time, not taking what you should have, always being polite. Not anymore — look where it got us. Sorry, but it's time we got what we worked for; we simply didn't realize that after you put in the work, you don't automatically get the reward. You've got to be greedy, you've got to push, you've got to do impolite things like taking the trophy.

Politeness is nice, and niceness is, well . . . nice. But when do you stop kicking yourself for being nice in the past and start smacking yourself into waking up to the present, pushing yourself to prepare for the future? Enough regrets, enough "I should haves," because pretty soon there are no more chances.

That's what happened. We got proud. We got pissed. We got a little scared of losing time. I learned self-confidence is not only acceptable, it is indispensable.

Be nice when it's time to be nice and when others are nice to you. But niceness has no place on the court because the other team wants you to lose. The court is where you can be all those things we're not supposed to be: aggressive, cocky, strong. It's okay; it's alright.

There's this feeling that you get. Once you get it, you can get it back again and again, just thinking about the game. It's when you can't distinguish between the emotions that are driving you, but you know that they're all there and they all want the same thing. It makes you grit your teeth, bite down on your back teeth so that your jaw is tight. Unsure if you're about to cry or about to attack, your nose flares and every muscle in your body tightens up. It happens when you take every last feeling of indignation and resentment, love and confidence, onto the court. When the court is your outlet for this feeling, you can't lose. For every time I felt I'd been manipulated or that I hadn't stood up for myself, hadn't proven that I deserve credit and respect, I pushed that much harder with my legs and wanted that much more. The cause of that feeling was different for each of us on the team, but we all had it and we quietly respected where it came from in everyone else. I don't need to know what or who has pushed Kristin around in her life or why it made her push twice as hard against Kim Frost. She just needs to know that I understand and that I can relate. Each time she grabs a rebound, I see the look. I see how she grits her teeth, how her upper lip curls just a little bit. The only sound that could possibly come from such a face would be a low growl. She has inside her what I have inside me. The fact that we all recognized tonight that each one of us is fighting against something different allowed us to fight for one common goal with all our hearts.

We weren't conceited, we were proud. And in between those two seasons, we wanted to be the best and we wanted everyone to know it. That's not selfish or cocky; that's the mentality of an athlete, and that's what I found!

And so, twelve months later, Kathleen Poe faced the opponent who had caused her to curl into herself on the floor, and this time, head high, she walked off the court.

The score: 63-41.

From *In These Girls, Hope Is a Muscle* by Madeleine Blais. Atlantic Monthly Press, 1995.

The Ethnic Experience: Holyoke and Bondsville

Cucumber pickers at the Joseph Zgrodnik Farm in Hadley, 1985. Photo by Jerome Liebling.

MARY DOYLE CURRAN

The Parish and the Hill *by Mary Doyle Curran (1917-1981) is the great "Holyoke book." It captures the story of three generations of Holyoke Irish, from the immigrants living in the "Flats" to the striving "lace-curtain" Irish trying to join the middle-class Yankees on Money Hole Hill.*

Mary Doyle Curran, born in Holyoke, uses the novel's narrator, Mary O'Connor, to relate the pain of the Irish seeking assimilation into American society. Curran taught English and Irish Studies at Wellesley, Queens College, and the University of Massachusetts at Boston. The following selections from The Parish and the Hill *describe the daily lives of the first generation of Irish immigrants and the social institution of the Irish wake.*

The Parish and the Hill

I remember Irish Parish. It was Ward Four in the old days before the Irish began coming in. After the first great famine in Ireland, they came as rapidly as they could make up the passage money — Kerry men and women — and the one spot of green they named Kerry Park. They built their shanties around the park overlooking the river. Soon Ward Four was crammed with Kerryites, all coming for the money, and, above all, for the food that could be picked from the trees simply by lifting one hand. No one had told them about the work that waited for them. It was not until some of the first ones, consumed by a longing for the green land, went home to Ireland, sick with the consumption laid on them by their jobs, that the others learned it was the same work that the Irish were doing in the dark mills of Liverpool and Manchester. It was in the mills that they would earn their living, or laying the rails for the railway that was to stretch from one side of the new country to the other. There were those Kerry men who would not follow the rails, for laying the rails took them with every step away from the Atlantic Ocean and that much farther from the old country. It was those who settled down in Irish Parish, and the mill owners were made rich by their decision. Shrewd Yankees that they were, they harnessed the water power and created the great dam in full view of Kerry Park. The Irish had that always before them to remind them that the tales of travelers can some-times be apocryphal.

These Irishmen soon found they had exchanged the English landlord for the Yankee mill owner; and they took off their hats, these shanty Irish, as reluctantly to this one as they had to the other. As time went on, the shanties disappeared, but the shanty Irishmen remained, housed now in the long row of red-brick tenements put up by the Yankee mill owners. The tenements were dark and small; children filled the five rooms to overflowing. There were five to a feather bed and three beds in one bedroom — the other bedroom, dedicated to the mother and father, held only one, though the youngest slept in a crib near the marriage bed, where the next occupant of the crib was being created. The marriage room also held the great chest stored with the linen brought from home. There was always the mingled musty smell of babies, tobacco, and bread in the house.

The front room was the one facing the street, and that was sacred to the dead, for it was here, in the early days, that the dead were waked. This room was filled with heavy furniture, bought at the local furniture store, and a few relics of the past: a colored picture of Ireland; perhaps a letter or two from home placed prominently on the table; a pot containing some of the old sod that someone, in a last moment of desperation, had seized before he got onto the boat. Here, too, would be the most precious wedding presents carefully preserved, but the focal point of the room was the great family Bible sitting on a table in the center. In this all the names of the living and dead were carefully inscribed by the priest. Only for a death or a birth was the Bible ever opened. It was never read, for these Irishmen had no need to read the Bible stories — didn't they hear them often enough in church, and didn't they have, for entertainment, plenty of stories in their own heads, stories that had little to do with the Bible?

The dining room, with its great round table in the center, was not used much; often an extra cot was set up in there for the oldest of the children. Occasionally, when the old people wanted to escape the din of the children, they went in there to talk; but this was seldom, for an Irishman talks best when there is competition. The kitchen was the lived-in room. Here the family gathered to eat, talk, and play. Around the glowing wood stove the family, old friends, and even the cat, gathered on a dark winter night. The stove was the heart of the room, replacing the open hearth of the old country. The men were given the favored place, in front of the stove, where they could toast their wool-socked feet in the oven. The women gathered in another circle off to the side, sewing or knitting, hastily giving a full, round breast to a child whose crying interrupted a story. The child, spasmodically clutching and unclutching its hands, would fall asleep, its face still buried in the breast.

The teakettle stood always simmering, adding its steam to the damp smell of the room made by the diapers drying to one side of the stove. There was never a stove that did not have its teapot standing on the back of it to keep the strong tea warm but not boiling. The men and women

At the Saint Patrick's Day Parade in Holyoke, 1986. Photo by Richard W. Wilkie.

both filled their bowls freely. On some occasions there was whiskey, or "poteen," as it was still called. The room was filled with the tobacco smoke that issued from the T.D.'s that both the men and the women smoked alternately. There was much talk of the cancer of the mouth that they thought was brought on by the rough stems of these clay pipes. It was a miracle that any of these women could hold a clay pipe, for most of them lost their teeth with the first child. Some of the older ones took snuff, carefully offering their paper packet to the one who sat next. The snuff was always accepted with a prayer for the dead — "The blessing of God be with the souls of your dead." Occasionally a thanksgiving was offered for a pipeful of tobacco, too. At seven-thirty the oldest children put the youngest to bed and came back to listen to the talk, until, overwhelmed by the heat of the room, they tumbled off the stools and were sent to bed. Determined to stay awake to hear the end of the story, they were soon asleep with ghosts and goblins haunting their dreams.

Usually these evenings ended at eleven o'clock, for there was no

Irishman wanting to be up after twelve. One could never tell what one would meet then. Too, they all had to get up early in the morning to get to the mill by six. When the windows were still dark with the night, the women would be up taking the hot soda bread out of the oven for breakfast and the men would be shaving themselves before the kitchen mirror. Excepting for the thump, thump, of the razor strap and an occasional fretful cry from the bedroom, this was one of the rare times that the house was silent.

Gradually the whole tenement came to life, though the streets outside were still quiet. Just as the first lightness appeared, the men would come out of the blocks with their lunchboxes in their hands and there would be greetings along the still dark street. Sometimes the women, too, would appear, with their shawls wrapped tightly around them to keep the cold away, on their way to church. The men would walk along with one another, but there was no talk — it was still too dark and too early for that. The women and men both hurried along so as not to be late for the daily Mass which began at five-fifteen and ended at five-forty, so that the men could get to the mill by six and the women back to the children.

The church would be very quiet and cold, and the people huddled there, waiting impatiently for the altar boy to light the candles so that the priest might appear and get on with the Mass. Though they wanted to start the day right, they didn't want it to take too long. The people would kneel, quietly saying their beads, their rattling the only sound in the church. They rose as a body when the priest appeared and began: "*Introibo ad altare Dei. Ad Deum qui laetificat juventutem meam.*" The women received daily communion; the men received it only on Sundays — they needed the warm breakfast to get them through the twelve hours in the mill. After Mass, they all came out, ready for talk and banter now, for it was lighter and the day had started right. Some of the old women stopped to light a candle, but the younger ones hurried home to their children.

While the men worked their shift in the cotton and paper mills, the women worked theirs in the home. They baked their own bread, and indeed cooked everything their families ate. Flour was bought by the barrel and potatoes by the bushel. On Saturday and Wednesday mornings, the whole house was filled with the smell of fresh-made bread. On Monday, it was filled with the smell of damp laundry. There would be a great kettle of starch on the stove and soapsuds foaming over the edge of the set-tubs used on Saturday night for bathing children and on Monday morning for beating clothes into cleanliness. The back yards of the tenements were filled in winter with freshly washed clothes, hanging stiff as boards, iced by the wind. The women hanging them, their hands red and stiff with the cold, kept up a constant barrage of talk. "There'll be no

drying today with the weather the way it is, and me with another tubful
to replace these."

For forty years the O'Sullivans lived in Irish Parish and there were
changes that took place, not within the old but within the young. No one
thought of the Hill in the old days, nor much about education either. The
seventeen children, with the exception of Agnes (God rest her soul,
marked for death by the words of the blasphemous comparing her to an
angel) had, as a matter of course, been sent to Sister School. The order of
Notre Dame, stern and severe in habit, taught them. They learned noth-
ing much except to read, write, and spell. My mother's handwriting was
medieval, each letter carefully and conscientiously drawn.

I was born in Irish Parish, but was lifted out of it, and with my family
was one of the group to move to Money Hole Hill. The influx up there
came gradually, and our move from Johnny O'Sullivan's block made us
aliens for many years. The slow migration really began in my grandfather's
day. It began with the marriage of Sidney Whitney to Bridie Flannagan.
Irish Parish acquaintance with the Hill had only been a geographical one
till then; but the Hill came to the Parish when it wanted a wife for its
foremost son; for beauty and health, and a fine aristocracy, an aristocracy
of the spirit, resided there.

Bridie was a paper cutter in the Whitney Mill. In six months, she was
a lady in the Money Hole Hill sense of the term. My grandfather could see
no difference and told her so — "a few more feathers in your hat," — he
would say. But he was secretly pleased that she came to hear his stories,
as she always had. But who wouldn't come to hear my grandfather tell
stories! "He would have scared the Devil himself and kept him from his
evil work," my grandmother used to say.

Bridie was one of the first wedges, but there was another. Nelly Finn
moved up to Money Hole Hill, but her invitation was not so legitimate.
Nelly was a great source of amusement to the ladies of Irish Parish whose
husbands couldn't afford her. In their secret hearts, they were rather
tickled to know that the men on Money Hole Hill were frail, even if their
wives did wear so much whalebone. The ladies of Irish Parish were fond
of Nelly Finn; the ladies on the Hill scorned her. They had their reasons.
Many were the nudges and sly winks when, after Mass on Sunday morn-
ings, she drove through Kerry Park, her parasol tilted rakishly, and as
many birds in her hat as there were in a bush. My grandfather was fond
of Nelly, too; he would wait for her to pass his corner on Sunday morning
and inquire, "How's business, Nelly?" Nelly became a myth for Irish
Parish. Long after her death, my mother would say, when I was pestering
her, "Don't bother me now. I'm as busy as Nelly Finn."

We moved to the Hill because of my father, who was a foreigner and had little understanding of Irish Parish for all his having been born in Ireland. My grandfather blamed it on County Cork — "It's English he is, not Irish at all," — he would grumble. Others moved because the old ties were disappearing, and the Irish had little but the church and the mill in common any more. When we moved, Irish Parish was still at one with itself. Ours was looked on as the first great apostasy; for my grandfather, now old and childish, was still considered one of the archangels of Irish Parish. Everyone protested his departure, and none more than himself; for in Irish Parish, at least, he could still be shanty Irish with impunity.

And so we left Irish Parish for less green fields; and we became outcasts from our own race, and aliens among the race of Yankees into whose hallowed circle we moved. There were, it is true, a few Irish on Money Hole Hill; and they were the worst of all, imitators of imitators, neither Yankee nor Irish, but of that species known as the lace-curtain Irish. They put the curtains up in their parlors, and decked out their souls in the same cheap lace. It was into this circle that a lace-curtain father moved a set of the most shanty Irish people that have ever been. My grandfather refused to go back to Irish Parish because he would not leave my mother, whom he considered the root and flower of our whole family. My mother would not leave because she could never abandon, defeated, a battle involving her race. She would remain, though ostracized by both sides; and before we left for the school of the Yankees and our lace-curtain cousins, my mother enjoined us to remember, in the battles which occurred every day, that we were O'Sullivans, descendants of the kings of Ireland, and we were not to come home crying. We never did; and to the end of my days, I shall remember my mother standing in the door, her black eyes flashing out a fire that still serves to warm the worlds of the Money Hole Hills that I have lived in since.

Wakes or "crepes," as they were known in Irish Parish, were a great source of amusement in our family because of my mother's unfailing attendance at all of them. Every night she read "religiously" the death and birth announcements in the paper. Later in the evening, she would put on her hat and coat to go out. My father would ask, "who is it tonight?" "Johnny Finn, my father's cousin, is being waked tonight," she'd answer. "But I didn't know he was related," my father would say. "Oh yes, he was a sixth cousin. His mother, Brigid, was Dinny Meehan's third cousin, who was" — and so on, and on, like a page of Genesis, begetting cousins, until she ended triumphantly with "and that makes him John O'Sullivan's fifth cousin."

Of course kinship was not really necessary to attend a crepe in Irish

Parish; but as the times changed, my mother grew more and more apologetic about her constant attendance. My aunts considered it a scandalous thing to do, attending every ragtail-bobtail crepe in town. My mother never said a word. She just went. In her eyes everyone was related to her; and literally there were nearly seven hundred of our relations in the city.

Attending wakes was part of my mother's social ritual. She was continuing a tradition. In the old days in Irish Parish, a wake was social. It was not the horrible death-watch it is now. People went to wakes, not to mourn the dead, but to comfort the living. The function of attendance was to give tongue to the dead and say to the living the consoling things the dead could not say.

I attended my first wake when I was ten years old. When my mother and I entered John D. Shea's Funeral Parlor, the dead man's wife and children were standing in a receiving line at the door. My mother went up to them. The wife murmured, "Mamie O'Sullivan, it's that glad I am to see you." My mother put her arms around her, kissed her, and said, "The thanks of God be with you, Mary O'Donnell. You've lost a fine man to Him. He'll be grateful to you, for he's needing such company in that lonely place." My mother had a heart like a homing pigeon. Without a thought she could find her way to the heart of others.

We turned from the family and walked to the casket. Again, as at the sight of Jerry Sheehan, I fell to my knees. Here, if ever I met it anywhere, in the face of the dead was the peace that passes understanding. I could hear my mother praying, as my grandfather had done, aloud. I prayed with her. As I prayed, I could hear my grandfather's words: "No man ever dies, Mary O'Connor. He just leaves quietly to go home."

After our prayers at the casket, we went to the back of the room. There were many people seated around, mostly women, all talking intimately in low voices. I had been so awed by the sight of death that I wondered how they could talk so easily. I soon found out. All the talk was about the dead man. Everybody came with his most beautiful memory of Seamus Flaherty. The whole conversation was a memento to the dead man, the most beautiful that could have been offered. His whole life was preserved, as was my grandfather's, in this oral tradition. It was from the old Irish women at such wakes that I learned of the early days in Irish Parish and my grandfather's youth.

The memories were not all proper and expurgated — what these old women did was resurrect the living from the dead in their warm, rich rememberings: "Do ye remember, Annie, the time Seamus caught us scrubbing? I was like to die for shame, and the scolding of him. 'Woman usin' snuff on their gums,' he said. 'Go get yourself a husband, Katie Flynn, or you'll be having bad dreams next.'" There was a sighing laughter.

"Ah, couldn't he sing, though," my mother added — "a voice like a very bird. Do ye remember Father Feeney, the one who thought he'd a voice, though he'd croak no better than a frog? Seamus sang the response one Sunday, and we all near half-killed with laughing. Father Feeney with his cracked *Gloria!*" Here my mother raised her voice, imitating him. "And the sweet bitterness of Seamus's response. Sure, himself was like a rooster. He apologized to the Ladies of the Sodality, saying that he was not in good voice, and Seamus was so slow in the response it confused him."

The men, after they paid their respects to the dead, usually gathered in the kitchen. Soon the smell of their cigar smoke seeped into the other room, and the clank of the whiskey glasses turned the wake into the kind of social festival it was. Every now and then, I could hear laughter, and I know that they, too, were remembering not the dead man, but the live one.

At twelve o'clock, the whole tone changed. There was a great, silent, somber tone now, and I sat in my chair, feeling the doom of the hour. The dead man was departing and the keeners began to sing the farewell. I trembled. That *coainim* was the most elemental cry I have ever heard. Only the wail of a child coming from the womb resembles it. These women were not professional keeners, as those who now attend Irish wakes. They were friends of the dead man, and their cries were those of people bereft of one whom they loved. The cry rose and fell with the passion of their woe. It was the wordless wail of man issuing from the womb of earth, the cry of the wounded, woeful animal. It was the cry of the living clutching, clasping at the departing spirit of the dead, begging, beseeching his return. It was the cry of those who knew there would be no coming back. It rose and fell, to the words, *Olagon! Olagon! Olagon!*

At twelve-fifteen, almost exactly, the keening ceased. There was nothing again but the deep silence, and the quiet sobbing of those who were left. The casket was closed. The dead man had gone home. Suddenly, from the back of the room, a voice began: "In the name of the Father, and of the Son, and of the Holy Ghost. . . . I believe in God, the Father Almighty, Creator of heaven and earth; and in Jesus Christ, His only Son, our Lord: Who . . . was crucified; died, and was buried." It was the beginning of the Rosary. A deep peace came over the room. The words rose as a tide of comfort, filling the room with their warm familiarity. "Hail Mary" — the great round went on — "Glory be to the Father." The solid round beads of the rosary formed a warm comfort in the pocket of my hand as I walked home with my mother.

From *The Parish and the Hill* by Mary Doyle Curran. The Feminist Press at The City University of New York, 1986; originally published in 1948.

TRACY KIDDER

Tracy Kidder reported on one year in Chris Zajac's fifth-grade class at
Kelly School in the Holyoke Flats, *in* Among Schoolchildren. *Chris Zajac is a*
talented, committed teacher striving to handle and inspire children in a wide
variety of personal situations. This profile of one class tells us much about
American education and how one teacher can make a difference. The book is also
a perceptive account of contemporary Irish–Puerto Rican relations in Holyoke.
      Kidder won a Pulitzer Prize and a National Book Award for The Soul of a
New Machine, *about the race to design a super mini-computer at Data*
General. *His books* House *and* Old Friends *are also set in the Pioneer Valley.*
He is a frequent contributor to the Atlantic Monthly *and the* New Yorker.

Among Schoolchildren

Kelly School is in an old industrial and residential part of Holyoke, a neighborhood long known as the Flats. Yankee investors, mostly from Boston, invented Holyoke in the 1840s out of the whole cloth of a small farm town. Immigrant Irish laborers built the city, damming the Connecticut River at its falls and making it flow through what would become the Flats, along an ingenious network of canals that fed falling water to the turbines of long blocks of tall brick mills. Holyoke was something new in America, one of the nation's first planned industrial communities, and the Flats was an essential part of the city's engine. For a time, around the turn of the century, Holyoke produced more paper than any other city in the world, staining the wide Connecticut a variety of colors all the way down to the city of Springfield.

Chris Zajac — née Christine Padden — spent the first two years of her life in this neighborhood. Her apartment building had stood just a couple of now half-demolished blocks to the north of the school. Her father worked about a half mile away, in the mill of a giant paper company called National Blank Book. He was a section leader, a subforeman, in the shipping and receiving department. He had walked to work among shoulder-to-shoulder crowds of men with lunch boxes, down streets that old-timers remember as having been clean. Perhaps they were cleaner in memory than they ever were in fact, but back then, in the late 1950s, the Flats still looked like a thriving part of a thriving city. But even by then Holyoke's industries had fallen into a decline, which by the 1970s became altogether visible.

As the city's population fell, from nearly seventy thousand at the peak to about forty thousand in the 1980s, the buildings of the Flats

Hispanic boy with chihuahua, Holyoke, 1986. Photo by Richard W. Wilkie.

deteriorated. Some mills were abandoned. In the name of urban renewal
— and partly in order to limit the size of the growing Puerto Rican
population— City Hall presided over the demolition of many old apart-
ment blocks. Most dramatically, the Flats burned. For years, flames lit
the nighttime sky over Holyoke. Fires started in old wiring. Pyromaniacs
and people bent on personal vendettas and professionals interested in
insurance money set fires, and several were fatal. The fires changed the
landscape utterly. Although they had abated now, the phrase "burned
out" was still occasionally used in the hallways of Kelly School to explain
why a child had vanished from the rolls.

Lately, the state and federal governments had put up money to rebuild part of the Flats, and landlords had actually renovated some apartment buildings. The far northern section of the neighborhood made local optimists declare, "It's coming back." The place was clearly in transition, but its next direction wasn't really clear. The train station in the Flats, which H.H. Richardson himself designed, now housed an auto parts store. On many streets, vacant lots accumulating trash and weeds surrounded lone, sooty red brick apartment buildings, which had the outlines of vanished neighbors etched on their side walls. They didn't look it, but even the most decrepit of those buildings had become valuable. Because so many buildings had disappeared and inexpensive housing was scarce in the region, and because the state and federal governments guaranteed a lot of rents, real estate speculators had lately moved in on the Flats and other run-down parts of Holyoke. They'd buy a tenement in the Flats or South Holyoke or Churchill, jack up the mostly subsidized rents, refinance the building, and, sometimes, sell it for a handsome profit. So far they had not greatly improved the majority of buildings.

Kelly School is in the Flats, but not exactly of the Flats. The people involved in its creation, back in the 1970s, had imagined Kelly School the cornerstone of the revival of the neighborhood, the phoenix rising out of the ashes of the Flats. They had built it into the side of a hill, on the high ground of those riverine lowlands: an imposing, complex structure of right angles, made of yellow brick with black asphalt trim along the eaves of its flat roofs. Its plexiglass dome stuck up like a tank turret. The designers gave it not just one but two fine, expensive gyms, in the hopeful thought that these would draw the community to its school. But the custodians locked up the school after hours now, because vandals had worked over the locker rooms.

Six hundred and twenty students had enrolled at Kelly School this year. Thirty were black, 11 Asian, 265 "white" ("Anglo" won't do in Holyoke, which annually stages the nation's second largest St. Patrick's Day parade), and 314 Hispanic, which mainly meant Puerto Rican. As always, the numbers would fluctuate throughout the year, but in a sense would remain the same; about a fifth of the students would leave, to be replaced by a roughly equal number of newcomers. About 60 percent of the children came from families receiving some form of public assistance. By design — the system was desegregated in the early 1980s — Kelly School's student body conformed statistically to the citywide population, and so did the student body in Chris's class.

Holyoke's borders enclose some working farms, some forest, and a gigantic mall beside the interstate, one site around which the new, suburban Holyoke is growing. Kelly School took in a fair cross-section of the

Holyoke tenements, 1980. Photo by Jerome Liebling.

city. Its territory included a suburban area, which looked like Anywhere, U.S.A. — one-story ranch houses, some modest and some grand. But only one bus from Kelly climbed into that region, and it didn't carry anyone from Chris's class.

Most of Kelly School's children came from neighborhoods in the old city. Seen from above, from the interstate, this old part of Holyoke is all smokestacks and church steeples. It has always been a city of labor and religion. Boosters advertise Holyoke as the birthplace of volleyball and as the place where the kitchen product Lestoil was invented. In the old days, an ethnographer could have mapped it by its churches: Mater Dolorosa and St. Jerome's in Irish and Polish Old Ward Four; Precious Blood and Perpetual Help in South Holyoke, where Masses were French Canadian in liturgy and music; Immaculate Conception and Holy Rosary in the French and Irish Flats. Holyoke's small black population always had a Baptist church, now situated near the projects on Jackson Parkway. Uptown Protestants still have an Episcopal and a Congregational church, and uptown Catholics have Blessed Sacrament and Holy Cross, Chris's mother's church. Sacred Heart — Chris's church — in formerly Irish Churchill, now holds Masses in Spanish as well as English. The ten thousand parishioners who used to go to French Precious Blood, in the lower ward of South Holyoke, have dwindled now to about forty, while clustered around that old Catholic church are many little storefront Pentecostal ones with Spanish names above their doors. Holyoke remains a balkanized city. The divisions used to be more numerous. Only one sharp ethnic division exists anymore — between Puerto Ricans, the latest newcomers, and practically everyone else.

Several children in Chris's class this year came from Old Ward Four, just uphill from the Flats, a mixed neighborhood now of whites and Puerto Ricans, generally poor. It is a greener neighborhood than the Flats, with more wood frame houses and far fewer vacant lots, but it too has apartment buildings and run-down sections. Chris's father grew up in Old Ward Four when it was simply called "the Ward." He lived with his parents in an apartment block near Dwight and Pine, now one of several notorious distribution points for narcotics. Chris had fond memories of visiting relatives in the Ward, but both she and her mother made a point of not driving through there anymore. The boarded-up storefronts and graffiti made them imagine Chris's father saddened. "If your father could see this now," Chris's mother had said to Chris the last time they had driven through that neighborhood together. And Chris had said, "He'd turn over in his grave."

The Zajacs went, as always, to Holyoke's elaborate St. Patrick's Day parade. The day was blustery, the sky the leaden color of the street down which, the parade wearing on, some marchers came lurching. When Senator Edward Kennedy hove into view, in tails and top hat and jauntily swinging a shillelagh, announced by many female voices up the street crying, "Teddy! Teddy! Teddy!" Chris whispered to one of her sisters, "I'm going to do it." She set her jaw, stepped off the sidewalk, and then she thought, "Oh, should I?" That cost her the chance. She'd just resumed her trot into the street when one of her elderly aunts, not hesitating for a moment, rose from her lawn chair, throwing off her lap robe, and dashed out to the senator. The aunt pumped his hand with both of hers. As the senator received the woman, with a slight bow and then a smile that he threw toward the sky, Chris veered away and trotted back to her place among her family on the sidewalk. She stood there muttering, making angry eyes at her aunt.

Chris and Billy put on their customary St. Patrick's Day party afterward at their house, nearly all of their extended families there, lots of corned beef and cabbage and some kielbasa, too. Billy merely tolerated the parade, and around this time of year if someone asked Chris a question such as, "What does St. Patrick's Day commemorate?" Bill would say, "Beer drinking," and Chris would fulminate briefly. What about the Polish, Billy? she'd say. Was beer unknown to them? The party was wonderful. Her best friend from college came. Chris got her mind entirely off school until around midnight, when she awakened with a start, thinking, "Has Felipe dropped his instrumental music lessons?" No, he hadn't. She went back to sleep.

Every now and then in uptown Holyoke, Chris got into an argument that went something like this: Some white acquaintance would say, "Goddamn Puerto Ricans." Chris would answer, "Look, I teach them. There are no more goddamn Puerto Ricans than goddamn anyone else." She'd describe radiant Puerto Rican children, such as Judith and Arabella, and the usual response was: "Yeah, but she's an exception. She's a good one." Chris felt uncomfortable in those arguments .

The ignorance of some of her townspeople appalled her. An angry parent visited Kelly School the first year of desegregation and declared, "Look, they even got the Puerto Rican flag here." In fact, the unfamiliar flag he had spotted was that of the Commonwealth of Massachusetts. Earlier this year a white parent stormed into Al's office complaining that his child was being taught some Spanish. While her own blind spots were not as large, Chris knew that she had some. Out in the city alone, she occasionally felt her mind close. In her car, passing by a group of young Puerto Rican men who stood on a street corner on a spring midafternoon, she felt uneasy, as she did sometimes driving to church. She knew that those men might work night shifts, and that most Puerto Ricans who stand on corners are not looking for trouble — for many, especially ones of agrarian backgrounds, conversation outdoors is infinitely preferable to seeing friends in a cramped living room. But Holyoke was Chris's city. She wasn't a latter-day, out-of-town VISTA volunteer coming down to the Flats to do her part for Democracy. She knew, of course, that a few vandals, and not Puerto Ricans in general, were responsible for the graffiti on buildings and on boarded-up storefronts. But she hated the graffiti and the signs of decay and disorder in neighborhoods that had once seemed safe and well kept. And through a car window it was easy to connect sights like those with Puerto Ricans. Driving through a once familiar neighborhood such as the one where her father grew up, she felt like a stranger in her own hometown. She would have felt uneasy getting out of her car.

Chris was born too late to experience any disadvantage from being Irish in Holyoke. She couldn't imagine how she might have felt if marked as "a shanty Irish girl" in the Yankee Highlands. Last year, though, on the class field trip, she imagined she got a taste of what it must be like to live in a world of hostile looks. Her class had arrived at an exhibit at the same time as an all-white class from a Boston suburb and some elderly white tourists. The white children from the suburb were rude and noisy. Her kids were very well behaved. But those elderly tourists smiled at the white children, and when her gold-skinned Puerto Rican students asked questions, the tourists recoiled, exchanging heaven-help-us glances. She could read their minds. "Ugh, Puerto Ricans. What are *they* doing here?" Her students didn't notice. Something of that maternal instinct that makes a she-bear dangerous swept over Chris, and for just a moment she was Puerto Rican, too. Oh, she would have liked to scold those bigoted old fools. "Look at these kids from Arlington you look at so fondly. They're terrible, *and* they're lily-white," she imagined herself saying. But the tourists didn't actually say anything overtly insulting, maybe because of the looks she gave them. The experience was new for her. She felt glad afterward to have discovered such angry, righteous feelings in herself.

Chris spent her first years as a teacher in a small uptown neighborhood school. Back then she had taught white children, some poor, some fairly well-to-do, many from working-class families like her own. She could easily imagine those children's lives outside school. She always knew some of their parents. She could look out the huge, old-fashioned windows of her classroom and say to some of her students that she saw their mothers hanging up laundry and might go outside right now and have a word with them if those children didn't shape up. She pined sometimes for that old school. These days, Chris would stand at her classroom window in the afternoon, especially on the afternoons before a vacation, and watching her walkers amble away across the playground, she would think, "I don't even know what I'm sending them back to."

And yet in the intimate setting of her classroom, the facts that half her classes nowadays were of Puerto Rican descent and more than half were poorer than she'd ever been did not seem like insuperable barriers. Unlike white parents, Puerto Rican ones tended to bring their children to the scheduled conferences with Chris, and to bawl out their children or praise them right there on the spot. When Chris entertained Puerto Rican parents in her room, no differences seemed much larger than that. She didn't find it hard to talk to Puerto Rican parents, even if an interpreter was needed. They wanted to know about their children's schoolwork and seemed especially interested to know if their children showed her proper respect. The word *"respeto"* means good manners practiced for their own sake. That was the general meaning Chris had in mind when she talked about respect.

She already knew Felipe's father, Eduardo, slightly. She had taught Felipe's sisters, who were good students. She thought Eduardo and his wife must be marvelous parents. Her first conversation this year with Eduardo, at her classroom door, had not altered her opinion. Eduardo had asked her — Felipe was standing there — how the boy was behaving. Chris had said, "Well, Felipe has his ups and downs." Eduardo had gazed sternly at Felipe, who had bowed his head and watched himself shuffle his feet.

From *Among Schoolchildren* by Tracy Kidder. Houghton Mifflin, 1989.

SUZANNE STREMPEK SHEA

Suzanne Strempek Shea's Selling the Lite of Heaven *(1994) is a novel set in the Polish community in the Bondsville section of Palmer. She relates the awkward courtship of a woman who works at a Fast Foto and a sensitive man who jilts her to become a priest. The heroine salves her disappointment in a series of humorous encounters with different characters seeking to buy the superfluous wedding ring. This selection describes an Easter Sunday of the Polish congregation.*

Strempek Shea writes for the Springfield Union News *and still lives in Bondsville.*

Easter Sunday

By 5:15 on Easter morning, the noon meal was nearly cooked and both my parents were fully dressed and polished for the day. The house smelled of simmering borscht and baking ham and Brut. On the kitchen table, set for the family breakfast that would be eaten after we returned from the 6 A.M. sunrise service, the everyday dishes were joined by my mother's black patent leather pocketbook, our three church envelopes, and a can of Progresso minestrone soup for the poor people's food basket. Though church is only a mile away, we would be leaving soon.

When I attend mass with my parents — they prefer the 8 A.M. Polish one in which even the sermon and the announcements are in the language that the relatives who took them in advised they try to lose to better their chances of blending in with the rest of America — we almost always are the first ones there. They are afraid of not getting a seat, or, worse, of having no choice but to sit in one of the vacancies way up front, in clear view of everyone else. I remember a time during my high school years when my mother began to refuse to wait for me if I was running late in my preparations. On several occasions, I had to chase the car as it pulled away, my mother crouched over the wheel, my father sympathetically looking back at me, then quickly at the driver, and again at me, my high heels clacking and my handbag flapping. It was pretty embarrassing and pretty much unnecessary, as aside from major Holy Days of Obligation, there always are lots of empty seats throughout the church.

Even so, my parents are determined each week to get their same pew — fifth from the last row on the left. The location allows for a quick exit, and is on the side of the church on which the priest — not the extraordinary minister — distributes communion. My mother never has accepted the idea of extraordinary ministers, and long ago made it clear that while she has no problem buying a pair of sensible pumps from him, she doesn't want that shoe salesman — that divorced shoe salesman, no less — placing on her tongue the Body of Christ.

So there we sat that Easter morning, five seats from the back, with only a handful of people beating us to the place. When my mother spotted their three or four cars parked in the prime spaces edging the front walk of the church, she said to no one in particular, "I told you," and raised high her eyebrows. I felt no guilt — any tardiness that prevented us from getting there right at the point when the nuns were unlocking the doors was not my fault. Today I had been ready on time. Everybody in the world went to this mass on Easter, and I knew Eddie would be one of them.

Slowly, the rest of the pews began to fill. Old sons held the door as their much older mothers maneuvered walkers over the threshold. Young mothers in tight floral dresses herded elaborately outfitted toddlers, and elbowed them when they played too much with the elastic strings holding the straw hats on their heads. To my left, my father, in the old brown suit he must have had forever, was praying on a set of rosary beads his own father had received on the day of his First Communion. The beads were dark and oval and I always have thought they looked like the coffee beans I once saw being ground up at the A & P. A long time ago I was snooping in their room for nothing special and I found the rosary in its place in a brown leather box on my father's dresser. I sat on the bed and swung it around, then admired the beads and their smoothness. Then I bit one, just to see if they were indeed some kind of food. I left in the first Our Father bead the straight impression of an incisor in what I finally found out was wood.

Now the beads were passing through my father's fingers at the rate of a clock's big hand: if you watched, you wouldn't see them moving. But all of a sudden you would notice he had gone through an entire decade.

I wondered what it was he prayed for. Were there things he'd wanted since he was a boy that he still hoped to get? Money? Property? Renown? Somehow, I couldn't see my father hoping to be famous, to be somebody who would get bothered for his autograph while scooping a bag of tenpenny nails from a bin down at Chudy's. He always had money — not in the bank, maybe, but I know there were wads of large bills jammed into at least three Chock Full o' Nuts cans on the top shelves of his workshop. He owned his own house, with three acres for his Macs and Spencers, so it couldn't be that. He was married, so it couldn't be love he wanted. Or could it?

To my right, my mother sat with her hands in her lap. If she had her Austrian crystal rosary with her, rather than leaving it in a velvet sack in her top dresser drawer, from where, my father and I are reminded periodically, it is to be taken on the day she dies so the undertaker can lace it through her fingers for eternity, I know her prayers would have something to do with me. And, I am certain, they would not be in thanksgiving.

One of the few women in our church who continue to wear a hat to mass in our church, my mother alternately darted and glared her eyes from beneath the small round brim of orchid and white satin hung with a drape of royal blue Russian lace.

I was staring at the foam rubber that poked through the cracked vinyl on the kneeler at my feet when she jammed her elbow into my side. "Hey!" I whispered sharply, and looked at her. Her own face was set straight ahead, but her eyes were flitting in some sort of code: to the right, back to the center, and to the right again. So I looked to the right, too, and saw Eddie taking a seat across the aisle and up a few rows. I felt my heart quicken and I lowered my head.

From the corner of my eye, I saw Eddie kneel in the silence broken only once in a while by a *ssshhhh* to some child or by somebody having a coughing fit. On Easter Sunday in my church, no music plays until the priest comes out in front of the little altar that the nuns, using papier-mache and gray paint, have transformed into the cave in which Jesus was buried — the same cave they used about four months before as the one in which he was born. The priest stands there in front of the empty hole and, in a big, long line of Polish, informs everyone that Christ has risen. Then the music swells up and the choir pipes out a harmonized Alleluia! Alleluia!

That is what it is doing right now, in a church so packed that people are standing on tiptoe outside next to the open windows to hear what is going on. The choir is blasting out Alleluia! We are responding Alleluia! Some of us, like me, who can't sing, only mouth the words. But all of us can feel the hope of a resurrection, of the fact that things can begin anew. One of us, and that is me, can feel the hope of something almost more unbelievable than God rising from the dead: the reality that Eddie Balicki has turned and that he has spotted me and that our eyes have met and that he right now is whispering Happy Easter, right to me.

Alleluia! the choir rings. Alleluia! on Easter Sunday. Christ is risen! And Eddie looked at you! Even said something!

Because I was with my parents, that one look and those two words were all I got of him that morning. There would be no staying behind for a prayer — they liked to be up and out of there and at the drugstore for the Sunday papers as soon as possible. They did oblige the priest's frequent request that everyone stay, not charge out of their pews immediately after the last amen, but that was about it. After the first chorus of "*Wesoly Nam Dzis Dzien Nastal,*" which exalts about the happy new day that is beginning, the three of us were pulled into the stream pouring out of the building, everybody smiling and greeting and looking forward to the rest of that happy new day.

I shuffled toward the door, but glanced back. Eddie had moved to the group that surrounded the empty crypt, and was standing there staring into the cave, resting his hand on the marble baptismal font next to it. I realized with a pleasing twinge that both of us, eight years apart, had been lowered into that very same marble bowl, howling because of our salted tongues, anointed foreheads, and dripping scalps, not realizing that we had just been made one of a holy nation, a people set apart.

From *Selling the Lite of Heaven* by Suzanne Strempek Shea. Simon & Schuster, 1994.

Northampton,
"Paradise of America"

Northampton's Main Street in 1836 from the porch of J.S. Vinton's inn. From *American Scenery* by Nathaniel P. Willis, 1839; courtesy of Eugene C. Worman.

HENRY JAMES

*Novelist Henry James (1843-1916) spent the fall of 1864 at Northampton's
Prospect House. Though he criticized the area as "stupid," he began writing his
first fiction during this stay. The visit became raw material for his first
full-length novel,* Roderick Hudson *(1875), which he wrote while living in
Rome, ruminating for the first time in a novel upon the qualities of American
vs. European life. His doubts about provincial Northampton reflect his overall
feelings toward his native country, yet he uses the Connecticut Valley to
symbolize the best of the American landscape, which he was prone to criticize,
yet ready, ambivalently, to prize.*

*Protagonist Rowland Mallet, an art connoisseur and a Civil War veteran,
visits his cousin Cecilia in Northampton and discovers a talented sculptor,
Roderick Hudson, working in obscurity there. Mallet invites Hudson to join
him in Rome, where he can develop into a serious artist.*

An American Landscape

Mallet had made his arrangements to sail for Europe on the first of
September, and having in the interval a fortnight to spare, he
determined to spend it with his cousin Cecilia, the widow of a
nephew of his father. He was urged by the reflection that an affectionate
farewell might help to exonerate him from the charge of neglect fre-
quently preferred by this lady. It was not that the young man disliked
her; on the contrary, he regarded her with a tender admiration, and he
had not forgotten how, when his cousin had brought her home on her
marriage, he had seemed to feel the upward sweep of the empty bough
from which the golden fruit had been plucked, and had then and there
accepted the prospect of bachelorhood. The truth was, that, as it will be
part of the entertainment of this narrative to exhibit, Rowland Mallet had
an uncomfortably sensitive conscience, and that, in spite of the seeming
paradox, his visits to Cecilia were rare because she and her misfortunes
were often uppermost in it. Her misfortunes were three in number: first,
she had lost her husband; second, she had lost her money (or the greater
part of it); and third, she lived at Northampton, Massachusetts.

The next day was Sunday, and Rowland proposed that they should
take a long walk and that Roderick should show him the country. The
young man assented gleefully, and in the morning, as Rowland at the
garden gate was giving his hostess Godspeed on her way to church, he
came striding along the grassy margin of the road and out-whistling the

music of the church bells. It was one of those lovely days of August when you feel the complete exuberance of summer just warned and checked by autumn. "Remember the day, and take care you rob no orchards," said Cecilia, as they separated.

The young men walked away at a steady pace, over hill and dale, through woods and fields, and at last found themselves on a grassy elevation studded with mossy rocks and red cedars. Just beneath them, in a great shining curve, flowed the goodly Connecticut. They flung themselves on the grass and tossed stones into the river; they talked like old friends. Rowland lit a cigar, and Roderick refused one with a grimace of extravagant disgust. He thought them vile things; he didn't see how decent people could tolerate them. Rowland was amused, and wondered what it was that made this ill-mannered speech seem perfectly inoffensive on Roderick's lips. He belonged to the race of mortals, to be pitied or envied according as we view the matter, who are not held to a strict account for their aggressions. Looking at him as he lay stretched in the shade, Rowland vaguely likened him to some beautiful, supple, restless, bright-eyed animal, whose motions should have no deeper warrant than the tremulous delicacy of its structure, and be graceful even when they were most inconvenient. Rowland watched the shadows on Mount Holyoke, listened to the gurgle of the river, and sniffed the balsam of the pines. A gentle breeze had begun to tickle their summits, and brought the smell of the mown grass across from the elm-dotted river meadows. He sat up beside his companion and looked away at the far-spreading view. It seemed to him beautiful, and suddenly a strange feeling of prospective regret took possession of him. Something seemed to tell him that later, in a foreign land, he would remember it lovingly and penitently.

"It's a wretched business," he said, "this practical quarrel of ours with our own country, this everlasting impatience to get out of it. Is one's only safety then in flight? This is an American day, an American landscape, an American atmosphere. It certainly has its merits, and some day when I am shivering with ague in classic Italy, I shall accuse myself of having slighted them."

He walked homeward, thinking of many things. The great Northampton elms interarched far above in the darkness, but the moon had risen and through scattered apertures was hanging the dusky vault with silver lamps. There seemed to Rowland something intensely serious in the scene in which he had just taken part. He had laughed and talked and braved it out in self-defense; but when he reflected that he was really meddling with the simple stillness of this little New England home, and that he had ventured to disturb so much living security in the interest of a far-away, fantastic hypothesis, he paused, amazed at his temerity. It was true, as Cecilia had said, that for an unofficious man it was a singular position. There stirred in his mind an odd feeling of annoyance with Roderick for having thus peremptorily enlisted his sympathies. As he looked up and down the long vista, and saw the clear white houses glancing here and there in the broken moonshine, he could almost have believed that the happiest lot for any man was to make the most of life in some such tranquil spot as that. Here were kindness, comfort, safety, the warning voice of duty, the perfect hush of temptation. And as Rowland looked along the arch of silvered shadow and out into the lucid air of the American night, which seemed so doubly vast, somehow, and strange and nocturnal, he felt like declaring that here was beauty too — beauty sufficient for an artist not to starve upon it.

From *Roderick Hudson* by Henry James. The Library of American, 1983.

HENRY WARD BEECHER

The Reverend Henry Ward Beecher (1813-1887) was one of his century's most influential public speakers. He graduated from Amherst College in 1834, which he attended because of its Congregationalist orientation. From his pulpit at Brooklyn's Plymouth Congregational Church, Beecher championed such causes as abolition and women's rights.

Beecher wrote many books, including novels. Norwood; Or, Village Life in New England *(1868) actually was set in Northampton and included glimpses of his neighboring alma mater. In* Norwood, *Beecher draws a vignette of the social structure of provincial towns and raises an ode to the great beautifier of New England communities — the American Elm.*

Village Life in New England

A traveller going north from Springfield, in Massachusetts, soon perceives before him an abrupt barrier, running east and west, which, if compared with the country on either side, might be called mountainous. The two westernmost summits are Mount Tom and Mount Holyoke. By a narrow passage between them comes through the Connecticut River. Passing between these hill-mountains, we enter a great valley or basin, some twelve miles wide and thirty long, which one might easily imagine to have been once a lake; the Pelham hills on the east, Sugar-loaf on the north, and the Holyoke range on the south, forming barriers on three sides, while its waters on the west were stayed by the slopes of those hills which, in the middle of western Massachusetts, are all that remain of the famous Green Mountains.

Look with my eyes, good reader, upon the town of Norwood, that, refusing to go down upon the fat bottom-lands of the Connecticut, daintily perches itself upon the irregular slopes west, and looks over upon that transcendent valley from under its beautiful shade trees, and you will say that no fairer village glistens in the sunlight, or nestles under arching elms! It is a wonder that Norwood was ever allowed to venture so near to the low grounds of the Connecticut; for it was early settled, not far from thirty years after the Pilgrims' landing. How the temptation to build upon the top of the highest hill was resisted, we know not.

Did the New England settler alight upon hill-tops, like a sentinel, or a hawk upon the topmost bough, to spy danger at its first appearing? Or had he some unconscious sense of the poetic beauty of the scriptural city set upon a hill — some Jerusalem, lifted up, and seen from afar, in all its beauty? Or was he willing to face the sturdy winds of New-England hill-tops, rather than to take the risk of malaria in the softer air of her valleys? Whatever the reason, the chosen spot in early days seems to have been a high and broad-backed hill, where the summer came last, and departed earliest; where, while it lingered, it was purest and sweetest; where winter was most austere, and its winds roared among the trees, and shook the framed houses with such awful grandeur, that children needed nothing more to awaken in their imagination the great Coming Judgment, and the final consuming storms, when the earth should be shaken and should pass away!

Norwood, a town of five thousand inhabitants, like hundreds of other New England towns, had in a general and indistinct way an upper, middle and lower class. A wholesome jealousy of their rights, and a suspicion among the poor that wealth and strength always breed danger to the weak, made the upper class — who were ranked so by their wealth, by their superior culture, and by the antiquity of their families in town — politically weaker than any other.

The middle class comprised the great body of the people, all dependent upon their skill and activity for a living, and all striving to amass property enough to leave their families at their death in independent circumstances.

The lower class of a New England village is chiefly composed of the hangers-on — those who are ignorant and imbecile, and especially those who, for want of moral health, have sunk, like sediment, to the bottom. Perhaps nowhere in the world can be found more unlovely wickedness — a malignant, bitter, tenacious hatred of good — than in New England. The good are very good, and the bad are very bad. The high moral tone of public sentiment, in many New-England towns, and its penetrating and almost inquisitorial character, either powerfully determines men to do good, or chafes and embitters them. This is especially true when, in certain cases, good men are so thoroughly intent upon public morality that the private individual has scarcely any choice left. Under such a pressure some men act in open wickedness out of spite, and some secretly; and the bottom of society wages clandestine war with the top.

But, fortunately for Norwood, the public sentiment, though strong and high in moral tone, had been by peculiar influences so tempered with kindness, that, far less than in surrounding places, was there a class of fierce castaways at the bottom.

The main street of Norwood was irregular, steadily seeking higher ground to its extreme western limit. It would have had no claims to beauty had it not been rich in the peculiar glory of New England — its Elm-trees! No town can fail of beauty, though its walks were gutters, and its houses hovels, if venerable trees make magnificent colonnades along its streets. Of all trees, no other unites, in the same degree, majesty and beauty, grace and grandeur, as the American Elm! Known from north to south, through a range of twelve hundred miles, and from the Atlantic to the head waters of the rivers which flow into the western side of the Mississippi, yet, in New England, the elm is found in its greatest size and beauty, fully justifying Michaux's commendation of it to European cultivators, as "the most magnificent vegetable of the Temperate Zone." Though a lover of moisture and richness, the elm does not flourish so well upon pure vegetable soils as on intervale lands, stronger in mineral ingredients than river meadows.

Single spots, finer than any in New England, there may be in other lands; but such a series of villages over such a breadth of country, amidst so much beauty of scenery, enriched, though with charming and inexpensive simplicity, with so much beauty of garden, yard, and dwelling, cannot elsewhere be found upon the globe. No man has seen America, who has not become familiar with the villages of New England and the farms of the Northwestern States. Yet every one will confess that a large part of this scenic beauty of New England is contributed by trees, — and particularly by the elm. The Elms of New England! They are as much a part of her beauty as the columns of the Parthenon were the glory of its architecture.

Their towering trunks, whose massiveness well symbolizes Puritan inflexibility; their over-arching tops, facile, wind-borne and elastic, hint the endless plasticity and adaptableness of this people; — and both united, form a type of all true manhood, broad at the root, firm in the trunk, and yielding at the top, yet returning again, after every impulse, into position and symmetry. What if they were sheered away from village and farm house? Who would know the land? Farm-houses that now stop the tourist and the artist, would stand forth bare and homely; and villages that coquette with beauty through green leaves, would shine white and ghastly as sepulchres. Let any one imagine Conway or Lancaster without elms! Or Hadley, Hatfield, Northampton, or Springfield! New Haven without elms would be like Jupiter without a beard, or a lion shaved of his mane!

And so, reader, as one loves to approach a mansion through an avenue of elms, we have led you through a short discourse of trees, to our homely story.

From *Norwood; Or, Village Life in New England* by Henry Ward Beecher. Charles Scribner and Company, 1868.

BRET LOTT

*Good writers abound in the Northampton area. One of them, Bret Lott,
captures a sense of place in* A Stranger's House *(1988). The novel tells the story
of a couple who buy and renovate an old house in Chesterfield. Following is a
selection breakfasting at the Miss Florence Diner. Bret Lott is now a professor
at the University of Charleston.*

Miss Florence Diner

W e went from the apartment first to the newspaper, where Tom
had to stop in and look over his desk, more a symbolic gesture
to his editor than any real devotion to the job. Then we went for
breakfast at the Miss Florence Diner, a brick-and-oak Deco place left over
from the forties or fifties, we could never decide which. Above the restau-
rant was a neon sign, the name spelled out in orange and set against a
large green chevron of sorts.

Inside, construction workers sat at stools along the counter, buffalo-
plaid shirts and down vests and scuffed workboots on, cups of coffee in
front of them. Most of the booths were full, men and women heading to
work, tabletops covered with plates of food: eggs, sausage, waffles, ba-
gels. Where each table met the wall was a miniature jukebox, above each
a glass case with a knob on the side. Inside the cases were pages and
pages of song titles; when you turned the knob the pages fell forward or
back to reveal more songs: tunes by Elvis and Linda Ronstadt and Bob
Seger and the Beatles and most anyone else.

We walked to the left along the booths, moving toward the back where
we liked to sit. At one booth sat two Smith girls, black turtlenecks on, pale
faces and chopped hair, cigarettes out. At another booth sat a business-
man in a three-piece charcoal gray wool suit, *The Wall Street Journal* in one
hand, a coffee cup in the other. At one other booth sat two old men, both
wearing flannel shirts, one bald, the other with a full head of white hair.
Both had their hands wrapped around their cups, and were staring out
the green-tinted window onto Route 9 and the cars heading into town.

We slid into our booth, and the waitress was there with two cups and
a pot of black, black coffee.

She didn't even ask, but went ahead and poured us each a cup; then
pulled from her apron a handful of half-and-half containers and dropped
them on the table. We'd had her before, and she always looked like this,
always had the same hairpiece on, a coffee pot in hand. The only thing
that ever changed about her was the addition or subtraction of her sweater,

depending upon what time of year it was.

"It's a nice frost today," she said, and smiled, nodding as if in agreement with her own observation.

"Not long before snow," Tom said, and broke open a container, dumped it into his coffee.

She said, "But then that's when winter really comes on, and I can wait for that. These frosts don't do anything other than make you drape your bushes at night and scrape your car in the morning. That's fine by me. That snow, though," she said, and scowled, shook her head. She hadn't yet looked at us, but held the glass coffee pot and stared at the cups as though they might move. She was waiting for us.

I said, "I'll have pancakes and sausage. Short stack."

"Same here," Tom said. "And o.j."

"Me too."

She gave a short, hard nod, turned and stopped to fill three more customers' coffee cups before she made it back to the cook station.

He was looking at the jukebox, and reached up, started flipping back the little laminated pages of selections. I reached across the table to him and pinched his forearm.

"Ouch," he said, and looked at me. He said, "How about Johnny Cash? 'I Walk the Line'?"

I leaned back and looked at everything, took in the smell of coffee and food, looked at the people and our waitress, now filling the cups of the construction workers. "I love this place," I said.

Tom reached into his pocket, his shoulders going up to get at, I imagined, the change buried in the corner of his pocket. "I'm glad you're so enamored of Miss Flo's, sweetheart," he said, his smile more of a grimace now that he was digging in the pocket. He pulled out a quarter, relief on his face, his smile easy now. "Because," he went on, "this is the caliber of the kinds of places we'll be able to afford from now on. This and Friendly's."

He reached over and dropped in the quarter, punched a letter and a number on the machine. Johnny Cash came booming out, his voice black gravel. Two of the construction workers looked over at us, men with flushed faces and small eyes and big hands. The businessman glanced at us over the top edge of his paper.

"Turn it down," I whispered loudly, and Tom laughed. He leaned back in the booth and put his hands behind his head.

"Come on," he said. "Enjoy this music. It's a luxury now."

I turned it down myself, fiddling with the little knob on the front of the machine. I didn't turn it down as low as I should have, and I sat back, too. Let them watch, I thought. Let anybody watch. We're buying a house today.

From *A Stranger's House* by Bret Lott. Viking Penguin, 1988.

RICHARD TODD

The tenure of New England Monthly, *lasting from 1984 until 1990,*
paralleled the 1980s boom in New England. The yuppie counterpart of Yankee
Magazine, New England Monthly *was published out of Haydenville, and*
printed several pieces on the increasing fashionableness of the Pioneer Valley.
Richard Todd, editor of New England Monthly, *sketched the contradictions of*
the late 1980s consumer economy in Northampton in this selection from the
magazine, adumbrating the economic collapse that would soon arrive. Todd
lives in Ashfield and works as a book editor for Houghton Mifflin.

Notes from the Transcendental Valley

I live right in the heart of New England, in a place we'll call Transcen-
dental Valley, and I have to say that things are very good here. Just
yesterday I walked down Main Street. The soap store, the candle
store, the balloon store were all full of customers. The sticker store, too —
lots of people, looking thoughtfully at the new bumper stickers. Trend:
stickers for the older driver. Among them, "AVENGE YOURSELF — Live long
enough to be a problem to your children" and "WE'RE $PENDING our kids'
inheritance." At the store devoted to saving the animals, more stickers:
"I ♥ Whales," "I ♥ Dolphins," "I ♥ Sea Otters."

Brisk business at the Juice Bar, with a new item featured: fresh wheat-
grass juice. Next door at the health store, babies in backpacks stared
gravely into the distance as their mothers deliberated over five kinds of
bottled water.

The only sign of economic distress I could see was at the store for
those who run. Jogbras were on sale, two for $28. The way I figure it, though,
they just overstocked on Jogbras. It could have happened to anyone.

The point is, we've got disposable income around here, and we've got
places to dispose of it.

One mystery, not talked about all that often: where does the money
come from? One theory holds that it comes from the young people. We're
a college town, and the school serves as our factory. Others say no, it's
the computers. The computers are built a couple of valleys to the east.
No one here builds them, but many think that the money oozes over
here anyway.

I don't know. To me, this place is looking more and more like the
island whose economy was founded on laundry. Everybody took in
somebody else's wash. Here, at noontime, the *dim sum* chef has lunch at

the restaurant of the Cajun expert, who goes off to enjoy *fajitas*. Everyone else plays racquetball until 1:30.

We live in a nearly perfect service economy. In this we may lead, but we march in step with the rest of the region. In the last five years, the time of its greatest prosperity in a century, New England actually lost manufacturing jobs. Not only in industries such as textiles, but even in high tech. Massachusetts alone lost 8,000 high-tech jobs last year. But the impact was muted by the growth of the service economy: again in Massachusetts, that meant 66,000 new jobs.

In 1973, Daniel Bell wrote in *The Coming of Post-Industrial Society*: "The post-industrial society, it is clear, is a knowledge society in a double sense: first, the sources of innovation are increasingly derivative from research and development ... second, the weight of the society — measured by a larger proportion of Gross National Product and a larger share of employment — is increasingly in the knowledge field."

Are we enacting that prophecy? Maybe, but Bell made it sound different from the way it now looks. In the information-driven society one imagines lots of beige offices, people making the big decisions that activate robots in some distant, benighted spot.

But it doesn't look like that. It looks more like candles . . . bumper stickers . . . *torta rustica*. There are no more shipbuilders in Massachusetts now that the Quincy shipyard is closing. But in the Commonwealth alone, 173,000 people work in restaurants. Of course, there is service and there is service. New England has 7,000 psychologists, too, and 42,000 lawyers.

But how does it all hang together? Where *does* the money come from? Walking down Main Street I remembered how this town used to be twenty-five years ago. In that era I once saw a family arrive on Saturday morning by buckboard. It was a warm day in winter, and they were taking advantage of the thaw to come down from a farm in the hills to shop. These were not recreational buckboardists; you could tell by their stiff dignity that the wagon was their only transportation.

I wonder what they needed. Whatever it was, they would not find it today. The thing about Main Street today is that although you can get what you want, you can't ever get what you need.

I stepped into the store for sweets. Odd how even candy stores have changed: once they sold romance; now they sell style. They have exemplary jelly beans here, beautifully displayed in plexiglass bins. They cost $1.99 the half pound. Feeling flush, I bought some banana and some watermelon jelly beans. (Odd flavors, but the colors go together beautifully, like the cream and green of an old MG.)

The reason I was feeling flush: like most other people around here I'd recently taken my banker's advice and refinanced my house. So these were really mortgaged jelly beans, and since over the next twenty-five years I would repay about 3.2 dollars for each one I had borrowed, they were costing me not $4 a pound but more like $13. And yet, disconcertingly, they seemed to me nearly free.

All these nice people making money from jelly beans and bottled water, making this such a wonderful place to live that more people want to live here, making my house worth more. Truly we are blessed, and my banker seems to feel it will go on this way forever.

From "Notes from the Transcendental Valley" by Richard Todd. *New England Monthly*, February 1987.

ELINOR LIPMAN

Elinor Lipman's "Harrow" in her novel The Way Men Act *(1992) clearly is Northampton. That's where Lipman lives, and she is very good at satirizing its "Left Bank life-style." Lipman's protagonist is Melinda LeBlanc, self-consciously without a college degree in a town dominated by prestigious "MacMillan College."*

Lipman, a Massachusetts native, also has written Then She Found Me, Isabel's Bed, *and a collection of short stories* Into Love and Out Again.

Left Bank Life-style

T he shops stand three across: mine in the middle, Dennis Vaughan's to my left and Libby Getchel's to my right, fronting on Main Street in Harrow, Massachusetts. We like the quaint sound of that, "Main Street," because all of us lived somewhere more irritating for a time and returned home with the conviction that a gentrified college town (cappuccino machines, poetry readings, bike paths), with shade trees and paper ballots, with stylish food and parking meters that still took dimes and nickels, would give us Quality of Life.

I arrange flowers for a living, a barren business for a single woman, just one of the reasons I'm in transition. After high school I went to the West Coast to be in the sun and to earn money for some mañana idea of college I had, picked carnations in Leucadia, and ended up on the allegedly artistic side of things, arranging them. I came back to work for my cousin Roger and his wife Robin, the sincerest couple in America. They flattered me and talked about my "art," as if what I do has lasting value. I admit to being good, certainly the best around here; but "here" is Harrow, home of MacMillan College, home to real artists, to tenured scholars of national standing, to people who write books, who *review* books.

Our friends in the big cities began to hear of Harrow from style section features on our Left Bank life-style. The out-of-state checks in our cash drawers are signed by culture-loving tourists, Tanglewood types, who believe they are discovering arts and crafts on this awninged, charming Main Street a season ahead of their friends. It makes me proud and a bit show-offish about living here. I am a native, a townie; I dart among the tourists, displaying my dry cleaning or my bag of groceries as if to say, "I *live* here, this place you choose as a weekend retreat, this Brigadoon, this movie set of a college town come to life. I live here, work here, dry-clean here, am known here. This is my home."

My name, legally, is Linda Louise LeBlanc, if you can imagine anything more forgettable. I became Melinda, chose it myself the summer between eighth grade and high school, suspecting that the next four years would require something sexier. They did. It was the same summer I successfully pierced my own ears with a sewing needle and an ice cube, and convinced my mother that the platinum streaks in my dark hair were caused by the sun. I dated, I graduated, I moved away to California; I came back, half believing that if I had once been the belle of Harrow, or at least the belle of Harrow High School, then I absolutely could go home again.

It was not a terrible idea: the town had changed. It was chic now, practically a vacation destination; and with the new Harrow came new Harrowites. I'd be a fresh face to them, someone's great idea of a lifetime partner, not just the ever-popular Melinda LeBlanc, good dancer and fun date, qualities that haven't worked so well for me in a very long time.

I moved in with my mother, a nice woman who passes out coupons and food samples on toothpicks at local supermarkets. We call my living arrangement temporary, because I'm not the type who lives at home at thirty. I agreed to be flexible, and tolerant of her ways: Yes it *was* her right to tape every incoming Christmas card to the banister, and to see that every horizontal surface in the living room had its own set of coasters. In turn she would not pass judgment on my friends, my eating habits, or my evening activities.

It helped that I took the rental unit, a linoleumed room with a claw-foot bathtub on the third floor, which she had painted and wallpapered one winter with extra income in mind, happy to evict the MacMillan lecturer/tenant when I said I'd return. The gray linoleum is patterned to look like carpeting, and the slanting eaves give it a garret feel. I painted the underside of the tub deep rose and begged one quilt and three rag rugs from my grandmother's lifelong output. I share the kitchen downstairs, which means microwaving my mother's leftovers and taking the plate up to my room. I like her company — it isn't that; I don't want to get used to having someone always there to talk to. Occasionally she telephones me at work over some extravagant menu item that requires purchases in exact numbers: lobster, cornish game hens, veal chops, take-out Chinese. Count you in or not? It means my traveling stepfather, who sells pacemakers up and down the east coast for a Minnesota company, has dropped in for one of his conjugal visits, and my mother thinks my being there would prolong the dinner hour.

We worked this out, my third-floor privacy, before I returned to Harrow. She had no idea how homesick I had been and how few concessions she had to make. I'll work for Roger and Robin at Forget-Me-Not, I said; I'll take classes at the community college. I'll think about a degree.

What I didn't say aloud was the real pull: that the only place I ever felt successful — even for lame, teenage reasons — was here.

Next door to Forget-Me-Not is Brookhoppers, a fly-fishing boutique and mecca for fly fishermen. Customers flock here from all over to buy Dennis Vaughan's hand-tied designer trout flies and to attend his weekend workshops at the Harrow Inn. It's the kind of shop nonfishermen pass and say, "This guy must deal drugs in the back room." Or, "This has to be a front for the Mob." But his disciples understand; they wait patiently for his attentions, declining help from anyone else with a, "No thanks, I'll wait for Dennis." He introduces himself, unnecessarily and modestly, as he moves from professor to stockbroker to radiologist to playwright, answering their questions as if each were fresh and penetrating.

Dennis is black, and attractive in a compact, wire-rimmed way that other men admire. He and his two salesmen wear earth-brown T-shirts with *Brookhoppers* silk-screened in speckled salmon across their hearts. The photograph on the back of his catalogue shows him in waders and a New Zealand sheepherder's hat, casting in a rocky turn of the Starkfield River. By popular demand, it is available as a poster for $14.99. Men have their secretaries write to say they hang it on the back of their office doors to soothe them while they close deals, traffic honking fifty floors below.

Two doors up from Dennis, on my right, is Rags for Sale, Libby Getchel's dress shop. The name is ironic, of course, because her dresses are one of a kind and expensive for Harrow. I had known her in high school where she was in the class behind Dennis and me, and hard to miss: Libby was broad-shouldered, taller than most of us, thin in a big-boned way that made her slow walk look Southern and sexy. She wore her straight blond hair chin-length with bangs as if a weekly trim nonchalantly undertaken with sewing shears were not carefully considered for effect. As a daughter of MacMillan employees, she could have gone to the college tuition-free but hadn't studied hard enough in high school. Instead she bought Vogue patterns and made her own dresses from translucent cotton blends, even in winter when her classmates wore wool and corduroy.

She returned to Harrow a year after I did, still wearing out-of-season party dresses; still wearing her blond hair at lengths that had nothing to do with fashion. She confided to me around that time, a time when we were still confiding in each other, that Dennis was a factor in her choosing Harrow for her store — I knew, didn't I, that they had meant a great deal to each other in high school?

I said no, I hadn't known —

"In a high school not particularly tolerant of an artistic kid who didn't conform, surrounded by professors' kids on one hand, and popular, cheerleading types on the other? Dennis was very nice to me."

I nodded, willing to downgrade my old popularity to be a better audience and friend. "How long did you two go out?" I asked.

Libby said never, unfortunately.

I asked why not.

"My own fault," she said. "A misunderstanding. A mistake I hope to correct."

I said, "Look, if I'd known at seventeen who'd be left to date at this age, I'd have kept a few lines open, too. But we're not Detroit — we can't very well announce a recall of all the defective parts of our life."

Libby didn't answer, and didn't have to. Her gray-green eyes explained that I was an ex-cheerleader, she was a proven nonconformist, and clearly there were no parallels.

From *The Way Men Act* by Elinor Lipman. Simon & Schuster, 1992.

TRACY KIDDER

In Old Friends *(1993), Tracy Kidder once again uses a Pioneer Valley setting to deepen our appreciation of particular social issues — this time, life in nursing homes. This nursing home is on the outskirts of Northampton on Route 9. Most of the story of two aging Western Massachusetts residents takes place there. The following selection records a visit to the Northampton Veteran's Administration Hospital by one of the nursing home's residents. It provides some insight into the workings of the VA Hospital, one of the city's long-standing institutions.*

Route Nine

"**R**oute Nine," Joe murmured as the car turned onto the two-lane highway. Joe smiled to himself. He didn't say much the rest of the way. He sat in the front seat and looked out the window.

They had to go only about a mile. A golf driving range went by on the right, and then a little bunch of stores, a liquor store among them. And then off to the left appeared the outer grounds of the VA Medical Center — beside the road a pretty pond and a wide, upward-sloping field, as closely mown and verdant as a fairway. The field ends at a stand of tall evergreens, framed against the sky on this blue and green and golden summer morning. Out beside the entrance there is also a garden, meant for the eyes of passersby. The garden is always immaculately tended, no matter what the state of the national economy. In the garden a cluster of pruned shrubbery spells out the initials VAMC just above which the hospital always plants a sign. The slogan changes periodically. Sometimes the sign reads, TO CARE FOR HIM WHO SHALL HAVE BORE THE BATTLE. Today it read, PRICE OF FREEDOM VISIBLE HERE.

Sometimes lone figures appear from among the trees at the top of the hill, old men or young, walking across the grassy hillside, down an unofficial path known locally as the Ho Chi Minh Trail. They are heading, it is generally assumed, for the liquor store across Route 9, though actually, most go to the convenience store instead. But the landscape was empty at this morning hour. Nothing besides pond and garden, field and woods, and the top of a smokestack, rising above the trees, was visible. Trees hid all the buildings of the medical center. Perhaps it was that fact, the impression that something was being hidden, which made these outer grounds seem eerie in their emptiness. Their military neatness proclaimed that this VA hospital wasn't like some others — the filthy sties to which some veterans had returned from Vietnam. But the landscape's prettiness and orderly solitude made contemplation of what lay behind the trees all the more appalling, like a flaming shipwreck on a calm and sunny sea. The wards of the hospital proper, the locked psychiatric wards, the drug and alcohol rehabilitation wards, the nursing home wards, in one of which Joe had lived during the longest four months of his life. To Joe, these spruce grounds were not pretty. They were dismal.

The car went up the drive on a winding way all overhung with trees, past old brick buildings and numbered parking lots, and then into a courtyard, surrounded by more brick buildings coupled together with walkways. It was an angular and complicated-looking place, worn by time and traffic. It was a place of boxes inside boxes. Joe had lived on C Ward, one of the innermost boxes, but today, he hoped, he wouldn't go much farther than the waiting room and a doctor's office. After the usual difficulties — swinging his feet out the door, rising slowly, his good arm quivering as he lifted himself — Joe transferred from car seat to wheelchair, was pushed on a brief passage through the summer morning, up a concrete ramp, and into the outer waiting room in front of the receptionist's window. Joe surrendered his VA identity card. The fact that his eyes never left it would by itself have proved he was a veteran, and remembered all the many ways of getting lost in paperwork. He could hardly have forgotten. From time to time he would receive notices from here canceling cholesterol checkup appointments that he'd already kept. He put the identity card back in his pocket and started waiting.

From *Old Friends* by Tracy Kidder. Houghton Mifflin, 1993.

Amherst and Hadley

A southwest view from 1854 of the Holyoke Range from Amherst College over South Amherst and Hadley. From *Gleason's Pictorial* magazine, 1854.

MARY HEATON VORSE

Mary Heaton Vorse (1874-1966) was a radical journalist and proletarian novelist of such works as Strike *and* Passaic. *She was a long-time member of the Provincetown artist colony and wrote* Of Time and the Town *about the bohemian community at the tip of Cape Cod.*

As a girl, Vorse spent her summers in Amherst. In A Footnote to Folly *(1935), she remarks on the provincialism of Amherst, which seemed aloof to the labor tensions and industrial poverty of nearby Springfield, Holyoke, and Chicopee.*

Summers in Amherst

I n my early days I lived isolated from firsthand knowledge of the industrial revolution. In the summers we lived in Amherst. My father had retired from business and worked in his garden and read his books. He was especially interested in American history which I read liberally with him. In the winter we lived in New York when we didn't go to Europe where I received most of my education.

I do not think I ever heard Socialism mentioned. It didn't occur to my parents that other systems of society than our own were possible. I never heard labor unions spoken of, or a discussion of the workers' struggle. My mother, who questioned the social system in Russia, did not question the system which made the slums. Yet she was disturbed by the spectacle of human suffering, and ran a small soup kitchen one hard winter, raising the funds and contributing largely to them.

Life, she felt, should be everywhere as it was in Amherst, where poverty was an accident and great fortunes unknown. We lived so far from industry that we didn't know the industrial revolution had happened. Yet within a few miles of us were the manufacturing towns of Holyoke, Chicopee and Springfield. Chicopee had and still has one of the worst infant death rates of the country. There was overcrowding; there was frightful poverty; social conditions were bad.

We in Amherst knew so little about these things that we might have been the original dwellers in the garden of Eden. We sat on our shady porches, reading indignantly about the sufferings of the Siberian exiles. Almost everyone voted the Republican ticket, went to the Congregational or the Episcopal church. Life was removed from the great forces that were forging America in workshops and steel mills. It was a little like living without the knowledge that there was such a thing as pain or death.

I should say that this is the greatest difference between the general state of mind of my childhood and the present state of mind. Today Amherst, in common with the rest of the conscious part of the community, discusses these social problems and asks to know about them. Today Amherst studies conditions in Holyoke and Chicopee.

Yet it is extraordinary how many middle-class, well-to-do, well-meaning Americans can still live without having the slightest idea of what is going on in the country. Still less have they any knowledge of the history of labor, of the ever-recurrent explosions which in strikes and so-called riots have starred the pages of industrial history.

The average man still sees the industrial explosions of his own day as something new and unprecedented, instead of events falling into a pattern as recurrent as the march of the seasons.

But if in Amherst we knew nothing about the conditions under which cloth was woven or coal mined or steel made, yet it was in the quiet of Amherst that my mind was prepared for thought. Like many New England families of that day, we combined a speculative and inquiring habit of mind with a conservative manner of living. My early training taught me not to fear the "pain of a new idea." It gave me the inclination toward a questioning and scientific attitude of mind. It taught me to value life and to hate injustice; to prefer warmth and simplicity in human relations to intellectual attainments.

But two things it did not give me. It gave me no wide knowledge or training. I know nothing well, not even the languages I speak. It taught me to think but not to act. On the other hand, I was taught to fear my own conscience rather than a differing public opinion.

The pleasant monotony of those long summers gave me an opportunity for wide reading; not only that, but I learned how to use a library, through the kindness of William Isaac Fletcher, a great librarian, and a founder of the modern library system.

Life in Amherst was very pleasant. There was kindness and friendship and the gay and mild excitement which are natural to a college town. As I look back, there crowd to my mind many people who opened windows for me and showed me new horizons. This was the time that led up to the peculiar excitement of the prewar years. There was a lively interest in thought everywhere. It was the prelude toward a wide questioning of a system which placed profits above people.

A college town is conservative. It changes less than other communities and yet it is not stagnant. Everyone travels; a stream of distinguished visitors passes through. I remember standing with the Emerson children goggling at their cousin, Henry James, who was visiting them, having precociously read his novels and being surprised to see him — already fat

— gather up one of the younger Emersons, saying, "Call me Cousin Henry!"

My father was always at home to his friends in the evenings. As I look back on the people who came to drink a glass of beer and chat with him, it seems to me that they were men of unusual individuality, men of character and achievement, informed with a gusto for living. Chief of these was H.H. Goodell, president of Massachusetts Agricultural College, a man of infinite humanity. There were such men as Professor John Tyler, with his great dome of a bald head fringed with flaming red hair, whose work on anthropology is still standard; John Bates Clark, who lived down the road from us; Austin Dickinson, with his red wig and his mole. Austin Dickinson was individual and pithy of speech, as were his sisters, Emily and Lavinia. Amherst bred people of personality and character. They had a precious quality, hard to grasp, which we call American: simplicity and candor combined with shrewdness and integrity. You can sense it, recognize it, but you cannot describe the essence of qualities which at their best made an Abraham Lincoln.

From *A Footnote to Folly: Reminiscences of Mary Heaton Vorse* by Mary Heaton Vorse. Farrar and Rinehart, 1935.

RAY STANNARD BAKER

Amherst has long been a place where writers escape — Noah Webster, Robert Francis, and Robert Frost, to name a few.

Perhaps the most enthusiastic celebrator of the pastoral Amherst life was Ray Stannard Baker (1870-1946), who also wrote under the pen name "David Grayson." After working as a journalist at McClure's profiling leading figures of his age, Baker decided to do what many writers and bohemians have done since: drop out of the city, move to the country, and write about the simple life. He spent "five happy years" writing and raising bees in Amherst before joining Woodrow Wilson's administration and serving as his press aide at the Versailles Peace Conference. Baker continued to keep Amherst as a second home and wrote much of his Pulitzer Prize-winning biography of Woodrow Wilson there.

Five Happy Years

A ny man who is rash enough to think of himself as happy should first define what he means by happiness — and then not be too sure.

Once, a long time ago, I collected a number of definitions of happiness and think the best of them was from the wise man of *Religio Medici*.

"For every man truly lives so long as he acts his nature, or some way makes good the faculties of himself."

Few men are ever really happy who do not know how to act their natures, or truly make good the faculties of themselves, and that never for long at a time.

Looking back along my years I can think of no period I enjoyed more deeply, none when I felt that I was more truly living, than the years from about 1910 to about 1915; and none that seemed unhappier than the years from 1915 to the end of 1917.

In 1910 we moved from our home in Michigan to Amherst, Massachusetts. I had been growing more interested every year in the country way of life. It seemed to me — to all of us — that we could live more naturally and freely in or near a small village than in the city. I had found that such a life was far better adapted to my particular kind of work; but I wanted more land to work with, and our growing family needed a larger house. Dr. Beal, now a widower, had retired from his professor's life and we wanted him to come and live with us. My dream was of a few acres with hills not far off, a field or pasture, an orchard, a possible cow, a pig or two, chickens and turkeys. I did not think of bee-keeping, which gave me finally so much satisfaction, until several years later. I wanted a place where I could work with my own hands and yet keep on with my profession.

I knew well enough from my experience in Michigan that any such experiment in true living must represent all sorts of compromises — what life is not a compromise? — but it was what I had dreamed about and what I longed for. Our land had to be near a town where there were good schools for our children. Our home had not only to meet the requirements of a large family, it must also be the home and workshop for a busy writer as well as a "part time" farmer.

Farm men and a woman work in their field off Route 9 near the center of Hadley. The Holyoke Range is in the distance. Photo by Jerome Liebling.

I had already fallen in love with New England. I had made numerous visits there. My own people had come from Vermont and Massachusetts and Connecticut; my boyhood had been full of the stories of the Green Mountain Boys and of the beauties of Lake George and Lake Champlain, of maple-sugaring in spring, and the trees hanging full in the autumn with apples and walnuts and chestnuts, of which we in the cold north-west knew nothing.

One perfect October week-end, with sunshine and clear cool air, the best New England knows, I visited an old and dear college friend of mine, Kenyon L. Butterfield, who then lived in Amherst, Massachusetts, and was president of the Massachusetts State College. On Saturday afternoon we climbed to the top of Mount Lincoln. The leaves were in their full autumn coloring, the chestnut burrs were opening and the nuts were falling. Men in the little fields were beginning to husk their corn. We saw a wild deer in a steep trail near Orient Brook. We flushed a covey of partridges. I thought I had never seen finer wooded hills, or clearer streams, or more comfortable old tree-shaded farmhouses with grassy lanes leading up to them from the country roads.

I fell hopelessly in love with the town and everything in it: and the next spring we moved there, all of us, with all of our belongings. We bought the back end of the old Smith farm, a field of about ten acres that had been in cultivation for a hundred years. At that time no road led into it or past it. Save for one magnificent elm near the top of the hill and a fine maple in the lower pasture, it was bare of any planting.

Here Dr. Beal realized *his* dream, that of building a home for his daughter and her family, big enough for all of us to live in. In one corner of it I was to have my first comfortable study with enough shelves for my books and a toby closet and drawers for my papers. And Dr. Beal was to spend a benign old age — he lived to be ninety-one — in his study at the other corner among his precious botanical specimens, with the portrait of his greatest hero, Louis Agassiz, hanging above his fireplace.

We have lived in this home ever since. Every tree, every shrub, every berry bush around the house and in the garden we planted with our own hands. We have lived with them through many summers and winters; we have cared for them; pruned and cultivated and fed them. We know them personally and intimately: all their little individual excellencies and beauties; all their waywardnesses — and we love them.

Some of the trees that we set out as saplings dug from a near-by hillside, have grown so tall that we can sit in the shade of them on hot summer days and they fend off the chilly blasts of winter. Our grandchildren now build secret tree-houses high among their leafy fastnesses and swing from their branches. What a miracle — all in thirty years!

I got acquainted with my near neighbors, many of them Polish farmers. I experimented with raising the usual crops grown in our valley: corn, potatoes, and even onions, always doing as much as I could with my own hands. It was an experience full of interest to me, full also of many other rewards — though not much money. I not only enjoyed the work but my health improved, and I found I could do more and better writing in a week in Amherst than I could in two weeks in New York.

I will admit that I sometimes found it difficult, especially during the first warm days of spring with so much going on out of doors, to keep sternly down for the required time to my writing. Often on pleasant summer mornings I was up at dawn or earlier. I had a table on the wide west porch where I could, whenever I lifted my eyes, look off across the valley to the hills. I made good progress with my writing for an hour or so, and then the country began to come alive around me. The sun rose higher, the grass put on its spangles of morning dew, and all at once the countryside seemed to awaken gloriously — the birds were singing, the dogs exchanging morning greetings across the fields, and the cows lowing, eager to be milked and turned out to pasture.

For some time, by sheer determination, I could keep my pen going — even though I might feel like whistling or singing with the best of them.

One temptation I could never resist. I sat where I could look out over my beehives, and when, sometimes in the warm forenoon, I heard the roar of a swarm rising in the sunny air, I stopped even in the middle of a sentence and ran down to see which colony it was coming from. After that, of course, I had to look up often to make sure where it was lighting, in what apple tree or on what currant bush, and presently, with what a rush of pleasure, I threw my pen aside and went out with my hive tools and with veil and gloves to cut down the great brown swarm and rehive it.

All these things, of course, interrupted me. I failed always to do as much writing as I had intended or hoped — I could never satisfy the voracious editors — and yet I never came back to my work on the porch, or in my study, without a fresh sense of the wonder and the beauty of life — a new appreciation that I was a humble part of it all, and new realization that it was infinitely desirable. I never spent such a morning as this without resolving never again to be dogmatic about anything in this world; I began to learn that life, after all, was first, and writing second.

––––––––––––

From *American Chronicle: The Autobiography of Ray Stannard Baker.* Charles Scribner's Sons, 1945.

DAVID GRAYSON

Under his pen name "David Grayson," Ray Stannard Baker wrote rural idylls set in Amherst, such as Under My Elm *and* The Countryman's Year. The Year *(1936) is a journal of the seasons in Amherst, starting in April and running through winter's end the following March. Grayson provides this account of New England maple sugaring at the end of winter.*

Maple Sugaring

March 25. Our friends having invited us to visit their sugarbush, we drove to Sunderland and walked three miles up Mount Toby. The wood roads were heavy with mud, with here and there patches of old snow: scarcely a sign of spring except the running sap and the swelling willow buds.

Hubbard's bush is in a rocky field on the flank of the mountain — an ancient wooden shack standing among magnificent old maple trees. When we came first in sight of it, it looked as though it were on fire, for the steam from the boiling sap was pouring out through every crack. It was indeed a stirring place — men and boys hallooing in the woods as they chopped fuel for the fire, or drove the sledges down the mountainside with barrels of sap, or ran in and out of the sugarhouse. As we came nearer we caught the ambrosial odor of the steaming syrup, and a moment later we were welcomed by Hubbard and his boys.

It was a perfect sugar day. Last night it froze hard, and today the sun shines warm: and every one of the hundreds of trees that have been tapped are dripping sap into the shining pails that hang from the spiles.

The sap is boiled in long shallow pans heated by a roaring fire of four-foot wood, there being a gradual flow from the pan where the sap comes in from the vat to the deeper pan where the syrup begins to grow thick and is of a deep golden color.

Hubbard is an expert — he is of the third generation of a family that has made sugar every spring for seventy years there upon the flanks of Toby — he knows by trial with a ladle when the syrup "aprons off" or "hairs off" whether it is ready to pour into the cans to sell as syrup or to boil down still further into sugar. We brought in pails and pans of snow to "sugar off" and ate our luncheon on a board table at one side of the saphouse. Afterwards, sitting by the steaming pans, there was mighty joking and storytelling.

Hubbard told me that a few of the prize maples in his bush are so large that they will produce three or four barrels of sap in a season. Each barrel will boil down to about a gallon of syrup: that is, each of these great trees will produce three and a half gallons of syrup, selling this year for about $2.00 or $3.00 — say $10 to a tree. Or, if the process is continued and sugar is produced, we have these results: a gallon of syrup weighing eleven pounds will boil down to make some eight pounds of sugar, selling at fifty or sixty cents a pound. The farmers here say there is "no real money in it"; but sugar making comes at a time of the year when ordinary farm work is slack (it will be ten days yet before they begin to put out their tobacco frames), and some of them say frankly that the spring makes them restless and they want to get into the woods and see the sap running. The fact is, they enjoy it.

From *The Countryman's Year* by David Grayson (Ray Stannard Baker). Doubleday, 1936.

MARY ELLEN CHASE

Mary Ellen Chase (1887-1973) was an English professor at Smith College and a prolific author who wrote more than twenty-five books of fiction, maritime history, and Biblical commentary. She was particularly taken with the Polish farmers of Hadley and wrote the novel A Journey to Boston *(1965) about their experience. It is a story of two Polish farm families and one of their daughters who marries a Yankee boy and turns from the Polish ways.*

In this striking passage on the Connecticut Valley from A Journey to Boston, *Chase extolled its brilliant light.*

The Bright Land

The wide valley of the Connecticut River must be one of the brightest lands in all the world. It is as bright as Florence, or as Fiesole, or as the brown hill towns of Umbria under the hot Italian sun; as bright as Provence even with the added light of the Mediterranean; as bright as the sparkling Spanish islands of Majorca, Minorca, and Ibiza. Perhaps this wide valley is at its brightest in Western Massachusetts, for, as the river broadens there on its way toward the sea, the land broadens also to make room for vast, sunlit fields of tobacco, asparagus, and onions.

People who live in Western Massachusetts, in the old towns of Amherst or Northampton, Hadley or Greenfield, Sunderland, Northfield, or Deerfield, or on the farms which nudge the shoulders of all such towns, are conscious always, at all seasons, of this amazing brightness, whether it is born of the sun during the long, hot summers, or of the incredible brilliance of the autumn colouring, or of the wide, sunswept reaches of snow which mark the slow, reluctant, tarrying winters. Perhaps, indeed, their awareness of it helps more than a little to dispel, or at least to lighten, the long, unintelligible darkness of threescore years and ten.

Not that rain does not fall in this region as it falls elsewhere on the earth. Yet, singularly enough, many of the rains are night rains; and even those of the days are, for the most part, gentle rather than violent, their drops and lines of water sparkling in the air, lingering on and within the thirsty grass, shining in pools upon the roads and pavements. A rare dismal day almost always has its bright moments and usually closes in a clear sunset. The dawns of this Connecticut Valley are bright dawns. The hesitating twilights are bright also.

Lesser gifts of Nature than the sun, the brilliant autumn trees, and the winter snow do their part in adding to this singular brightness. The spring and the summer fields, stretching east and west from the river, unless they have been ploughed and sown, are often bright with buttercups or charlock. The tangled roadsides glow with the yellow of loosestrife, St. John's-wort, and the lesser celandine. Yellow is, in fact, a predominant colour in these regions, a warm rich yellow filled with light.

The people themselves do their part in adding to the brightness of their valley. During the summer they grow velvety marigolds in their garden plots; and in the autumn these same gardens show masses of chrysanthemums, mostly in various shades of yellow. Certain tobacco farmers contribute immeasurably to this effect of light and brilliance by their net-covered fields, which from a distance look like shimmering lakes of clear water. Even the long red or gray tobacco barns, with their shuttered sides open to the wind which sways their drying leaves, per-haps because of their grace and symmetry and their ample room for great patches of sunlight to rest upon them, *seem* at least to be a part of this all-pervading, all-embracing brightness. One never looks upon them with-out wondering with gratitude at the wisdom shown in their length and contour, at the way in which they suit the wide fields where they stand with hot sun penetrating the long, perpendicular openings in their sides and glowing upon their wooden clapboards.

People serve in other ways to enhance this incomparable brightness. Perhaps the very fact that many of them are Polish does its share. For there is a remarkable vitality in the Polish nature, a strength and a mental agility which have made them lively citizens of their adopted country, eager to do their part toward the common welfare. Apathy, or careless-ness, or indifference are traits far removed from the Polish mind and personality at its best. Polish Americans are ambitious for themselves and for their children, experimental and enterprising in their work, generous, outgoing, ardent, alive.

The Polish women wear many-coloured scarves on their heads as they kneel upon the brown soil to set the dark-green tobacco plants in the spring or to cultivate the sharp shoots of the onions as the summer days advance. Such women have a way of moving slowly forward upon their knees. They seldom rise and walk. And, as they work, their bright heads lend brightness to the earth as their mothers' and their grandmothers' heads used to do in the old fields at home.

The men who work on the land along with their women folks do their share also in adding to the brightness of this region and not only through their net-covered tobacco. Many farmers grow pumpkins and squashes among their other crops so that their fields in early autumn glow with the yellows and the oranges of these stout and homely fruits. They pile them, too, in barnyards and on lawns and at roadside vegetable stands. In September and October one never walks or drives through this Connecticut Valley without smiling at these ungainly mounds of squashes and pumpkins heaped in uneven, bulging pyramids on green grass, or against barnyard fences, or under bright trees, or before the doors of farmhouses.

From *A Journey to Boston* by Mary Ellen Chase. W. W. Norton & Company, 1965.

MADELEINE BLAIS

In These Girls, Hope Is a Muscle *is Madeleine Blais's account of the 1992-1993 Amherst High School Girls Basketball team and their state championship (see the Sports section for another excerpt). The book masterfully and comically captures the sense of place in the Five College area, including Amherst's "self-absorbed loftiness" in this selection. Blais also teaches journalism at the University of Massachusetts at Amherst.*

Politically Correct in Amherst

Amherst is a college town, home to Amherst College, the University of Massachusetts, and Hampshire College, with the usual self-absorbed loftiness that makes such places as maddening as they are charming and livable. The communities surrounding Amherst range from the hard and nasty inner-city poverty of Holyoke, the empty factories in Chicopee, and the blue-collar solidity of Agawam to the cornfields and strawberry patches in Whately and Hatfield and Hadley and the shoppers' mecca that is Northampton. They tend to look on Amherst with eye-rolling puzzlement and occasional contempt as the town that fell to earth.

When the chamber of commerce sponsored a contest for town motto, Coach Moyer submitted several that he still thinks should have won — "A Volvo in every garage," "Where adolescence lasts forever," and his personal favorite, "Amherst: Where sexuality is an option and reality is an alternative." Townspeople often refer to Amherst, fondly, as "Never-never land." The chamber of commerce ended up choosing as its motto "There's no place like downtown Amherst." Downtown consists mostly of pizza joints, Chinese restaurants, ice-cream parlors, bookstores, and not much else. It has the world's slowest deli. The businesses that don't begin with the word *Pioneer* often end with the word *Valley*. It's hard to find a needle and thread, but if you wish, you can go to the Global Trader and purchase for four dollars a dish towel with a rain-forest theme.

Amherst is an achingly democratic sort of place in which tryouts for Little League, with their inevitable rejections, have caused people to suggest that more teams should be created so that no one is left out. There are always some parents who sit on the bleachers reading their well-thumbed copies of William James's *Essays in Pragmatism* or rereading Trollope, who look up just in time to greet their child's good catch or hard drive to the center with an airy cry of "Deft!" rather than "Way to go!"

Coach Moyer finds it ironic that the same people who disparage athletic competition, sometimes wrinkling their noses as if the very word had an off odor, were sufficiently driven to get 800s on their Graduate Record Exams. They use words like *deobscurantize* when they mean *make clear*, and at parent-teacher meetings for kindergarten-age children they ask if their youngster will be taught not just how to spell, but also the history of spelling.

"In Amherst," says Coach Moyer, "people are so sophisticated that when one first grader said to the other, 'Guess what, I found a condom on the patio,' her friend wanted to know, 'What's a patio?'"

Coach Moyer has proposed some politically correct trash talk just for those who seek to avoid the rough language of the fray:

"I'm going to meet you outside the game and refuse to mediate."

"You ignore your inner child."

"And so's your co-parent."

Every year in August the Rotary Club hosts a Teddy Bear Rally on the town common: 190 booths featuring bears as well as bear furniture, bear clothes, bear books, and other bear sundries.

The church Moyer's wife attends uses an "inclusive language" hymnal, invented in Amherst, which replaces patriarchal references to *Our Father* with the word *creator* and which tones down imagery with a male bias, employing small subtle shifts, such as "Onward, Christian Stalwarts."

It's the last place in America where you can find people who still think *politically correct* is a compliment. The program notes for the high school spring musical, *Kiss Me, Kate*, pointed out politely that *The Taming of the Shrew*, on which it is based, was "well, Shakespearean in its attitude toward the sexes."

Political action is approved, even among the very young.

A few years ago a second-grade class at Fort River School mounted a successful campaign to get the state's Turnpike Authority to abolish the symbol that had lined the road that goes from Stockbridge to Boston since its opening in 1957, a pilgrim's hat with an arrow shot through it. These days it's just a plain old pilgrim's hat. Jen Pariseau has a theory about how Amherst got to be so PC: "It all goes back to this guy Jeffery Amherst."

The man from whom the town took its name in 1759 was commander in chief and field marshal of the English armies.

"Some people say he was a womanizer and a drunk. The one thing we know for sure is that he tried to wipe out the Indians by giving them blankets infected with smallpox. Ever since, we've been trying to make up for him."

In the sixties Amherst College managed to lose all its Jeffery Amherst dinner plates, with their frieze shoving the white military officer from England in an eternal rout of the Indians. But it has yet to lose its fight song, a somewhat airbrushed version of the life of Lord Jeff, "a soldier of the king." After touchdowns at football games and at the parties afterward you can hear it being sung, in a low register filled with, often, inebriated conviction, a tribute to an old order in which boys were boys, men were men, and girls didn't go to Amherst College. Women entered Amherst College for the first time as transfer students in 1975 and as freshmen in 1976, a fact that used to merit a sentence in the catalogue but is no longer considered newsworthy.

Oh, Lord Jeffery Amherst was the man who gave his name
    To our college on the hill;
And the story of his loyalty and bravery and fame
    Abides here among us still —
Abides here among us still.
You may talk about your Johnnies and your Elis and the rest,
    For they are names that time can never dim,
But give us our only Jeffery, he's the noblest and the best,
    To the end we will stand fast for him.

The town is, for the most part, smoke free, nuclear free, and eager to free Tibet. Ponchos with those little projectiles of fleece have never gone out of style. Birkenstocks (called Birkies), clogs, capes, Doc Marten's, woven tops, and tie-dyed anything are all still the rage. With the exception of Cambridge, Massachusetts, Amherst is probably the only place in the United States where men can wear berets and not get beaten up. The common nickname for the area is the Happy Valley. In good weather, freeze-dried hippies, men and women in their forties and fifties, clinging to their long hair and their beards the way World War II marines used to cling to crew cuts, line the sidewalks with their wares: multicolored candles shaped like pyramids, tin earrings, colorful beads, incense.

From *In These Girls, Hope Is a Muscle* by Madeleine Blais. Atlantic Monthly Press, 1995.

Educational Life

Deerfield Academy boys in the early 1950s gazing westward from the ridge east of Deerfield overlooking tobacco barns, the Deerfield River valley, and the distant Berkshire hills.
Courtesy of Deerfield Academy.

NOAH WEBSTER

When Noah Webster (1758-1843) moved to Amherst in 1812, he was one of the best-known intellectual leaders in America. His Grammatical Institute of the English Language *(1783-85) called for distinct "American" language and provided the nation's first "speller," which sold 60 million copies over a century. He moved from New Haven to Amherst because of the lower cost of living and an opportunity to cultivate fruit trees. He served in the Massachusetts legislature and organized a meeting setting the stage for the Hartford Convention, at which New England considered seceding from the United States over the War of 1812.*

Webster was one of the founders of Amherst College. He viewed the college as an orthodox Congregational counterweight to the Unitarian excesses of Harvard. Webster completed work on his magnum opus, An American Dictionary of the English Language, *in 1828.* '

Founding Amherst College

(To Jeremiah Evarts)   Amherst, June 27, 1820

Dear Sir,

Since the decision of the legislature against the removal of Williams College into this county, the Trustees of Amherst Academy have determined to put into operation the charitable fund entrusted to their care. The way seems now to be open and free from embarrassment from contending claims. Our committee and agents have made a beginning in the collection of materials for a building. Some persons in Franklin County have agreed to furnish lime gratuitously, and the people of this town and Pelham and Leverett have volunteered their services to convey stone for the foundation, boards, etc., and nearly a hundred loads of stone are already on the ground ready for laying. There is a spirit of enterprize among us which is very encouraging, and I hope it will not be checked. But although labor and materials are cheerfully furnished to the extent of the abilities of our people, we *cannot proceed* without some pecuniary aid. The people in the country have little money — or rather none that they can spare for such an object — and I am apprehensive that the business must stop for the want of perhaps a thousand dollars. I have just conversed with one of the committee, who is of this opinion.

As I deem this a *very important* object, I take the liberty in my private capacity to ask you whether in this exigency we can find a few friends in Boston who will send us aid. You will be able to decide the question without much trouble by showing this letter to the Reverend Mr. Dwight, to Mr. Hubban, and a few others. We wish to procure bricks to be made this summer, and the lapse of a few weeks will render it impossible; but we cannot contract for a sufficient number without money for part payment, and money we cannot obtain in this region.

Excuse me for giving you this trouble, and believe me with much esteem and respect, Your Friend,

N. Webster

A print of Noah Webster from an original painting by Chappel, published in 1867.
Courtesy of the Jones Library, Amherst.

(To William Leffingwell)   Amherst, Massachusetts, September 27, 1820
Dear Sir,

By the pamphlet which accompanies this, you will see what we are doing in this quarter to aid the propagation of the Gospel. We have collected in small subscriptions from our common people, chiefly, a fund of 50,000 dollars to educate pious young men, and the Institution is to be in this town. We are erecting, by voluntary contributions, a building of a hundred feet in length, and the burden of this falls on the inhabitants of this neighborhood. Labor and materials are supplied cheerfully, but some money is necessary, and in the present state of markets the people in the country cannot get money. We want our Christian friends in this and the neighboring states to take an interest in this Great Enterprise, which has for its object the common benefit of the world; and we do hope that this infant institution will grow up to a size which shall contribute to check the progress of errors which are propagated from Cambridge. The influence of the University of Cambridge, supported by great wealth and talents, seems to call on all the friends of truth to unite in circumscribing it. This is a cause of common concern, and we beseech our prosperous friends in Connecticut who love to do good not to forget us. Any contribution however small will be gratefully received and soundly applied.

Please accept for yourself and family, the affectionate regards of, dear Sir, Your friend and obedient Servant,

N. Webster

From *Letters of Noah Webster*, edited by Harry R. Warfel. Library Publishers, 1953.

EMILY DICKINSON

The longest Emily Dickinson (1830-1886) spent away from her family in Amherst was a year at Mount Holyoke Seminary in 1847-1848. In the following letter, written six weeks into the fall term, she describes her initial homesickness and then her surprise at enjoying Mount Holyoke. One of twelve surviving letters from Dickinson's Mount Holyoke year, this letter sheds light on Emily Dickinson at a formative stage and describes the Mount Holyoke of pioneer Mary Lyon, who established the path-breaking female seminary in 1837 and directed it until her death in 1849.

Student Life at Mount Holyoke Seminary

My dear Abiah.   South Hadley, 6 November 1847

I am really at Mt Holyoke Seminary & this is to be my home for a long year. Your affectionate letter was joyfully received & I wish that this might make you as happy as your's did me. It has been nearly six weeks since I left home & that is a longer time, than I was ever away from home before now. I was very homesick for a few days & it seemed to me I could not live here. But I am now contented & quite happy, if I can be happy when absent from my dear home & friends. You may laugh at the idea, that I cannot be happy when away from home, but you must remember that I have a very dear home & that this is my first trial in the way of absence for any length of time in my life. As you desire it, I will give you a full account of myself since I first left the paternal roof. I came to S. Hadley six weeks ago next Thursday. I was much fatigued with the ride & had a severe cold besides, which prevented me from commencing my examinations until the next day, when I began.

I finished them in three days & found them about what I had anticipated, though the old scholars say they are more strict than they ever have been before. As you can easily imagine, I was much delighted to finish without failures & I came to the conclusion then, that I should not be at all homesick, but the reaction left me as homesick a girl as it is not usual to see. I am now quite contented & am very much occupied now in reviewing the Junior studies, as I wish to enter the middle class. The school is very large & though quite a number have left, on account of finding the examinations more difficult than they anticipated, yet there are nearly 300 now. Perhaps you know that Miss Lyon is raising her standard of scholarship a good deal, on account of the number of applicants this year & on account of that she makes the examinations more severe than usual.

You cannot imagine how trying they are, because if we cannot go through them all in a specified time, we are sent home. I cannot be too thankful that I got through as soon as I did, & I am sure that I never would endure the suspense which I endured during those three days again for all the treasures of the world.

Mary Lyon (1797-1849), born in Buckland, began Mount Holyoke in 1837 as a three-year female seminary modeled after the curriculum at Amherst and Williams. It was renamed Mount Holyoke College in 1888. From The Power of Christian Benevolence Illustrated in the Life and Labors of Mary Lyon *by Edward Hitchcock, 1860.*

I room with my Cousin Emily, who is a Senior. She is an excellent room-mate & does all in her power to make me happy. You can imagine how pleasant a good room-mate is, for you have been away to school so much. Everything is pleasant & happy here & I think I could be no happier at any other school away from home. Things seem much more like home than I anticipated & the teachers are all very kind & affectionate to us. They call on us frequently & urge us to return their calls & when we do, we always receive a cordial welcome from them.

I will tell you my order of time for the day, as you were so kind as to give me your's. At 6. oclock, we all rise. We breakfast at 7. Our study hours begin at 8. At 9. we all meet in Seminary Hall, for devotions. At 10 $^1/_4$. I recite a review of Ancient History, in connection with which we read Goldsmith & Grimshaw. At 11. I recite a lesson in "Pope's Essay on Man" which is merely transposition. At 12. I practice Calisthenics & at 12 $^1/_4$ read until dinner, which is at 12 $^1/_2$ & after dinner, from 1 $^1/_2$ until 2 I sing in Seminary Hall. From 2 $^3/_4$ until 3 $^3/_4$, I practise upon the Piano. At 3 $^3/_4$ I go to Sections, where we give in all our accounts for the day, including, Absence — Tardiness — Communications — Breaking Silent Study hours — Receiving Company in our rooms & ten thousand other things, which I will not take time or place to mention. At 4 $^1/_2$. we go into Seminary Hall, & receive advice from Miss. Lyon in the form of a lecture. We have Supper at 6. & silent-study hours from then until the retiring bell, which rings at 8 $^3/_4$, but the tardy bell does not ring until 9 $^3/_4$, so that we dont often obey the first warning to retire.

Unless we have a good & reasonable excuse for failure upon any of the items, that I mentioned above, they are recorded & a *black mark* stands against our names: As you can easily imagine, we do not like very well to get "exceptions" as they are called scientifically here. My domestic work is not difficult & consists in carrying the Knives from the 1st tier of tables at morning & noon & at night washing & wiping the same quantity of Knives. I am quite well & hope to be able to spend the year here, free from sickness. You have probably heard many reports of the food here & if so I can tell you, that I have yet seen nothing corresponding to my ideas on that point from what I have heard. Everything is wholesome & abundant & much nicer than I should imagine could be provided for almost 300 girls. We have also a great variety upon out tables & frequent changes. One thing is certain & that is, that Miss. Lyon & all the teachers, seem to consult our comfort & happiness in everything they do & you know that is pleasant. When I left home, I did not think I should find a companion or a dear friend in all the multitude. I expected to find rough & uncultivated manners, & to be sure, I have found some of that stamp, but on the whole, there is an ease & grace a desire to make one another happy, which delights & at the same time, surprises me very much. I find no Abby. or Abiah. or Mary, but I love many of the girls. Austin came to see me when I had been here about two weeks & brought Viny & Abby. I need not tell you how delighted I was to see them all, nor how happy it made me to hear them say that "they were *so lonely.*" It is a sweet feeling to know that you are missed & that your memory is precious at home. This week, on Wednesday, I was at my window, when I happened to look towards the hotel & saw Father & Mother, walking over here as dignified as you please. I need not tell you that I danced & clapped my hands, & flew to meet them for you can imagine how I felt. I will only ask you do you love your parents? They wanted to surprise me & for that reason did not let me know they were coming. I could not bear to have them go, but go they must & so I submitted in sadness. Only to think Abiah, that in 2 $^1/_2$ weeks I shall be at my *own dear home* again. You will probably go home at Thanksgiving time & we can rejoice with each other.

You dont know how I laughed at your description of your introduction to Daniel Webster & I read that part of your letter to Cousin. Emily. You must feel quite proud of the acquaintance & will not I hope be vain in consequence. However you dont know Govr Briggs & I do, so you are no better off than I. I hear frequently from Abby & it is a great pleasure to receive her letters. Last eve, I had a long & very precious letter from her & she spoke of see^g a letter from you. You probably have heard of the death of *O. Coleman.* How melancholy!! Eliza. had written me a long letter giving me an account of her death, which is beautiful & affecting & which you shall see when we *meet again.*

Abiah, you must write me often & I shall write you as often as I have time. But you know I have many letters to write now I am away from home. Cousin. Emily says "Give my love to Abiah."

From your aff
Emily E. D —

———————

From *The Letters of Emily Dickinson*, edited by Thomas H. Johnson. Harvard University Press, 1958.

SYLVIA PLATH

Poet Sylvia Plath grew up in Wellesley, Massachusetts, and went to Smith College in 1950. Though poetically inclined, she followed the mainstream college route of the day in academic and social life. A letter from her freshman year describes the rituals of dating Amherst College boys. Another letter describes a portentous visit to the grounds of the Northampton State Hospital with her friend Myron Lotz.

Student Life at Smith

October 19, 1950

This weekend I went out Saturday with Bill. We doubled with Ann Davidow — that nice girl I told you about. We went over to Amherst as usual. Honestly, I have never seen anything so futile as their system of dating. The boys take their dates up to their rooms, usually to drink. After the first hour, the groups break up, and couples wander from fraternity to fraternity in search of a crowd into which they can merge or a "party" which they can join. It is like wandering from one plush room to another and finding the remains of an evening scattered here and there. I cannot say I give a damn about it. Bill, at least, is very sweet and thoughtful — nowhere as superficial as most of the boys I've run into over there. We were both quite tired and not in the mood for any party glitter, so we went to the suite, and I curled up on the red leather couch and dozed while he stretched out in a chair. He had built a fire and put on some good records, so for about two hours I rested, my eyes closed. We didn't even talk. At least both of us were tired at the same time. I almost have to laugh when I think back on it now. What would my housemates say if they knew what an entertaining evening I spent? I don't suppose they would realize that I had a better time under the circumstances than I could have had by straining to achieve a bright, empty smile in a crowd all night.

Sunday night I did the rather unwise thing of accepting a blind date to Alpha Delta (God, these Greek names are foolish!).

My date had pictures and scrapbooks of his girl — a Smith girl spending her junior year abroad — around the room. So I was more or less just a date. It's funny, but the whole system of weekends seems more intent on saying: "I went to Yale" or "Dartmouth." That's enough — you've gone somewhere. Why add, "I had a hell of a time. I hated my date." You see, I don't think people with ideals like our mutual friends, the Nortons, frequent the bars where I have hitherto made my appearance (drinking Cokes). As for what I wore — my aqua dress Sat., and my red skirt and black jersey last night. This next weekend I have vowed to stay home and sleep and study. I wonder if I will ever meet a congenial boy. Oh, well —

Northampton State Hospital, built in 1856, as it appeared in 1994. It was closed as a hospital in late 1993. Photo by Richard W. Wilkie.

Dear Mother,   December 15, 1952

We changed then, for the cocktail party, and walked over to the professor's house. On the way we decided to keep on walking for a while longer, and so walked up to the mental hospital, among the buildings, listening to the people screaming. It was a most terrifying, holy experience, with the sun setting red and cold over the black hills, and the inhuman, echoing howls coming from the barred windows. (I want so badly to learn about why and how people cross the borderline between sanity and insanity!)

Sunday, as we went walking out in the fields, we saw some airplanes landing close by, and so hiked over to watch them landing like toy gliders at a small airport. As we approached the field, a tall, lean, blue-eyed man with a moustache came toward us. We chatted for a while and he showed us his private plane, and we listened to the pilot describe his experiences. He looked at us: "I'm going up this afternoon, want to come?" I stared at Myron, who gave me an understanding, benevolent grin: "She'd sure like to, sir," he told the pilot. So we went back, and they strapped me into the two-seater little plane ... We taxied across the field, bumping along, and it felt like being in a car. I didn't believe we would go up, but then, suddenly, the ground dropped away, and the trees and hills fell away, and I was in a small glass-windowed box with a handsome, mysterious pilot, winging over Northampton, Holyoke, Amherst, watching the small, square, rectangular colored fields, the toy houses, and the great winding, gleaming length of the Connecticut River. "I am going to do a wing-over," he said, and suddenly the river was over my head, and the mountains went reeling up into the sky, and the clouds floated below. We tilted rightside up again. Never have I felt such ecstasy! I yelled above the roar of the motor that it was better than God, religion, than anything, and he laughed and said he knew. "You fly it," he told me, and I took the stick and made the craft climb and tilt. For half an hour we were up.

Today I am probably going to the infirmary because of my insomnia, so don't worry if you get a notice. I have an appointment with the psychiatrist this afternoon about my science, and will ask her if I can go up there for a few days to rest and get rid of a slight sore throat. Also, Mary Ellen Chase called me this morning and I hope to see her sometime this week, too.

    x x x Sivvy

From *Letters Home by Sylvia Plath: Correspondence 1950-1963*, edited by Aurelia Schober Plath. HarperCollins, 1975.

JILL KER CONWAY

Jill Ker Conway, former Smith College president, has become a best-selling author, with her memoirs The Road from Coorain *and* True North. True North *describes the Australian educator's adult life, including teaching women's history at the University of Toronto and becoming president of Smith College in 1974.* True North *has a splendid passage on Conway's first visit to Smith, the interview for its presidency, and her thoughts on preserving women's colleges.*

Smith's First Woman President

I t was touching to read the history of the foundation of Mount Holyoke. Mary Lyon's battle to raise the money for her institution showed a hard marble woman at work, harvesting the pennies New England farm women could scrimp together from within their already frugal housekeeping budgets, coaxing bigger gifts from churches and from large donors. It had taken so long for the pennies to add up to the necessary sum to start the building in South Hadley, where the aim to educate women on their own terms first found architectural expression.

Sophia Smith's benefaction for the college which bore her name had been generous, but there had been the same painstaking scrimping by early classes of Smith alumnae to contribute the extra pennies needed to add up to the cost of building the first gymnasium for women. The endowments that supported women's colleges had grown slowly, and never rivaled their Ivy League counterparts. It troubled me to think of them being casually turned over to male direction, because I knew no male-directed institution would suddenly allow the needs of women to drive financial priorities. And I knew from my daily work at the University of Toronto what efforts of will and political finesse were required to redirect any allocation of resources in times of surplus, let alone in times of scarcity.

In the summer of 1973, Natalie, whose accounts of her life as a student at Smith made the great women scholars who'd given her her love of learning seem like household presences, told me that the presidency of Smith would soon be vacant, and that she had written a long letter to the Search Committee setting out why she thought I'd be the right person for the job. She had, by then, become a member of the History Department at Berkeley, after much pondering what would be the most creative choice for the future. Although her departure broke up one of the most creative partnerships of my life, I'd urged her to make the move. It was an indicator of the intellectual environment we lived in at the University of Toronto that neither of us could find a collaborator within our own fields. I knew Natalie was a dazzling scholar, and that she should be teaching in an institution where there was a large cadre of graduate students up to her level of work. Beyond feeling pleasure that my most admired colleague wanted me to be custodian of the institution she cherished, I gave the matter no more thought. I was busy learning to swim in the choppy seas of my new administrative life, rooted in Canada, and far too preoccupied to think of change.

When the letter from the Smith Search Committee turned up on my desk in December, I knew I had to schedule a meeting with them, if only as a courtesy to my friend and collaborator. The few documents which accompanied the invitation tickled my curiosity. Smith's educational budget for its 2,800 undergraduate students was larger by far than the entire Faculty of Arts and Sciences at the University of Toronto, four times Smith's size in enrollments. I wondered what it would be like to think about educating students drawing on such resources.

I liked the delegation from the Search Committee I met at the Century Club in New York. They were a mixture of trustees, alumnae, students, and faculty — all full of intellectual energy and enthusiasm. They seemed worried about the trend to coeducation among similar male colleges like Williams and Amherst, but energetically convinced that Smith's mission was to educate women. I thought their worries misplaced. I was working with women students in an institution of some sixty thousand students. I taught, by preference, at night, when the part-time women came in droves to the downtown campus. I knew what their battles were, how hard it was for them to feel entitled to take the time for expansive nonutilitarian learning.

One of my favorites was a tiny blond woman in her forties, mother of four, alone in life because of divorce. She worked in a suburban computer center and was often late for class. I tried to convince her that her time was worth money, and that a cab to and from the commuter station to the University campus would give her that extra hour in the library she needed. But she had no past experience of spending money as an investment in herself and her talents and couldn't change her ways. She continued to arrive at my class white-faced and tired from her long commute by public transport. She needed to change worlds to see herself differently, a vision that could only come from the moral support of her peers, and a counseling service expert in unraveling the conflicts and self-denigration of older women. My few minutes' pep talk after class wasn't enough.

I thought there were thousands of women like her in every major city in North America who would jump at the chance to have four years to devote to self-development. The discussion was lively, but I went away unconvinced that this was the job for me. I thought I could help the cause by what I was writing on the history of education, but I liked what I was doing in Toronto too much to think about the subject more.

Beyond a polite thank-you for making the time to meet with them, I didn't hear from the Search Committee again until April 1974, by which time they had slipped from my consciousness. It was John who insisted that I accept the invitation to visit the Smith campus and learn more about the college. "I know more about this kind of New England institution than you do," he said. "You should take it very seriously. I've had my ten years in Canada. I'll go with you wherever you want to move now. It's your turn."

John and I had wandered about the Smith campus on an August visit to the Connecticut Valley in the late 1960s. We had admired its leafy central core landscaped by Frederick Law Olmsted, its focal point the tranquil water of Paradise Pond, its residential center of gravity the neo-Georgian quadrangle to the north of the old campus. But we had seen it in the depths of summer somnolence, while en route to visit the MacLeish family in Conway — never in full session with the students who were its raison d'être.

Spring comes to the Connecticut Valley a good two weeks before the first crocuses in Toronto, so on my April visit I left a grey city to see a campus ablaze with crocus, daffodils, scilla, and rich strawberry and cream magnolias. Brighter than the spring flowers were the faces of the young women I saw everywhere. I could spend months at a time at the University of Toronto without ever hearing a female voice raised. Here the women were rowdy, physically freewheeling, joshing one another loudly, their laughter deep-belly laughter, not propitiatory giggles. The muddy afternoon games on the playing fields produced full-throated barracking. I was entranced.

The student who took me for a tour of the campus thought I was a parent of a potential freshman, so I had to quickly invent a suitable female relative from whose point of view I could ask questions. My guide was a sophomore from the Midwest. She planned to major in economics, but she had interests in religion and philosophy, and might elect a double major. She was planning to live and work in Washington D.C., perhaps for the government, perhaps for a research organization. Her house in the Quad evoked a strong response in me, impressive though the science labs, library, art studios, music building, and athletic facilities had been. The space was ample and well furnished, the notice board awash with political notices, the rooms sizable, each door alive with signs, posters, ironic comments, cartoons. There was a notice for a house meeting that evening, and, in response to my inquiry, I learned that each house was self-governing in all but a few respects. Office was elective, and hotly contested. I realized that this was a real alternative society, a place of true female sociability, where women ran things for themselves.

The faculty I met displayed the justifiably wary curiosity of people presented with a total stranger as a potential President. The women clearly fit Natalie's description of the scholarly figures who had transmitted their love of learning to her. The men were more recognizable as academic types, so that I thought I could guess where they'd done their graduate study. I'd recently been spending a good amount of my time at the University of Toronto cutting budgets, scaling down or closing services, thinking about how to make do. This didn't seem to be part of Smith's experience. In fact, the Trustees and the Search Committee spent most of the time I was with them asking what I'd plan to raise money for, what I thought could be improved. They assumed everything was possible, even as they worried about bucking the trend to coeducation. Educational quality was what everyone cared about, and there seemed to be no limits to the efforts everyone was prepared to expend to achieve that.

While president of Smith College, Jill Ker Conway planted a tree for Environment Week in April, 1981. Courtesy of Smith College Archives.

What worried them was whether Smith could raise money effectively if it insisted on adhering to its mission to educate women. Could it continue pricing its tuition competitively while not admitting men? What would happen to the quality of its academic life if women from elite prep schools were all counseled to enroll at Harvard or Yale? Would there be enough women of talent to go around in the coming decade of the eighties, when the cohort of young people was dramatically reduced in size?

I thought the case for women's education in an all-female student body was easy to make. One had only to explain the historical trends which had confined middle-class women to domesticity, unravel the ambiguous motivations which inspired coeducation, push people to think whether the classroom experience for young women and young men was really the same, and point to the outcomes in the careers of graduates from women's colleges. In any event, one could also point out that women's colleges were the only truly coeducational ones so far as faculty were concerned. It was the Harvards and Yales which were single-sex institutions in that dimension. As for the worry about numbers of applicants, that seemed part of the preoccupations of a small segment of American society. A college for women should be concerned with the whole age spectrum of potential students, not just entering eighteen-year-olds. And even among the eighteen-year-old population I thought it foolish to be so preoccupied with entering test scores. That preoccupation was part of the American quest for security in a formless society which eased its anxieties through developing statistical measures for everything. I was from a tradition where one sought to educate not only the very gifted but to expand the potential of those who were not precociously high achievers. There was a very large cohort of women who could benefit from a Smith education, and whose motivation, character, and capacity for growth were as important as the way they tested at age sixteen or seventeen. Smith had always been a leader in women's education, and there was no reason why it shouldn't continue to be so in the changed mores of the 1970s. I was glad that Trustees, students, faculty, and alumnae had all been polled and had voted overwhelmingly that Smith should remain an institution for women. I thought Smith could take the lead in reaffirming that purpose for other women's institutions.

From *True North* by Jill Ker Conway. Alfred A. Knopf, 1994.

PATRICIA WRIGHT

How many visitors to the University of Massachusetts have wondered why a campus of concrete high-rises sits in the middle of the countryside? Why does a rural university have the tallest library in the world? These are the questions tackled in Patricia Wright's "A Complex Edifice." Ms. Wright, a writer for the UMass alumni magazine, explains how the university administration, confronted with having to build a campus to accommodate 25,000 students in the 1960s, enlisted the talents of architects Marcel Breuer, Kevin Roche, Hugh Stubbins, and Edward Durrell Stone — yet with dubious results.

The Architecture of UMass

I t was a decade bristling with cranes, crawling with heavy equipment, and pocked with construction pits. It was a decade in which the discouraging dictum, "You can't get there from here," took on special meaning on the campus.

It was a decade that should have been recorded by time-lapse photography — so we could watch, even now, the rise of the concrete titans of the sixties and early seventies, among the modestly scaled, loosely spaced brick structures of the preceding hundred years.

"My God, we had to accommodate all those students!" exclaims Oswald Tippo, provost of the university during the early seventies. "Fifteen hundred more students every year, 100 to 150 new faculty a year, classrooms to accommodate them, dorm rooms to accommodate them!"

It was a decade in which the baby boom seemed to have hit the ground running. Thousands of Massachusetts high school graduates had no options for higher education in the Commonwealth, says John Lederle, then president of the university. "I'd go to the legislature and say, 'Look, these kids are born, they have as much right as you had to get an education!'"

And so there came to pass the modern campus of the University of Massachusetts. To serve a student population that by now has quadrupled in size — from about 6,000 in 1960 to some 25,000 today — the campus underwent revisions that can only be described as cataclysmic.

Incredibly, almost no campus buildings went down to make room for such bruisers as the Campus Center, the University Library, the Fine Arts Center, the Graduate Research Center, Whitmore Building, Herter Hall, and Southwest.

"I think they may have taken down one old wooden building," says art history professor and architectural historian Paul Norton. "But nothing of significance. Not since I came here, and that was in '58."

It would be wrong to imagine the campus mutating in a single spas-modic decade from bucolic "Mass Aggie" to a sort of academic Brasilia, new-risen from the fields. It had been about 55 years since the university was an agricultural college, 40 since it graduated from state college status.

There had been gradual physical growth in the central campus. Goodell and Hicks were built in the thirties, Machmer and the Student Union in the fifties. But large tracts of land remained between buildings, and no building was much taller than a tree. Up through the fifties the campus retained much of the pastoral quality it had possessed when the land around the central pond was devoted to growing hay.

It would be wrong, too, to assume — as many visitors do, seeing for the first time the overpowering contrasts of style and scale that were wrought by the big sixties buildings — that an existing rational order was disrupted when they were built.

On the contrary. The institution had commissioned and been offered numerous master plans, beginning in the 1860s with the proposals of no less an authority than the great American landscape architect Frederick Law Olmsted. But, beginning with Olmsted's, the plans had mostly been ignored.

This was the sad observation made many years ago by professor of landscape architecture Frank Waugh, himself the author of a series of little-heeded plans. It was the observation decades later of landscape architects Sasaki, Walker and Associates: "There appears to have been a tendency," a Sasaki report remarked tactfully, "to plan and design indi-vidual buildings with insufficient regard for the context and environment in which they have been placed." The results, according to the report, were "little apparent order" and "lack of articulated space."

One problem, aside from a sort of rural relaxation about building placement, was that the campus had evolved in a series of concentric rings around the campus pond.

A more conventional growth pattern for college campuses is the multiplication of quadrangles. That might have happened here as well if the Olmsted plan had been adopted and the college had grown up around a rectangular "common" on the eastern ridge, where Morrill Science Complex is now.

In the course of concentric development, buildings went up in front of buildings which had gone up in front of other buildings — in such ways that it's often hard to tell which is the front and which is the back, and how we're supposed to get in.

"I believe they've probably had troubles with that all along," says Paul Norton. "I was looking at Old Chapel recently and wondering which side the architect thought was the front. It could be taken to be the pond side, it could be taken to be the other side. I think maybe he didn't know!"

Successive plans tried to come to grips with this problem of a concentric campus with an untraversable space — the pond — at its core. More than one early 20th-century plan envisioned a great, bold pedestrian boulevard running east to west across campus, bridging the pond and connecting major building groups.

These plans never came to fruition and really there was no great pressure for them to do so. The campus population was growing slowly. It was nothing that could not be accommodated in the growing accumulation of smallish, "reddish," as Norton calls them, Georgian revival buildings.

Until the sixties. That's when the university experienced what professor of landscape architecture Julius Fabos calls "the semimadhouse" of monumental expansion.

Fabos had studied with Hideo Sasaki, who was known as the best campus planner in the country. In the early sixties Sasaki's firm was hired by the university to coordinate site and circulation planning around the new buildings. In Fabos' view, the Sasaki firm did well in developing the concept of a pedestrian campus. The idea was an academic core restricted to foot traffic, with automobiles — and dormitory-dwelling students — parked at the periphery.

Sasaki failed to find a politically acceptable alternative to North Pleasant Street, a busy local artery that still sends heavy traffic hurtling through the east side of campus. But he was successful in eliminating the vehicle route that had swung along the west side of the pond since the 19th century; in planning the relationship of the new southwest residential complex to the rest of campus; and in producing an "appropriately scaled approach" to the campus in the form of Commonwealth Avenue and Haigis Mall.

But for all Sasaki's skill and prestige, says the European-born Fabos, he "couldn't hold in line these people." By "these people" Fabos means "the prima donnas" — the corps of famous architects called in by the university for its new, urban-scale structures.

To name only the most well-known architects, Marcel Breuer designed the Campus Center. The University Library was designed by Edward Durrell Stone. The Fine Arts Center was designed by Kevin Roche. Hugh Stubbins designed the Southwest Residential Area.

All of these architects had national and international reputations, and none but Stubbins were from Massachusetts. This could not have occurred in previous decades when only Massachusetts architects were assigned by government officials. In the sixties this system was changed to allow the Board of Trustees its own choices. And the board was interested not only in quickly increasing the carrying capacity of the campus, but in distinguishing it architecturally.

Was the university trying to project a new image for itself in the design of these new buildings? Lederle and Tippo say no.

"I think we wanted buildings that would be appropriate to a comprehensive state university in a beautiful setting," says Tippo. "I don't think we were trying to impress anybody."

"We just wanted functional architecture that would take advantage of the latest ideas," says Lederle. But he adds, "I do think there was a concern with making these buildings worthy of the institution and worthy of the money we were putting into them."

Julius Fabos, on the other hand, believes that bringing in "these giant architects to design these giant buildings" was "the physical expression of bringing the institution up to the level of other institutions in the Northeast."

So, like Harvard and Yale, the University became a kind of showcase for prestige modern architecture — designer architecture, one might call it. But unlike Harvard and Yale, Massachusetts was opting for a radical shift of style and scale at its very core.

The issue of height is still argued. Was a 28-story library tower really necessary, or five 22-story dorms? The general case for high-rises was compactly stated several years ago by Associate Vice Chancellor for Administration and Finance Jack Littlefield. Tall buildings, he said, "may give you funny feelings about the horizon, but they leave you more grass and trees."

Others disagree. Especially where the library tower is concerned. Paul Norton says it would have been better to take down South College than to indulge the "terrible idea" of building a library 28 stories tall. Physical plant director Roger Cherewatti, who must cope with the considerable maintenance and operational headaches the tower presents, says it should be "written in the architects' bible: Thou shalt *not* build a library more than four stories tall! Unless the chancellor tells you to!"

As for Southwest, the imposing collection of high and low rise dorms indisputably compresses large numbers of students onto a very small amount of land. Some 5,400 of them are presently housed and fed on the equivalent of four city blocks. They also appear — from the outside at least — to be housed very handsomely, in towers rising from the Massachusetts landscape like the residential blocks of the earlier 20th-century French architect Le Corbusier.

Le Corbusier proposed such apartment towers for much the same reasons that have been used to justify Southwest: to minimize land use while maximizing occupancy and access to light and views.

However, several generations of students have objected to Southwest. Julius Fabos thinks it's because the designers were thinking about the external sculptural impact of the buildings, rather than the psychological and sociological impact on the students inside. (He thinks this produced "an elegant monstrosity.") Paul Norton, who considers Southwest elegant but not monstrous, thinks that student tastes simply changed, and at exactly the wrong moment.

Old Chapel, W.E.B. Du Bois Library, and the Student Union at the University of Massachusetts at Amherst, 1992. Photo by Richard W. Wilkie.

"Students weren't objecting to that kind of housing at the time it was being planned and built," he says. "But just as it was completed, they wanted to live in different ways. They didn't want two students to a room. They wanted suites, or they wanted to live together, or they wanted — anything but what they were given over there! But it wasn't Stubbins' fault."

Norton is arguing, in other words, that unpredictable factors derailed the architect's good intentions at Southwest. Nobody, least of all Paul Norton, makes that argument for Kevin Roche's Fine Arts Center, an extraordinarily bold and handsome structure that has been plagued by maintenance and functional problems. Most of these problems, says Norton, were entirely predictable. As head of the art department at the time, he was one of those predicting them. For example, he protested bitterly against the rigid row of studios in the building's long upper beam.

"Well, it's ridiculous," he says. "Ridiculous! It's ridiculous to put all those art classrooms way up in the air; all those hundreds of students, every day, having to go up flights and flights of stairs just to get into a classroom; and when you get up there you can't see anything, there's no *reason* to be up there! You're just up there!

"And then the classrooms as a series of boxes — 600 feet of boxes all lined up in a row. That was exactly what we did not want! We wanted open space that could be converted to larger or smaller spaces by a class. I didn't care whether it had dirt on the floor, that would have been fine. What we wanted was flexibility.

"It goes back to the way the plans were accepted," Norton concludes. "I was there. Roche brought up a bunch of very nice slides and a model he'd made and explained it all very carefully to the Board of Trustees. Immediately after that presentation, the board went into a closed room and accepted the plans.

"After that, it didn't matter what you said to Kevin Roche. He didn't have to listen to anybody, and he didn't!"

If a competition were established for best anecdotes about arrogant architects on campus, Kevin Roche anecdotes would probably win hands down. The classic is recounted, second hand, by physical plant director Cherewatti. A member of Cherewatti's staff once ran into the architect off campus.

"He went up to him, and he said 'Mr. Roche, what were you doing with that building? It is the most unfunctional building I ever saw! I mean there's 20-foot slanted ceilings and leaks and nothing leads properly — I still get lost!'

"And Roche said, 'Well you know I wasn't designing a building — I was designing a *piece of sculpture.*'"

Roche was not the only offender. Oswald Tippo says university administrators came to see architects as "a very aggressive group of people — very aggressive. They had this horrible feeling they were right about absolutely everything!"

What Julius Fabos calls prima donna behavior among the architects was coupled, in this period of explosive growth, with the administration's desire to make decisions quickly and to avoid having them scuttled by revisions. "There comes a point when you have to say 'No more changes,'" says Lederle.

This led, sometimes, to casting in concrete decisions that are now regretted. Few but Lederle still defend the notion of a high-rise library. "I'll have to take responsibility for those bricks that are falling off too," says the good-natured former president. The building has a brick veneer "because I said we're not going to have a nothing-but-concrete campus."

Lederle himself has reservations about Marcel Breuer's Campus Center. "It's sort of — *cavernous*," he says. The 12-story structure suppresses student services into a long underground concourse, with layers of hotel rooms and convention facilities stacked overhead. "It's not very warm. I said at the time I couldn't imagine students liking this building."

Julius Fabos speaks with distaste of the Campus Center, too. "You don't need to be a landscape architect," he says, to see that the fortresslike structure on its great raised base "is less than well integrated with the rest of campus."

Still, there are things to like about the Campus Center, with its fine proportions and sucked-in windows, and the beautiful views from its upper decks. There are things to like about all the new buildings. The "brutalist" aesthetic most of them represent has been called "tomato cannery style" by at least one unimpressed visitor to campus. (The term brutalism in recent architecture refers to the assertive use of concrete, not to psychological intentions.) But for other people, these powerfully shaped buildings have great visual interest especially in a strong sun that shows off their crisp edges, stripped surfaces, and Brobdingnagian geometry.

As a collection of buildings, too, there is something to be said for the new architecture of the central campus. Undeniably, our sense of scale is put through hard paces by the juxtaposition of the tiny Old Chapel and the towering University Library. But none of the "designer" buildings shoulders aside older structures so ruthlessly as the Morrill Science Complex, begun in 1960, shoulders aside poor little Clark and Wilder Halls. None of the premier buildings was so carelessly placed as many in the previous generation.

In fact, the Campus Center, the library, and the FAC create a powerful, if as yet uncrystallized, new crescent around the west side of the pond. If ever knit together in a thorough and imaginative landscape plan, they could come closer to performing one of their original functions — effective redefinition of the campus core.

That kind of landscape planning and execution, it's generally agreed, has always been give short shrift. "It seems you never get enough money along with the building itself to facilitate the outside," says Lederle. "There are always the typical cutbacks," says Fabos. "And the ideal environment becomes much less ideal."

Fabos, however, is the most encouraging person you can talk to about the possibilities for reclamation.

Listening to him talk about the importance of the landscape, you begin to realize it's not just that we can avoid past mistakes in future buildings — although people are thinking about that.

("I dug out the Scope of Services statement for the designer of Southwest," says Roger Cherewatti, "and it was two sentences. 'We want dorms for 6,500 kids, and we want them to have dining commons.' Well for our new sports arena we put together a *45-page* scope of work. Every inch of that arena is going to function at its peak. That's the difference.")

And it's not just that we can adjust as we go along for conspicuous flaws in the present system — for example, for the circulation problems that are signaled by the hundreds of footsore shortcuts crisscrossing the campus lawns. Although people are thinking about that, too.

("We do have an undersized path system for the number of people who move around campus," says Beverly Nuckles, who was a student at the university in the sixties and recently returned as a planner. "It will be interesting to see what happens when we try and correct the paths that are undersized, by expanding them just a little to take up the volume that we have.")

There's also the possibility, says Fabos, of *comprehensive landscape redesign*. It was done at the University of Pennsylvania, he says, with spectacular results. Some people credit campus improvement with helping reverse Penn's decline in enrollment.

Can spaces that weren't well thought out to begin with — and that are now defined by works of immovable architecture — really be turned around by redesign of the landscape? Can our curious collection of somewhat haphazardly placed early buildings, and almost overwhelmingly scaled recent buildings, ever be crystallized into a coherent whole?

Fabos says emphatically, yes. He gives an example that's especially apt for a campus where (as former president Lederle says sadly) we've still got cars stashed everywhere.

"It is like the difference between a space where 20 cars can park anywhere — so they park anywhere — and a space which is organized so they know where to go," Fabos says.

"With vegetation, with trees, with lights, with pathways, these spaces begin to make sense. And it's not so expensive. We're talking ten or fifteen million dollars for the whole thing.

"Basically the cost of one building! For the cost of one new building, we could make this visually a first-class campus."

————

From "A Complex Edifice" by Patricia Wright. *Contact*, The University of Massachusetts, Winter 1987.

JULIUS LESTER

Julius Lester, a long-time faculty member at the University of Massachusetts, has been noted for his writings on black studies. Lester's provocative Look Out, Whitey, Black Power's Gon' Get Your Mama! *was the first book to explain black power. His* To Be a Slave, Black Folktales, *and* Long Journey Home: Stories from Black History *have covered a broad portion of the black experience.*

One of the most discussed aspects of Lester's life has been his conversion to Judaism. When he began teaching a course at UMass on blacks and Jews it set off a contentious dispute within the university. This selection from Lovesong *(1988), Lester's account of becoming a Jew, narrates the incident from Lester's point of view and includes a vignette of writer James Baldwin teaching at UMass. This book caused such consternation that Lester was reassigned from the Afro-American Studies to the Judaic Studies Department at UMass.*

Campus Politics

I am going to offer the course next semester on blacks and Jews. I draft an outline and give it to Haim Gunner, who teaches in the Environmental Science Department at the university and is one of the leaders of the Jewish Community of Amherst. We met when we appeared on a panel last year as part of a day-long conference about anti-Semitism and racism on campus.

He and his wife, Yaffa, invite me to their house for lunch to talk about the course. We have been chatting casually for a while when the doorbell rings. Haim returns with a man whose mournful face is ringed by a white beard. It is the rabbi who conducted the bat mitzvah. He is introduced to me as Yechiael Lander, the Hillel rabbi at Smith College and Amherst College, and part-time rabbi of the Jewish Community of Amherst.

Why is he here? Is there something so offensive in my course outline that Haim and Yaffa thought it better for the rabbi to tell me?

I am nervous and uncommunicative during lunch. Finally, when the dishes are cleared and coffee is served, Haim says, "I took the liberty, Julius, of making a copy of your course outline and showing it to Yechiael. I hope you don't mind. "

"Not at all," I lie.

"I like what you want to do," the rabbi says. "I like the way you explore definitions of oppression and the various forms it takes — political, economic, cultural, etcetera — and then see in what ways the histories of Jews and blacks converge and diverge. However, you must include something in the course about Judaism. "

"I wouldn't be comfortable doing that," I say nervously.

"Well, you must. "

"Are you sure it would be all right?" I ask timidly.

He looks at me as if I am ridiculous. "Well, of course."

What I am asking is, Does he trust me to teach Judaism? I know nothing. And I am black. Would Jews trust a black person talking about their religion? I look at him. I think he trusts me more than I trust myself.

"I read your article as part of my sermon at services at Amherst College on Yom Kippur," he says. "Thank you for writing it. It meant a lot to me and to a lot of the students. I know that I'll be able to fill your class with students from Smith and Amherst alone."

"Well, before you do that, I have to put together a whole new course."

I ask him, Yaffa and Haim what books they would recommend I read. When I leave, I have a two-page reading list.

Paul Puryear, the chairman of the Afro-Am Department, calls me into his office. Paul, who chain-smokes, is a heavyset, dark-skinned man with a beard. He is one of those in the department who has not stopped speaking to me. A blunt, outspoken man, he, too, is a Southerner bred in the creed that morality was the standard applied to one's own behavior first and only reluctantly to that of others.

"Close the door and sit down," he says, chuckling.

I do so.

"Did you hear about the departmental faculty meeting Friday?" he asks, lighting a cigarette.

"No. I didn't know there was one."

He laughs. "You weren't supposed to. I thought maybe somebody had told you about it."

I shake my head. "Nobody's talking to me."

"They still mad at you? Well, wait until I tell you what they tried to pull."

"I'm not sure I want to know."

"Oh, you'll enjoy this. They called a special meeting. I'm the chairman of the department and I didn't know a thing about the meeting. I happened to be here in the building and somebody who wasn't in on the plot asked me what the meeting was about. I said, 'What meeting?' He said, 'There's a faculty meeting at three. You didn't call it?' I said, 'Uh-uh.' To myself I said, I'd better go to the meeting and see what's up. I mean, they don't come to the scheduled meetings. Something heavy must be going down for them to call a meeting on their own. So I got to the meeting. It was obvious they didn't want me there, but what could they do? Well, the subject under discussion was your new course, the one on blacks and Jews."

"What?" I exclaim.

"They were planning to take a vote to ban you from teaching the course."

"Who was there?" I want to know.

He shakes his head. "I'm not going to tell you that."

"I just want to know who my enemies are, Paul."

He shakes his head. "Think about it. You can figure out who all was involved."

"Well, they can vote until they're dead but they can't stop me from teaching that course."

"That's what I told them. I said, 'Ain't you fools ever heard of academic freedom?' I told 'em that if you wanted to teach the course, there wasn't a thing they could do about it and if they wanted to make an issue of it, I'd fight them all the way to the chancellor."

"What reasons did they give for not wanting me to teach the course?"

He chuckles. "They said you wouldn't teach it from the quote correct political point of view unquote. They said you were too pro-Israel."

"How did things end up?"

"When they saw I wasn't going to let them get away with it, they decided that A.B. should teach a course on blacks and Jews that would be politically correct, quote, unquote."

"Paul, you're kidding!"

He laughs. "Next semester we're going to have two courses on blacks and Jews. Wasn't nothing I could do. If I wouldn't let them stop your course, not that they could have, I couldn't turn around and stop A.B. from doing one."

"No. I understand that."

"But you ain't heard the best part."

"You mean there's more?"

"He's teaching his blacks and Jews course at the same time and days as yours." He laughs loudly. "How many course you scheduled to teach next semester?"

"Two."

"Well, drop the other one. I expect you're going to have a large enrollment for the black and Jews one and I don't have the money to assign you a T.A." He chuckles.

I thank him. He had done more than I would have expected, especially since he probably doesn't agree with a word I wrote.

I leave his office and walk down the hall to mine and call Saul Perlmutter, the university Hillel rabbi.

"I need to talk with you as soon as possible," I tell him.

I met Saul when he invited me to speak at a Hillel Sunday brunch several years ago. He invited me back another year and has been helpful in recommending books on Judaism and Jewish history for my course.

I got to his office in the Student Union Building and tell him of my almost violent encounter with A.B., of the departmental effort to sabotage my course, and ask him to recommend my course to any Jewish students who ask. He agrees and suggests I also contact Leonard Ehrlich, chairman of the Judaic Studies Program, to see if it will cross-list my course.

I present the revised course outline to the chairman of Judaic Studies. A few days later he calls. The Judaic Studies Program's curriculum committee has voted to include the course as one of its department offerings.

A.B. has three students in his "Blacks and Jews" course; there are eighty in mine. The price of such vindication, however, is reading eighty papers, and since I will be assigning four papers, that's three hundred twenty papers, which will amount to between fifteen hundred and two thousand pages.

The students are disappointed that there are only ten blacks in the class. In the ten years I've taught here, I've never had many black students in my classes, though. A black student told me once it was because my wife is white. On such reasoning and humanity the future of blacks may depend.

It's a good class, ninety percent Jewish, ranging from one very outspoken Orthodox young man to Reform Jews to anti-Zionists to Jews whose only relationship to anything Jewish is that they were born from a Jewish mother. There is also a German exchange student.

The students are bewildered by the joy with which I lecture about Judaism, the passion in my lectures on Jewish history. Some have come during office hours to tell me that my enthusiasm is making them look anew at the Judaism they had all but rejected.

I cannot rid myself of the desire to convert. Would I want to if I were not so isolated from blacks now? I don't know. But I do feel lonely and abandoned by my people. If I converted now, I'm afraid I would be doing so only because I am angry at my own people. I know that if Jews did not accept me, I would be devastated. I can only become a Jew when I know that is what God wants of me, when I know that being a Jew is right for me, even if no Jew in the world accepts me.

I doubt that Jews would accept me in my complexity any more than blacks have. When Hannah Arendt published *Eichmann in Jerusalem*, she became a nonperson among Jews as I have among blacks. Would Jews have responded any differently to a Jew who defended the black re-

sponse to Young's resignation than blacks have to me? I don't think so.
I must accept that this loneliness is how God wants me to live.

James Baldwin is teaching on campus this academic year. I have spent
a lot of time with him. We know each other as only writers can and we
have talked and argued almost until sunrise many nights about our
definitions of ourselves as writers, about blacks, about Israel; we've
swapped stories and gossip about other writers and our misadventures
in the world of publishing. He has been at the house often, almost every
Shabbat evening, in fact. He has sat at our Shabbat table and read the
words from Psalms that are part of our Sabbath evening ritual. He has
seen me hold the kiddush cup as we chanted the blessing, raise the loaves
of challah as we chanted *ha-motzi*. And we have certainly discussed my
being Jewish, to which his initial response was "Well, I'm not surprised."
(Is there some conspiracy of people who have known for years I should
have been Jewish but wouldn't tell me?) The personal bond between me
and Jimmy is quite deep because we know the penalties writing extracts,
how its demands diminish our human capacities even as what we write
seeks to expand the capacity for being human in us.

So why am I surprised? Why do I feel betrayed? Why do I feel he
dishonored the love and caring my wife has shown him? Why am I sorry
that my children shared their purity with him?

One of the courses he teaches is my "History of the Civil Rights
Movement." Every Tuesday he lectures in a large auditorium and on
Thursday the class of some three hundred or so meets in sections taught
by individual faculty members. Last Tuesday Jimmy devoted his lecture
to the Jesse Jackson affair.

He began with a diatribe, albeit an eloquent one, blaming the media
for reporting it. I was sitting in my customary seat in the back of the
auditorium and my mouth dropped. No one put words in Jesse's mouth,
did they? After denying he said it, Jesse finally admitted he had. But
Jimmy's view was that Mondale and Hart say things like that about
blacks but the media won't report it. His sense of history is supposed to
be better than that. When former vice-president Spiro Agnew referred to
someone as a "Fat Jap" it was reported widely, to Agnew's embarrass-
ment. Nixon's Secretary of Agriculture, Earl Butz, had to resign for telling
an anti-black joke in a setting similar to the one in which Jackson made his
"Hymie" reference. Jimmy insisted on blaming the messenger, however.

He then went on to hold Jews responsible. Exactly how Jews were to
blame escaped me. Maybe because we were so ungracious as to say that
we were insulted by being referred to as "Hymies." But I was shocked
when Jimmy referred to Jews as being nothing more than "white Chris-

tians who go to something called a synagogue on a Saturday rather than church on Sunday."

I love Jimmy. It was reading *Notes of a Native Son* my sophomore year at Fisk that told me that I, too, could be a writer, because Jimmy wrote with a lyricism and love closer to me than the anger of Richard Wright. I know he is not an anti-Semite, but his remarks in class were anti-Semitic, and he does not realize it.

Julius Lester joined the faculty of the University of Massachusetts at Amherst in 1971. He is now professor of Judaic Studies. Photo by Milan Sabatini.

At the conclusion of his lecture, he called for questions or responses. Then the real horror began. His words had given black students permission to stand up and mouth every anti-Semitic cliche they knew and they did so, castigating Jewish landlords and Jews in general. Jimmy listened and said nothing. I was grateful when an Afro-Am faculty member stood up to say that Jewish involvement in the Civil Rights Movement should not be denigrated, minimized or castigated as paternalism.

When class ended, I was scarcely out of my seat before I found myself surrounded by Jewish students, most of whom I did not know, most of whom had tears in their eyes. One young woman from Smith College seemed to speak for all of them when she asked, fearfully, "Do you think what he said is true?"

I responded with characteristic eloquence: "Jimmy was full of shit this morning!"

In my section of the class on Thursday, my students were so disturbed that we spent the entire class discussing Tuesday's lecture. The Jewish students were hurt and angry; the white students were bewildered, and the black students were silent. I suppose I could have been more diplomatic and circumspect. But then I wouldn't be me. I told them I thought Jesse Jackson was really auditioning for a role as one of "Charlie's Angels," that Baldwin was wrong in his analysis of the Jackson affair because his outrage was misdirected. Why weren't he and other blacks angry at Jesse?

I did not expect what I said to remain in class. Neither did I expect people in the Afro-Am Department not only to stop speaking to me, yet again, but also this time to include a hostility in their silence which frightens me. The hostility was open when one department member stuck his head in my office and said, "I thought Jimmy's lecture Tuesday was quite good. I thought he handled the discussion very well." The look of cold defiance in his face was chilling.

I wish they would sit *shivah* and be done with me.

From *Lovesong: Becoming a Jew* by Julius Lester. Henry Holt and Company, 1988.

CHIP BROWN

In 1970, Hampshire College opened in Amherst. It was an expression of the educational and social experimentation of the Sixties. Hampshire did away with grades, required courses, and traditional majors. The college stressed independent study and research projects.

Twenty years after the birth of Hampshire College, Class of '71 graduate Chip Brown reviewed in the New York Times Magazine *the college's history, stating with surprise that an experimental college has survived into the Nineties. Brown's account covers the political battles that have marked Hampshire's evolution.*

What's New at Frisbee U.

Hampshire College was born 20 years ago this fall in an apple orchard in western Massachusetts. As the many journalists who described its infancy were wont to say, the school had a silver spoon in its mouth and a Frisbee in its hand. It was a college that gave no grades, had no departments, and didn't offer tenure to faculty members. Academically, students were free to do whatever they wanted. The year it opened, Hampshire was one of the hardest schools in the country to get into.

If the question mark had not existed, Hampshire would have invented it. The heart of the curriculum was asking questions: students learned "modes of inquiry." The new philosophy was summed up in the motto *Non Satis Scire*, To Know Is Not Enough. The poet Archibald MacLeish spoke to the hope surrounding this "new departure" in education when he delivered the address at Hampshire's inaugural convocation. "I think," he said, "we may be present at a greater moment than we know."

Now, two decades and 5,000 alumni later, Hampshire finds itself one of the last of a breed. Its survival alone is something of an accomplishment. Experimental colleges have retrenched or vanished. The University of California at Santa Cruz had modified its curriculum. New College in Sarasota, Fla., merged with the state university. Nationwide, the trend is toward fewer electives, more structure. Best-selling books like "The Closing of the American Mind" blame the experiments of the 60's for the decline in academic standards.

Does Hampshire instill anything traditional methods do not? It's always hard to measure the value of educational method, but the nature of Hampshire's program makes assessment doubly hard. When students have such a large role in their own illumination, how much do you credit the college?

As one of the guinea pigs in the experiment, I've always thought a good argument could be made that the social aspect of Hampshire — the shock-the-parents coed bathrooms, group living in the "modules" and the obligation to cook, clean, and fetch groceries from the Mixed Nuts co-op every week — had as much impact on undergraduate experience as the interdisciplinary curriculum and "modes of inquiry." But maybe not. And maybe even wanting to measure the worth of an education is wrongheaded, born of a consumerist mentality that views the mind's development as product refinement. In any case, this spring I packed a couple of Frisbees in the car, assumed a mode of inquiry, and drove up to the orchard in Amherst to revisit the experiment, such as it was 20 years ago, and such as it is today.

It used to be that we were taller than the trees. Now the saplings that line the blacktop driveway are robust oaks. I wandered around in the reverie of an April morning. The land sloped west toward a valley full of chopped-out cornfields and renascent pasture. Students drifted in and out of the library. Book cache, television studio, cliff face for instruction in rappelling, it is still the eye of the college. The basement bulletin board was a montage of campus life unchanged by time: panic-and-stress work-shops, film festivals, poetry readings, for-sale signs, notices of missing pets (Simon the cat had disappeared from Module 54).

For a school with little respect for tradition, much seemed the same. The old Frisbee field had been replaced by a warren of solar-heated arts and academic buildings, but Ultimate Frisbee was still the reigning sport, as it was in the early 70's, when Hampshire had one of the best teams in the country. The Dionysian spirit was alive and well in the unofficial "clothing optional" floor of Merrill House. The "Trip or Treat" Hallow-een party had made its way into college guidebooks.

Backpacks and sneakers, blue jeans with holes in the knee, a certain scruffy air: students look the same, too, though today, 70 percent come from public school and 30 percent from private — the reverse of 1970. The campus is still predominantly white, despite the college's expressed com-mitment to a racially and ethnically diverse community. At $20,240 a year, a Hampshire education is one of the dearest in the country. Nearly half the students receive some sort of financial aid from the college.

Clothes, intellectual positions and even behavior are governed by the code of the "politically correct," which is to say antisexist, antiracist, antihomophobic, antispecist. One of the unforeseen aspects of Hampshire turned out to be how sexually uptight the place was, even in the any-thing-goes atmosphere of the early 70's. And some of those inhibitions endure as students sacrifice spontaneity to project correct behavior. No one would undo Hampshire's commitment to feminist values, which has produced on-site day-care facilities and position of power for women, but all that right thinking can sometimes have puritanical overtones.

A photograph by Jerome Liebling, a Hampshire professor, of the naked torso of his baby daughter — part of Liebling's impressive exhibit on display in the library gallery — had recently come under attack in an anonymous letter in the student paper. The writer argued that because a child cannot consent to having her genitals photographed, the picture constituted child abuse: "God help me if I see any more child pornography condoned on this campus again."

"Sometimes it's hard to be a heterosexual male here," said Halstead York, who was having breakfast in the dining hall with his friends Jeri Chittick, Rebecca Drury and Elizabeth Rosenthal.

"Students are trying so hard to be open-minded they're close-minded," said Jeri.

"A lot of the issues I believe in," said Rebecca. "I consider myself a feminist, but people on campus don't think I am."

Despite the social climate, the students were all happy about Hampshire. "I've learned a lot here," said Jeri. "How to ask questions, how to get away with doing what you want to do. You learn that you should say what you want to say. You learn that on papers you should get comments and not just a 92 and 'put in more commas.'"

"I took a class at UMass and nobody asked questions," said Elizabeth. "Nobody cared about the reading. They asked, Are we going to be tested on this? It was like a big high school."

"I went to a class here and the teacher said, 'Why do you want to take this class?' and I had to figure out why," said Jeri. "You have to stand up for yourself. "

"I wish there were more of a conservative streak, " said Elizabeth.

It's almost impossible to convey the fervor of the early years. "Nothing was ever so much fun, " recalled Francis D. Smith, who was hired in 1967 and served as the college's dean of Humanities and the Arts. "This was *ab ova*, from the egg, from the beginning."

Hampshire was the child of four prestigious institutions in the Connecticut River valley: Smith, Amherst, Mount Holyoke and the University of Massachusetts. A committee of educators from the four-college consortium had been kicking around the idea of a new college since the 1950's. They foresaw an explosion of knowledge no traditionally structured curriculum could adequately cover. Educating might be cheaper and more effective if students were taught to teach themselves.

Harold F. Johnson, a lawyer and wealthy Amherst College graduate, read about the proposed "New College" in an alumni bulletin, and decided to put up $6 million. The Ford Foundation made a large grant. Franklin Patterson was hired as the college's first president in 1966, and went to work drafting Hampshire's bible, "The Making of a College." He overlaid the curriculum reforms from the 1958 "New College Plan" with the pressing social, political and intellectual concerns of the day. The college should help counteract the alienation in American society, strive to humanize technology and be a force for social change. Patterson's teen-age son designed the insignia, the 10-leafed Hampshire tree. Ground was broken on the library, and Hampshire set about recruiting faculty and students. "We didn't know if anybody would come," recalled Charles R. Longsworth, the founding vice president who succeeded Patterson as president, and who had helped draft the final plan.

They needn't have worried. Hampshire was hot. SAT scores were not required. Candidates brought their creative work to their admission interviews — everything from light shows to loaves of bread. Some 2000 applicants vied for 270 places. An amazing 97 percent of students accepted actually matriculated.

Jim Johnston tried to transfer to Hampshire in 1971 but was told the college didn't take transfer students. Undeterred, he drove to the campus with a portfolio of silk screens and prints, wangled his way into the dining hall, and converted one wall into an art gallery. He even sent out invitations, including one to the admissions office. He got in. "They could have just as easily had me arrested, " he recalled.

Professors were equally excited by an institution that did not want to regiment them in departments or dictate what they had to teach. Hampshire received a thousand applications for 50 faculty positions. The physics professor Herbert Bernstein, then a fellow at the institute for Advanced Studies in Princeton, read about Hampshire in the Whole Earth Catalog and was so intrigued he offered to work for nothing. He was hired, at a salary of $1.

At first, everyone knew more about Hampshire wasn't than what it was. "There was this feeling of excitement and anticipation that something really great was going to happen, but you didn't know what it was," said Kim Shelton, a documentary film maker who was part of that pioneer class. "You had the feeling of being on an expedition with all these really great people."

What emerged was kind of a graduate school for 18-year-olds. Instead of grades, students got written evaluations. Progress was measured by passing a series of exams in three "divisions." In Division I, students had to demonstrate a grasp of modes of inquiry in each of the college's four "schools": Humanities and Arts, Social Sciences, Natural Sciences, and Communications and Cognitive Science.

For Division II, students had to organize their course work and research around a particular theme. Someone interested in weaving, for example, might jump off into an exploration of the chemistry of dyes; write a paper about the religious implications of weaving in aboriginal societies; work up a computer-based experiment in pattern recognition; or perhaps compose a sonnet sequence about the joys of being a Luddite. Instead of majors, there were concentrations. And the final exam — the Division III project — was the equivalent of a thesis defense.

As the college tried to establish methods and standards, it was in a quandary over how to evaluate popular personal-growth courses like "Dimensions of Consciousness." "We'd want to get evaluations of students' work in and the answer would come back, 'You don't evaluate personal growth, you recognize it,'" recalled Richard L. Muller, the dean of the school of Communications and Cognitive Science.

There was a lot of what was charitably called "creative floundering," which led to attrition rate of 40 percent — lower than the national average, but well above the rate at other schools in the valley. Some Hampshire students sauntered around with an air of preppie entitlement that irked faculty, but by and large they quickly showed that they were interested in doing serious work, and they held their own in classes at the other four colleges. (The five-college consortium was the most important legacy of Hampshire's sponsors.) They earned reputations for being talkative in class (perhaps to a fault), quick to make use of a professor's office hours, and intent on adapting the course to their needs.

"In my experience Hampshire students are different from the rest of the students in the valley," said Benjamin DeMott, an Amherst professor who served on an advisory committee during Hampshire's gestation. "The ones I've taught seem much more interested in an independent way in their own education. There's no notion that a teacher is there to inspire or entertain. The teacher is a resource who has some information to impart. The teacher becomes a kind of coach. When I have one of these kids in my classes, I'm impressed."

Hampshire's darkest hours came in the early 1980's. A number of faculty members had noticed a shift in the mid-1970's, when for the first time students seemed more conservative than teachers. By the mid-1980's, applications plunged to where the college was admitting 1 applicant for every 1.23 who applied. The lower caliber of student added to criticism that standards were lax. Hampshire, which depends on tuition and fees for 80 percent of its $24 million budget, was finding its efforts to attract new students hampered by stereotypes about Frisbees and drugs. The college came off badly in a widely publicized story about a student who'd written his thesis on the aerodynamics of the Frisbee.

After much discussion, the college decided to make a "commitment to quality." It cut the number of students from 1,200 to 900. The board of trustees resolved to operate at a deficit, spending some of the small endowment of $10 million. To combat the hippie image, Frisbee photographs were declared verboten in official publications.

"We knew we were taking an enormous risk," recalled Adele Simmons, who recently left after 12 years as president to head the John D. and Catherine T. MacArthur Foundation in Chicago. "I would go to bed at night planning the phone call to the president of UMass to talk about merging."

Almost immediately things turned around. By last fall, Hampshire's enrollment was back over 1,200 and the applicant pool for a class of 350 students was over 2,000.

Today, there's more structure than meets the eye. There are filing deadlines. Exam days. An advising center. "We know more about what we're doing now," says Nancy Lowry, dean of the School of Natural Sciences. Students have to pass all Division I exams by taking courses instead of doing independent projects.

As always, a lot of weight falls on the faculty adviser to keep the student pointed in the right direction. It's clear now that teaching students to teach themselves entails more, not less, work for the faculty. The 11-to-1 student-faculty ratio is not low enough, and students often have to cajole overworked faculty members onto their exam committees — a hurdle that some shy young people have a hard time leaping. Since there is no tenure, faculty members are often embroiled in controversies over the reappointment of their colleagues, forced to make tough decisions whether to renew the contracts of good teachers who lack scholarship and good scholars who can't teach. A Humanities and Arts professor who wasn't reappointed sued the college, charging discrimination; the threat of litigation now keeps some faculty from making candid appraisals.

Hampshire's affable new president, Gregory S. Prince, arrived last fall from Dartmouth, where he was an associate dean of faculty. At 51, he has the golden shine of a Cheever character before everything goes to hell. Every Monday, he meets with students over breakfast in the dining hall. He invited me to sit in.

And so it was that the president of the college was sipping orange juice while a student harangued him about Becky the Tumorous Horse.

"Greg, I don't understand why Becky was taken from the farm center," said Karin Bond, the spokeswoman for a delegation of three grim-faced students. "Why was Becky removed?"

Prince explained that his wife had removed Becky to their family farm in New Hampshire, where the horse could be cared for at no expense to the college, and that it had been a college-wide decision to put the rest of the horses up for sale and phase out the costly research program.

"Greg, your wife has definitely wanted that horse from the moment she saw her," said Karin.

"Karin, that just isn't true," said Prince, explaining again that his wife was providing care for Becky at no expense to the college, etc. etc.

"What's the difference in expense to the institution between raising horses and raising sheep?" Karin shot back. Her complexion was getting pale. She began to weep. The other students at the table shifted uncomfortably.

"This is what I wanted to do with my life, Greg, and you're taking it away from me!" she cried, banging the table with her fist. She began to shout. "Why can't I have this program when I spend $20,000 a year to go to school here!"

"That's a different question, Karin," said the president. Karin sobbed for a while. Eventually it seemed there was nothing more to say. Prince looked dejected. The breakfast had never gone worse, and to add insult to injury an alumnus was gleefully scribbling notes.

"Anyone else have anything on their mind?" said Prince. He turned to Jill Davidson, a first-year student with a bandanna on her head. "Why are you here this morning?"

"I'm embarrassed to say my father wanted me to come. He heard students could have breakfast with the president."

The vaunted "new departure" has not changed the face of higher education, but Hampshire's example has not gone unremarked.

"Though much of the bubbly countercultural experience of Hampshire has troubled me, I've always defended the college — all the more so now that everybody is running scared," said David Riesman, the Harvard sociologist and author who wrote about Hampshire in "The Perpetual Dream: Reform and Experiment in the American College." "Hampshire has been influential — one of the most visible examples of an experimental curriculum on the East Coast. I see it as extremely helpful."

Riesman cited Hampshire's exceptional record in science education. At most colleges, including Harvard, students fade away from science. At Hampshire, more graduate with an interest in science than enter with one. Hampshire was one of the first colleges to offer an undergraduate program in the cognitive sciences — the rubric for a forward-looking amalgam of philosophy, psychology, neurobiology and computer studies.

Alumni are perhaps the best testimony of the effectiveness of the Hampshire method. Eighty percent of Hampshire graduates are accepted into their first choice of professional or graduate school. Twenty percent own their own businesses. In Hollywood, where Hampshire alumni have been nominated for nine Academy Awards, there is something called the Hampshire mafia, which include the documentary film makers Ken Burns, whose five-part Civil Wars series is scheduled to run on PBS this September, and Robert Epstein, who made "The Times of Harvey Milk."

But a number of graduates from the early years feel they have gaps in their education. One survey found many rued the lack of history. Another deficiency became known to my parents as the Molière problem. The Molière problem first reared its head one Thanksgiving when Molière's name came up, and I, with my degree, made the mistake of saying "Who's Molière?"

"Who's Molière?" said my mother, looking like she'd just put her finger in a wall socket. "Who's Molière? Twenty thousand dollars of college tuition and you don't know who Molière is?"

What can I say? I was reading Faulkner. I was on a Faulkner binge, and might still be if I hadn't come down with mononucleosis. Getting students to moderate their enthusiasms — to give up sweets and study something they're not particularly interested in, for the sake of a balanced diet — is still a problem Hampshire is working on.

The progressive agenda of 1970 is still before the college in the form of multiculturalism. Hampshire recently adopted something called the "Third World Expectation." (The new departure in jargon establishes requirements but calls them expectations.) It is "expected" that courses and exams, whether in lighting design or physics, will include some discussion of how the issues under consideration bear on the third world. Every teacher I talked to welcomed the idea.

By such means, Hampshire hopes to enlarge the perspective of students, and foster a sense of community. And yet the very qualities that make students successful at Hampshire are an ability to go it alone, to work independently. The contradiction of the college has always been that a student is pulled one way by the philosophy, which prizes community, and another by the structure, which emphasizes self-reliance. Hampshire is not a community of people holed up in a big ivory tower; it's 1,200 ivory towers.

"No one shares the same body of knowledge," says Anton Mueller, a book editor who graduated in 1981. "Everyone is an expert on a topic, but there's little basis for common discussion, so sitting in a class can be frustrating."

Much of Hampshire's initial popularity came from the idea that faculty and students were involved in the making of a college — that there was indeed a college to be made. Hampshire's goals and structure were still forming. Would it be just a trendy factory, training people for the Information Age? Or could it offer a fractured society the model of a Utopian collective, where one person's success didn't depend on another's failure. Today, the Utopian visions have faded. Students sit on the board of trustees and the faculty reappointment committee, but have no part in the making of a college. The college has been made.

If Hampshire's aspirations are not so grand, neither are they so grandiose. "The goal of a Hampshire education is to elicit the best in students — to help them develop artistic and intellectual creativity," said Olga E. Euben, the former admissions director who is credited with bringing Hampshire to the 90's and who is now retired. "These are individualistic values, but they incorporate a social and moral and political sense. Even when Hampshire graduates are doing banking, they're doing it with a twist."

"I don't know what you really learn at Hampshire," says Jim Johnston, who has given up staging guerrilla art shows in favor of composing and film producing, "but what you're left with is an attitude about life, a willingness to take chances."

Toward sundown my last day Hampshire, I hiked into a field beyond the apartments of Enfield House to pay my respects to an old sugar maple. I think of it as the living version of the leafy insignia on the Hampshire letterhead, for I once spent the night in its branches. There were about a dozen of us, all member of David Roberts's "The Literature of Great Expeditions" class. Roberts, now an author and magazine writer in Boston, had put his class up a tree to simulate the ordeal of Maurice Herzog, who led a French mountain-climbing expedition that he wrote about in "Annapurna." It would have been colder to sit on snow at 22,000 feet, but maybe not as uncomfortable as being wedged on belay 60 feet up in the crotch of a maple. Hardly anyone slept; the temperature sank into the teens. Some of us would be picking splinters for weeks.

And yet all of us were overtaken by a sense of fellowship. A joke would come from one of the perches, laughter would sweep the limbs, and then the sounds of the night would rush in again, binding us all in the charged silence of a flock. I can't say I learned anything indispensable that night (I could have spent it with Molière instead), but I have never forgotten it, and so perhaps I did. The grass at dawn was stiff with frost. Ad we limbered up for the descent to earth, one of the bivouackers who was an exchange student from Amherst spoke up. "I'll have to tell people the best time I ever had at Amherst was at Hampshire," he said. The whole tree laughed, and then everybody went home.

From "What's New at Frisbee U." by Chip Brown. *New York Times Magazine,* June 10, 1990.

JOHN MCPHEE

The function and style of the New England prep school is the topic of selections by John McPhee and Edward Hoagland, both Deerfield Academy grads and travel and nature writers. McPhee's 1966 account of long-time headmaster Frank L. Boyden is in the "Mr. Chips" vein, unabashed in its admiration for the legendary Deerfield headmaster of more than sixty-five years.

Headmaster Frank L. Boyden

Boyden has the gift of authority. He looks fragile, his voice is uncommanding, but people do what he says. Without this touch, he would have lost the school on the first day he worked there. Of the seven boys who were in the academy when he took over in that fall of 1902, at least four were regarded by the populace with fear, and for a couple of years it had been a habit of people of Deerfield to cross the street before passing the academy. Boyden's problem was complicated by one of the trustees, who was so eager to close the school that he had actually encouraged these boys to destroy the new headmaster as rapidly as they could. The boys were, on the average, a head taller and thirty pounds heavier than the headmaster. The first school day went by without a crisis. Then, as the students were getting ready to leave, Boyden said, "Now we're going to play football." Sports had not previously been a part of the program at the academy. Scrimmaging on the village common, the boys were amused at first, and interested in the novelty, but things suddenly deteriorated in a hail of four-letter words. With a sour look, the headmaster said, "Cut that out!" That was all he said, and — inexplicably — it was all he had to say.

A few days later, a boy asked him if he would like to go outside and have a catch with a baseball. The two of them went out onto the school lawn and stood about fifty feet apart. The boy wound up and threw a smoke-ball at him, apparently with intent to kill. Boyden caught the ball and fired it back as hard as he could throw it. A kind of match ensued, and the rest of the students collected to watch. The headmaster and the boy kept throwing the baseball at each other with everything they had. Finally, the boy quit. "Of course, I was wearing a glove and he wasn't," says the headmaster, who is a craftsman of the delayed, throwaway line.

Most schools have detailed lists of printed rules, and boys who violate them either are given penalties or are thrown out. A reasonable percentage of expulsions is a norm of prep-school life. Deerfield has no printed rules and no set penalties, and the headmaster has fired only five boys in sixty-four years. "For one foolish mistake, a boy should not have a stamp put on him that will be with him for the rest of his life," he says. "I could show you a list of rules from one school that is thirty pages long. There is no flexibility in a system like that. I'm willing to try a little longer than some of the other people do, provided there is nothing immoral. You can't have a family of three children without having some problems, so you have problems if you have five hundred. If you make a lot of rules, they never hit the fellow you made them for. Two hours after making a rule, you may want to change it. We have rules here, unwritten ones, but we make exceptions to them more than we enforce them. I always remember what Robert E. Lee said when he was president of Washington College, which is now Washington and Lee. He said, 'A boy is more important than any rule.' Ninety per cent of any group of boys will never get out of line. You must have about ninety per cent as a central core. Then the question is: How many of the others can you absorb?"

To say that Deerfield has no set rules is not to say that it is a place where a boy can experiment at will with his impulses. The academy has been described, perhaps fairly, as a gilded cage. The essential underlying difference between Deerfield and schools like Exeter and Andover is that Exeter and Andover make a conscious effort to teach independence and self-reliance by establishing a set of regulations to live by and then setting the boys free to stand or fall accordingly. Exeter and Andover boys can cut classes, within established margins, and they are provided with time they can call their own. Deerfield boys have several free hours each Sunday, but most of their time is programmed for them, and attendance is constantly taken. The headmaster's respect and admiration for Exeter and Andover are considerable, and he likes to quote a conversation he once had with an Andover headmaster, who said, "Maybe you're right. Maybe we're right. There is a need for both schools." Andover and Exeter, looking ahead to the college years, try to prepare their students for the freedom they will have, so that they can enjoy it and not suffer from it. Boyden believes that the timing of a boy's life requires more discipline in the secondary-school years than later, and that there is no point in going to college before you get there. "Boys need a sense of security," he says. "Discipline without persecution adds to that sense of security. People sometimes don't realize this, but boys like a control somewhere. We try to give them what you might call controlled freedom. We're the last bulwark of the old discipline. We're interested in new things, but I'm not going to throw away the fundamentals."

All discipline ultimately becomes a private matter between each boy and the headmaster. Most of the boys feel guilty if they do something that offends his sensibilities. Unlike his great predecessor Arnold of Rugby, he does not believe that schoolboys are his natural enemies; on the contrary, he seems to convince them that although he is infallible, he badly needs their assistance. A local farmer who was in the class of 1919 says, "When you thought of doing something wrong, you would know that you would hurt him deeply, so you wouldn't do it. He had twenty-four-hour control." A 1928 alumnus says, "It didn't matter what you did as long as you told him the truth." And 1940: "Whatever it was, you didn't do it, because you might drop a little in his eyes." He will give a problem boy a second, third, fourth, fifth, and sixth chance, if necessary. The rest of the student body sometimes becomes cynical about the case, but the headmaster refuses to give up. "I would have kicked me out," says one alumnus who had a rather defiant senior year in the early nineteen-fifties. The headmaster had reason enough to expel him, and almost any other school would have dropped him without a thought, but Boyden graduated him, sent him to Princeton, and, today, does not even recall that the fellow was ever a cause of trouble. Boyden is incapable of bearing grudges. He wants to talk things out and forget them. He is sensitive to the potential effect of his forbearance, so he has sometimes taken the risk of calling the student body together and asking for its indulgence. A boy once drank the better part of a fifth of whiskey in a bus returning from another school, reeled in the aisle, fell on his face, and got sick. The headmaster called the school together and said that for the sake of discipline in the academy at large he would have to let the boy go unless they would guarantee him that no episode of the kind would happen again. The headmaster was beyond being thought of as weak, so he got away with it. People often wonder what on earth could make him actually drop a boy, and the five cases in which he has done so are therefore of particular interest. All have a common factor: the offender was unremorseful. One of them was guilty of nineteen different offenses, including arson. Nevertheless, if he had told the headmaster that he was wrong, he could have stayed in school.

A boy of considerable talent once told the headmaster that he could write his English papers only between midnight and dawn. His muse, the boy claimed, refused to appear at any other time of day. The difficulty was that after the boy's inspiration ran out he invariably fell asleep and missed his morning classes. Like all geniuses, this boy was likely to attract imitators. The headmaster addressed the student body. "Are you willing to let Mac Farrell stay up all night writing his English papers?" he said. "Mac Farrell alone?" The boys agreed.

The headmaster has often put himself in an uncomfortable corner for a boy who is different. He once had two students — artistic cousins of

Mac Farrell — who liked to paint and particularly liked to go out at night and do nocturnes. They did the cemetery by moonlight and the old houses in the edge of the glow of street lamps. The headmaster knew that this was going on, but he overlooked it. His own favorites have always been responsible, uncomplicated, outstanding athletes, and he cares even less about art than he knows about it, but, in his way, he was just the right headmaster for these two boys. "With a person as unDeerfield as myself," remembers one of them, who is now Curator of Graphic Arts at Princeton University, "he was sympathetic and understanding. He was patient and — what can I say? — incredibly wise in the way that he handled me."

Certain boys at Deerfield in earlier years would commit long series of petty crimes and believe that all had gone undetected. Then, finally, the headmaster would stop such a boy, pull out a small notebook, and read off to him everything he had done wrong since the first day of school. For years, the headmaster roved the campus late at night, like a watchman. Until the late nineteen-thirties, he made rounds to every room in every dormitory during study hours every night. Since then, he has made spot visits. He never gives a boy bad news at night. He never threatens. He uses shame privately. He more often trades favors than gives them. If a boy asks something of him, he asks something in return. There is no student government, nor are there faculty committees, helping to run Deerfield. The headmaster holds himself distant from that sort of thing. Senior-class presidents are elected on the eve of Commencement. Students who are in the school now say they would not want student government anyway, because they feel that it is a mockery elsewhere.

From *The Headmaster: Frank L. Boyden of Deerfield* by John McPhee. Farrar, Straus & Giroux, 1966.

EDWARD HOAGLAND

*Edward Hoagland's "'Company Men for Whatever Company Employs Us'"
is a contrarian slant on Deerfield Academy. He expresses how uncomfortable he
felt as a budding artist at Deerfield. Ironically, Hoagland attended Deerfield in
the late 1940s, at the same time as John McPhee. Like McPhee, Hoagland writes
insightful nature books, including* Notes from the Century Before *(on
British Columbia) and* Red Wolves and Black Bears. *His novels include* The
Circle Home *and* Seven Rivers West.

Going Home to Deerfield Academy

Do you remember how funny schoolmasters' names used to sound?
They probably still do, but especially was this so at pricey prep
schools four decades ago. Poland, Cate, Crow, Bohrer, Suitor, Poor,
Cook, Coffin, Hatch, Conklin — these were flesh-and-blood men I knew
at Deerfield Academy in western Massachusetts in the late 1940s. Mr.
Conklin, with a polished pink pate, was a pretty good geology teacher
who ran a dogsled during the winter and whose means of maintaining
order among teenage boys was to speak louder, *louder*, and LOUDER
until the whole science building rang with the rage in his tenor voice. Mr.
Poland, angularly bony, with crested eyebrows, was an avid birdwatcher
long before anybody had thought up the term, and taught biology suc-
cessfully at nearly a whisper. Mr. Bohrer (in chemistry) was not boring,
but Mr. Coffin taught Latin by rote in a stiff high collar and a gruff dry
bark. Mr. Hatch — leaning back in his swivel chair with his feet crossed
on his desk — hatched me as a writer by alternating the rhapsodic with
the Socratic methods of teaching English and by Navy war stories and
evocative chat about the nub of ideas and the aims of an artist.

Mr. Crow, a small, bird-boned, feline-mannered historian, was a stu-
dent of wealth and waxed most eloquent when he got on the subject of
the rights of the rich. Mr. Poor carried a clipboard everywhere, hurrying
so fast with a posture so straight he looked as if he might topple over
backwards. He supervised attendance-taking seventeen times a day, and
on Sundays sat in the balcony of the church we went to and wrote down
the names of boys who fidgeted; Saturday nights in the winter, at the
basketball games where the roll call of the school was once again checked,
he sat opposite the bleachers to note down (he said) who didn't stand and
cheer at appropriate baskets. Mr. Cate, on the other hand, Dickensianly
rotund and ruddy, was Deerfield's "greeter." He greeted the parents,
gave them the tour, smiling widely, and tried to massage them a little as

he led them into the big doorless office of our famously diminutive and intuitive headmaster, located in the hallway of the main school building, where all the boys passed by many times every day.

Frank Boyden (appropriately named, since his life was devoted to raising boys) was a man who trusted the evidence of his eyes and above all in *character*. He thought he could not only recognize the nature of it at a glance in a tongue-tied new boy but mold it almost irrevocably as well. In this latter conceit he was probably wrong. In the several alumni gatherings I've poked my head into over the years I've never had the feeling that we Deerfield graduates are any less grungy, shifty, petty-minded, and nondescript than any average grouping of men who have gone to a well-heeled school. A preponderance of us have become simply company men for whatever company employs us, veneered with a corporate piety, skin-deep.

The Head, or "the Quid," as we also called him (we didn't know why, but the name went back to the school's early days; when the students were local farm boys and had to spit out their quids of chewing tobacco when he came in sight), had a mild-looking, rather froglike face. He wore wire-rimmed glasses and double-breasted dark suits with ties of the same color. He catnapped more than he slept, drove a horse and buggy on campus and traveled by limousine everywhere else. He was whimsical, arbitrary or even worse in his treatment of some of the masters, once firing a bachelor for getting married (bachelorhood was encouraged), and pushing out my friend Mr. Hatch after twenty-five years' service for suggesting that the older faculty should be covered by a pension plan. But he was kind to the boys, employing no disciplinary measures beyond a clap of the hands and what we called his "toilet face" to impose silence on the school when it gathered. Individually, his appeal was always to our consciences, and somehow it worked. When an errant boy showed up at his desk, he would peer at him intently, directly into his eyes no matter how the boy hung his head (the headmaster's phenomenal shortness was a help in accomplishing this), and blush for and with him, telling him that he, the headmaster, had been hurt as well as disappointed by his behavior, until the boy flushed red with shame.

"We are not a high school," he would say at Evening Meeting if graffiti had appeared on a wall somewhere, and by morning the anonymous culprit would have turned himself in. We were mostly good boys, no question about it. When a straw ballot was taken before the 1948 presidential election, Thomas Dewey got four hundred and some votes, Henry Wallace eight votes, Harry Truman only three, and Norman Thomas, the socialist candidate, one (mine) — a result so remarkably skewed as to prove how astute Mr. Boyden was at picking the sort of conservative body of students he wanted. Indeed, Deerfield still admits no girls, the last of the old-line New England male schools to refuse to go coed, and partly as a result, applications for admission have fallen by twenty percent in the past three years. And yet nearly as many of today's students say they approve of the policy as disapprove.

The profane in my day was represented by "the bank," a board lean-to dug into a bank of earth, out of sight, overhanging the hockey rink. This was where juniors and seniors who wished to smoke were allowed to do so (smoking is outlawed now); and it was a long, cold, conspicuous walk that athletes didn't make, or the designated class leaders, the faculty favorites, or the handful of scholars we had. Those who did venture there were boys as skeptical of the values of Deerfield as I and my closest friends were, but who expressed their independence by the slouch in their walk, by where they walked, and by the dirty jokes they told when they got there, dragging on their butts and blowing smoke rings; some had even lost their virginity over summer vacation.

David Dunbar, a young history teacher presently at the school, says he "works on intellect in the morning in the classroom and character on the soccer field in the afternoon." That was Mr. Boyden's theory too. Mr. Boyden coached football and baseball himself, relying on such basics as the off-tackle plunge and the bunt toward first base. The school's library was in an incredibly cramped, squalid basement room, but the gym was immense, a temple of brick where I enjoyed watching high-caliber diving and swimming. He was right that if people don't get a special appreciation of sports in secondary school it's not likely to be made up for during the busier years of college. Also, he insisted that we all put our hands in the soil of the potato fields surrounding our campus for a couple of days in the early fall, harvesting five thousand bushels. Even his varsity football team missed practice to dig potatoes, and I'm sure he thought it was one of the distinctions between how he trained us and how his rival headmasters at Hotchkiss and Choate operated, not to mention still more snobbish schools like Groton and St. Mark's. Mr. Boyden, who stayed on as Head for a total of sixty-six years (he quit at eighty-eight) and who had converted Deerfield from a local day school with fourteen students by taking on a good many boarders who had been kicked out of older prep schools (such families are often rich), seemed free of class snobbery with regard to boys of conventionally Anglo-Saxon parentage, but he relished telling us that we had outworked the itinerant Mexican harvesters in the next potato field, as if it wasn't just our youth that had accomplished this, but our genes and our breeding.

Though he wanted a kindly tone to prevail, we were boys, and sometimes unkind. One student was turned into a living football on occasion, when two teams vied to push him across a "goal." Another was tied to a radiator, which then was turned on. The boys most rewarded were the big, bland, presentable ones who took nothing too seriously, said the right things, and went along to get along. At the hymn-singing on Sunday evenings these tallest, handsomest, best-dressed boys sat in the front row of the mass of students in the common room of the Old Dorm, facing a succession of well-tweeded clergymen from comfortable churches, and I suspect that at times we all had the feeling they were placed there to hide the rest of us in our grubbiness, stumpiness, and misshapen, nose-picking inadequacy. The school laid such emphasis on the trappings of idealism — on picking up any papers we saw blowing about, so visitors would get a good impression, on finishing up any job once begun, on sportsmanship on the playing field — that it's odd to realize in retrospect how free of any deeper substance it floated: it was not charitable, philanthropic, or particularly "Christian." At least I can't remember Christianity ever being preached to us as derived from the Christ who, infusing the work of Tolstoy and Dostoyevski, had quite mesmerized me by that point.

I had happy days there (I used to arrive on the train with my pet baby alligator concealed in a blanket), but I should confess that my position at Deerfield was ambiguous enough that in my third year, as a senior, I was assigned to the dormitory corridor apportioned for misfits and known as The Zoo. We weren't such a bad group — my friend Eddy Mumford, the class poet, and me, the class novelist; a boy whose ambition was to run a bus business and who helped buy the local bus line that served Deerfield in his graduation year; another not-too-out-of-sync boy with a prominent Adam's apple whose passion was photography but who later became a flying instructor; and the scion of one of America's major smokestack fortunes who had not yet found himself. We had three or four heirs of major fortunes in our class, all mildly floundering. I, perhaps, wasn't, being within a few years of publishing my first novel, but I didn't know that then, and for many years afterward had bad dreams about trying to get into the dining hall in the wrong-colored shirt. (To eat supper one had to wear white.) More important, many of us suffered later on, I think, from a fear of women, a remoteness and intransigence with them and an incomprehension of them, that was due to our not having rubbed shoulders with them in adolescence.

It's unnatural, anyhow, that boys of thirteen or fourteen should be uprooted from home. "Red" Sullivan, a ginger-haired, salty-tongued Irishman with a puckery mouth, was a father figure to the freshmen from broken households and dealt also with the upperclassmen who wanted to smoke. He was thought, too, to be able to talk with the local construction workers and delivery people, "speaking their language." Mr. McGlynn's stock in trade, on the other hand, was his wit. He was a tamed radical but still had a few uncommon ideas, always alert with a verbal conundrum to pose to the boys he liked. Mr. Cook, who called the whole school's roll every evening (sitting on the floor with our legs scrunched into the lotus position, we became expert at inserting our "Here!" with split-second precision into the rush of four hundred nineteen names), taught French grammar and appeared to be more bored than any man I had ever seen before. Like many of the masters, his face was that of an overgrown boy, though his eyebrows had long since turned bushy and white, but unlike most of them, he had no zeal for the crush of earth, grass, and bodies on the athletic fields or the parade ground of twenty-four tennis courts, or for running back and forth all afternoon until one's face grew gray and gaunt. Mr. Cobb — who like Mr. Cook was married and a relaxed, good fellow — had been an officer in the shore patrol in the Navy during the war and "handled" the boys everybody had failed, such as the sophomore who hanged himself from an apple tree by the railroad tracks one morning, wearing only his skivvies, just before the first train went by.

Students at Deerfield now have a freer schedule, I found on a visit last fall — a less narrowly meat-and-potatoes curriculum. Philosophy, art history, religion, and drama are taught. Extra sports such as wrestling are offered, and the hockey rink is indoors. The new headmaster, Robert Kaufmann, is a Harvard Business School-trained administrator, and the older teachers have been let off from most of their coaching duties and dorm supervisory load. As Deerfield has come to seem more traditional in the spectrum of private schools, more boys are now being accepted from Saudi Arabia than from New York City. (The big issue here, when other students were marching to end the Vietnam War, was whether seniors should be allowed bicycles.) On the other hand, in my day we had no black students, and one Japanese represented the Asian world, whereas today there are twenty-five blacks, and boys from twenty-six foreign countries, enrolled. The masters still work under one-year contracts till the end of their teaching lives, but the lawns and buildings look yet more grandiose, and the fields we marched down to en masse, with our overcoats draped across our left arms to cheer for the football team, have expanded also. I remember wanting to swim the river that borders them but never doing it, a regret that may have fueled some boldness on my part later on. I regret not having been a better friend to a roommate or two, as well; and I regret my failure at a piquant moment when I discovered a skunk wandering around with his head stuck inside a peanut butter jar but didn't manage to pry the jar all the way off. I broke the bottom so the creature could breathe, but let him hurry away still jaggedly collared.

When I go to reunions and stand underneath the big striped tent, with Malcolm Forbes's hot-air balloon outside giving rides to alumni children, and the crowd of hundreds of grown-ups emitting its primal, involuntary, gleeful sigh as hundreds of lobsters are thrown alive on the coals of a bonfire to writhe and roast, I wonder what we all have learned since, apart from something about the precariousness of life. At best, we know a bit about love and how to work purposefully, but the experiences of adolescence seem random and hazardous in retrospect. I left Deerfield determined to become a writer at all cost, expecting even harder obstacles ahead than there really were, and wanting to be my own man, which also seemed a more difficult feat to attempt at a school like that than it did afterward.

"'Company Men for Whatever Company Employs Us': Going Home to Deerfield Academy" by Edward Hoagland. *New England Monthly*, May 1987.

The Environment,
Natural and Built

A view from Patton Hill to Mount Monadnock in New Hampshire across the Connecticut River Valley over Greenfield, Bernardston, and Northfield. Photo by Geoffrey Bluh.

THOMAS CONUEL

The story of Quabbin Reservoir remains one of the most poignant in Western Massachusetts lore. Four towns — Dana, Enfield, Prescott, and Greenwich — were wiped out in 1938 by waters forming a new reservoir for Greater Boston. Thomas Conuel, writing for the Massachusetts Audubon Society in Quabbin: The Accidental Wilderness *(1981; revised 1990) describes how modern water engineering created both the largest reservoir in the world and the most extensive wilderness area in southern New England.*

Quabbin: The Lost Valley

On a September evening in Barre, Massachusetts, ten miles from the eastern edge of Quabbin Reservoir, the parking lot of the Wildwood Nature Center was crowded with cars. The nature center's main hall, a long rectangular room filled with straight-backed chairs, was darkened, and the shades were drawn. A slide show was in progress and there was standing room only. Warren "Bun" Doubleday stood in front of sixty people and began another lecture on what is commonly referred to as "the lost valley," the four towns that once comprised the Swift River Valley and now lie buried beneath the waters of Quabbin Reservoir.

With a pointer Doubleday tapped an engineering drawing projected on the screen and explained how Winsor Dam and Goodnough Dike were constructed. He described intake tunnels and earthen dams and, in clear, precise language, the enormous engineering effort that went into the construction of Quabbin Reservoir. Next came slides of the Swift River Valley towns. There were slides of Dana, Enfield, Prescott, and Greenwich and their houses, churches, and stores. "This is Nellie Hart's house," Bun narrated, "and here is the old Methodist Church, and this is my grandfather's house." There were slides of the railroad that was known locally as the "Rabbit Run" because it stopped so often that the forty-mile trip from Athol to Springfield often took three and a half hours. And there were pictures of the ponds and lakes of the Swift River Valley.

When the slide show was over, Doubleday rolled a short black and white film. As it ran, he provided a narrative. He, his wife Sigrid, and a pilot climbed into a small airplane and flew over the construction site that became Quabbin Reservoir. After the slides of the Swift River Valley, the movie was a mild jolt. The bulldozed and barren landscape looked as if it had been bombed. Trees after cutting were stacked like matchsticks. Cellar holes gaped where buildings once stood. There was not a house in sight. The land was uniformly devastated.

Bun Doubleday (nobody calls him Warren, and the origin of the nickname is obscure) narrated the home movie in a measured voice that at first reminds one of Maine. But he is not from Maine. He was born and raised in Doubleday Village in North Dana, the village named after his great-grandfather, Nehemiah Doubleday.

A vigorous man in his early seventies who looks considerably younger, Doubleday has close-cropped white hair, bright, alert eyes, and wears dark-rimmed glasses. His stories, like his laugh, are dry and quiet. He is part of a small and ever-dwindling group of original residents of the Swift River Valley towns. When the reservoir was built, 3,500 residents were displaced. Nobody is quite sure how many former residents still remain in the area, but the number is small.

Bun Doubleday's family came to the valley from Connecticut in 1795. Nehemiah Doubleday was co-owner of the Doubleday and Goodman Sawmill on the west branch of Fever Brook in North Dana. The sawmill burned in 1915, but its remains still can be seen on a site about two miles from one of the access roads into Quabbin Reservation. Nehemiah built the house in which he and succeeding generations of the Doubleday family lived, and that house was the last to be razed when North Dana was leveled in 1938. It was a large, neat colonial with a red barn beside it and two maples in the front yard. During the drought in 1965 the stone steps of the house could be seen protruding upward through the mud flats and low water of North Dana.

Myron Doubleday, Bun's father, ran the town grocery store. He retired at the age of forty-five, when the MDC bought out the store. In those days, Bun Doubleday recalled, a man of forty-five who lost his job could not get another one. The creation of Quabbin Reservoir effectively put his father out of business for life.

The valley that Bun Doubleday's ancestors came to live in at the end of the eighteenth century was part of Narragansett Township Number 4, land granted to veterans of the Narragansett Indian Wars in 1675. Greenwich was the first town incorporated from the township in 1754.

Now the floor of Quabbin Reservoir, Greenwich was once an unusually beautiful town with green hills surrounding broad, flat fields. Located in the northeast corner of Hampshire County, it was divided into two parts, Greenwich Center and Greenwich Plains, each with its own post office. Greenwich Plains was a low, rich, fertile valley. On the heights, at the edge of the plain, were the mountains, Mount Pomeroy, Mount Liz, and Mount Zion. Today the mountains are islands jutting through the waters of the reservoir.

As Greenwich grew, it subdivided. The town of Enfield, settled around

1730, grew from the south parish of Greenwich. By 1816 Enfield was incorporated and named after Robert Field, an early settler. Like Greenwich, Enfield was situated on the former hunting grounds of the Nipmuck Indians, who had been gradually replaced by the white settlers. The west and east branches of the Swift River cut through Enfield. In later years the river helped power the mills that made Enfield the wealthiest of the valley towns. High hills towered above Enfield. One of these, Great Quabbin Mountain, 500 feet above the floor of the Swift River Valley and 1,000 feet above sea level, was a landmark and is today the lookout summit in the public area of Quabbin Reservation.

Dana was located on the banks of the Swift River in Worcester County. It had been carved from the towns of Greenwich, Petersham, and Hardwick and was incorporated in 1801 and named after Judge Francis Dana of the Massachusetts Supreme Court. Four villages made up the town: Dana Center, North Dana, Storrsville, and Doubleday Village. Scattered through the town were three ponds: Pottapaug, near the center of town, "a large and beautiful sheet of water . . . a resort for fishermen"; Sunk Pond in the southwest corner of town, and Neeseponset-Town Pond in North Dana.

By 1822 the town of Prescott was incorporated. It was a mere sliver of a town bounded by the hills of Mount L, Mount Russ, and Rattlesnake Mountain and by the west branch of the Swift River. Historically, Prescott was dealt a modest dollop of fame in the person of Daniel Shays, who lived in the east parish of Pelham before it was incorporated into Prescott. Shays was born in 1747 in Hopkinton, Massachusetts. He moved to the Swift River Valley and during the American Revolution organized a company and eventually became a captain. He was described as a natural leader, courageous, independent, and ambitious. When the war ended, Shays returned to farming in the Swift River Valley and in 1786, along with his friend Luke Day of West Springfield, led a rebellion of farmers against the repressive debtor laws that allowed creditors to strip farmers of their possessions.

History has looked kindly upon Shays and Luke Day. Both are now regarded as having been hardworking farmers striking out against incompetent government officials who were willing to sit by while war veterans lost their homes and farms to stay-at-home war profiteers. Unfortunately, though the cause was worthy the results were disastrous. The farmers' rebellion at first prevented the sitting of local courts in Northampton and Springfield, thus effectively ensuring that no adverse judgments against farmers could be handed down from those courts. Shays and Luke Day then organized a march on the state armory in Springfield, hoping to capture the armory and its supplies of guns and cannons. That foray ended in a rout when government troops fought back and drove the army of farmers out of the state. His army in ruins, Daniel Shays fled back through Pelham and the Swift River Valley and barely escaped being trapped there by government troops. He slipped away and is said to have lived out the remainder of his life in upstate New York. Shays and his fellow rebels were later pardoned by the government.

When the state built Quabbin Reservoir, it also constructed a road along the western edge of the reservoir and named it the Daniel Shays Highway. One wonders what Shays, a modest man by all accounts, would think if he could know that the memorial to his name is a twenty-mile stretch of two lane blacktop.

The nineteenth century was a fine time to live in the Swift River Valley. The four towns prospered, and villages sprang up near the towns. The valley was full of farms, grain mills, and small manufacturing firms. In Greenwich there was a gristmill, built in 1745, and an assortment of cottage industries. There were factories in Dana, including the Swift River Box Company, and small industries that churned out straw bonnets, billiard legs, and soapstone fixtures. Prescott was known for its fruit farms, its charcoal kiln, and its soapstone industry. For travelers there were the Conkey Tavern, the Atkinson Tavern, the Quabbin Inn, the North Dana Inn, and the Swift River Hotel.

But the twentieth century was less kind to the valley. By 1910, rumors abounded that the Swift River Valley was destined to become a reservoir for Boston. Property values dropped; businesses folded; and when the rumors became fact, the valley towns succumbed almost meekly to the wishes of the water planners from Boston. Prescott was the first to go. In 1830, 758 people had lived in Prescott. In 1927 only 250 people lived there. After a final town meeting in 1927, the town was turned over to the Metropolitan District Commission, which ran it until its official demise on April 28, 1938. Enfield, Greenwich, and Dana remained relatively unchanged until the end in 1938.

The *Springfield Morning Union*, in an often-quoted story, reported the demise of Enfield as follows:

> "Under circumstances as dramatic as any in fiction or in a movie epic, the town of Enfield passed out of existence at the final stroke of the midnight hour.
>
> A hush fell over the Town Hall, jammed far beyond its ordinary capacity, as the first note of the clock sounded; a nervous tension growing throughout the evening had been felt by both present and former residents and casual onlookers.
>
> The orchestra, which had been playing for the firemen's ball throughout the evening, faintly sounded the strain of Auld Lang

Syne . . . muffled sounds of sobbing were heard, hardened men were not ashamed to take out their handkerchiefs."

It is easy to see why the Swift River Valley was considered expendable by state water planners. No major businesses would be ruined, no major highways disrupted, no prominent landmarks buried by the waters of Quabbin. The Swift River Valley was a small, out-of-the-way place, totally lacking the political or financial power that could have saved it. Even to this day MDC officials concede that the greatest problem in building Quabbin Reservoir, and a problem that builders of any future reservoir the size of Quabbin will face, is the tricky emotional problem of moving not just a family or two, but obliterating a whole community with its history and sense of shared lives.

Construction of what was to become Quabbin Reservoir was begun in 1928, completed in 1939, and the reservoir filled for the first time in 1946. The first phase of construction did not involve the Swift River Valley directly. Because Wachusett Reservoir was perilously low, a 12.5 mile aqueduct was built between the Ware River in Barre and Wachusett. A horseshoe-shaped tunnel, twelve feet wide and large enough to drive a truck through, was blasted through underground rock 200 feet deep and then lined with concrete. The first water from the Ware River arrived at Wachusett in 1931, just in time to prevent Wachusett from drying up completely. By that time, after two dry seasons, Wachusett was 81 percent empty.

Construction of the second tunnel, this one to run westward from Barre to the Swift River Valley, began in 1931. That tunnel is thirteen feet high, eleven feet wide, and ten miles long.

Meanwhile, the state was surveying the Swift River Valley, photographing buildings, acquiring land, and preparing to move cemeteries and build dams. The task of creating a reservoir the size of Quabbin was immense. Metropolitan District Commission engineers, under the direction of Chief Engineer Frank Winsor, tackled the problem of impounding the waters by allowing the valley's topography to determine the shape of the reservoir. At the southern tip of the Swift River Valley, there are two gaps in the hills. The Swift River flowed through one gap on its way out of the valley, and Beaver Brook through the other. The gaps were made by prehistoric rivers that once cut through the valley and the surrounding hills. Glaciers had left over 100 feet of deposition above the bedrock of the old riverbeds. The dams that would impound the waters of Quabbin Reservoir had to be built so that their foundations would reach down through the layers of glacial deposits and rest on the solid ledge of the prehistoric riverbeds below.

First, tunnels were built to divert the waters of the Swift River away from the sites of the dams. Then, concrete caissons were lowered to the riverbed. The first experimental caisson was a block of concrete that was sixteen feet high, nine feet wide, forty-five feet long, and reinforced with steel rods. It had a steel edge and at the bottom contained a hollow chamber six feet high. In that chamber, working with pumps and compressed air, MDC laborers excavated sand, mud, and silt from the riverbed and passed it to the top of the caisson in buckets. As the laborers dug, the caisson settled deeper into the riverbed, eventually coming to rest on bedrock 135 feet below the surface. The caisson was groated with concrete to the rock of the riverbed and formed an impermeable barrier. Other caissons were then lowered onto the first caisson and groated in place. The caissons, when in place, formed a concrete wall nine feet thick.

Winsor Dam and Goodnough Dike were then built above the solid cores of watertight concrete. Both are earthen dams, the materials used in their construction having been excavated from the valley itself. The MDC engineers compacted fifteen feet of fine sand over the tops of the concrete caissons and then built a pool of water over the top of what was to be the dam. They then installed pumps in the pool and dumped measured amounts of soil into a mixing box in the pool. The pumps circulated the water through pipes that could be directed to any area of the construction site. The water, mixed with soil from the mixing box, flowed through the pipes out over the top of the dam, with the coarser soils coming to rest near the edge of the pool, while the finer soils were carried toward the center. The fine soils, which are impervious to water, in this way created a watertight center in the dam.

Winsor Dam and the Goodnough Dike are about three miles apart on the southern, most public edge of the reservoir. Winsor Dam, named in memory of Frank Winsor, who died shortly before the construction of the reservoir was finished, is 2,640 feet long, 170 feet above riverbed, and 295 feet above rock ledge. It contains 4 million cubic yards of earth fill and has a 400-foot spillway. Goodnough Dike is only slightly smaller, 2,140 feet long, 135 feet above the bed of old Beaver Brook, and 264 feet above rock ledge.

The reservoir that stretches behind these dams is 18 miles long, with a water surface area of 38.6 square miles and a shoreline of 118 miles. The distance from Boston, at the eastern edge of the state, to Pittsfield, at the western edge, is 140 miles, only 22 miles more than the shoreline of the reservoir. The maximum depth of the water in front of Winsor Dam is 150 feet, and the average depth of the reservoir eight miles away from the dams is 90 feet. The entire watershed of Quabbin is 186 square miles, supplemented by an additional 98 square miles of watershed in the adjoining Ware River basin.

Of the $65 million appropriated for the construction of Quabbin Reservoir, $41 million was spent on the construction of the dams and tunnels. With the remaining money the MDC built roads and an administration building and two baffle dams to circulate the water from the Ware River through Quabbin. The baffle dams built in Greenwich, now near shaft 12, are simple earth dams that, along with a channel dug by the MDC, circulate the waters from the Ware River northward toward Mount Zion and in the process clean the water of debris. The final figure for the construction of Quabbin was $53 million.

In 1938 a hurricane swept through the valley, flattening stands of trees but doing no damage to the newly constructed dams. By 1939, cleanup crews were finishing with the reservoir, picking up construction and hurricane debris and removing the last structures in the Swift River Valley. The dams were finished and roads were built in and around the administration building in Enfield. The aqueduct from Quabbin to the Ware River was completed, and in the northern part of the reservoir a series of small dams were added to improve circulation in some of the shallow areas of the reservoir.

In July 1939 the waters of the Swift River began backing up and spreading over the low areas of the valley. By 1946 the reservoir was full and Quabbin Reservoir had replaced the Swift River Valley on the map of Massachusetts.

From *Quabbin: The Accidental Wilderness* by Thomas Conuel. University of Massachusetts Press, 1990.

A view north from the southern end of the Quabbin Reservoir; the water covers what was once the town of Enfield, Massachusetts. Photo by Richard W. Wilkie.

JAMES TATE

Poet James Tate practices his craft in the Pioneer Valley. Tate, a Kansas City native, lives in Pelham and has taught at the University of Massachusetts since the late 1970s. He won the Pulitzer Prize in 1992 for his Selected Poems *and a National Book Award in 1994 for* Worshipful Company of Fletchers. *"Quabbin Reservoir" appeared in the volume* Distance from Loved Ones *(1990).*

Quabbin Reservoir

All morning, skipping stones on the creamy lake,
I thought I heard a lute being played, high up,
in the birch trees, or a faun speaking French
with a Brooklyn accent. A snowy owl watched me
with half-closed eyes. "What have you done for me
philately," I wanted to ask, licking the air.
There was a village at the bottom of the lake,
and I could just make out the old post office,
and, occasionally, when the light struck it just right,
I glimpsed several mailmen swimming in or out of it,
letters and packages escaping randomly, 1938, 1937,
it didn't matter to them any longer. *Void.*
No such address. Soft blazes squirmed across the surface
and I could see their church, now home to druid squatters,
rock in the intoxicating current, as if to an ancient hymn.
And a thousand elbowing reeds conducted the drowsy band pavilion:
awake, awake, you germs of habit! Alas, I fling
my final stone, my calling card, my gift of porphyry
to the citizens of the deep, and disappear into a copse,
raving like a butterfly to a rosebud: I love you.

"Quabbin Reservoir" from *Distance from Loved Ones* by James Tate. University Press of New England, 1990.

TONY HISS

Tony Hiss writes admiringly of the efforts of the Center for Rural Massachusetts at the University of Massachusetts at Amherst to maintain the rural quality of the region against suburban sprawl. The Center's design manual Dealing with Change in the Connecticut River Valley *has formulated a way to accommodate new growth without compromising the sense of place.*

The Experience of Place *(1990) by Tony Hiss explains how powerfully special places can affect us and how they can best be preserved. Hiss, a writer for the* New Yorker, *has written five other books and many articles.*

Thinking Regionally

In *Dealing with Change in the Connecticut River Valley: A Design Manual for Conservation and Development*, a recent book by Bob Yaro and three associates (Randall Arendt, Harry L. Dodson, and Elizabeth A. Brabec), the Center for Rural Massachusetts presents a full-length analysis — complete with photographs, site plans, model bylaws, and vivid full-color drawings of future construction — of how a large, three-hundred-year-old working landscape can absorb high suburban densities of development over a forty-mile stretch of river terrain without jeopardizing future private property values or sacrificing its ancient partnership sense. All the new housing would be detached single-family homes, as in most existing suburbs (research by the Center for Rural Massachusetts has shown that the average New England family still dreams of having a house and a lawn that are all its own), but the net gain in density would actually be higher than what is permitted in most suburbs and closer to what you'd expect to find in a residential neighborhood of a small city, because the *Design Manual* makes room for the same number of people that could ordinarily be accommodated only by blocks of attached row houses. Yet in the *Design Manual* studies, none of this growth would bring about the look of even a low-density suburb; the whole region, all forty miles of it, would still look like a working landscape and function as a working landscape.

The basic design ideas in the *Design Manual* are that most new houses, shops, and offices should be gathered together in clumps, usually at the far edges of open fields, and that wherever it is possible, existing villages and woods should be used as closets for higher density — places where new construction can be neatly stowed away without diverting attention from partnership values. The proposed bylaws give meticulous consideration to the question of just how visible new projects can get, stipulating, say, the kind of "softly illuminated" nighttime signs that would be appropriate in front of roadside stores, so that you'd still have a sense of driving through moonlight and starlight.

The landscape under examination in the *Design Manual* is the Pioneer Valley — a local name for the Massachusetts portion of the Connecticut River Valley and, more specifically, for the small towns and broad expanses of richly productive riverfront farmland between Holyoke and the Vermont–New Hampshire border, which have remained essentially unchanged since the seventeenth and eighteenth centuries. The long view north along the river, particularly from a vantage point such as the summit of Mount Holyoke, at the southern end of the rural portion of the valley, became a famous tourist attraction in the early nineteenth century, so the Pioneer Valley, like the Hudson River Valley, is a place where even the partnership sense has been carefully documented over the years, by landscape painters and by writers. For instance, there's *The Oxbow*, Thomas Cole's gigantic, panoramic, thundercloud-laden canvas of the gliding sailboats and golden haystacks and grazing sheep, the plumes of smoke from farmhouse chimneys, and the soaring, wheeling birds he saw from the peak of Mount Holyoke in 1836 — a painting that hangs in the Metropolitan Museum of Art. Standing on that peak several years earlier, Timothy Dwight, the president of Yale University who became America's first epic poet, called the scene before him "the richest prospect in New England, and not improbably, the United States," and "a collection of beauties to which I know no parallel." And in his book *Travels in New York and New England*, Dwight wrote: "When the eye traces this majestic stream, meandering with a singular course through these delightful fields, forcing its way between these mountains, exhibiting itself like a vast canal . . . it will be difficult not to say that with these exquisite varieties of beauty and grandeur the relish for landscape is filled."

Pioneer Valley farmland is now more vulnerable to development than it used to be — the major farming business in the area, the Consolidated Cigar Company, which used to grow the kind of large-leaf tobacco used for wrapping cigars in the fields next to the Connecticut River, picked up stakes in the mid-1980s and moved its operations to Latin America. But the valley by now has a long history of making room for change while maintaining its sense of roominess, and has already absorbed some conspicuous nonfarming uses without compromising its integrity. It contains five major colleges — Smith, Amherst, Mount Holyoke, Hampshire, and the University of Massachusetts. And since the late 1960s, the valley has attracted so many craft workers — more than a thousand of them, including potters, weavers, woodcarvers, calligraphers, jewelers, glassblowers, blacksmiths, silversmiths, printers, book-binders, and people who make musical instruments — that it has acquired a new reputation, as an East Coast Santa Fe.

Now the natural countryside in the Pioneer Valley is coming under the guardianship of several new Connecticut River regional environmental programs. In Connecticut, Massachusetts, Vermont, and New Hampshire — the four states along the river's 407-mile course from the Canadian border to Long Island Sound — over $900 million in federal, state, and local funds have been spent since 1970 to improve water quality in the river, and in 1987 the Nature Conservancy, which operates the largest privately owned nature-preserve system anywhere in the world, set up a Connecticut River Protection Program to save 7,000 acres of wild areas near the river, such as floodplain forests and riverside grasslands — "the best of the river's remaining natural communities," according to a recent issue of *The Nature Conservancy Magazine*, including all "those that still possess enough biological integrity to maintain themselves as functioning systems well into the future." Dennis Wolkoff, who is the Nature Conservancy vice president in charge of the Eastern Regional Office, says, "The Connecticut River is the ecological thread that ties New England together."

There is so much at stake in the Pioneer Valley that the *Design Manual*, with its proposals for concealing density, has been causing something of a sensation in planning circles: A development company known for carving up whole mountains into small lots bought 110 copies of the book for the use of its acquisitions and planning staff; the American Society of Landscape Architects gave the book a design award in 1988 as one of the best landscape books of the year; and both the water commissioner of Texas and the director of a national rural planning institute in West Germany have asked for copies. But Bob Yaro, who considers himself a close student of Benton MacKaye, has a slightly different, and more complicated, explanation for the instant success of the *Design Manual*.

Yaro thinks that the conclusions in the *Design Manual* are workable only because two more MacKaye hunches about development have turned out to be true: Areas can conceal density only by working directly with connectedness; and the process of working with connectedness is politically acceptable, because it's basically a democratic procedure rather than something outsiders can control or impose — all they can do is tap into local people's hidden expertise about connectedness ("The job is not to 'plan' but to *reveal*"). What MacKaye couldn't guess was that in a post-interstate boom, there would be a couple of additional, equally compelling reasons for building a region around connectedness: It's cheap; and you can get it done quickly, while there's still a landscape around you to work with. And there was a gap in MacKaye's thinking — the gap that led him to have doubts. He didn't see the full force of the discouragement built into people after two hundred years of development decisions that ignored connectedness. Yaro discovered early in his career that to attract people's interest to regionalist projects he needed to take the psychology of regional planning one step beyond MacKaye's work: Often, he found, before you could hope to make the public value of a place part of the local process of thinking about land-use decisions you had to take a preliminary step, which involved reconnecting people to their own sense of connectedness. Ever since, the first part of any Yaro project, urban or rural, has involved revalidating connectedness and helping it to find a voice.

Part of Yaro's approach has to do with learning how to avoid any oncoming development storm. "When I was growing up, in the 1950s, my grandparents had a farm outside Hartford, in a place called Andrews Corners, where their farm was actually one of the four corners of a crossroads," Yaro told me one afternoon last year at the University of Massachusetts faculty club. "The farm was surrounded by orchards, and there was a skating pond for the winter and blueberry bushes for July and August picking. By the time I was a teenager, the three other corners were being filled in, and there were supermarkets and gas stations standing on old farmland. By the time I got out of college, my grandparents' farm had become a regional shopping mall. Almost all the regionalists I know have had this kind of experience, growing up — it's what gets them started. Part of the appeal of a movie like the first *Back to the Future* is that it lets you see instantly what going back thirty years can do — the suburban mall vanishes, and old fields and barns reappear. One of the few human rights that aren't officially guaranteed in this country is an agreement that the places you grow up caring about will be there for you when you're ready to start a family of your own."

Yaro paused, and then said, "Until very recently, it seemed as though we had two land ethics in the United States — five percent of the nation was set aside as national parks, and treated as special places where we talked about things like 'America the Beautiful' and 'We, the People.' This was neutral territory, but it seemed that different rules had to be obeyed through most of the rest of the land: either 'Take the Money and Run' or 'Private Property: Keep Out.' But all the time, the first land ethic was in place inside vast numbers of people, who would have told you if you asked them — and I have — that they never thought about the land and didn't have an opinion on the subject. But given the right setting, the right evocation, the right stimulus, many of those people who put themselves in the 'Don't Know' column turn out to be very articulate and outspoken concerning the special qualities they care about in their own communities. People can become vehicles for places. These are the feelings and this is the understanding now bubbling up from real people who live in real places — and as a result, there's a ferment in the country about land values that hasn't been seen since MacKaye was writing, in the 1920s. Even the environmental movement, when it emerged in the 1970s, didn't tap all these concerns; at first, we were paying so much attention only to clean air and clean water that I used to think that any visitors from outer space would immediately ask each other, 'Are these creatures really terrestrial beings?'"

From *The Experience of Place* by Tony Hiss. Alfred A. Knopf, 1990.

TRACY KIDDER

Tracy Kidder's book House *(1985) makes the seemingly elementary tale of building a house in Amherst touch on an amazing array of topics. The book starts with Jonathan and Judith Souweine commissioning architect Bill Rawn to design a house. From there* House *expatiates on types of lumber, taste in house layouts, the socio-economic backgrounds of craftsmen, and architect-client relationships. This excerpt describes the Greek Revival buildings in Amherst that inspired the style of the Souweines' house.*

House

At a single sitting, out of the void of virtually unlimited possibilities, Bill had summoned a floor plan that fulfilled Judith's and Jonathan's most important wishes for a house. Bill felt warmed up himself. This basic form could answer his wishes, too. This layout — the rectangular box with a front door in the gable end, more or less facing the road — had a historic precedent. Elaborated in his mind, its roof, its paint, its moldings on, it was a kind of American house that he had long admired casually. They had not stopped at one today, but he seemed to remember passing by some.

"What this house wants to be is Greek Revival," said Bill.

"It does?" said Judith. "How does it know?" She smiled. Her smile is a bit of jewelry that she wears when she teases. It notifies her victims that she feels mischievous and merry because of them and not at their expense. Her smile had always worked that way on Bill. Again and again, and especially when speaking architect's lingo, Bill uses terms that sound obscure and pompous to Judith; she retorts and grins, and often he just goes on, stammering and insisting that he really is "exceedingly serious."

Occasionally, Bill invites her jibes on purpose. This time he had not meant to amuse. He really thought he'd had a brainstorm and he had expressed it in the manner of one of his favorite architects, Louis Kahn, who liked to say that bricks and other building materials wanted to become certain kinds of structures.

Judith stopped smiling. "Gee," she said, "what's Greek Revival?"

On Sunday, having seen residential Amherst through the Souweines' eyes, Bill showed them the town through his.

For most of two centuries Amherst was a village. Elderly natives remember its dirt streets. In the 1960s, in a hurry, it turned into a big, busy town. The palpable reason, on the north side of Amherst's borders, is a skyscraper farm, the campus of the University of Massachusetts. It has a library twenty-seven stories high. Seen from a bucolic angle, rising against the sky above the tobacco barns of neighboring Hadley, the university's drab-colored towers look completely incongruous, like a city just landed in a big field. The sight has never amused Bill, the contextualist. The campus disgraces his profession, he has said. With the university's towers have come many modern subdivisions, tidy and pleasant. Bill and the Souweines visited some yesterday. Today, Bill led his friends on a search for something older — Greek Revival buildings. He found them all over Amherst.

Bill has an explorer's enthusiasm and a mapmaker's eye for places. Jonathan vividly remembers Bill taking him on a walking tour of lower Manhattan and transforming the place for him. When in the mood, Bill can read a landscape as though it were a novel. Today, though, he kept the focus narrow. In downtown Amherst, among remnants of the old village, Bill found a row of Greek Revival buildings. He and the Souweines ended up there.

They stood a few blocks away from the house where Emily Dickinson lived, their backs to the old village green. It was a fine, sunny, thawing winter day. Bill and Jonathan and Judith ambled down the sidewalk on Greek Revival row. "1838," "1842," "1837," said signs fastened on the corners and near the doorways of the buildings they stopped to examine. Bill, who had never studied the form closely, began picking out its salient features, making the old style his own even as he explained it to Judith and Jonathan.

First in the row stood Amherst's College Hall — an example of what Bill decided to call "civic Greek Revival." It was an imposing public edifice, with a portico for an entrance. The building's roof extended out over this grand porch and was supported by several ample Doric columns. The rest of the row consisted of houses. Some were large and fine, some small and comparatively plain. None had a portico or true columns. Instead, the houses had pilasters at their corners, some of which were molded to suggest the bases and the capitals and the fluting of real columns. Clearly, Bill pointed out, pilasters don't support a thing except the idea of a temple. Front doorways mattered. The moldings around them should suggest columns. Although some of these did not, Bill thought that Greek Revival entry doors ought to open onto the street, through one of the narrower ends of the rectangular structure. A proper Greek Revival roof should not be very steeply pitched. When you look head on at the narrower, gabled end of a Greek Revival house, you should see a pediment, a completed triangle, with the roof forming the two sloping sides and a ledge of wood or brick making up the triangle's base. In most plain, traditional American houses, the base of that triangle is not completed. Bill decided that the completed triangle was crucial.

Bill also valued the frieze — the wide surface, sometimes decorated with moldings, sometimes plain, that separates the tops of second-story windows from the line of the roof. The frieze sits on top of the pilasters. The frieze, Bill noted, provides an ample separation between pilasters and roof line. "The frieze raises the house. It's like pushing up your shoulders and standing very frontal."

Looking at those houses, Bill felt blessed with more than his usual luck. Last night the Greek Revival form had seemed to pop out onto his tracing paper, as if he himself were just an intermediary. And today, he had found that form all around town — a contextualist's dream made manifest. "Suddenly, it's not just a house on a landscape. It's a house that's part of the town, that wasn't imposed from outside, that fits in, you know, in a symbolic way."

Bill felt sure he had found the right beginning for a contextualist, postmodern house that would suit him and the site and his old friends. It remained for Bill to help his old friends agree.

On weekends in Amherst, Bill continued to lead his friends on tours. He gathered that Judith and Jonathan admired the Greek Revival houses he showed them and also that she and especially Jonathan worried about the stylishness of those houses. Judith, he observed, was the more immediately receptive. Jonathan's thoughts, as Bill read them, were: "Oh, yeah, because I sort of like these old farmhouses." Bill told them that what he had in mind departed only modestly from the basic form of the farmhouse. Many of the Greek Revival buildings he showed them were, in fact, quite simple. "Not a lot of pretension, but a little decoration. Those are just boxes with a little decoration."

The New England farmstead most comely to Bill was a structure that had evolved, a main house with many ells attached to it. Reproducing the rambling New England farmstead and all its intersecting roof lines would surely cost a great deal more than building just a box and one ell and attaching the appropriate ornaments. Besides, from the start they had all agreed that this house would have a porch, and there is nothing like a porch for adding informality. Greek Revival meant simplicity and economy, Bill told Jonathan and Judith.

They drove in circles, cruised slowly down streets, stopped and looked, got out and gazed. "There's one," Jonathan would say of a farmhouse with a touch of the Greek. And Bill would answer, "No. Not quite." He offered counterexamples. In Sunderland, just north of the university, they found another Greek Revival row. South of Amherst, about midway between the village green and the Souweines' new land, Bill spotted a Greek Revival church. It delighted him first of all because of its location. "It's just such a marvelous symbolic connection between the town and the Souweines' land." He also liked the building for itself. (Later, on a warm spring day, Judith finds Bill lying on the ground beside that church, in deep contemplation of it. Bill wears only sneakers and jogging shorts and for a moment Judith has the impression that he is lying naked before the building. She is greatly amused, and calls Bill an architectural voyeur.) Bill showed them all those buildings and more, partly on the theory that educating his clients in the essence of the form would strengthen his position later on, when the inevitable budget crunches occurred and the Souweines started talking about eliminating pieces of the design. At least they would know what they were losing, he figured. To his various arguments for Greek Revival — practical, contextualist, and aesthetic — Bill added a political one. "We're not celebrating something from France or Rome or Greece, but something American and populist, and something so simple. A box with some ornament." Bill explained later, "We all come out of this sixties thing that we haven't totally rejected, and that's wrapped up in some sense of social conscience." Greek Revival was in fact a simple style compared to many others, but Bill knew that the house he had in mind would look elegant beside most other new ones in the area. "You're convincing them to do a fancy kind of house. But we're all attached to this kind of liberalism that they feel so strongly." Greek Revival flourished in America during the age of Andrew Jackson, Bill recalled. "New populism. What nicer political heritage could there be for the Souweines than that? A time when this country opened itself to new people, when the proletariat got its first view of power in this country."

From *House* by Tracy Kidder. Houghton Mifflin, 1985.

MARK KRAMER

In Three Farms: Making Milk, Meat and Money from the American Soil *(1980), Mark Kramer describes a dairy farm in Conway which has been in the Totman family for four generations. He sketches crackerjack dairyman Lee Totman and explains how the family farm in New England has been on the decline for more than a century. This is a story of economic, technological, and environmental change.*

Kramer writes from personal knowledge of agriculture, having lived on a Western Massachusetts farm and taught agricultural history and politics at the University of Massachusetts at Amherst. A journalist writing for the Atlantic Monthly, *Kramer also has written* Invasive Procedures: A Year in the World of Two Surgeons.

Conway Dairy Farm

There are two steel engravings, a matched pair like the masks of comedy and tragedy, in Solon Robinson's 1879 agricultural masterpiece, *Practical Hints for Farmers*, and they sprang to mind the very first time I passed the Totman farm. The engravings, on facing pages, bear the capitalized legends FARMER SNUG'S RESIDENCE DURING HIS LIFETIME and THE SAME PLACE UNDER FARMER SLACK'S MANAGEMENT.

Farmer Snug kept his place tidy. An inspector's checklist would read very nicely: Fences — mended. Barn — neat as a pin and bursting with provender, farmer seen through open mow doorway, working hard. House — upright and commodious, with porch straight and true.

Yankees traditionally build porches that will sag after a decade, and tack them on houses built to stand a century. I think it is a custom smiled upon by church fathers, because it insures that the porch will be a barometer of the morale of whatever occupants may be therein. To knowledgeable Yankee passersby, Farmer Snug's straight porch is the equivalent of a gold star in Saint Peter's ledger, pasted up in the column headed "Hard Work and Keeping after Things." New England is a harsh climate not only for crops but for neighbors and porches as well. Any flagging of morale — any passing of days skulking indoors in a state of depression instead of working diligently outdoors in the soothing earnestness with which the industrious look upon themselves, any slackening of righteousness — and down goes the porch.

Farmer Slack's porch — on the way down. Fences — down already. Shutters — on five of eleven windows in view, shaken free of hinges now. Barn — empty, mow door off track. Pigs — out. Trees — the trees have scarcely bothered to leaf out. And on the sagging porch, an adult male who appears to be able-bodied and of working age lounges indolently.

As anyone who has ever lived in an agricultural region can attest, Farmer Slack dwells in every rural town. Farmer Snug is a rarer bird, but he does live in Franklin County, and Lee Totman is his name. I have tried to understand his phenomenal success. His virtuosity is startling in a way that is hard to communicate to nonfarmers. He is more than just a good farmer. He is *right there*.

He doesn't waste moves. He is always set up for the job he needs to do. He plans only as much as his equipment and help permit. He takes shortcuts where they pay and lavishes attention where that pays better. His manure truck is an old unregistered jalopy; his equipment shed is made of old telephone poles and sheet tin. But his milking time is usually about twenty minutes longer than it needs be if he is in a rush, and he spends hours in seeming idleness, just watching his cows carefully. He has, for the multitude of chores which make up a farmer's day, the sort of sense of essential motion that a Japanese calligrapher brings to the drawing of letters. Things are well set up, and usually go right. When Lee's tractor does get stuck in the mud, he laughs.

The right equipment is always near at hand to get it out quickly and easily. Lee is always at work. He is always on the farm; when he needs something he has it delivered. When he does have to go into Greenfield, he goes for as short a time as possible — he says the buildings seem to shake and vibrate as he passes between them. On Mother's Day and on his wife's birthday, he drives to Deerfield — all of six miles — and gets chocolates from the local pharmacy.

At work he is as happy as a hog with a full trough, obstinate, singleminded and intent — intensely concentrating on the chore of running the farm right. In spite of his seeming hardheadedness, he brings to each day's plan an alertness, a flexibility — in solving problems, in reordering priorities in the light of developing events — that combines a realistic comprehension of the cost of doing things with the drive to do what he finds ought to be done. He does this with a stern consistency, with a seemingly carefree, silent and smiling staunchness day after day, decision after decision. He dwells in the world as one who fully accepts personal responsibility for each of his actions; it is the world of the just, which by the way he sleeps the sleep of, snoring some.

Lee stays home and makes things work right because he *can* do it; the perfection of the farm expresses and proves his being; away from the farm things must seem unsatisfactorily wild. As a consequence of his success in building a world that yields to his logic and his effort, he doesn't give much of a damn what other people think and say about him.

However, he enjoys appreciation as much as he despises sloth on those few occasions when he allows it to cross his path or inconvenience him. He has a few friends, with whom he and his wife visit once in a while. They are people whom he finds good cause to admire.

Lee is the apotheosis of capitalistic America. If he is admirable for his organization, his concentration, the focus and death-defying outpouring of constructive energy, and if for these qualities he seems to some to be endowed with a Zen-like aura of certainty, of instinctual correctness in every act, there is a wonderful irony to that thought: Lee Totman's organizing precept, central referent, the wellspring of his ways, mother lode, his straight, his narrow, his guardian angel, his pole star, is one single elegant question.

What's the payoff?

The Lee Totman Farm, Conway. Photo by Geoffrey Bluh.

He does not seem to be an avaricious man. It is a spiritual question. If the answer looks good, he goes to work. "I'm not so ambitious," he is fond of saying, "that I like to take extra steps. There is too much else to do. Routine is what's important around here. Perhaps I'm good at routine, and if I am it's because I'm lacking in imagination. I see that some of the very intelligent people I know concentrate on many goals — they should never farm because it would restrict them too much. I'm pretty happy just working at this one thing."

Perhaps it is his immunity to innuendo, to criticism of any agricultural sort, his impeccable standing as a first-rate farmer beyond even a suspicion of posturing that so aggrieves some members of the farming community. For Lee, will works. Lee imagines that will works for everybody, which of course it doesn't.

To make hay at all, much less to make it well and to get it in with style, is an act that goes against the laws of nature. The same rain that waters rich grasslands half the year around also supports forest plants. And in New England, field plants lose competitions with forest plants in just a decade. New England wants to be forest. In the earliest days before land was cleared by the Indians and many generations before explorers invaded and Empire settlers colonized the Indians' clearings, the region's only naturally occurring grasses were marsh grasses and salt hay. The earliest white settlements centered around seaside, riverside, and island barn sites. Natural freshwater marshes — extensive ones occurred around Hartford, Springfield and the lower Merrimac River — drew settlers. As Betty Thomson points out in *The Changing Face of New England*, it is flooding that drives the pervasive forest from this rare natural mowing land. Salt marsh floods twice daily, rivers seasonally. Some southern trees have learned to grow on floodland, but in New England, the marshes alone are given naturally to grasses.

The grasses that so trouble Lee Totman by invading stands planted with tenderer species, the grasses we now call "native," are not native, then, at all. Ms. Thomson quotes an early settler named John Josselyn, writing in 1672 to say over forty different weeds "sprung up since the English planted and kept cattle in New England." There is some thought that before these jostling imports arrived, fields — and woods too — supported varieties that did not exhibit the same glaring struggle obvious to us now — that the protocols were mostly settled, that a stable population of triumphant species went about its business less conspicuously at war.

To manage the open land on a farm successfully requires a tactful and energetic exercising of human will over the natural course of wind, rain, and time. What Lee Totman's beautiful hayland wants to be is a maple-beech hardwood forest. Given a respite of just a hundred fallow years, that's what it would be again, arriving at this climax condition after incarnations in transit as fields of moss, strawberries and blackberries, then as stands of quaking aspen, white and yellow birch. Finally, hemlock and white pine, ash, white and black birch and cherry would move in, never quite to leave, but to grow and fall before the aggression of great broad maples and smooth-skinned beeches. Today fusarium wilt attacks the maples and "split bark syndrome" decimates stands of beech. The only near virgin forest to be seen is an awesome museum piece, the woodlot of the Harvard Forest at Petersham, Massachusetts.

Nature on its own arranges things in other ways than Lee Totman does. Were the farm to vanish, the soil on the forest floor would soon have a pH of about 5.5 (quite acid) and would support a different micro-bial community from the ones that live in Totman's stately and often-limed fields of alfalfa (pH — a neutral 7 on the nose). The killdeer, robins and cowbirds who like plowed ground would give way to the woodcock, wild turkey, and partridge of the deep woods. Hare and squirrel would be fewer, bear, elk and wolves would resume their residence. This is how the forces of nature had things worked out for tens of millennia. This is northern Massachusetts's self-maintaining condition, maple-beech forest that won the good Lord's competition to stay in place. On the Totman farm, maple-beech is the state known as "the scheme of things."

To undertake to diverge from it is to assume a great undertaking indeed. The modern world, as represented by Lee Totman at work on his tractor, shoulders this chore as a matter of course although every step wades against the inexorable tides of nature. The war against the jungle is manifest off the farm in such simple sights as lawnmowers and cement sidewalks. We humans wage this battle with a blithe finesse, with a heedless and unself-critical expenditure of energy that might signal to some wise observers in flying saucers that *Homo sapiens* is a race of very lively creatures, given with pluck and abandon to great works that make things different from what they would be otherwise.

While Totman's dairy farm does not exactly dare the encroaching jungle, as might some aboriginal rain-forest clearing, the spirit of the affront is the same. The main difference is in latitude. In the north, nature moves with softer, slower, and gentler but no less persuasive force than it does in the tropics. Thawing and freezing; supplanting of species by tougher species that slowly edge in, causing stress, disease and slow death; grinding down by course of wind and water and snow — all replace the fierce tropical battles of rain, heat, stingers, poisons, thorns and stickers, horny hides, raging floods, armies of ants and parasites that eat neighbors in minutes, which together spend the additional energy of the tropical sun. But whatever the intention, whatever the latitude, the battles of nature are the same; the methods up north are somehow more in the spirit of slow, considered and vindictive Yankeedom. The land shapes the people and the people shape the land.

The Totman farm now consists of about a hundred acres of cropland and pasture, and about two hundred acres of woodlot. After Lee took over, he cleared about ten or fifteen additional acres of bottomland. It had grown back before the lower farm was annexed to the Totman farm in the 1940s.

A hundred years earlier, between 1820 and 1840, virtually the entire hill where the farm sits was cleared land. It happened during a brief flowering of Yankee agriculture that now appears rather magical. The boom started in the 1810s, when roads broadened the region's commercial life, and it grew by bounds in the 1830s and early forties, when railroads and mills spread along the valleys and riversides.

The crop of choice turned out to be sheep, especially the merino sheep first imported in large numbers, along with the native shepherd from the Spanish Escorial royal flock, by one William Jarvis, American consul and chargé d'affaires in Lisbon. Farmers whose villages had been sufficient unto themselves turned for the first time to making money. By 1830, half the farms in Massachusetts were said to be mortgaged. Boston's supply of fowl, butter, and eggs nearly ceased in 1837 because most farmers had turned to sheep. Fortunes were made selling wool, breeding stock and meat, and other fortunes were made at the mills. In 1842 President Tyler, pressured by mill owners, altered a tariff law, allowing the importation of European wool. It sold at prices farmers at home could not match. The boom faded, sometimes leading farmers into tasteful retrenchment in other agricultural pursuits, but more often leading them into poverty as wool prices failed to meet farm costs. Many farm families joined the migration to lands not yet depleted by intensive agriculture, lands that lay over the Alleghenies to the west. As the Western Reserve was settled, the cleared woodlots of New England began to close in — maple-beech on the rise. By the time Joshua Totman moved into Conway in the 1860s, the most marginal rank of farms was already abandoned. The mill owners continued to prosper working the imported wool; many farmers' children moved off the land and took mill jobs.

The oldest folks in Conway remember when a few more of the now wooded hills were cleared land, but the time when most of the land in the area was clear has passed beyond memory. Fred Call of Colrain, just north of Conway, tells of his father complaining about the shame of abandoning productive land in the mid-1800s. Today about 70 percent of the state is wooded and the situation is quite stable. Land lost to farming nowadays — 10,000 to 20,000 acres a year of the ground that's still farmed — is lost chiefly to roads, housing developments, and shopping centers that sell food imported from other regions. Massachusetts imports all but 15 percent of its food. Even milk is shipped into Massachusetts. The only crop the commonwealth produces in excess of local wants is cranberries for Thanksgiving. It happened because neglecting the land paid better than caring for it.

From *Three Farms: Making Milk, Meat and Money from the American Soil* by Mark Kramer. Little, Brown, and Company, 1981.

ARCHIBALD MACLEISH

Archibald MacLeish's connection to the Pioneer Valley began in 1927 when he bought a house in Conway. Even while he taught at Harvard and served as Librarian of Congress and Assistant Secretary of State, the Pulitzer Prize–winning poet maintained his Conway rural getaway.

In 1963, upon the passing of Robert Frost, MacLeish succeeded him as Amherst College's Simpson Lecturer. MacLeish also wrote several pieces related to the region, including the verse play "An Evening's Journey to Conway, Massachusetts" and the libretto to an Andre Kostelanitz opera "Magic Prison," based on Emily Dickinson's meeting with literary editor Colonel Thomas Wentworth Higginson after eighteen years of correspondence.

MacLeish's "A Lay Sermon for the Hill Towns" from Riders on the Earth *(1978) is a particularly eloquent argument for sustaining the life of the community in the face of insatiable new "development."*

A Lay Sermon for the Hill Towns

Lay sermons should be satisfied with lay texts. I have taken mine from a letter written in the town of Conway, Massachusetts, on the seventeenth day of July in the year 1892. It was written by my grandmother, Julia Whittlesey Hillard, whose husband, my grandfather, was, in that year, the newly settled pastor of the Conway church, having previously served in a sequence of churches beginning at Hadlyme near the mouth of the Connecticut River in the 1850's and ending, forty years later, here in the Hoosac Hills, looking out over Deerfield and the narrowing valley.

I mention this migration because it has a good deal to do with my grandmother's letter. Most parsons stay more or less put once they have found a congregation, but not Elias Brewster Hillard. My grandfather was the son of a sea captain in the North Atlantic trade and he had inherited the habits of the quarterdeck: he not only spoke out; he spoke out in the wind's teeth. When the Civil War came along he found himself in a milltown in Connecticut where uniforms were manufactured for the union armies, most of them shoddy. The millowner was, of course, a deacon of the church, and placed, as such, in a conspicuous seat where my grandfather's sermon on shorn lambs could reach him. The result was foreseeable though not necessarily foreseen: the Hillard family moved on in the predestined direction — north, away from the prosperous communities and fashionable churches, bringing its growing brood of children and an ever-increasing reputation for candor.

It was my grandmother, of course, who suffered from all this, though she never said so even to herself. She was a small woman, delicately made, who had borne nine children in almost as many towns and who had paid at last with her own health for her endless labors at the laundry tub and the stove and the sink and the broom, to say nothing of her duties in the church and the Sunday School and the sickroom of the many towns. Five years before the wanderers came to rest in Conway she had been ill, and if she was not recovered it was not because her life had changed but because Conway, she thought, had healed her with its hill-town air, its hill-town sun, and its northwest wind out of Vermont and the Adirondacks. The letter of July 17, 1892, was about that miracle.

She had been corresponding all her adult life with a beloved teacher. "Dear Miss Guilford" had not heard of Conway, Massachusetts, and must be told at length in a Sunday letter. "I reserve," my grandmother wrote, "the more leisurely writing time that Sunday brings as my own and to spend at my own sweet will." Which was gallant enough in a little lady who never had time of her own — but which proved, before she had written her way down the first, brief page, to be overly optimistic. She caught herself, as she put it, "nodding" and went off to get aged mother to bed, after which she decided to finish her never-finished washing and go to bed herself — "and what a good harbor that is when night comes."

But the letter was still a Sunday letter when she went on with it — Sunday the 24th of July instead of Sunday the 17th. And the subject was still the same. Dear Miss Guilford must imagine this Conway she has never seen. And what is she to imagine? Conway people in this generation will be surprised. She is to imagine Arcadia. "That," my grandmother writes, "is the name by which we know it." And where does Arcadia begin? Back of the little parsonage which still stands where it stood then — halfway up the hill that climbs south out of the village street. "The houselot is a very large one with much of hill and dale in it, and a bird's nest of a house amidst the trees and shade (not too much, however; the sunshine pours in on every side)." And off she goes, dragging Miss Guilford almost literally by the hand.

My grandmother had never heard, I suppose, of Emily Dickinson. Nobody had in those days, not even within thirty miles of Amherst. And yet there is an echo in her words of that childlike voice with its unchildlike meaning — "You come with me in at the large gateway and up the rising, slightly winding, path to the little house with its porches and vines and flowers — past that and past the garden on its high terrace to your right, and past the dull red barn on your left, and up a grassy path through a shady orchard with all the time such lovely views opening before and around you that you pay no heed to the way by which you came but feel, when here, that you have been translated and know a new heaven and a new earth." And so the journey goes on, my grandmother running ahead and dear Miss Guilford following after as best she can. "Here we are at the top of a steep, grassy, wooded hill sloping to the village. This is Arcadia."

But not all of Arcadia as it turned out. There was something more — a healing something which had saved her from "that long and fearful illness . . . Conway with its tonic air and its simple, wholesome affectionate life has worked wonders for me. And how devoutly thankful I am! For it means so much — and not to me alone, but to all my precious family and to our dear people . . . I prize my new strength very highly and I try to make a conscience of guarding it."

But even this last and deeply personal confession was not enough. There was something more that had to be said, had to be shown. "I wish I had a camera that could take a picture of Conway life for you. It is a busy little place with four churches — Congregational and Methodist and Baptist, yes, and Catholic — very earnest, warm-hearted Christians, intelligent, intellectual, spiritual, ready for every good work, appreciative and responsive. Our life and work here are more a labor of love than in any of the homes yet. And I do believe we were never loved as we are here, or had so fruitful a field of service before. And is that not wonderful when you consider the ages we have come to? I am 57!"

Arcadia indeed — more than Arcadia — a good and healing life in a very human community sustained by the earth and the streams and the sun and the labor that belongs to a land of little valleys and great shouldering hills. But that was 1892 when my grandmother was fifty-seven and I had just been born a thousand miles away in Illinois. And where are we now? My grandmother is long dead and I am eighty-four, and the town . . . there are those who believe that the town too is close to the end of things: close to the loss of its identity as a town like so many of those famous settlements below us in the valley which have dissolved into the endless anonymity of subdivision and expressways. Where is Hatfield now? An exit on Route 91. Where does Amherst begin? Where a white post on Route 9 tells you you are "Entering Amherst."

Well, it is always possible, I suppose, that the hill towns will disappear in the same way: turn into bedroom towns which will turn into rural slums which will be "restored" by public housing in which no one would willingly live. It is possible, but it is not inevitable. And the reason it is not inevitable is the reason my grandmother discovered as she led Miss Guilford to Arcadia. A town is not land, nor even landscape. A town is people living on the land. And whether it will survive or perish depends not on the land but on the people; it depends on what the people think they are. If they think of themselves as my grandmother thought of the people of Conway in 1892, if they think of themselves as living a good and useful and satisfying life, if they put their lives first and the real estate business after, then there is nothing inevitable about the spreading ruin of the countryside. The hill towns will survive as long as they are inhabited by people who think of themselves as living their own lives, think of their neighbors as people who will keep the fields open and the woods green and the little rivers running for their lives' sake, and for the sake of human life.

Economic inevitability is not only Marxist dogma. It is also, and increasingly, American fantasy. To preserve something for life's sake when money can be made by destroying it is sentimental to the American business mentality, and the American business mentality is now established as the norm of American thinking. My grandmother would not have agreed, and it's no use trying to dispose of my grandmother by throwing words like "sentimental" at her memory. No woman who bore nine children in as many parsonages, and then brought them up on a minister's stipend, cooking and washing and sewing for the lot, was ever sentimental or could afford to be. Women like that were far more practical than real-estate operators. And what they were practical about was human values: the kind of thing the real estate developer has never thought of. "Development pays, doesn't it?" says the developer. Yes, it pays, sometimes, but what does it do to life in the town? says my grandmother. "Life in the town!" says the developer. "Let them watch television!" Which wouldn't mean much to my grandmother but might mean something to some of us.

No, the crisis in the American hill towns is not a hill-town crisis. It is an American crisis. Sooner or later, and sooner rather than later, the country people, the practical mothers and grandmothers, are going to have to challenge the business mentality which turns land into real estate and small towns into dispensable relics of the past which developers can exploit for profit. They are going to have to teach the impractical and sentimental business mentality what a town actually is: what one town was to Julia Whittlesey Hillard — a place where she was made whole, where her life was recreated, a place of which she could say: "Our life and work here are more a labor of love than in any of the homes yet. And I do believe we were never loved as we are here." That is practical talk. It puts first things first. It means something.

"A Lay Sermon for the Hill Towns" from *Riders on the Earth* by Archibald MacLeish. Houghton Mifflin, 1978.

Permissions and Sources
(Continued from the copyright page, p. iv.)

Explaining the Pioneer Valley
Excerpts from *The Old Patagonian Express* by Paul Theroux. Copyright © 1979 by Cape Cod Scriveners Co. Reprinted by permission of Houghton Mifflin Co./Seymour Lawrence. All rights reserved.

The Connecticut River and the Valley
GEORGE W. BAINE and HOWARD A. MEYERHOFF • From *The Flow of Time in the Connecticut Valley: Geological Imprints* by George W. Baine and Howard A. Meyerhoff, revised edition, 1963. The Connecticut Valley Historical Museum, with the Pratt Museum, Amherst College. Reprinted by permission of the Connecticut Valley Historical Museum.

TIMOTHY DWIGHT • Reprinted by permission of the publishers from *Travels in New England and New York* by Timothy Dwight, edited by Barbara Miller Solomon with the assistance of Patricia M. King. Cambridge, Mass.: The Belknap Press of Harvard University Press. Copyright © 1969 by the President and Fellows of Harvard College.

BASIL HALL • From *Travels in North America in the Years 1827 and 1828* by Basil Hall. Cadell & Co., Edinburgh, 1829.

BEN BACHMAN • From *Upstream: A Voyage on the Connecticut River* by Ben Bachman. Copyright © 1985 by Ben Bachman. Reprinted by permission of Houghton Mifflin Co. All rights reserved.

The Colonial Frontier
SAMUEL ELIOT MORISON • From "William Pynchon: Founder of Springfield, Massachusetts" by Samuel Eliot Morison. *Massachusetts Historical Society Proceedings*, February 1931 (Vol. LXIV). Reprinted by permission of the Massachusetts Historical Society.

THOMAS PYNCHON • From *Gravity's Rainbow* by Thomas Pynchon. Copyright © 1973 by Thomas Pynchon. Used by permission of Viking Penguin, a division of Penguin Books USA Inc.

JOHN PYNCHON • From *The Pynchon Papers, Volume I: Letters of John Pynchon, 1654-1700*, edited by Carl Bridenbaugh, 1982. Reprinted by permission of the Colonial Society of Massachusetts.

JOHN WILLIAMS • From *The Redeemed Captive* by John Williams, edited by Edward W. Clark (Amherst: University of Massachusetts Press, 1976), copyright © 1972 by Edward W. Clark. New material copyright © 1976 by The University of Massachusetts Press.

LUCY TERRY PRINCE • "The Bars Fight" by Lucy Terry Prince, 1746. Published in *A History of Deerfield, Massachusetts* by George Sheldon. Pocumtuck Valley Association, 1895.

CONRAD AIKEN • "Deerfield" by Conrad Aiken, in *Massachusetts: A Guide to its Places and People*, Federal Writer's Project of the Works Progress Administration. Boston: Houghton Mifflin Company, 1937.

Reform and Renewal
JONATHAN EDWARDS • From *Jonathan Edwards: Representative Selections*, edited by Clarence H. Faust and Thomas H. Johnson. Hill and Wang, 1962.

ROBERT LOWELL • "Jonathan Edwards in Western Massachusetts" from *For The Union Dead* by Robert Lowell. New York: Farrar, Straus & Giroux, Inc., 1964. Copyright © by Robert Lowell. Copyright renewed © 1992 by Harriet Lowell, Sheridan Lowell, and Caroline Lowell. Reprinted by permission of the publishers.

JAMES MACGREGOR BURNS • From *The American Experiment: The Vineyard of Liberty* by

James MacGregor Burns. Copyright © 1992 by James MacGregor Burns. Reprinted by permission of Alfred A. Knopf, Inc.

FREDERICK DOUGLASS • From *Life and Times of Frederick Douglass* by Frederick Douglass. Revised edition, 1893. The Library of America, 1994.

OLIVE GILBERT • From *Narrative of Sojourner Truth* by Olive Gilbert, 1875 edition.

WASHINGTON GLADDEN • From *Recollections* by Washington Gladden. Boston: Houghton Mifflin Company, 1909.

EDWARD BELLAMY • "How I Wrote 'Looking Backward'" by Edward Bellamy. *The Ladies Home Journal*, April 1894.

CORINNE MCLAUGHLIN and GORDON DAVIDSON • From *Builders of the Dawn: Community Lifestyles in a Changing World* by Corinne McLaughlin and Gordon Davidson. Walpole, N.H.: Stillpoint Publishing, 1985. Copyright © 1985 by Corinne McLaughlin and Gordon Davidson. Reprinted by permission of the authors.

JOYCE HOLLYDAY • From "'We Shall Not be Moved'" by Joyce Hollyday. Reprinted with permission from the May 1990 issue of *Sojourners*, 2401 15th St. NW, Washington, DC 20009; (202) 328-8842.

Famous Visitors

GEORGE WASHINGTON • From *The Diaries of George Washington, Volume V, July 1786—December 1789*, edited by Donald Jackson and Dorothy Twohig. Charlottesville, Virginia, 1979. Used by permission of the University Press of Virginia.

RALPH WALDO EMERSON • Reprinted by permission of the publishers from *The Journals and Miscellaneous Notebooks of Ralph Waldo Emerson*, edited by William H. Gilman et al. Cambridge Mass.: The Belknap Press of Harvard University Press, Copyright © 1961 by the President and Fellows of Harvard College.

NATHANIEL HAWTHORNE • From *The American Notebooks* by Nathaniel Hawthorne, edited by Claude Simpson. Centenary Edition of the Works of Nathaniel Hawthorne: Vol. 8, Columbus, Ohio: The Ohio State University Press, 1972. Reprinted by permission of the publishers.

CHARLES DICKENS • From *American Notes* by Charles Dickens. Macmillan, 1893.

HENRY WADSWORTH LONGFELLOW • From *The Complete Works of Henry Wadsworth Longfellow*. Houghton Mifflin Company, 1893.

The Inspiration of Poets

EDWARD TAYLOR • From *The Poems of Edward Taylor* edited by Donald E. Stanford. Yale University Press, 1963.

WILLIAM CULLEN BRYANT • From *Poetical Works* by William Cullen Bryant. Thomas Y. Crowell, 1893.

EMILY DICKINSON • Reprinted by permission of the publishers and the Trustees of Amherst College from *The Poems of Emily Dickinson*, Thomas H. Johnson, ed., Cambridge, Mass.: The Belknap Press of Harvard University Press, Copyright © 1951, 1955, 1983 by the President and Fellows of Harvard College.

JANE LANGTON • From *Emily Dickinson is Dead* by Jane Langton. Copyright © 1984 by Jane Langton. Reprinted by permission of St. Martin's Press, Inc., New York, NY.

HELEN HUNT JACKSON • From *Verses* by Helen Hunt Jackson. Boston: Roberts Brothers, 1888.

FREDERICK GODDARD TUCKERMAN • From *The Complete Poems of Frederick Goddard Tuckerman* edited by N. Scott Momaday. Copyright © 1965, 1993 by Oxford University Press, Inc. Reprinted by permission.

ROBERT FROST • "Fire and Ice" from *The Poetry of Robert Frost* edited by Edward Connery Lathem. Copyright 1923, © 1969 by Henry Holt and Co. Copyright 1951 by Robert Frost. Reprinted by permission of Henry Holt and Co.
Letter to *The Amherst Student*, March 25, 1935, reprinted from *Robert Frost: Poetry and*

Prose, ed. Edward Connery Lathem and Lawrance Thompson (New York: Holt, Rinehart & Winston, 1972) with the permission of The Estate of Robert Frost.

ROBERT FRANCIS • Prose excerpts from *The Trouble with Francis: An Autobiography* by Robert Francis (Amherst: University of Massachusetts Press, 1971), copyright © 1971 by Robert Francis.
"Apple Peeler" from *The Orb Weaver* © 1960 by Robert Francis. Wesleyan University Press by permission of University Press of New England.
"Two Ghosts" from *Robert Francis: Collected Poems*, 1936-1976 (Amherst: University of Massachusetts Press, 1976), copyright © 1976 by Robert Francis.

SYLVIA PLATH • All lines from "In Midas' Country" and all lines from "Above the Oxbow" from *The Collected Poems of Sylvia Plath* by Sylvia Plath. Copyright © 1959 by Ted Hughes. Copyright renewed. Reprinted by permission of HarperCollins Publishers, Inc.
All lines from "Child's Park Stones" from *The Collected Poems of Sylvia Plath* by Sylvia Plath. Copyright © 1980 by Ted Hughes. Reprinted by permission of HarperCollins Publishers, Inc.

ADRIENNE RICH • From *The Fact of a Doorframe: Poems Selected and New, 1950-1984* by Adrienne Rich. By permission of the author and W. W. Norton & Company, Inc. Copyright © 1984 by Adrienne Rich. Copyright © 1975, 1978 by W. W. Norton & Company, Inc. Copyright © 1981 by Adrienne Rich.

JOSEPH BRODSKY • "The Hawk's Cry in Autumn," 1975, translated by Alan Myers and the author, from *To Urania* by Joseph Brodsky. New York: Farrar, Straus & Giroux, Inc., 1988. Copyright © 1988 by Joseph Brodsky. Reprinted by permission of the publishers.

ARCHIBALD MACLEISH • "Conway Burying Ground" and "New England Weather" from *Collected Poems 1917-1982* by Archibald MacLeish. Copyright © 1985 by The Estate of Archibald MacLeish. Reprinted by permission of Houghton Mifflin Co. All rights reserved.

RICHARD WILBUR • "Orchard Trees, January" from *New and Collected Poems*, copyright © 1982 by Richard Wilbur, reprinted by permission of Harcourt Brace & Company, originally appeared in KQ.
"Fern-Beds in Hamshire County" from *Walking to Sleep: New Poems and Translations*, copyright © 1967 and renewed 1995 by Richard Wilbur, reprinted by permission of Harcourt Brace & Company.

PAUL MARIANI • "A Break in the Weather" from *Prime Mover: Poems 1981-1985* by Paul Mariani. New York: Grove Press, Inc. 1985. Reprinted by permission of the author.

Politics

CALVIN COOLIDGE • From *The Autobiography of Calvin Coolidge*. Cosmopolitan Book Corporation, 1929.

JOHN FOSTER [FOSTER FURCOLO] • From *Let George Do It! A Comedy About America Politics* by John Foster (Foster Furcolo). Harcourt, Brace & Company, 1957. Reprinted by permission of the author.

LAWRENCE O'BRIEN • From *No Final Victories: A Life in Politics from John F. Kennedy to Watergate* by Lawrence F. O'Brien. Copyright © 1974 by Lawrence F. O'Brien. Used by permission of Doubleday, a division of Bantam Doubleday Dell Publishing Group, Inc.

JOSEPH NAPOLITAN • From *The Election Game and How to Win It* by Joseph Napolitan. Copyright © 1972 by Joseph Napolitan. Used by permission of Doubleday, a division of Bantam Doubleday Dell Publishing Group, Inc.

Springfield, "City of Homes"

JONATHAN DANIELS • From *A Southerner Discovers New England* by Jonathan Daniels. Copyright © 1940, 1968 by Jonathan Daniels. Reprinted by permission of Brandt & Brandt Literary Agents, Inc.

Sports

The Ethnic Experience: Holyoke and Bondsville

Northampton, "Paradise of America"

JAMES C. O'CONNELL has written the *Inside Guide to Springfield and the Pioneer Valley* (Western Mass. Publishers, 1986); *Shaping an Urban Image: The History of Downtown Planning in Springfield, Mass.* (with Michael Konig; Connecticut Valley Historical Museum, 1990); and numerous articles on cities and travel. A native of Springfield, Massachusetts, he lives on Cape Cod with his wife, Ann Marie, and sons Chris and Charlie. He has a Ph.D. in urban history and currently serves as Economic Development Officer at the Cape Cod Commission.

RICHARD TODD, formerly editor of the award-winning *New England Monthly* and executive editor of the *Atlantic Monthly,* lives in Ashfield, Massachusetts, where he both writes articles and edits books for Houghton Mifflin Company.

RUTH OWEN JONES has published numerous articles about the history of the Pioneer Valley and was picture researcher for the *Historical Atlas of Massachusetts* (University of Massachusetts Press, 1991) and *From Colony to Commonwealth: Massachusetts, an Illustrated History* (Windsor Publications, 1987). She lives in Amherst, Massachusetts.

MICHAEL MCCURDY is an artist, illustrator, and author. His wood engravings and drawings appear in trade books and limited editions for both adults and children. His most recent titles include *The Gettysburg Address* and David Mamet's *Passover.* He lives in Great Barrington, Massachusetts.